Praise for *John: Verse by Verse*

"For over two decades I have benefited from Dr. Osborne's careful and erudite treatment of Scripture. I am excited to add this treatment of one of my favorite of New Testament books to my library, and would commend it to every preacher, scholar, and serious Bible student."

—**J. D. Greear**, pastor, The Summit Church (Raleigh-Durham, NC)

"The journey from text to sermon can be a perilous one with many obstacles and detours along the way. I recommend that preachers carefully study the text itself in its context to discern its thrust and structure and only then to consult several carefully selected commentaries, reading the more scholarly, technical ones first and then the more popular ones. Would it not be wonderful if there were a commentary that was at once as accurate as the most technical and yet as down-to-earth as the most popular? Would it not be a gift to have a commentary whose author knows the text—indeed the whole Bible—so well and reverences it so highly that he can consistently point the preacher to the text's meaning, clarifying what is puzzling, underscoring repeated themes, summarizing key emphases? Would it not be even better if such a commentary provided a logical outline of the whole book that could point toward a faithful consecutive exposition of it? Ah, good news! There is just such a commentary! Grant Osborne does all these things and more in his verse-by-verse unpacking of the Gospel of John. It is no substitute for doing your own careful study, but if you have ever lost your way or gotten bogged down in getting from text to sermon, this commentary may provide just the help you need."

—**Greg R. Scharf**, professor of homiletics,
Trinity Evangelical Divinity School (Deerfield, IL)

"As a senior statesman of evangelical biblical scholarship, Grant Osborne is not only a remarkably careful exegete, but also a clear, engaging and accessible communicator. Everything he writes is for the benefit of the church, not just the ivory towers of academia. This commentary on John, like the others in this series, is a model of this balance. It demonstrates a deep awareness of the questions scholars raise about the Fourth Gospel, yet presents them in language every reader can understand. Commentaries that prove to be most enduring are those that find this balance between accuracy and accessibility. By this standard, the volumes in this series are destined to become classics."

—**Mark L. Strauss**, University Professor of New Testament,
Bethel Seminary San Diego

T0375047

JOHN

Verse by Verse

JOHN

Verse by Verse

GRANT R. OSBORNE

LEXHAM PRESS

John: Verse by Verse
Osborne New Testament Commentaries

Copyright 2018 Lexham Press

Lexham Press, 1313 Commercial St., Bellingham, WA 98225
LexhamPress.com

Print ISBN 9781683590750
Digital ISBN 9781683590767

Lexham Editorial Team: Jeffrey Reimer, Elliot Ritzema, Danielle Thevenaz, and
    Rebecca Brant
Cover Design: Christine Christophersen
Typesetting: ProjectLuz.com

CONTENTS

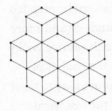

SERIES PREFACE

There are two authors of every biblical book: the human author who penned the words, and the divine Author who revealed and inspired every word. While God did not dictate the words to the biblical writers, he did guide their minds so that they wrote their own words under the influence of the Holy Spirit. If Christians really believed what they said when they called the Bible "the word of God," a lot more would be engaged in serious Bible study. As divine revelation, the Bible deserves, indeed demands, to be studied deeply.

This means that when we study the Bible, we should not be satisfied with a cursory reading in which we insert our own meanings into the text. Instead, we must always ask what God intended to say in every passage. But Bible study should not be a tedious duty we have to perform. It is a sacred privilege and a joy. The deep meaning of any text is a buried treasure; all the riches are waiting under the surface. If we learned there was gold deep under our backyard, nothing would stop us from getting the tools we needed to dig it out. Similarly, in serious Bible study all the treasures and riches of God are waiting to be dug up for our benefit.

This series of commentaries on the New Testament is intended to supply these tools and help the Christian understand more deeply the God-intended meaning of the Bible. Each volume walks the reader verse-by-verse through a book with the goal of opening up for us what God led Matthew or Paul or John to say to their readers. My goal in this series is to make sense of the historical and literary background of these ancient works, to supply the information that will enable the modern reader to understand exactly what the biblical writers were saying to their first-century audience. I want to remove the complexity of most modern commentaries and provide an easy-to-read explanation of the text.

But it is not enough to know what the books of the New Testament meant back then; we need help in determining how each text applies to our lives today. It is one thing to see what Paul was saying to his readers in Rome or Philippi, and quite another thing to see the significance of his words for us. So at key points in the commentary, I will attempt to help the reader discover areas in our modern lives that the text is addressing.

I envision three main uses for this series:

1. **Devotional Scripture reading.** Many Christians read rapidly through the Bible for devotions in a one-year program. That is extremely helpful to gain a broad overview of the Bible's story. But I strongly encourage another kind of devotional reading—namely, to study deeply a single segment of the biblical text and try to understand it. These commentaries are designed to enable that. The commentary is based on the NIV and explains the meaning of the verses, enabling the modern reader to read a few pages at a time and pray over the message.

2. **Church Bible studies.** I have written these commentaries also to serve as guides for group Bible studies. Many Bible studies today consist of people coming together and sharing what they think the text is saying. There are strengths in such an approach, but also weaknesses. The problem is that

God inspired these scriptural passages so that the church would understand and obey *what he intended the text to say.* Without some guidance into the meaning of the text, we are prone to commit heresy. At the very least, the leaders of the Bible study need to have a commentary so they can guide the discussion in the direction God intended. In my own church Bible studies, I have often had the class read a simple exposition of the text so they can all discuss the God-given message, and that is what I hope to provide here.

3. *Sermon aids.* These commentaries are also intended to help pastors faithfully exposit the text in a sermon. Busy pastors often have too little time to study complex thousand-page commentaries on biblical passages. As a result, it is easy to spend little time in Bible study and thereby to have a shallow sermon on Sunday. As I write this series, I am drawing on my own experience as a pastor and interim pastor, asking myself what I would want to include in a sermon.

Overall, my goal in these commentaries is simple: I would like them to be interesting and exciting adventures into New Testament texts. My hope is that readers will discover the riches of God that lie behind every passage in his divine word. I hope every reader will fall in love with God's word as I have and begin a similar lifelong fascination with these eternal truths!

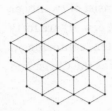

INTRODUCTION TO THE
GOSPEL OF JOHN

The Gospel of John is a remarkable piece of work. If we want a biblical book that is clear, filled with the gospel and good basic theology, and a good read for the young seeker or convert, we give them the Gospel of John. And if we want to study an incredibly deep theological masterpiece that stretches the brightest mind, we open the Gospel of John. It is at one and the same time the easiest to understand and the most complex of all the Gospels. It takes a brilliantly gifted writer to do that.

John is the most accessible and yet the most complex of biblical books because the author gives us the basic gospel as well as the process by which God brings every person ever born to a faith-decision—I call this the "encounter Gospel," the most evangelistic of them all. At the same time, it is a teaching Gospel, intended to give the mature Christian the deepest theological truths to chew on. Further, it is brilliantly creative, a wondrously well-written dramatic masterpiece. If I were teaching a course in college or seminary on creative writing, John's Gospel would be set alongside Shakespeare as a model of brilliant characterization and plot.

The longest stories in the **Synoptic**[1] Gospels consist of twenty or so verses, while John's dramas (chapters 1, 3, 4, 6, 9, 11) are forty or more verses in length and powerfully written, centering on the encounter of various characters with Jesus as the Christ and Son of God.

AUTHOR

At the outset, the most important thing to remember is that this is a biblical book and as such is *the word of God*. As I wrote in the series preface, there are two authors: the human author and the divine Author. Even as I argue that the human author was indeed the apostle John, the more important item must be realized—John was writing under inspiration from the Triune Godhead, and every single word stems from God. In one sense that is all we need to know. Yet still it is important to realize that the channel through whom God decided to give us this material was John, one of the Twelve. When we search for meaning, we are not just asking what John intended to say but what God wanted John to say. The "why" of a text is more than the human author's intention but includes also divine inspiration.

It is critical to know the author of a document and their basic perspective in writing so as to interpret what they say and determine the historical truth of the details. This is why we need commentaries—we cannot do this on our own. All four canonical Gospels, however, are anonymous—they never tell us their authors. So to determine the author of John, we must turn to two sources of information—who the earliest witnesses believed wrote it, and how the author presented himself in his writing.

EXTERNAL EVIDENCE FOR AUTHORSHIP

The traditions contained in the New Testament did not end with the books themselves, for the churches planted by the apostles

---

1. Terms in bold type are discussed in the glossary (page 491).

continued to bear fruit, and there was an ongoing continuity into the **patristic** period of the second to the fourth centuries (around AD 101–400). The traditions that anchored the beliefs of these churches developed in a straight line from the New Testament witnesses. Therefore, the best sources for who wrote the four Gospels would be the church fathers. The earliest of them personally knew Matthew, Mark, Luke, and John, so their witness regarding authorship has to carry a great deal of authority.

From the earliest time we know about, the only title for the Fourth Gospel in Greek manuscripts and other early writings was "The Gospel according to John." So right away the possible field of authors is narrowed to first-century Christians named "John." The earliest church fathers (Justin Martyr, Ignatius, Polycarp) do not mention John by name, though Polycarp quotes 1 John 4:2 (*To the Philippians* 7.1), and Justin Martyr alludes to John 3:3–5 (*First Apology* 61.4–5). This Gospel was a favorite of **gnostic** writers (often cited in the *Gospel of Truth*). Its misuse by these gnostics led to an early reluctance of orthodox authors to quote John.

Still, Tatian used the Gospel of John as the historical basis of his harmonization of the Four Gospels in his *Diatessaron*, and Athenagoras also alluded to it in the second century (*Plea for the Christians* 10). Theophilus of Antioch quotes it (AD 181), and Irenaeus (AD 180) attributes it to the apostle John (*Against Heresies* 3.1.1), as does the Muratorian Canon and the Anti-Marcionite prologue (both late second-century works). Irenaeus says he heard Polycarp talking about being tutored by John (*Against Heresies* 3.3.4). After that period, there was near-unanimous acceptance of the apostolic origins of this Gospel, apart from a group called the *Alogoi*. These opposed the Gospel because of its use by the Montanists, who said their founder was the Paraclete of John 14:16.

The final important witness is Eusebius, the fourth-century historian who listed two early church leaders named John. He quoted Papias, from early in the second century, who spoke of a

"John the elder" behind this Gospel (*Ecclesiastical History* 3.39.4–5). Many see this as a different John from the apostle, but I and others argue that Papias did not separate elders from apostles (compare 1 Pet 5:1 on Peter as "fellow elder") and was writing of the apostle John. In short, the external testimony from the first four centuries strongly favors the apostle John as the author.

INTERNAL EVIDENCE FOR AUTHORSHIP

The text of the Gospel itself also shows us certain things that help identify the author. He is a Jew, most likely from Galilee, a disciple of Jesus, and a person who wrote about Jesus as one who was present for the events he narrates. That narrows the list considerably. Clearly, the author was also "the disciple whom Jesus loved" (= Beloved Disciple, or BD) from John 13:23; 19:26; 20:2; and 21:7, 20, calling himself "the disciple who testifies to these things and who wrote them down" (21:24). This BD has been variously identified as:

- Lazarus (called "loved" in John 11:3, 36);
- John Mark (Acts 12:12), who was an associate of Simon Peter (1 Pet 5:13) and the author of the second Gospel according to tradition;
- Thomas, featured in John 11:16; 20:24–29;
- the elder John (see above);
- the apostle John; or
- a fictional creation used to portray the ideal disciple and author.

Looking at the evidence from John, it is highly unlikely the BD is a fictional creation. He *is* the ideal disciple, but I would argue it is an actual person being portrayed as such. Also, in 21:2 he is one of the seven who experienced the miraculous catch of fish. Almost certainly, this group is meant to be part of the twelve disciples, so that rules out John Mark, Lazarus, or a separate "elder John." Moreover, in every episode the BD is paired with Simon Peter, and this would favor him being a member of the inner circle of three that is so often portrayed in the Gospels—Peter, James, and John. James died young (Acts 12:2), so that does not fit the one prophesied to have a long life ahead him in John 21:20–23. So all in all, the apostle John is by far the most likely to be the BD, and that would favor him as the author of this Gospel.

Nevertheless, many critics strongly doubt that John could have written this on the grounds that (1) a nearly illiterate fisherman who grew up on the shores of the Sea of Galilee could hardly have written so sophisticated a literary work as this; (2) the detailed knowledge of Judean geography and topography demands that the author be from Judea rather than Galilee; and (3) a Galilean fisherman would not have been so close to the high priest that he would have had access to Herod's courtyard in 18:15.

While these arguments have some merit, they are not ultimately successful because most Jews were fairly literate from regularly reading the Torah, and John had spent a great amount of time, perhaps years, in Judea. His family had a priestly background (see commentary on 18:15–16 below), and many of the great writers of history had modest backgrounds. In other words, there is no valid reason why John the son of Zebedee could not have written this masterpiece.

A final objection to John's authorship comes from a theory that has been popular in recent decades called the Johannine Circle. According to this view, John developed a group of disciples who helped him gather and write his material, and it is this group that is responsible for the Fourth Gospel. John was the initial author, but most of the material came from a series of editors, adding stories and details again and again from the preaching of John's community. However, this is quite speculative and depends on the supposition that we can detect in this Gospel a series of "aporias" or clumsy transitions that point to later material. The truth is that in the last thirty years, a series of works have shown the incredible literary unity of this work. It is brilliantly tied together, and in actuality there are no clumsy transitions. This is a brilliantly conceived and executed work with a wonderfully intact plot development (see, for instance, the intro to chapter 21). So I conclude that the Fourth Gospel was written by a single author, the apostle John.

PROVENANCE AND DATE

The earliest possible date for the writing of this Gospel is probably the late 60s, if the author knew of the Gospels of Mark and possibly Matthew, as most suppose today. The latest possible date used to be toward the end of the second century (argued by those who supposed the apostle John was not the author), but that is no longer tenable because of the discovery of two papyri: Egerton Papyrus 2, containing a fragment of an unknown gospel based on John's Gospel and dated AD 130–150; and an early papyrus fragment of John ($\mathfrak{P}$52; John Rylands Papyrus 457), dated AD 110–120. This means the range of possible dates would be AD 70–100.

Most scholars today assign it to the 80s or perhaps the early 90s due to John 21:23, the rumor about John living until Christ returned. If John wrote the book of Revelation, as I argue in that commentary in this series, he was alive at least until the late 90s. Arguments for an early date stem from the absence of any reference to the destruction of Jerusalem and the temple in AD 70, and arguments for a late date stem from the phrase "expelled from the synagogue" in 9:22; 12:42; 16:2, and the Jewish decision to do so in AD 85. Both arguments have a certain viability but prove little. The Jewish ban probably existed in Jesus' day as well. The complexity and depth of John's theology has also mandated a late date for some, but issues like the preexistence and deity of Christ were held much earlier in the early church than many critics have thought. My view is that a date in the middle of these possibilities, say in the early 80s, would best fit the evidence. However, there is no certainty to be had.

Some have seen the provenance (place of origin) of this Gospel as being Alexandria (due to similarities with Philo) or Antioch (due to similarities with the Syriac *Odes of Solomon*), but neither is that likely. The best option by far (and the traditional one) stems from the testimonies of Irenaeus in the second century (*Against Heresies* 3.1.2) and Eusebius in the fourth (*Ecclesiastical History* 3.1.1) that John wrote during his ministry in Ephesus. That fits the book of Revelation as well (and his letters) and provides the most likely place of writing.

AUDIENCE AND PURPOSE OF WRITING

We certainly must begin here with John's own statement of his purpose in 20:31: "But these are written that you may believe that Jesus is the Messiah, the Son of God, and that by believing you may have life in his name." The question is how to interpret "that you may believe," whether it means saving faith on the part of non-Christians, primarily Jews, or growing faith on the part of Christians. This is critical, for it matters a great deal whether John is evangelistic in intent or is primarily a teaching Gospel.

It is quite common today to think that all four Gospels, including John, were written almost entirely for Christians. For example, sociological approaches to the Gospels have developed theories that each evangelist had his own community in mind. (This is called in German *Sitz im Leben*, the "situation in the life" of the individual community.) However, a growing number have started to challenge this as unduly speculative and believe that all four Gospels were written for the church as a whole. This makes a great deal of sense, for there is no evidence in the second century for such tightly controlled communities as ones dedicated to Matthew's or Luke's or John's teachings.

A side effect of this debate is the neglect of the possibility that the Gospels could have an evangelistic purpose. This is an overly narrow assumption. While Mark and Matthew could be understood as not showing a deep interest in reaching the lost, Luke and John at least both have a developed **soteriology** (doctrine of salvation). I will discuss John's interest more below, but it is clear that there is a developed emphasis on evangelism in this work.

John wanted both to awaken faith in unbelievers and to bolster faith in believers. In chapters 1–12 encounters with Jesus and faith-decisions are quite numerous, and salvation dramas are in the foreground—Jesus with John's disciples in chapter 1, with Nicodemus in chapter 3, with the Samaritan woman in chapter 4, and so on. However, this is not the only thing John is interested in, for he also carefully chronicles the conflict of believers with Jewish adversaries and shows the disciples growing in their faith and in their sense of mission.

LITERARY STYLE

This Gospel has a unique and highly literate style of writing. John's discourses are written in high prose and at times have a poetic air about them. At the same time, his Greek can seem clumsy, using too much parataxis (coordinate clauses instead of subordination) and asyndeton (clauses connected without conjunctions), neither of which was considered good style. He loved variation and double meaning, favoring synonyms for stylistic variation (for instance, four word-pairs in the well-known "do you love me" passage of 21:15–17).

John's use of key terms again and again makes this Gospel a treasure house for word studies and for theological themes—for example, *witness, command, life, truth, world, abide, light, darkness,* and *reveal*. Further, his narratives are filled with misunderstandings (Jesus speaks on the heavenly plane while his audience interprets on the earthly plane) and irony (with the forces of evil forced to do God's bidding).

One of the best-known aspects of John's Gospel is its differences with the Synoptic Gospels. Over 85 percent of this Gospel is material unique to John. For a while many thought John did not know about the others, but recently the tide has shifted and it is now believed that he decided to remain independent. There are several places that demonstrate some dependence, especially on

Mark (John 3:24; 5:33–35; 7:1; 11:2, 56–57; 18:24, 28). John uses the Synoptic tradition but is largely independent of it.

The result of this independence is that many key events in Jesus' life are not present. The baptism of Jesus is told second-hand in 1:32–33, and the temptation by Satan, the transfiguration, and Gethsemane are all omitted. There is no mission discourse, no Olivet Discourse, no exorcisms, and none of the lengthy parables. In their place are several added sections, like the calling of John the Baptist's disciples in chapter 1, the two Cana miracles, the encounters with Nicodemus and the Samaritan woman, the conflict narratives of chapters 5–8, the raising of Lazarus, and the Good Shepherd *mashal* (extended metaphor).

The style used in the discourses differs markedly from Synoptic material. The "messianic secret" of Mark, where Jesus asks that nothing he is doing be told (see, for example, Mark 3:11–12; 8:29–30), is reversed in John by the "I am" sayings, as Jesus tells everyone who he is. Mark is secretive; John is confrontational. Many critical scholars wonder if we have the same Jesus in John, but the differences do not really warrant so radical a conclusion. It is true that Mark is more secretive, but Matthew and Luke contain both secrecy material and stories in which Jesus reveals who he is. So the style progresses from secretive Mark to outspoken John, with Matthew and Luke a happy medium on the scale. The truth is that Jesus at times held his cards close to the vest and other times proclaimed the truth from the housetops. John brings out the latter side of Jesus.

The divinity of Jesus, though not as explicit and forceful in the Synoptics, is still present in all the Gospels. There is no contradiction. Consider what has been labeled the "Johannine thunderbolt" in Matthew 11:27: "All things have been committed to me by my Father. No one knows the Son except the Father, and no one knows the Father except the Son and those to whom the Son chooses to reveal him." You cannot get much closer to the language of John than this. Also, note the incredibly high **Christology** of Matthew 26:64: "From now on you will see the Son of Man sitting at the right hand of the Mighty One and coming on the clouds of heaven." John does have the "highest" theology of the four, but it is not a new theology.

HISTORICAL RELIABILITY

Over the last couple centuries no Gospel has been as doubted as this one with respect to the historical truthfulness of its material, due both to its differences with the Synoptics and to the depth of its theology (for example, its presentation of the deity of Christ). Its distinctive portrayal of events like Jesus' numerous trips to Jerusalem during his public ministry or the raising of Lazarus as the driving force of passion week makes many doubt its accuracy.

More recently, there have also been quite a few articles in critical journals on the historical reliability of the Gospel of John, but when one reads them more closely it is not the Gospel that is seen as historical but the community behind John's Gospel. These scholars have redefined the meaning of *historical* to the point that it no longer refers to the events behind the Gospel narrative but rather to a scholarly re-creation of the community assumed to exist at the time of writing. It is this "historical community" that made up the stories on the basis of their community needs.

However, along with many recent scholars I have become convinced that if anything John has greater emphasis on the historical reliability of his material than any of the other three Gospels. His is definitely the most chronological of them, since it is built around three Passovers (2:13; 13:1; 18:28).

His eyewitness style stands out throughout his narrative. His narration of Jesus' trips to Jerusalem certainly happened just as he says, for pilgrimages at festival time were commonplace for faithful Jews. As we learn more and more about the times and customs of the period when Jesus walked this earth, John is increasingly corroborated for the accuracy of his portrayals. With his frequent use of "witness" and "truth," it is clear that John's intention is to write a verifiable historical document, and he demonstrates an interest in apologetics by writing with an eyewitness flavor that can be verified as authentic.

OUTLINE

John's primary interest is in theological history, and the structure of his Gospel reflects that interest, including a prologue (1:1–18) and epilogue (21:1–25), a preparatory period (1:19–51), a series of events detailing Jesus' public ministry (2:1–12:50), a lengthy farewell address (13:31–17:26), a passion narrative (18:1–19:42), and a two-pronged resurrection narrative (20:1–21:25), with chapter 21 functioning as both an epilogue and part of the resurrection material.

I. Prologue: The Word made flesh (1:1–18)
  A. The essence of the Word and creation (1:1–5)
    1. The divinity of the Word (1:1–2)
    2. The Word in the old creation (1:3)
    3. The Word in the old and new creations (1:4–5)
  B. The witness of John the Baptist (1:6–8)
  C. The coming of the incarnate Word (1:9–14)
    1. The coming of the true light (1:9)
    2. The rejection of the Word by the world (1:10–11)
    3. The Word as accepted (1:12–13)
    4. The incarnation of the Word (1:14)
  D. The greatness and grace of the Word (1:15–18)
    1. John's further testimony (1:15)
    2. Grace received from the Word (1:16–17)
    3. The revelation of God by the One and Only Son (1:18)
II. John witnesses about Jesus (1:19–34)
  A. The revelation of John's identity (1:19–23)
    1. Their questions (1:19–22)
    2. John's witness about himself (1:23)

B. The revelation of John's mission (1:24-28)
  1. The question about his baptism (1:24-25)
  2. John's answer (1:26-28)
C. The witness of John about Jesus (1:29-34)
  1. Initial testimony to the Lamb of God (1:29-31)
  2. The deeper witness of the Spirit (1:32-34)
III. Jesus begins to form his band of disciples (1:35-51)
  A. The first three disciples come to Jesus (1:35-42)
    1. John's continued witness (1:35-36)
    2. Interaction with the two disciples (1:37-39)
    3. The aftermath: Andrew brings Peter to Jesus (1:40-42a)
    4. Jesus' prophecy and witness about Peter (1:42b)
  B. Philip and Nathanael come to Jesus (1:43-51)
    1. Jesus takes the initiative (1:43-44)
    2. The invitation to Nathanael (1:45-46)
    3. Jesus encounters Nathanael (1:47-49)
    4. Jesus the Son of Man (1:50-51)
IV. The public ministry of Jesus: signs and teaching (2:1-12:50)
  A. Glory revealed: the beginning stages of Jesus' ministry (2:1-4:54)
    1. The new wine and the new temple (2:1-25)
      a. The first sign: turning water into wine at Cana (2:1-12)
      b. Confrontation in the temple (2:13-25)
    2. Nicodemus and the new birth (3:1-21)
      a. Introduction: encounter at night (3:1-2)
      b. First dialogue: the new birth (3:3-4)
      c. Second dialogue: water and Spirit (3:5-8)
      d. Jesus confronts Nicodemus's ignorance (3:9-12)
      e. Jesus' heavenly authority (3:13-15)
      f. Commentary: life and light confront the world (3:16-21)

3. The Baptist testifies to the glory of Christ (3:22–36)
   a. The Baptist's final witness (3:22–30)
   b. Commentary: the glory of the Son (3:31–36)
4. The Samaritan woman and return to Cana (4:1–54)
   a. Return to Galilee through Samaria (4:1–6a)
   b. Initial encounter: request for water (4:6b–9)
   c. Second encounter: offer of living water (4:10–12)
   d. Third encounter: water of life (4:13–15)
   e. Fourth encounter: awareness of her marital situation (4:16–18)
   f. Fifth encounter: growing awareness and worship (4:19–22)
   g. Sixth encounter: true worship is in Spirit and truth (4:23–24)
   h. Seventh encounter: Jesus identifies himself as the Christ (4:25–26)
   i. The disciples' return and the woman's witness (4:27–30)
   j. The mission discourse (4:31–38)
   k. The harvest: Jesus as savior of the world (4:39–42)
   l. Healing and conversion at Cana (4:43–54)
B. Jesus and the festivals of the Jews (5:1–10:42)
   1. Healing of the lame man on the Sabbath (5:1–15)
      a. Jesus and the man at the pool (5:1–5)
      b. Healing on the Sabbath (5:6–9a)
      c. The Sabbath controversy (5:9b)
      d. Interaction with the leaders (5:10–13)
      e. Reaction to Jesus (5:14–15)
   2. Conflict over Jesus' claim to be Son of God (5:16–47)
      a. Thesis: sharing the Father's work (5:16–18)

VI. The arrest, trial, and passion of Jesus (18:1–19:42)
- A. The arrest of Jesus (18:1–11)
  1. Betrayed by Judas (18:1–3)
  2. Jesus goes forth as a sovereign (18:4–9)
  3. The arrest (18:10–12)
- B. The interrogation by Annas and Peter's denials (18:13–27)
  1. Jesus before Annas (18:13–14)
  2. Peter's first denial (18:15–18)
  3. Interrogation by Annas (18:19–24)
  4. The final two denials (18:25–27)
- C. The trial before Pilate (18:28–19:16a)
  1. Outside: the Jews demand Jesus' death (18:28–32)
  2. Inside: Pilate questions Jesus about his kingship (18:33–38a)
  3. Outside: Pilate finds Jesus not guilty (18:38b–40)
  4. Inside: the soldiers scourge Jesus (19:1–3)
  5. Outside: Pilate again finds Jesus not guilty (19:4–8)
  6. Inside: Pilate talks with Jesus about power (19:9–11)
  7. Outside: the Jews obtain the death penalty (19:12–16a)
- D. The crucifixion and burial of Jesus (19:16b–42)
  1. The crucifixion of Jesus (19:16b–37)
  2. The burial of Jesus (19:38–42)

VII. The resurrection of Jesus (20:1–21:25)
- A. The appearances in Jerusalem (20:1–31)
  1. The empty tomb and the great race (20:1–10)
     a. The dilemma of the missing body (20:1–2)
     b. The race to the tomb (20:3–4)
     c. The entry into the tomb and apologetics (20:5–7)
     d. Seeing and believing (20:8–9)

MAJOR THEOLOGICAL THEMES

At the core of this Gospel is the wondrous good news that Jesus Christ the Son of God became incarnate and descended to earth in order to reveal God and bring God's salvation to fallen humanity. It is impossible to separate soteriology (the doctrine of salvation) from Christology (the doctrine of Christ) at the center of this book. Since this is mainly an encounter Gospel in which Christ enlightens every person (1:4, 7, 9) and challenges them about the truths of God, soteriology is placed first. The light of God in Jesus forces people to make a decision based on faith. No one can remain neutral about Jesus; each one must decide to accept or reject Christ, and their eternal destiny awaits that faith-decision.

SALVATION

The dramas in this Gospel (chapters 1, 3, 4, 5, 9) stress what I call a "faith-decision," demonstrated in the conversion of the five disciples in 1:35–51; the challenge to Nicodemus in 3:1–15; and the conversions of the Samaritan woman in 4:1–42 and of the man born blind in 9:1–41. The decision to reject Jesus is found in the healing of the lame man in 5:1–15. The emphasis in John is on the universal nature of this encounter. Jesus sheds his light on every person (1:4, 7, 9) and is "Savior of the world" (4:42), indeed of "all" humanity (1:7; 5:23; 11:48; 12:32).

John develops his theology through key terms, as Jesus' mission is to the "world" (105 of its 186 occurrences in the New Testament are in John), with Satan the "prince [ruler] of this world" (12:31; 14:30; 16:11). The Jewish people have lost their place as the covenant people and are part of this world (1:10–11), but in spite of its rebellion and obstinacy, God loves this world and sends his Son to save it (1:29; 3:16–17; 4:42; 6:33). The world is characterized by unbelief (3:36; 16:9), but Christ has defeated Satan (12:31; 16:11) and brought salvation.

The faith encounter is seen in clusters of terms that occur in virtually every chapter: (1) "believe/faith" (ninety-eight times versus thirty-four total in the Synoptics), always a verb to stress the dynamic nature of faith commitment; (2) two verbs for "know" (used a total of 141 times) centered on the intimate mutual knowledge of the Father and Son extended to God's people; (3) five verbs for "see" (used a total of 114 times), often signifying spiritual insight and coupled with the first two terms to depict the life of discipleship; (4) "life/eternal life" (sixty-six of its 135 times in the New Testament), stressing the result of faith-decision, with eternal life not just a future gift but also a present possession of the believer; (5) "truth" (eighty-five of 163 times in the New Testament), indicating both intellectual truth and moral truth, the latter stressing authentic patterns of living in light of the final truth that has been revealed in Christ.

JESUS CHRIST, BOTH GOD AND MAN

There is a remarkable balance in John between Jesus' humanity and his divinity. Jesus' deity is expressed powerfully in 1:1, 14, 18; 10:30; and in his "I am" sayings, especially those in the absolute form, which can be translated, "I, Yahweh, am he" (8:24, 28, 58; 13:19). These are direct allusions to God's revelation of himself as Yahweh at the burning bush in Exodus 3:14–15 and of 'anoki hu' (I am he) in Isaiah 43:10; 47:8, 10; 51:12 to signify "God and God alone."

Yet as the Son of the Father, Jesus is not only one with him but also subordinate to him. This is implicit in the prologue (John 1:1–18), with Jesus as the revealing Word, and explicit in Jesus as the Sent One or agent of God in 3:17 (thirty times in the Gospel) and in 5:19–30, where John makes clear his dependence on the Father in life and judgment. He is fully God and at the same time is submissive to God his Father. Note the primary concepts:

- *The Living Revealer*—This is the meaning of *logos*, the "Word," as Jesus came into this world to make his Father known to it, so that sinful people could meet God and encounter him at every level of their being.
- *The Son of Man*—This title speaks of the one who will be "lifted up" on the cross to glory (3:14; 8:28; 12:32). He is the descending and ascending Redeemer (1:51) who reveals the **Shekinah** glory to humanity (1:14) and becomes the gate to heaven (6:62). Scholars debate whether Jesus used this title as a circumlocution for "I" in line with Ezekiel (who uses it ninety-three times of him as a mortal human being) or in an exalted sense for the one who has dominion over all the earth in line with Daniel 7:13–14. In John it has both emphases but primarily Daniel's use, stressing the **apocalyptic** glory of Jesus through suffering.
- *The Messiah, Son of God*—The revelation of Jesus as "the Messiah, the Son of God," in John 20:31 is the major purpose of this Gospel. The Father-Son relationship dominates this work. Jesus is "the one and only Son" (1:14, 18; 3:16, 18) who

shares his Father's glory. He is the royal Messiah, the "King
of Israel" or "King of the Jews" (1:49; 12:13; 18:33; 19:3, 19)
whose throne is the cross. He is also the means of atonement for the world (1:29; 6:51; 10:11, 15; 11:50–52; 15:13; 17:19).

The Holy Spirit

The Spirit is first of all a member of the Trinity, sent by the Father
(14:16, 26) and the Son (15:26) to reveal divine truths. He is given
"without limit" to Jesus (3:34) and remains on him (1:32–33) and is the
source of the "living water" (4:10) that flows from him (7:37–39). As
part of the divine mission to the world, the Spirit is the "Advocate,"
the representative of the Godhead sent to the world to convict it of
its sin (14:16; 16:8–11) and to Jesus' followers to guide and empower
them in their mission to the world (14:15–17, 26; 15:26; 16:12–15). He
indwells the hearts of believers as "the Spirit of truth" (14:17; 15:26;
16:13), guiding them to the divine truths revealed in Jesus.

Mission

In John, God's salvation is revealed to the world in four stages:
(1) God reveals himself to the world by (2) sending his Son as his
agent or envoy to reach the world. Then (3) both Father and Son
send the Spirit, and finally, (4) the Triune Godhead sends his followers to bring the message of salvation to the world. Virtually
every aspect of the Fourth Gospel depicts a part of this mission,
and it involves not just the disciples of Jesus but all future believers
as well. We are all engaged in carrying on Jesus' mission to bring
forgiveness of sin and eternal life to fallen humanity.

Eschatology

Eschatology throughout the New Testament deals with more than
the last things, the end of human history. The New Testament
authors teach that the last days have already begun, a reality that
touches every area of believers' lives. For John, every single doctrine he presents flows through this great truth.

Some scholars teach that John has replaced the final eschatology of the Synoptic Gospels with a realized eschatology centered on the present blessings of believers. According to this way of seeing things, the Olivet Discourse is replaced by John's Farewell Discourse (13:31–17:26), and the return of Christ with the coming of the Holy Spirit (14:16–17, 26). However, this is not actually the case. John clearly has an interest in the second coming and the arrival of eternity (5:25, 28–30; 6:39–40; 14:2–4; 21:22). It is far better to see in John's emphasis on present blessings an anticipation of their final realization, namely, God's promises fulfilled at the return of Christ.

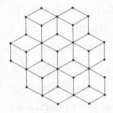

PROLOGUE: THE WORD MADE FLESH

(1:1–18)

The purpose of a prologue in any of the Gospels is to introduce the drama of Jesus and the key themes that will flow through the writer's presentation. This is probably the most remarkable prologue ever written, and one could easily take an entire book to present in depth all that John says. Jesus is the Living Revealer (Word) of God and is God himself. In Jesus God has taken on human flesh (incarnation), and in him the **Shekinah** (God "dwelling" among his people) walks planet Earth. Moreover, Jesus has brought the light of salvation into this world, and sinners by believing in him can become the children of God. However, sin is the great obstacle between God and humanity, and sinners must turn to Christ and be reborn to be forgiven. Many of the key terms in this Gospel are introduced here: *life, light, darkness, sent, truth, world, believe, know, receive, witness, new birth, love,* and *glory.* These terms will come up again and again throughout John's narrative.

It is not necessary to say, as some have, that this prologue was written after the Gospel was finished, perhaps by another author. The language and style fit the rest of the narrative quite closely, and they were clearly written together. Others have labeled this a hymn with prose insertions, and they debate which parts are the hymn and which the insertions—for instance, verses 1–5 (6–8), 9–14 (15–18), or 1–2, 3–5 (6–9), 10–12a (12b–13), 14 (15–18).

However, while it is poetic, it is likely best categorized as high prose rather than a preexisting hymn. I would conclude that the prologue is particularly beautiful prose with a depth of theology unmatched in any other writing. Every time I teach or write on this material (like now), I am thrilled just at the privilege of digging into it once again.

JOHN BEGINS WITH THE ESSENCE OF THE WORD AND CREATION (1:1–5)

John has deliberately constructed the story of the "new creation" by Jesus after the opening words of Genesis, "In the beginning God created the heavens and the earth" (Gen 1:1). It all started not with the material that made up the old creation but with the Word: "In the beginning was the Word." Jesus was there at the origins of the universe and that he was involved in that creation, which we will see in verses 3–4. This is also a statement of preexistence, that Jesus as the Word existed before time and creation began. As creator of both physical and spiritual life, he was the divine agent responsible for both the original creation of the world (v. 3) and the spiritual re-creation of the world (v. 4). The Son of God as the preexistent Word is the basis of all the incredible claims John makes in this section. The first two verses relate who he was before creation, verse 3 tells what he did in creation, and verse 4 states what he is doing in the new creation to bring spiritual light and life into this world.

Jesus as the "Word" (*logos*) in Greek thought would denote the principle of reason that governs life and makes thinking possible. However, John's use here is much closer to Jewish concepts of the Word as the divine Wisdom that God used to create the world (Prov 8:30–31) and was seen as God's living voice in his relation to the world. So this means Jesus is the "Living Revealer" of God, the very voice of God in this world (Ps 33:6).

THE DIVINITY OF THE WORD (1:1-2)

This first verse relates three things about the Word: He is preexistent (NLT, "already existed"), he enjoys a special relationship with God, and he is himself deity. Each step is more intense than the previous one. The Word first exists before creation comes into being, then has a special relationship with God, and finally is in his very nature God himself. Think what is going through John's mind as he pens this. This Jesus with whom he walked throughout Galilee was actually the eternal Word, God himself in human flesh. He created the very world in which he walked, and when he spoke it was the very voice of God John heard. Only a being who had that special relationship with God and was there at the beginning could have created this world, and John walked with him!

The idea that the Word was "with" (Greek: *pros*) God connotes both presence (they were together) and special relationship—the idea of *pros* is often "side by side" with another. In the second and third statements, Jesus' humanity (relationship with) and divinity (identity with) are brought together. He is the God-man.

The Greek for "The Word was God" (*theos ēn ho logos*) has been misused by Jehovah's Witnesses, who interpret the absence of the article before God to mean "a god." There are several serious errors in this. To begin with, there is no actual relationship between the Greek and English articles. The absence of the article in Greek rarely meant "a," and it normally established an abstract aspect, namely, that Jesus partook of divinity or "Godness." At the same time, it was common in Greek to designate the subject by using the article (so "the word" was the subject) and to show the predicate nominative by leaving off the article (so "God" or "divinity" come after the verb), resulting in "the Word was God/divine." This is proved when the same thing takes place in 1:18, when *theos* without the article is used for God the Father ("no one has seen God at any time"). So this cannot be translated "the Word was a god" in this context. It is a perfectly clear statement of divinity.

The second verse combines the first two clauses of verse 1, reemphasizing the special relationship of the Word "with God" at the origin of creation. In this sense, it states that the act of creation in Genesis 1 is renewed in the new creation established by the Word. The gospel reality constitutes this new creation and was the purpose of God and the Word "in the beginning."

THE WORD IN THE OLD CREATION (1:3)

As a corollary to the deity of the Word, John tells us that he was the agent of God in the very act of creation. Christ as Creator is an exciting truth found also in 1 Corinthians 8:6; Colossians 1:16; Hebrews 1:3; and Revelation 3:14. To emphasize this truth, John states it positively ("Through him all things were made") and negatively ("without him nothing was made"). Every single aspect of the created order came into being "through" (*dia*) him. This is even more wondrous for us, for we know that there are more galaxies out there than there are stars in our galaxy, and there are more complex cells in our body than have ever been imagined before. With all our knowledge, we know that the created universe is beyond scientific understanding, and the Word has made it all! Christ is both Creator and Sustainer of all there is.

When John says "in the beginning" in 1:1, he does not mean that the Word came into being along with creation as parallel births. The Word preexisted creation and was the power that brought creation into being. John uses expansive language—"all things" and "nothing"—to stress the whole of creation. The verb *egeneto* means "to come into existence" and here stresses the act of creation ("were made"). The technical phrase we now use to describe this is *creatio ex nihilo*, "created out of nothing," meaning that there were no materials out of which God made the world. Everything mentioned in the six days of creation of Genesis 1 was the product of the creative work of the Word.

It is unclear whether the phrase that ends verse 3 in most versions ("that has been made") actually ends verse 3 (as in NIV, KJV,

NASB, LEB, NET) or should start verse 4 (with NRSV, NLT, NJB), thus reading, "What has been made in him was life." My opinion is that the parallelism of the lines and the developing thought fits the latter better than a redundant "nothing was made that has been made." I disagree that in the second option "what has been made" would have to mean the incarnation. I believe it is the new creation, and that fits very well in the context.

The Word in the Old and New Creations (1:4–5)

Life and light are at the heart of the Genesis 1 creation, and they form the core of the new creation as well. So in these verses there is a double meaning in the move from physical life and light to spiritual life and light in Christ. The Word has bridged the gap between the two. Life is encased in the Word, and in God's gift to sinful humanity the life and light of God have become incarnate. Spiritual life is now available to all, and that life has become "the light of all mankind," meaning it illuminates every human being with the light of God. All of creation culminates in the new life found in Christ.

The two key words "life" and "light" permeate all of John's writings. "Life" appears thirty-six times in John and seventeen in Revelation, nearly half of the total number in the New Testament. The earthly life of the old creation has been transformed into the heavenly, eternal life of the new creation.

The imagery of "light" is another major concept, appearing twenty-three times in John. The light-darkness motif is a dominant theme in the Gospel. Here it is part of what is called the "universal salvific will" of God, presented in verses 4, 7, 9, and here. Putting the three together, God sheds his salvific light on all humanity (v. 4) so that they may experience that light and believe (v. 7), and that means every single person is convicted by the light of God (v. 9). The doctrine is best defined in 2 Peter 3:9, where Peter states that God does not want "anyone to perish, but everyone to come to repentance." This looks to the revelation of God in Jesus, as all of us are confronted with our utter sinfulness by the light of Jesus and his sacrificial death so our sins could be forgiven. Here we are at the very heart of John's gospel message.

John introduces the darkness-light dualism in verse 5. The light of God "shines in the darkness" through the Word, building on Genesis 1:2–3: "The earth was formless and empty, darkness was over the surface of the deep. ... And God said, 'Let there be light.'" The darkness here is greater and more sinister, for it is the darkness of sin (as in John 3:19; 8:12; 12:35), but as in Genesis it has felt God's salvific light. Throughout John the war between light and darkness rages.

However, John expresses the eternal truth clearly: "The darkness has not overcome it." There is a debate here, for the verb *katelaben* can mean either "understand, comprehend" (as in KJV, NASB, NIV 1984) or "overcome, extinguish" (so NIV, NRSV, NLT, ESV). The former would fit the influence of 1:10, in which the world does not "recognize" or "know" the true light. There are also some who think there is a double meaning here, as the world does not understand the light and so opposes it.

While this is probably true, the main thrust in this context of conflict is on the inability of darkness to keep the light of conviction from shining in the lives of those the Spirit encounters (as in 12:35, "walk while you have the light, before darkness overtakes you"). Throughout this Gospel the light of Christ confronts the darkness of sin and forces the sinner to make a decision to accept or reject the light, and nothing can stop that light from shining.

JOHN THE BAPTIST ARRIVES AS A WITNESS (1:6–8)

John explained the heavenly reality behind this extraordinary new creation in verses 1–5. Now the prologue turns to the earthly witness to this light of God, the Word. The Word was not a purely supernatural phenomenon but actually appeared on the stage of this world. He was heralded by John the Baptist, who is introduced in verse 6: "There was a man sent from God whose name was John."

"There was" might better be translated "there came," using the verb (*egeneto*) that in verse 3 described creation ("was made"). This may carry a small bit of that force and describe John as created for this very purpose. He was part of the new creation. In the same way that God was the source of the light, he was the source for the witness. The Baptist was "sent from God" as his official envoy to prepare for the arrival of the Word, whom we now know is Jesus the Christ. He is the first of the "sent ones," a semi-technical description of a *shaliach* or (sent) ambassador to represent God and his ultimate Sent One, Jesus.

The ministry of this John is described in verse 7 as his being a "witness," which is a frequent theme that speaks of official testimony to the reality of the Christ (5:31–40; 8:14–18). As a witness he was sent from God to testify "concerning that light"—Jesus as the Word. There is a judicial flavor to this concept: Jesus is presented in the courtroom of this world, and the witness to this reality is none other than John the Baptist.

The purpose of this testimony dominates this Gospel: "so that through him all might believe." The verdict is clear, and it is proved that Jesus is indeed the Word, the light of God. This continues the message of verses 4–5, namely, God's desire that "all mankind" might respond to the light by making a faith-decision for Christ. This doesn't teach universalism, for every person will not be saved, but every person will be encountered by the light (v. 5) and be convicted by it (see 16:7–8). The mission theme of John's Gospel begins here, preparing the reader for 1:35–39, where two who hear the Baptist's witness do indeed believe and follow Jesus.

John wants to make sure there is no misunderstanding and so tells us in verse 8, "He himself was not the light; he came only as a witness to the light." The entire focus of the prologue is to introduce the world to the Word, Jesus, whom we will see as "the true light" in verse 9. Some have thought this reflects a later time when a Baptist cult existed that placed John above Jesus (perhaps this is also behind Acts 19:1–7). That is no more than a possibility, though.

This verse centers on the purpose of John and to place his ministry in proper historical perspective as preparation for Jesus' coming.

THE WORD BECOMES INCARNATE (1:9–14)

THE COMING OF THE TRUE LIGHT (1:9)

It is not the Baptist but the Word that is "the true light," meaning the one who can truly light the way to God. In John, "true" means the "genuine" or "authentic" revelation of God, and as such the Word alone can "give light to everyone." Only the true light is able to enlighten the sinner with the light of God, meaning he is the only source of salvation. Moreover, he illuminates "every person," culminating the theme from verses 4 and 7 on the universal convicting power of God. Again, this does not mean that everyone will be saved. The light shining on every single person means all are brought to the place of decision, but then the light of God separates humanity into believers and unbelievers depending on their response. Every human being experiences the light of God in their lives, but many, probably the majority, reject the light. They cannot extinguish it (v. 5), but those who "love darkness instead of light" will "hate the light" (3:19–20).

This true light became incarnate and "was coming into the world." He was no Olympian deity who dwelt on a mountain far removed from his subjects and cared very little for them. No, he became one of us and was crucified for us so he could bring us to God. As the world was rebelling against God, it was also the focus of God's salvific love (3:16) and the recipient of the sacrifice of the God-man in order to save that very world (3:17; 6:51; 12:47). He became incarnate to take away the sins of the world (1:29), bring life to the world (6:33), and be the Savior of the world (4:42).

THE REJECTION OF THE WORD BY THE WORLD (1:10–11)

We are now introduced to the truth about the world. The term *kosmos* ("world") appears seventy-eight times in John's Gospel, 105 times in all of his writings (John, 1–3 John, and Revelation). This is more than half of all the occurrences (186) in the entire New Testament. The world is dominated by sin and rebellion, with Satan "the ruler of this world" (12:31; 14:30; 16:20). Hostility typifies the world's reaction, yet at the same time it is the recipient of God's salvific love (3:16), and Jesus was sent to save it (1:29; 3:17; 4:42; 6:33). These two verses cover the reactions of the world as a whole (v. 10) and of the Jewish people in particular (v. 11), implying that the Jewish people are now part of the world.

The Word entered this world in order to experience rejection and to die in order to save it. John begins verse 10 with the double truth of his incarnation ("He was in the world") and act of creation ("the world was made through him"). It would be expected that the world of humankind would love and worship the very one who had created them and their world (v. 3) and who had loved them enough to become one of them. Instead, they failed to recognize him. The verb behind "recognize" (ginōskō) doesn't just mean they *failed to know* who he was but rather that they *rejected* who he was. To "know" him would demand repentance and conversion, a complete change of perspective on life. They were unwilling to take that step. They demanded Christ meet them on their own terms, and so were unwilling to accept the revealed Word and the salvation-offering Savior.

John turns to a significant part of this created world in verse 11, saying he also came to *ta idia*, "that which was his own" or "those who belonged to him." The Old Testament speaks of the Jewish people as "his treasured possession" (Deut 7:6), so this shows how his own people, the Jews, reacted to the Word. They relinquished their special relationship, for they too turned against Christ and so throughout the Gospel of John are part of the world. Yet they have far less excuse than the rest of the world, for they were the covenant people and understood the work of creation, yet they too rejected their Creator. God's own Son, their expected Messiah, arrived, and they "did not receive him." They repudiated him. "Did not know" and "did not receive" are sister terms, stating the reality of their deliberate rejection of the "true light."

THE WORD AS ACCEPTED (1:12–13)

John divides the world into two groups—those who reject and those who accept. In verse 12 God gives those who accept and believe a new status and authority: "Yet to all who did receive him, to those who believed in his name, he gave the right to become children of God." Receiving and believing are the antithesis of "not knowing/receiving" and are virtual synonyms, with "believe" another key term in John, occurring ninety-eight times versus a total of thirty-four in the **Synoptic** Gospels and fifty-four in all of Paul's writings. It is always a verb, stressing the dynamic process of faith-decision. This belief is "in his name," meaning the full reality and person behind "the Word." To believe is to immerse one's self in all that is Jesus as the Word of God.

Here we see the result of the revelation of the Word and the new creation that is effected. The first eleven verses have led up to this moment, and we now realize our part in this drama. To "give the right" means for the Word to bestow "authority" (*exousia*) on the believers as "children of God." They have the right to belong to a new family, and their status changes from peasant to prince. The new birth makes them part of the royal household of heaven. In the new creation, believers are royalty.

In verse 13 John shows the extent of this new authority, controlled not by human effort but only by God. He uses the metaphor of birth to present this truth, preparing for the new-birth imagery of 3:3–8. This new birth is "not of natural descent, nor of human decision or a husband's will, but born of God." This new-creation reality, this spiritual rebirth, cannot be brought about by human passion or family planning. Only God can accomplish it. It comes about not by natural means but by supernatural intervention. We participate via faith in Christ.

THE INCARNATION OF THE WORD (1:14)

In my opinion, this is the single greatest sentence ever written in the history of the human language, the deepest theological statement ever written. No finite human being could ever enter the realm of God and join his family. It could only come to pass if God himself were to enter the realm of humanity and provide redemption. Here John tells how this came to pass: "The Word became flesh," not only the high point of this prologue but also the high point of history. God has become incarnate in the Word and entered this world. The Creator has become a creature and "made his dwelling among us." Moreover, by "becoming flesh" Jesus took on himself human nature in its fullness, the full reality of being human. He entered the realm of darkness and became light in the darkness. It is impossible for finite minds to comprehend the incarnation. To think of God of very God encased in human flesh, fully God and fully human, is a mystery beyond us. Like the Trinity, we don't fully understand it but fully rejoice as we accept it.

The phrase "made his dwelling among us" is *eskēnōsen* in the Greek, literally "tabernacled among us." This pictures the Old Testament Shekinah, the glory of God dwelling among his people in the tabernacle and temple. This presence of God with his people was seen in the pillar of fire by night and the cloud by day in the exodus (Exod 13:21) and then filled the tabernacle, making it the most sacred object in the universe, the physical manifestation of God's holy presence (Exod 25:8–9; Ezek 43:7; Zech 2:13; 8:3). In Jesus as the Word, the Shekinah walked planet Earth; he was a walking holy of holies. I guarantee John was weeping with joy as he wrote this!

If "we have seen his glory," no wonder there was no longer a need for the temple. All that the temple meant was wrapped up in Jesus. The glory of God, once sealed in the temple on penalty of death, was now opened up to all in Jesus. This glory is further defined as "the glory of the one and only Son." In the KJV this was

translated "the only begotten," for the Greek term is *monogenēs*.
This can be used of an only child (Judg 11:34 LXX;[1] Luke 7:12; Heb
11:17), but that is not the force here. The components of the word
are *monos* and *ginomai*, and here they mean "the only one of a kind,"
stressing the uniqueness of "the one and only Son," the God-man
who alone shared the divine glory.

Finally, this glory-filled Word "came from the Father, full of
grace and truth" (echoing Exod 34:6). Virtually all agree the background to this is found in Exodus 33–34, where Moses asks to see
God's glory (Exod 33:18) and God passes in front of him, declaring
himself to be "the God of compassion and mercy ... [full of] *unfailing love and faithfulness*" (NLT). "Grace and truth" reflect the two
primary Hebrew terms used of God in the Old Testament, *chesed*
("gracious lovingkindness") and *emet* ("genuine covenant faithfulness"). The Word embodies God's gracious love and his absolute faithfulness.

WE SEE THE GREATNESS AND
GRACE OF THE WORD (1:15–18)

As the unique glory of God tabernacling on earth, the Word is
now seen in his greatness. We begin with the further witness of
John the Baptist.

JOHN'S FURTHER TESTIMONY (1:15)

John's testimony employs a play on words where the temporal
becomes a statement of status, "The one who comes after me
[*opisō*, temporal] is before me [*emprosthen*, status], because he
is first [*prōtos*, status] over me" (my translation). The Word was
born after John but surpassed him. John was the forerunner to
the Messiah, but Jesus was the vastly superior figure, for he is
the one whose coming had been anticipated for generations. The

---

1. "LXX" is an abbreviation for the **Septuagint**, the Greek Old Testament commonly used in the early church.

notation that he "existed before me" refers back to the preexistence spoken of in 1:1. The Word had absolute primacy and priority over John.

GRACE RECEIVED FROM THE WORD (1:16–17)

In verse 14 the Word was seen as "full of grace and truth," and John now builds on that, saying, "out of his fullness," showing that God's people ("we all") have "received" the benefits of his fullness in the salvation gifts that come from God. The Word has filled us with his divine blessings, the greatest of which is himself. The gift enumerated here is "grace in place of grace" (*charin anti charitos*).

This is a difficult phrase to understand, depending on the meaning of the preposition *anti*. There are three major options: (1) accumulation, translating "grace upon grace" or "one gracious blessing after another" (NLT); (2) correspondence, meaning "grace for grace" and implying that the grace shown the believer corresponds to the grace of the Word; (3) replacement, translated "grace instead of grace" (or as in the NIV, "grace in place of grace already given"), that is, the grace of Christ replacing the grace that had come through the law. The first has been more popular, but I favor the third. This fits the more usual meaning of *anti* as well as the thrust of the next verse, with the new covenant blessings replacing the old covenant ones.

In verse 17 John explains the "grace instead of grace" further. The phrase "the law was given through Moses" explains the grace of the old covenant, and "grace and truth came through Jesus Christ" presents the grace of the new covenant. The previous source of divine grace was Moses, who gave the law. It was a temporary gift, meant from the start to be replaced by the greater gift of Christ (see Gal 3:21–4:7). This greater and more permanent gift was the full expression of God's unfailing love and faithfulness as found in verse 14, and it came "through Jesus Christ." The rest of John's Gospel will explore the implications of this final gift of Christ.

THE REVELATION OF GOD BY THE ONE AND ONLY SON (1:18)

This verse is a mirror image of verse 1, framing the prologue with statements about the deity of Christ as the revelation of God. In 1:1, "the Word was God," and here we have "the one and only Son, who is himself God." Here the emphasis is also on the intimate relationship between Father and Son—"[face to face] with God" in 1:1 and "in closest relationship with the Father" here. In both verses the Son is called "God" and is "the Word," the Living Revealer and virtual voice of the Father.

John begins verse 18 with a reference to Exodus 33:18–23 (see the mention of Moses in the previous verse). In that passage, Moses asked to see the glory of God and stood in a cleft of the rock as God passed by, covering his face lest Moses look upon it and die. "No one has ever seen God" doesn't mean no one has ever had a true vision of God (see Exod 24:9–11; Isa 6:1–13; Ezek 1–3) but that no one can ever be face-to-face with God—see the Lord as he really is—and live through it. The point is that now for the first time in history people can see the very face of God in Jesus, "the one and only Son, who is himself God" (see 1:14). In this we are at the very heart of the concept of the Trinity. Jesus is at one and the same time fully God and fully human and the Revealer of God as the God-man.

In the final part of this verse, "In closest relationship with the Father" is literally "in the bosom of the Father," a metaphor for a supremely intimate relationship. The Father and Son are one in being and one in loving intimacy. This intimacy expands and encloses the followers of Jesus as well, for the Word "has made him known." In other words, the intimate depths of the Father are revealed by the Word, and so that intimacy expands to include all the saints. I love to teach this verse in seminary, for the Greek word for "made known" here is *exēgēsato*. The technical term for deep Bible study is *exegesis*, so I can translate this verse, "the one and only Son, who is himself God and is in closest relationship with the Father, has *exegeted* him."

I could meditate on this passage for hours and hours. It is impossible to exhaust its riches. Each of the sections is filled with insights and a depth of meaning unmatched in anything else (even other passages in Scripture) I have ever read. In the opening part we see two wondrous truths: the Word himself was God of very God, and the Word himself actually created this universe, Father and Son acting in concert. These twin realities are the high points of all Scripture, telling us that we need not overly worry about the state of this world. Evil is doomed, for sin entering this world and bringing death along with it (Rom 5:12–14) is a temporary tragedy certain to be destroyed when the divine Lord returns in glory— that very same glory with which he entered this world.

The Word created this world (v. 3), and the Word has already portended the end of evil by bringing about a new creation and introducing spiritual light and life, the antithesis of evil. With this supernatural light, every person is encountered and convicted by the Spirit and makes a faith-decision to accept or reject the divine offer of salvation. Nothing can stop that from taking place (v. 5). The inauguration of the new creation is the coming of John the Baptist (vv. 6–8), created to be the forerunner, the witness that introduces Jesus the Word to the world and initiates his messianic ministry.

The Word did not only bring about the new creation, he became the "true light" that brought people to it and convicted them of their sins (v. 9). However, the majority rejected the light, including "his own" people, the Jews, who refused to receive him. In this way the Jews ceased to be the covenant people and became part of the world (vv. 10–11). However, those in the world and in Israel who did believe were given a new authority to be the new royalty of the new creation community, to be part of the family of God (vv. 12–13).

Most significant of all, this divine Word took on human flesh (v. 14) and became incarnate, and in so doing the Shekinah, the

glory of God dwelling among his people, walked in Galilee and
Judea as the God-man, Jesus the Word of God. In him the gracious
lovingkindness and the genuine faithfulness of the covenant God
became human and brought God's salvation into this world. As we
meditate on this stupendous reality, the troubles of this world are
put in perspective and we realize that as we trust wholly in him,
we are truly part of this new creation and can rise above the evil
around us and walk in victory and triumph.

This in fact is the thrust of the final section (vv. 15–18). The
fullness of God has come in Jesus the Word, and we are part of it.
The gracious lovingkindness of God and his genuine faithfulness
are not just theological concepts but living experiences, transforming our daily pressures and showing us again and again that
God really is in control, and we really can rise above these earthly
pressures and affirm God in a new way. Christ the Word has "made
him known" not just theoretically but experientially, giving us an
entirely new perspective on life.

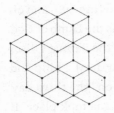

JOHN WITNESSES ABOUT JESUS
(1:19–34)

The reason for John the Baptist's existence was to be a "witness" as the messianic forerunner (John 1:7), the "voice crying in the wilderness" of Isaiah 40:3 (John 1:23). This passage relates the official beginning of Jesus' ministry, and it starts with John the Baptist baptizing in the Jordan (about AD 26/27).[1] The Jesus story, his messianic ministry, begins here. There are two sets of interrogations, the first centering on who he is (vv. 19–23) and the second on what he has come to do (vv. 24–28).

John's ministry here consists of four testimonies about himself and Jesus: (1) in 1:15–17 he stated that Jesus is the "greater one" who surpasses him and brings grace and truth; (2) in 1:19–23 he testifies that he is not the Messiah but the "voice" clearing the path for the Messiah to come; (3) in 1:32 he witnesses that the Spirit has descended on Jesus and anointed him as Messiah; (4) in 1:34 he proclaims that Jesus is the Chosen One of God.

The narrative that begins here takes the reader through the first week of Jesus' public ministry. John uses the language of "the next day" to talk about the events of 1:19–2:1, yielding six days' time that we could call the opening week of the season of the new

---

1. Luke 3:1 places it in the fifteenth year of the reign of Emperor Tiberius, who was co-regent with the emperor Augustus in AD 11/12.

creation. On the first day, John was interrogated (1:19–28), and on "the next day" (1:29) John bore witness to Jesus as the Lamb of God. Then the "next day" (day three, 1:35) several of the Baptist's disciples followed Jesus. On the "next day" (day four, 1:43), Philip and Nathanael became disciples (1:43–51). Finally, on "the third day" after these events (2:1) the wedding feast of Cana took place. It took two days to travel to Cana of Galilee for the wedding, so on the seventh day the wedding started. The seven days would be: 1—verses 19-28; 2—verses 29-34; 3—verses 35-42; 4—verses 43-51; 5-6—trip to Galilee; 7—the wedding starts.

JOHN'S IDENTITY IS REVEALED (1:19-23)

The Baptist was extremely popular from the beginning and was considered the first prophet to appear in centuries, attracting crowds from all over Judea (Matt 3:5). Because of this popularity, an official delegation from Jerusalem was sent, consisting of "priests and Levites," who were at the lower end of the religious hierarchy. The priests regularly performed the temple rituals, and Levites were the attendants in the temple and acted as the temple police. They would have been sent by the Sanhedrin and chief priests to question the Baptist. The Jerusalem officials were worried that with all the rumors about him as a prophet, he might have been another of the many messianic pretenders who had appeared of late.

THEIR QUESTIONS (1:19-22)

The interrogation begins with John's rejection of their primary question ("who he was"). The imagery depicts this as a virtual courtroom scene, with John told to identify himself for the judge (the interlocutors representing the Sanhedrin). The language in verse 20, literally "he confessed and did not deny" (NIV: "He did not fail to confess, but confessed freely") is redundant and gives his official response to the inquiry. His statement at the end of verse 20 shows the question behind the delegation's question: "I am not the Messiah."

The rest of their questions will also center on the messianic hopes of the nation. The Jewish people longed for a Messiah, but there was a lot of confusion as to exactly what that meant. The Essenes at **Qumran** (the writers of the Dead Sea Scrolls) expected two messiahs—a royal one and a priestly one—along with a prophet. Still, most Jews awaited a single "Anointed One" (the meaning of the Greek *christos*, translated "Messiah" here in the NIV). He had already confessed to Jesus in 1:15 as the "greater" one, and now made it perfectly clear he was not the expected Messiah.

So the delegation goes down the checklist of expected messianic figures in verse 21 by asking him, "Are you Elijah?" Elijah is seen as a messianic figure in Malachi 4:5, which states that Elijah would come "before that great and dreadful day of the LORD comes." Since the Baptist dressed and acted like Elijah, this was a natural query.[2] The next question, "Are you the prophet?" stems from "the prophet like Moses" of Deuteronomy 18:15, 18, considered the Messiah of the Torah at Qumran and by the Samaritans.

But John says no to both questions. Interestingly, Jesus in Matthew 11:14 and 17:12 does call him Elijah. It is likely that Jesus saw more significance in his ministry than John did. The old adage proves true: "Nobody is perfect."

They finally run out of questions and so repeat the "Who are you?" of verse 19, explaining that as an official delegation they have to give an answer to the officials who sent them. Finally, they allow John to speak for himself.

JOHN'S WITNESS ABOUT HIMSELF (1:23)

John responds obliquely, alluding to Isaiah 40:3, rather than giving a direct answer. It shows, however, John's awareness that he transcends a rabbinic role, and also that he, along with Jesus, is in the

---

2. Matt 3:4 and Mark 1:6 say he wore a camel-hair coat and leather belt; see 2 Kings 1:8.

process of fulfilling the Old Testament messianic prophecies and expectations. This fulfillment of Isaiah's cry is found in all four Gospels (Matt 3:3; Mark 3:3; Luke 3:4), and it speaks of the removal of all obstacles (the leveling of roads, the removal of mountains) by the intervention of God for the return of Israel from exile. Isaiah's witness is added to the Baptist's witness to the significance of this One who will follow and transcend all previous prophetic ministries.

Still, the Essenes of Qumran used this verse in an **eschatological** sense for the study of Torah as preparation for the coming of the kingdom (1QS 8:13-16), and this became the theme verse for the early church calling itself "the Way" (Acts 9:2; 19:9, 23; 22:4). Like Qumran and the early church, John saw himself fulfilling Isaiah's promise of a "voice in the wilderness" that would "clear the way [NIV: "make straight the way"] for the Lord." In Isaiah "the Lord" was Yahweh, but for John and the early church it was Jesus, the Son of God. The Baptist believed his was an active ministry of removing all obstacles for the arrival of the Messiah and the kingdom he would bring with him. The primary obstacle was the failure of God's people to remain faithful to him and his demands, so as in Mark 1:4, the voice came "preaching a baptism of repentance for the forgiveness of sins."

JOHN'S MISSION IS REVEALED (1:24-28)

THE QUESTION ABOUT HIS BAPTISM (1:24-25)

When they reported back, several of the officials from the Pharisees were not satisfied with John's response. The Pharisees were a group of pious lay religious leaders (called the Hasidim in the Maccabean period, 170-100 BC) who contemporized the Torah by developing an oral tradition so as to enable the common people to understand and keep the regulations and remain faithful to God. As a result, they were very concerned about remaining faithful to the Jewish laws and had problems with John's practice of baptism.

If he was not the Messiah or Elijah or the prophet, what right did he have to baptize (vv. 24–25)? This was a valid concern since his practice differed significantly from the rest of Judaism. They had regular washings for ritual purity (Mark 7:1–4), and the group at Qumran went into the pool every morning to signify cleanliness before God. John's, however, was a one-time initiation, conducted by John himself rather than self-administered. Where did he get the authority for it if he was not the Messiah or a prophet?

If at this time the Jews were baptizing Gentiles who converted (there is no absolute evidence for its existence before AD 70), this would be even more significant, for John would be saying the Jewish people had virtually become Gentiles needing to repent of their sins. I am personally open to that possibility, for this was only forty years before the written evidence.

JOHN'S ANSWER (1:26–28)

John could have answered by contrasting water baptism with Spirit baptism (see Matt 3:11; Mark 1:7–8; Luke 3:16), but instead he compares himself to the greater one (John 1:15), someone they "do not know" or recognize. There is a double meaning here: On one level they have seen Jesus and not realized who he was, but on a deeper level this is an allusion back to 1:10–11, where "not knowing" signifies one they have rejected and do not want to know. They believe they are taking the high road as the religious experts, but John is in effect telling them they are part of the world and do indeed need the baptism of repentance.

Once more (after 1:15) he states that Jesus is "the one who comes after me." This points to John as older than Jesus (see their birth accounts in Luke 1) but even more as the one who began his ministry first so as to prepare for Jesus. This one John is introducing transcends him; he is so superior that he is the one "the straps of whose sandals I am not worthy to untie." Since rabbis received no pay for their services, it was common for their disciples to perform small services for them. There was a rabbinic saying that a disciple would do everything for his rabbi that a slave would do except "untie the straps of his sandal" (b. Ketubbot 96a), for this was too demeaning a task. John's point is that he isn't even worthy to be Jesus' slave.

The author closes by telling us where this took place, the "Bethany on the other side of the Jordan." This is not the Bethany of John 11, a suburb of Jerusalem and the home of Jesus' close friends Mary, Martha, and Lazarus. Still, a Bethany scene begins and ends the narrative of Jesus' ministry (John 12 begins the passion narrative), so John may want to frame the story of Jesus' ministry with Bethany scenes.

THE WITNESS OF JOHN ABOUT JESUS (1:29-34)

INITIAL TESTIMONY TO THE LAMB OF GOD (1:29-31)

In verse 29 John sees Jesus "coming toward him," and the language pictures this as the first steps in Jesus' public ministry. His incarnation in 1:9, 14 ("coming into the world") moves into its second phase with his "coming" at the start of his ministry. John's testimony is crucial for the theology of his Gospel: "Look, the Lamb of God, who takes away the sin of the world!"

There are three options for understanding the metaphor behind this affirmation: (1) The **apocalyptic** Lamb who will triumph over evil and crush the sins of the world by force; (2) the Suffering Servant of Yahweh from Isaiah 53 (the Aramaic word for "servant" can also mean "lamb"); (3) a sacrificial lamb, possibly drawing on the imagery of the Passover lamb, the scapegoat, or the lamb of the daily sacrifices, but all centering on the sacrificial element.

While the Suffering Servant could be part of this (see the parallel in Isa 53:7 and the image in John 1:34 below), the main thrust is the lamb metaphor. The major argument for the apocalyptic Lamb is Matthew 11:2-19, in which John sends from prison to ask if Jesus is "the one who is to come." This could be taken to mean that

John the Baptist had serious doubts about Jesus' sacrificial messianic ministry, which would favor the apocalyptic option. However, these are the Baptist's later doubts and could be the type of temporary uncertainty we all pass through now and then. Overall, the sacrificial view is perfectly viable in light of the Baptist's general preaching on sin and repentance. There is no emphasis in this Gospel on conquering the enemies of God and destroying sin in that way. The sacrificial death of Jesus "taking away" sin by providing forgiveness is a much more apt image than the apocalyptic annihilation of sin. So I see a blending of the latter two views: Jesus the Suffering Servant is the atoning sacrifice that takes away sins.

All this does not mean the Baptist understood all the implications perfectly but that he had a dawning understanding of Jesus' greater purposes. The Spirit was using him to introduce the reason for Jesus' coming. The lamb was one of the primary animals in the sacrificial system, and in John's statement that Jesus "takes away the sin of the world" there is a nascent idea of atonement. But did he understand Jesus bearing the sins of the nation? Did he understand Jesus as the Suffering Servant of Isaiah 53? Mainstream Judaism at this time did not interpret the Suffering Servant as the Messiah but rather as a symbol for the nation. Still, the Spirit could have revealed this to John; we know that the community at Qumran did understand the servant this way. We cannot know how much he realized, but still the most natural way to interpret John's testimony here is sacrificially.

To explain this remarkable witness to Jesus, the Baptist in verse 30 reminds his listeners of what he had said in verse 15, that this Jesus "has surpassed me because he was before me." Jesus' transcendent greatness means that the forerunner must give way to God's greater work in him. Though born later and beginning his ministry later, Jesus was both preexistent and chosen of God. As great as this first prophet to appear in four hundred years was, his ministry must be defined as witness to the true identity of Jesus (John 1:7, 15, 19–20).

In verse 31, John relates the moment when he first understood Jesus' true identity. Until that time, he "did not know him." This doesn't mean they had never met, for they were relatives, probably cousins (Luke 1:36), though we don't know how much time they spent together when they were growing up. Until the baptism itself John, like all Jews, longed for the Messiah to come but had no idea who he would be. John understood his baptism as signifying repentance (Mark 1:4), but he also knew that baptism could be an anointing for ministry, so he "came baptizing with water [so] that he [Jesus] might be revealed [as the Messiah] to Israel." But until Jesus arrived and the Spirit took over, he had no idea this was the appointed moment.

THE DEEPER WITNESS OF THE SPIRIT (1:32-34)

John the Baptist's moment of realization regarding Jesus' messianic nature and his status as the Lamb of God would have come when he baptized Jesus. The story is not narrated, for John the evangelist wants to put it in the mouth of the Baptist and make it part of his witness. So in 1:32-33 he testifies, "I saw the Spirit come down from heaven as a dove and remain on him." This means that John is the official witness of Jesus' anointing (the meaning of *christos*, "Messiah/Christ"), but it was also a sign to the Baptist himself. In the Old Testament kings are anointed by a high priest or prophet, but Jesus is anointed by the Holy Spirit. As Jesus in this Gospel is the Revealer of God, the Spirit in this Gospel has a revelatory function, infusing Jesus with power and making him known to all (14:26; 15:26). The Spirit inaugurates Jesus' ministry here, and John now knows him as the designated Messiah.

The physical form of a descending dove combines several things, especially the Spirit of God hovering over creation in Genesis 1:2, thus a new creation; and the dove returning to Noah's ark in Genesis 8:8-12, thus inaugurating a new world order. Thereby we have a new age inaugurated in the coming of God's Son. The Spirit/dove, which John saw "remain on him," depicts this new covenant reality as the eternal kingdom of God arriving with Jesus. This echoes Isaiah 11:2, "The Spirit of the LORD will rest on him," a primary theme found also in Acts 10:38: "God anointed Jesus of Nazareth with the Holy Spirit and power." The new age has dawned, and God's power has come in Jesus on his people (1 Pet 1:5).

In 1:33 John says again that the Baptist "did not know him" until that moment when the Spirit descended and revealed the full reality of Jesus to him. He states it in a most interesting way: "The man on whom you see the Spirit come down and remain is the one who will baptize with the Holy Spirit." This means the Spirit's witness transcends and deepens the Baptist's testimony. There are two transcendent things here: the Spirit's witness transcends John's, and Jesus' baptism with the Spirit transcends John's baptism with water. John's witness and his baptism were in reality both preparations for greater events that would arrive with Jesus. This becomes explicit in 7:38–39, where out of believers in Jesus flow "rivers of living water," namely, the Holy Spirit. Through him, the Spirit flows to all humankind (see 16:8–15), proof that the new creation has truly arrived.

The Baptist's conclusion in 1:34 is in a sense a fourth official "witness" (after 1:15, 19, 32) building on 1:7–8, "I have seen and I testify that this is God's Chosen One."[3] This is an allusion to Isaiah 42:1, "Here is my servant … my chosen one in whom I delight." This passage was also part of God's affirmation of Jesus in Mark 1:11. It continues the servant and sacrificial images from 1:29 and points forward to Christ as the Suffering Servant destined (chosen) to die as the atoning sacrifice for sin. The thrust is God pouring out his Spirit on his Chosen One, calling him to his Suffering Servant ministry on the cross.

---

3. There is a difficult text-critical debate between the readings "Chosen One of God," preferred in NIV, NJB, REB, NLT, and "Son of God," preferred in KJV, NASB, NRSV. The latter has the better manuscript support and is a major emphasis in John, but I agree with those who prefer "Chosen One" here because it is the less-likely reading—that is, it is unlikely that later scribes would have replaced the major title "Son of God" with one that appears nowhere else in John.

This is the opening scene of Jesus' ministry and begins a set of inaugural events, the fourfold witness of John the Baptist to Jesus as the Chosen Servant here (1:19-34) followed by the beginning of the formation of Jesus' community of disciples in the next set of verses (1:35-51). The witness of the Baptist here starts with his responses to the official delegation from Jerusalem that he is not the Messiah but merely the "voice" from Isaiah clearing the way for the true Messiah to arrive (1:19-23). The critical point is that the Old Testament messianic prophecies are in process of being fulfilled in the arrival of the Messiah.

Then in 1:24-28 the Baptist relates what he does, leading to the further witness that his ministry is unworthy of being compared to Jesus' superior ministry. His whole point in 1:19-28 is that neither he nor his ministry should be especially lauded, for he is the forerunner sent to prepare for the true Messiah and to remove all barriers to his coming. He has come to witness to the far greater one whom God will soon send. This is an invaluable passage for us, for it is easy to be complacent about our relationship with Jesus, almost as if he is our fraternity brother or something. We need the same sense of awe John felt when he contemplated the coming of this Being from heaven who transcends anything this world can offer.

John was related to Jesus but did not realize who he was until the Spirit revealed it to him at the baptism of Jesus, as he relates in 1:29-34. Then he knew that Jesus was incomparably greater and that his baptizing Jesus was actually the messianic anointing the Jewish people had wanted for centuries. At that time, the Spirit descended on Jesus and the understanding dawned in John. This one was the Chosen One, the one destined by God to be the Suffering Servant and the atoning sacrifice that would lead to forgiveness of sins.

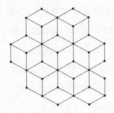

JESUS BEGINS TO FORM
HIS BAND OF DISCIPLES
(1:35–51)

This scene traces the first stages of Jesus' ministry as he was choosing his band of disciples and fashioning his team. This builds on 1:12, for these are those who "did receive him" and are now made part of his family, becoming "children of God." Many have the mistaken impression from Mark 1:16-20 that he began choosing them while they were fishing on the Sea of Galilee, but that event probably took place six to nine months into his ministry as he was about to move to Capernaum. In actuality, the day after his baptism by John, on the fourth day of that opening week (see the introduction to 1:19-34), Jesus went to spend some time with his cousin and found his first disciples among John's followers.

THE FIRST THREE DISCIPLES
COME TO JESUS (1:35-42)

John's Continued Witness (1:35-36)

"The following day" is the day after John's original testimony to Jesus as "the Lamb of God" and "the Chosen One," day three of this inaugural week (see 1:19, 29, 35, 43; 2:1). On this occasion, he is accompanied by "two of his disciples," a common phenomenon

for rabbis. (Jesus and his disciples were also considered a rabbinic group.) In all four Gospels, John the Baptist is the messianic
forerunner and is supplanted by the "greater." In Luke, Jesus is
the greater prophet; in Mark and Matthew, Jesus is the greater
teacher/rabbi, and here Jesus is the greater Revealer of God. So it
is natural that the core of John's followers gravitate to Jesus.

Now for a second time John sees Jesus and exclaims to those
around, "Look, the Lamb of God!" It seems clear that John has
thought further about his witness in 1:15, 30, about Jesus' greatness and is passing on his ministry (and disciples) to the greater
man of God to be part of his far greater calling. He wanted his followers to know the significance of this transcendent One. There is
interesting imagery in the narrative flow of Jesus' "coming toward"
John in 1:29 and "passing by" him here. As the man, so also the ministry—Jesus is now taking over center stage and will be the focus
from this time on. The Lamb of God is the core of salvation history and the plan of God for the salvation of the world.

INTERACTION WITH THE TWO DISCIPLES (1:37-39)

John does not appear again in this episode (we will see him again in
3:22-30). His part is finished for now, and Jesus takes over his ministry and disciples. The interaction between Jesus and these two
begins a narrative style that is fairly unique to John, with double
meaning and an enigmatic format. The earthly interaction is actually enclosing a spiritual interaction in which the offer of salvation
is enacted. Every word here is part of an earthly scene but has a
spiritual/heavenly counterpart. When the two disciples hear the
Baptist's witness, they begin to follow Jesus—they are in process
of becoming followers. John often uses "follow" (mainly the verb to
describe ongoing action) to describe discipleship (1:43; 8:12; 12:26;
13:36-37; 21:19-22). It is their initiative here. This reflects rabbinic
practice, where the disciples chose the rabbi rather than vice versa.

We know one of them was Andrew from verse 40, but the
other is unidentified. It might be Philip (v. 43) or perhaps John

the "beloved disciple" and author of this Gospel.[1] Since he never names himself in this Gospel, that would make sense and fit the eyewitness touches in this scene. We will never know until we get to heaven.

The double meaning continues in verse 38. Jesus turns and asks, "What do you want?" (literally "What are you seeking?"). Again there is far more meaning than appears on the surface. This will be asked again in 18:4, 7, and 20:15, and it always demands a thoughtful response regarding the deep desires that drive the individual. In a real sense he is demanding, "What do you really want out of life?" The motif of seeking Jesus is at the heart of the evangelistic purpose of John.[2]

Their response, "Rabbi, where are you staying?" seems evasive at first glance. It is not much of an answer. Yet note that even though they had never seen Jesus before, they were already willing to accept him as their rabbi on the basis of John's testimony. Their question also contains far more than appears on the surface. On the earthly level, they seem to say only "Where are you lodging?" But the term menō ("staying") is a major concept in John and implies a desire to "dwell" or "remain"; we will see it later in the "mutual indwelling" theme of 15:4–10. At the deeper level, they are expressing a desire to follow Jesus and "remain" with him.

Jesus' response in 1:39a, "Come and you will see," is then an invitation to salvation. Philip uses these exact words in 1:46 to invite Nathanael to become a follower of Jesus. Both terms are used in John to depict a faith-decision: "come" in 3:21; 5:40; 6:35; 7:37; and "see" in 6:40; 9:39; 16:16; 17:24. The clear implication is that these two followers of John had been searching for what Jesus was now offering them.

---

1. See "Author" in the introduction.

2. See "Salvation," in the discussion of major theological themes in the introduction.

Behind this is time spent at Jesus' feet hearing the message of salvation, implied in 1:39b, "So they went and saw where he was staying, and they spent that day with him." They did not just move from one place of residence to another; they found a new home with God in Christ. They heard the true Rabbi or Teacher, the Word of God, and he "made his dwelling among" them (1:14 reenacted as salvation). One of John's narrative techniques is not to describe directly the conversion of the individuals but to present it in the picture language of the story (as with Nicodemus or the Samaritan woman). This is the case here as well. We see the faith-decision depicted in the drama behind the scenes. It becomes clear in the witness of Andrew to Simon in verse 41, "We have found the Messiah."

This scene is important enough for John to tell us how much time they spent together: "They spent that day with him ... [until] about four in the afternoon." Literally, this is translated "the tenth hour," but this was more likely Jewish reckoning (beginning at dawn, so about 4:00 in the afternoon) rather than Roman (beginning at midnight, so ten in the morning). This would be the most significant day of their lives.

THE AFTERMATH: ANDREW BRINGS PETER TO JESUS (1:40–42A)

This is "evangelism explosion" at its best—each one seeks one. One of the two disciples who comes to Jesus is now named: Andrew the brother of Simon, who also becomes one of the Twelve (Mark 3:18). He could not wait to share his newfound faith and so immediately goes to his brother Simon, who was undoubtedly also a follower of the Baptist. The first thing he says is, "We have found the Messiah." John then explains—probably for Gentile readers who did not know the term—that this means in Greek *christos*, "anointed one."

For the Jewish people a Messiah was expected from Old Testament prophecy; he was the expected deliverer who would

be anointed by God to vindicate God's people and destroy their enemies. The redemptive overtones and idea of a "Suffering Servant"
Messiah from Isaiah 53 were unknown in Judaism, as mentioned in
the discussion of 1:29 above. While the Baptist may have glimpsed
some of this, it is unlikely that his disciples would have done so.
Still, Andrew's confession here shows an amazing level of understanding for a mere Jewish fisherman. It shows how deeply spiritual and knowledgeable he was. He would have been perfect as an
integral member of the Twelve. He then went to his brother Simon
Peter and "brought him to Jesus" (v. 42). As with the two in verse
39, Peter's conversion is not narrated but implied.

JESUS' PROPHECY AND WITNESS ABOUT PETER (1:42B)

Another incredible scene takes place, as Jesus encounters one of
the great future leaders of the church for the first time. The verb
behind "looked" (emblepō) means to "look intently" or "directly,"
and we can picture Jesus looking deep into Peter and discern-
ing who he really is. He was not named "Peter" but "Simon bar-
Jonah" or "Simon son of John." In Judaism, the name of the father
became a kind of surname for a person. However, Jesus is omniscient (another theme of John's—we will see it again in 1:47 and
4:16–19) and gives Simon a second name that will typify his true
place in the church—Cephas (the Aramaic form) or Peter (the
Greek equivalent), the "rock."

When parents named a child, they chose a name that had a
meaning that would signify what they hoped for their child. Jesus
on the basis of his foreknowledge gave Simon his true name that
portended his destiny as the rock of the church. This points back
to the episode in Genesis when God gave Jacob the new name Israel
(Gen 32:28). It is a second occasion of divine intervention in renam-
ing a person who would change the destiny of God's people. In
actuality, this spoke not only of Simon's future as Peter but also
of the messianic authority Jesus possessed in giving him that new
name. This was truly prophetic, for throughout Jesus' ministry

Peter was not a rock but shifting sand, always saying or doing the wrong thing. However, God was at work, and after Pentecost when the Spirit came, he did indeed become "the rock of the church" (also prophesied in Matt 16:18).

PHILIP AND NATHANAEL COME TO JESUS (1:43–51)

Here Jesus takes the initiative (in 1:37 the two disciples come to him) and encounters Philip, who then, like Andrew, brings someone else to Jesus. This is unusual because in the Jewish world, disciples chose which rabbi they wished to follow (much as students today decide which seminary to attend). Jesus is the God-man and so like his Father chooses whom he wishes. He also decides to leave for Galilee, perhaps for the wedding at Cana of chapter 2 and perhaps to begin ministry there.

John differs greatly from the **Synoptic** Gospels here. They divide Jesus' time strictly between Judea and Galilee. Jesus is in Galilee for his entire ministry and does not come to Judea until passion week, the week of his death. In John, Jesus emulates his parents, who, it says in Luke 2:41, went every year for Passover. In these early chapters Jesus is a jet-setter, traveling back and forth often: in Judea (1:29–42), then Galilee for the wedding (2:1), then back to Jerusalem for Passover (2:13), then back to Galilee by way of Samaria (ch. 4). The Synoptics are more topical in their arrangement, but John catches the historical flow well.

JESUS TAKES THE INITIATIVE (1:43–44)

Before leaving for Galilee, Jesus takes the time to choose another for his discipleship band—Philip (Mark 3:18), who likely had also been a follower of the Baptist. Now Jesus says "Follow me" in the present tense, implying a call to ongoing discipleship, and as with Andrew the hint is that Philip is converted. We know little about Philip. We know he became one of the Twelve (Mark 3:18), but John is the only Gospel that describes his actions at all (6:5–7; 12:21–22; 14:7–9). He is probably not the same person as the Philip of Acts

6:5; 8:4–7, 26–40. According to later tradition, he was martyred at Hierapolis near Laodicea in the Roman province of Asia.[3]

We are told in 1:44 that he was from Bethsaida, Andrew and Peter's hometown, a fishing village northeast of Capernaum on the other side of the Jordan River on the northern shore of the Sea of Galilee. Mark 1:29 tells us that Peter moved to Capernaum during Jesus' ministry, so this was the hometown where they all grew up. Likely the three of them became followers of John the Baptist together.

THE INVITATION TO NATHANAEL (1:45–46)

Following the evangelistic pattern set by Andrew, Philip brings his friend Nathanael to Jesus. Nathanael is never called one of the disciples, but many believe he is the Bartholomew of Mark 3:18, since (1) Bartholomew is coupled with Philip in the lists; (2) Bartholomew actually means "son of Tolmai," and so there is room for a first name (as "Simon son of John" in 1:42 above); (3) in 1:50 Jesus says he will "see greater things," likely the miracle at Cana, meaning he immediately became a disciple. So Nathanael may have joined Simon, Andrew, and Philip in becoming the first of the Twelve to follow Jesus.

Philip's invitation was also similar to Andrew's in 1:41: "We have found the one Moses wrote about in the Law, and about whom the prophets also wrote." This follows the tendency in the New Testament to use scriptural fulfillment to prove the reality of Jesus as Messiah, a practice still used in apologetics today. The point is that the Law and the Prophets (a way of speaking about the entire Old Testament) point to Jesus as Messiah. The emphasis on the Law probably has in mind Deuteronomy 18:15, with Jesus as "the prophet like Moses."

---

3. See the Acts of Philip, a collection of stories about Philip that was probably composed around the fourth or fifth century AD.

Philip identifies Jesus formally: "Jesus of Nazareth, the son
of Joseph," mentioning both his hometown and his father. This
was normal procedure, especially since the name Jesus was quite
common, so he would need to be distinguished from others of the
same name. Nathanael's reaction in verse 46 is curt: "Nazareth!
Can anything good come from there?" There are two possible
reasons for this: (1) This is a local saying from Cana, Nathanael's
hometown, reflecting rivalry between the two villages. (2) Since
the Messiah was to come from Bethlehem (Mic 5:2), Nazareth was
too insignificant to be the home of the Messiah. It had no more
than two thousand inhabitants and is mentioned nowhere in the
Old Testament or the Jewish historian Josephus. Both reasons are
probably behind Nathanael's outburst, and it is paralleled by the
reactions elsewhere to the fact that Jesus was a "Nazarene" (see
Matt 2:23; Acts 4:10; 24:5).

Philip can only respond, "Come and see," echoing Jesus' challenge to the two in 1:39. Once more, there is a double meaning.
Nathanael is challenged to see for himself, and it constitutes an
invitation to the salvation offered by Jesus. It is impossible to know
how much of this Philip understood, but he had become a follower
of Jesus and this was his first foray into his future ministry, so he
likely understood more than we might think.

JESUS ENCOUNTERS NATHANAEL (1:47-49)

Once again, Jesus took the initiative when he "saw Nathanael
approaching." His challenge is similar to his encounter of Simon
in 1:42, demonstrating his divine omniscience. He looked deeply
into Nathanael's character and walk with God (even though he had
never met the man) and said, "Here truly is an Israelite in whom
there is no deceit." To understand all that Jesus meant by this, we
must turn to the story of Jacob in Genesis 27. The name Jacob connotes "deceit." That certainly characterized Jacob, who tricked
his brother Esau out of his birthright, so that the latter then said,
"Isn't he rightly named Jacob? This is the second time he has taken

advantage of me: He took my birthright, and now he's taken my blessing" (Gen 27:36).

Later, after he successfully wrestled God, the Lord renamed him Israel, giving him the name that would depict the nation itself. Here Nathanael is called a "true" or "genuine" Israelite, an Israelite who is not like the old Jacob (filled with deceit) but like the new Israel, a man who "strives with God" (the meaning of Israel) and is completely trustworthy. In other words, this is an Israel with all the Jacob removed. Nathanael is a model disciple, completely honest and reliable.

Needless to say, Nathanael is shocked and responds in 1:48, "How do you know me?" He is overwhelmed that a complete stranger has demonstrated a deep knowledge of him. Jesus' retort is enigmatic: "I saw you while you were still under the fig tree before Philip called you." In other words, it just took a glance and Jesus knew not only who Nathanael was at the core of his being but also that he would be invited by Philip. There has been all kinds of speculation about a deeper meaning for the fig tree here, like saying that it was the place where rabbis studied Torah or was an Old Testament symbol for home (Isa 36:16; Zach 3:10). None are overly helpful, and this is probably a simple historical reminiscence—Jesus saw him under a fig tree and knew what kind of person he was. The stress is not on the fig tree but on Jesus' supernatural insight.

Nathanael proves Jesus right by making an astounding leap of faith and understanding into Jesus' true nature and stature. He calls Jesus "rabbi," as did the two in 1:38, but then he goes far beyond what anyone would ever dream of calling a rabbi. When he calls Jesus "Son of God" and "king of Israel," he even goes beyond Andrew and Philip, who recognized Jesus as Messiah (1:41, 45). John's depiction of these early followers is remarkable. In the Synoptics, the disciples never show any understanding of Jesus' true nature until Peter's confession in Mark 8:27–30 and parallels, and then it is to him as Messiah. Here at the very start, they affirm him as not only Messiah but also Son of God and King of Israel.

This section (1:35–49) contains an extraordinary set of **christological** titles attributed to Jesus by his followers—Lamb of God, Chosen One of God, Messiah, prophet like Moses, Son of God, King of Israel. Many critics consider the Fourth Gospel unhistorical at this point, believing this stems from the early church and not the incidents recorded here. However, nothing here is beyond historical plausibility. The disciples' affirmations explain why they leave the Baptist to follow Jesus, and all the titles have to do with messianic expectations—the very topic the Jerusalem delegation asked John about in 1:19–25. These titles exemplify the flowering of faith and understanding in these disciples, and the scene makes sense as it is.

At the same time, when Nathanael called Jesus "Son of God," he hardly meant everything the title came to mean to the early church. He intended it in terms of the royal Messiah, as when David is called a "son" of God in 2 Samuel 7:14; Psalm 2:7; 89:27, or when Israel was labeled a "child" of God in Deuteronomy 1:31 and Jeremiah 31:9. The further theological dimensions—the oneness with the Father, the uniqueness of the one and only Son— are found in the prologue and intended by John but not part of Nathanael's original understanding. "King of Israel" is found in Isaiah 44:6 and Zephaniah 3:15 but was not a messianic title. With its sister expression, "King of the Jews," it is also found in John 12:13; 18:33, 39; 19:3. Nathanael likely used it in the sense of a conquering king defeating Israel's enemies.

JESUS THE SON OF MAN (1:50–51)

Jesus uses Nathanael's insight to take him further on the path of messianic understanding. He begins by acknowledging the reality of Nathanael's faith: "You believe because I told you I saw you under the fig tree." He had taken an incredible step, moving from Jesus' supernatural insight to the realization of who he was. But Nathanael can go further. What Jesus says here must be understood in light of John's view of true faith—actual belief takes place when one has both heard Jesus' teaching and observed his works. Nathanael had experienced the first part—he believed as far as he was able when he heard what Jesus told him after he was sitting under the fig tree. But there was more to come; soon he would "see greater things than that," and his faith would deepen. Remember the key phrase "Come and see" of 1:39. The "greater things" will begin with the Cana miracle in 2:1-11, which implicitly says Nathanael will be one of his disciples accompanying him to Cana.

In verse 51 we see the first of the *amēn* sayings in John. The Synoptics use a single *amēn* for these sayings, but John uses a double form for greater emphasis: *amēn amēn*, "truly, truly" (NIV: "very truly"). This phrase was used in the ancient world to affirm or confirm the truthfulness of a statement. Thus it would often be found at the end of a prayer as a type of assent to the contents of the prayer. When Jesus uses it, it functions as his divine imprimatur to emphasize the importance of his point. "Very truly I tell you" can be translated, "I tell you the truth" (as in the NLT), and in John's double form it would stress the absolute truth Jesus is giving. The *amēn* sayings are "Jesus creeds" in a real sense—particularly important truths for his followers.

The rest of verse 51 also gives us the opening Son of Man saying in John. Jesus drew the title from the "one like a son of man" in Daniel 7:13-14, where he is a heavenly figure "given authority, glory and sovereign power" over all the nations. In other places, the Son of Man figure has an earthly aspect, drawing imagery from Ezekiel's "son of man" (for instance, 2:1, 3, 6, 8); in Ezekiel it means "mortal human being." The title occurs thirteen times in John and is often associated with Jesus' heavenly origin and status.

This first Son of Man saying is the core of **eschatology** in John, telling how in Jesus heaven and earth are brought together into unity. The introductory "you will see" is repeated from verse 50. The "you" is plural: Jesus includes all his followers in this saying. This is the ultimate "greater thing" promised to Nathanael.

"Heaven open" is an **apocalyptic** image, and the Jewish people believed that when the heavens opened God would intervene in human history, and his kingdom would come. At Jesus' baptism, the heavens are "torn open" when the Spirit descends (Mark 1:10), and in Revelation 4:1 the open door in heaven signifies the final events ushering in God's final kingdom.

Here the open heaven refers to the presence of Jesus as he brings the kingdom into this world (Mark 1:15). Jesus' phrase "'The angels of God ascending and descending on' the Son of Man" reflects the motif of "the stairway between heaven and earth" (NLT). Like the reference in 1:47, it must be understood by considering the story of Jacob, but here it is Jacob's ladder or stairway in Genesis 28:12. Jacob in his vision saw a stairway reaching from earth up to heaven with the angels going up and down it, symbolizing his new authority and access to God's throne. Jesus is pictured here as the final Jacob and new Israel, the one on whom the angels ascend and descend as they unite heaven and earth.[4] Jesus is the one who has united heaven and earth, in a sense providing in *himself* the first step to the "new heaven and new earth" of Revelation 21:1. The rest of John's Gospel develops this image in several directions, but the key is that Jesus brings heaven and earth together in himself.

This wonderful passage is one of the best examples in Scripture of the process of disciple-making. In 1:35-37 John the Baptist is the perfect forerunner, knowing when his ministry and purpose have culminated, when it is God's time to pass the baton to the "greater

---

4. Some have doubted that this is in the imagery since this verse does not mention a vision or a stairway. That is to demand more detail than is warranted. The mention of angels ascending and descending is a clear allusion to Genesis 28, and the Jacob imagery stems from 1:47 and continues here. I have little doubt that this is the thrust of Jesus' saying here.

one," Jesus. This humility is desperately needed in the church—we have far too many who demand to be the head and cannot serve in subordinate roles. John not only passes on his ministry but also sends his disciples to Jesus.

In 1:38–42, the two disciples hear John's testimony and decide they want to be followers of Jesus. He asks them what the true goals of their lives are, and they declare that they want to remain with him and become his disciples. He takes them with him, and they "see" who he really is, as they are converted and become his followers. Andrew, realizing he is indeed the expected Messiah, goes and brings his brother Simon. Jesus with his divine insight sees deep into Simon's soul and predicts he will become the rock of the church. This section depicts the evangelistic program of the church, and all of us should study it.

The second half of this passage provides an even more significant story, with Philip and Nathanael closely paralleling Andrew and Simon, each convert bringing others to Jesus. Again this a model for the church today. The way Jesus converts Nathanael is astounding, as his omniscience once more leads him to see into the depths of his person and future value for God. Nathanael is a contemporary Jacob, personifying the church as a new Israel. He is not only a model disciple. He is the first to see the "greater things" and experience the true reality of Jesus.

Verse 51 belongs with the prologue as teaching the divine power and authority of Jesus. Now we see that he is Jacob's ladder, bringing not only the kingdom but also heaven itself down to earth and uniting them in himself. In eternity there will not be two places (an earth down here and a heaven up there) but one true entity, a "new heaven and a new earth" in one. In Jesus, at the spiritual level, that is already the case. For his followers, heaven is their dwelling place now (Eph 2:6–7), and they are already citizens of heaven (Phil 3:20). This becomes the central image for the theology of John.

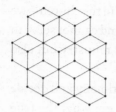

THE NEW WINE AND
THE NEW TEMPLE
(2:1–25)

We now arrive at the first major section of the Gospel, which narrates Jesus' public ministry (2:1–12:50). This is built around seven signs that are carefully organized to accord with Jesus' discourses. These signs are miracles used by God to signify the person and work of Jesus. As a result, many call this "the book of signs," for in these God reveals the glory and authority of Christ. The Jewish people here encounter the light of God in Jesus (1:4, 7, 9) and receive the invitation of God through these sign-miracles to investigate his true identity. The signs demand faith-decision, which intensifies the conflict as the Jewish people continually reject Jesus and his message. At the same time, his glory becomes more and more evident for those with the eyes of faith (1:12).

The first section of the book of signs (2:1–4:54) is framed by two Cana-miracles (2:1–12; 4:46–54), the first two signs. The theme is the fulfillment of the old ways and old covenant and their replacement by the new covenant and salvation Christ has brought with him. In him we have the new wine, the new temple, the new birth, the living water, and the new worship.

THE FIRST SIGN: JESUS TURNS WATER
INTO WINE AT CANA (2:1-12)

The weeklong opening part of Jesus' ministry is finished, and he likely was taking a small break to attend a wedding in Cana, a small village a few miles north of Nazareth in Galilee. This was also the home of Nathanael (see 21:2). Weddings normally began with a procession bringing the bride to the groom's house, a wedding supper, and a week of festivities. Jesus came with his mother and disciples (five so far, see 1:38-50), so the bride or groom may have been relatives or at least close friends.

THE WEDDING AND THE SERIOUS PROBLEM (2:1-3A)

At some part of the festivities, they ran out of wine. The groom was responsible for such things, and his whole family would have been disgraced. Hospitality was very important in the ancient world, and weddings were among the most serious of social obligations. Some even think his family could have been sued by the bride's family for such a thing. This was a desperate situation.

JESUS AND HIS MOTHER (2:3B-5)

Apparently the hosts of the wedding approached Jesus' mother. We don't know why (perhaps she was a close relative), but she immediately came to Jesus with the problem, saying, "They have no more wine." It is also difficult to know what she expected him to do. He had not performed any miracles as of yet. The reaction of his hometown when they rejected him in Mark 6:1-6 shows he had never done any such thing while he was younger.[1] Still, she felt he would find the answer. Jesus was a village carpenter (Mark 6:3) and so a resourceful person. Probably his father, Joseph, who was older, had died and Jesus had taken over his practice. So Mary as a widow had learned to depend on Jesus for help, and she turned to him now.

---

1. Later compositions like the Infancy Gospel of Thomas tell stories like Jesus changing clay pigeons into real ones as a child, but these stories are apocryphal.

Jesus' reaction in verse 4 is startling. On the surface it seems rude and disrespectful, but the context must be considered carefully. First, he calls Mary "woman." When Jesus gives her over to John's care in 19:26 he also calls her "woman," and there is a great deal of love in that scene. He is not being rude here, and when we combine this with the following ("Why do you involve me?"), he is clearly trying to distance himself from her and the situation. The question is literally, "What is this to me and to you?" It is used by demons in Mark 1:24; 5:7, to say, "Get away. Stop interfering." Jesus was reluctant to do anything. It is not disrespect but disengagement; he did not want to get involved, as the NIV's "Why do you involve me?" shows.

The reason is found in "My hour has not yet come." In John the "hour" refers to the time of destiny, the passion events (7:30; 8:20; 12:23; 17:1). Jesus is reluctant to begin at this time the series of events that would culminate in the cross. He had hoped for a brief hiatus and to enjoy the wedding with his disciples. He didn't want to initiate the tumultuous road that God willed for him quite yet. The much greater wedding feast (the wedding supper of the Lamb) was awaiting, but he did not want a public declaration via a messianic miracle to take place at this time.

We see here the human side of Jesus, including his acquiescing to his mother's request. Mary shows a mother's trust in her son when she ignores his mild rebuke and simply tells the servants who stood with the empty wine jugs, "Do whatever he tells you." She is a model disciple, leaving everything to Jesus and trusting in his wisdom. In a sense, Jesus is saying, "I don't want to do it, but I will." Jesus' subsequent actions show that her trust was well placed. This drama moves from Jesus' reluctance to one of the greatest messianic miracles in the Gospels.

The Miracle of the Wine (2:6–10)

Jesus turns not to the wine jugs but to "six stone water jars, the kind used by the Jews for ceremonial washing." Their purpose was to render the unclean ritually pure, which would take place when a person dipped their hands and feet in the water (Mark 7:1–5). The jars were thus constantly exposed to impurity. When Jesus had them filled with water and then turned it into wine, a double miracle took place: (1) The unclean was made clean. The reason the jars were made of stone is because earthen jars that were made unclean were to be broken; there was no such prescription for stone jars (Lev 11:33–35). (2) The water was changed into wine; perhaps the best wine ever served at a wedding.

When the wine was served, the servants first took some to the master of the banquet (who was in charge of the festivities, including the food and wine), who tasted it beforehand and called it the "best wine" of the entire festivities. He was very surprised to taste such quality wine late in the week. His explanation in 2:10 provides further background to wedding practices then. It was customary at weddings to buy some expensive and some cheaper wines. The good stuff was provided at the outset, and then "after the guests have had too much to drink" and their palates were somewhat dulled, the cheaper wine would be served. Jesus had saved the best for last.

THE AFTERMATH (2:11–12)

John steps in and tells us that this is the "first" (the Greek literally means "beginning," as the inauguration of these events) of the (seven) signs Jesus performed, which determine the organization of chapters 2–12. The **Synoptic** Gospels call miracles "acts of power" (*dynamis*), while John labels them "signs" because they signify the power of God in Jesus as well as show his true nature. Jesus performed an incredible messianic miracle, not just changing water into wine but changing it into 180 gallons of the best wine ever tasted. No wonder it "revealed his glory" (2:11). As signs to his glory they unveil God's work in him. Moreover, as Jesus reveals the Father, the sign-miracles reveal his true glory (see 1:14, 16, "we have seen his glory").

After seeing this messianic sign, "his disciples believed in him." This is an evangelistic challenge for the reader; we see here that the only proper response to Jesus is a faith-decision. Discipleship begins with faith. Faith and **Christology** are two central themes in this Gospel. In 20:30–31 this in fact is presented as the major purpose of the book: "These are written that you may believe that Jesus is the Messiah, the Son of God, and that by believing you may have life in his name."

John concludes with a brief side note about Jesus' activity in the ensuing days (v. 12). It is likely that this was a planning visit, during which Jesus traveled about sixteen miles northeast, "down" to the lower elevations of the lake. Jesus at some stage near this time moved to Capernaum for his Galilean ministry. (In Matt 9:1 it is called "his own town.") It was ideally located on the northern shore of the lake and was the central town in that region, a large fishing village with a major north-south road passing by it and a great deal of trade taking place there.

JESUS CONFRONTS IN THE TEMPLE (2:13–25)

The first issue in looking at John's account of the temple cleansing is how to harmonize it, occurring as it does at the start of Jesus' ministry, with the Synoptic Gospels, where it occurs at the end. Most scholars believe there was only one clearing of the temple, at the end of his ministry, and it led to his arrest. That would mean that John, for thematic reasons of his own, places it at the beginning. This is not a problem for those with a high view of Scripture, because a high view of Scripture recognizes that the Gospels do not aim at chronological order. Topical organization was seen as perfectly fine.

However, with that said I see no problem with two cleansings. The purpose of the event here at the start of Jesus' ministry makes perfect sense and has a different purpose than the one at the close of his public ministry. In the Synoptics the cleansing points to divine judgment on Israel for its apostasy, while here the focus is messianic zeal for the purity of God's house. Both fit right where they are, and John's narration almost makes it one of the "signs" of Jesus' messianic nature. I conclude, then, that there were indeed two clearings of the temple. There are two sections, the cleansing itself (vv. 13–17) and the confrontation with the leaders (vv. 18–22).

THE CLEARING OF THE TEMPLE (2:13–17)

This is the first of three Passovers in John (with 6:4; 11:55), breaking John's narration of Jesus' ministry into two parts over a roughly two-year period. These and the other festivals Jesus attends according to John make perfect sense even though they are mentioned only in this Gospel. Jesus regularly attended Jewish festivals with his parents (Luke 2:41), and he would have continued this practice as an adult. It shows his piety, for Passover was a spring pilgrimage festival, and Jewish men were expected to attend each year.

The affront to God's house (2:13–14)

When he arrived, he saw the usual chaos caused by the sale of the animals ("cattle, sheep and doves") needed for the various sacrifices, and the exchange of foreign coins. The number of animals needed was staggering, and they were the source of huge profits. The population of Jerusalem swelled from a population of 50,000–70,000 to at least 250,000 during the Passover, and all those people came to make sacrifices.

They also had to give the half-shekel temple tax, which had to be paid in pure Tyrian silver. Many Roman coins had images of the emperor or other pagan symbols on them, so they were considered idolatrous and could not be placed in the temple. Most pilgrims exchanged their coins in the temple precincts for convenience's sake, but it was scandalous to many for the chief priests to exchange idolatrous coins in the temple itself—so most of the common people agreed with Jesus here. The priests also often charged high interest; it was supposed to be 2–4 percent but was often much higher.

All this was taking place in the court of the Gentiles, where a market that should not have been there was set up. The buying of sacrificial animals and exchanging of coins was necessary, but not in the temple precincts. The chief priests had replaced worship with commerce, and the resulting chaos was more than Jesus could take.

Jesus' reaction to the desecration (2:15-16)

Jesus clearly was outraged by the hullabaloo, believing they had desecrated the temple with this buying and selling. So he made a whip out of some ropes and chased them all out of the temple, the sheep and cattle as well as the sellers. John gives the details in verse 15: "he scattered the coins ... and overturned their tables." Often in the Old Testament there was also a call for purifying the temple in light of spiritual impurity (Ezek 43:7; Zech 14:21; Mal 3:3). In fact, the Sanhedrin had established money changers on the Mount of Olives for this very reason, but the chief priests were greedy and wanted the profits for themselves. No wonder this was a scandal.

In verse 16 there is a stress on Jesus' authority as Messiah and Son of God, as he charges the sellers, "Stop turning my Father's house into a market!" He was uniquely God's Son, so this was not just the temple but "my Father's house." When they narrate the cleansing of the temple, the emphasis in all the Gospels is not so much on Jesus' use of force as on his righteous indignation, his moral and spiritual outrage.

His messianic zeal for his Father's house must have astounded the bystanders. There were no legal repercussions for his actions, undoubtedly because the people were on his side. Even after the second cleansing, the leaders could not kill him because they were "afraid" of the people (Mark 11:18).

The moral of the story (2:17)

The disciples caught the true meaning of Jesus' actions when they at a later time "remembered" Psalm 69:9, "Zeal for your house will consume me." This is one of the most often-quoted psalms to support Jesus' passion (see 15:25; 19:28). Psalm 69 tells David's belief that one reason for the opposition against him was his passion and zeal for God and his temple (69:7–9). In the psalm, "consumes" is in the present tense, while here it is future, pointing to Jesus as the coming Davidic Messiah. Jesus, the Son of God and Messiah, is filled with zeal, and this messianic zeal means he must purify his Father's house of the shameful actions of these profit-driven leaders.

THE CONFRONTATION WITH THE LEADERS (2:18–22)

The demand for a sign (2:18)

In verse 18, the leaders respond. "The Jews" in John nearly always means the leaders of the Jews, as here. They have brought shame to God's house, and now they challenge God's Son to prove that his authority to clear out the money changers has precedence over their authority. Jesus has already produced one "sign" (2:11), and now they want another.

This is a telling reaction. They are not denying the legality of his actions or trying to arrest him. Their only question is the source of his authority, and this is a valid question, for they no doubt believed the Messiah would provide such "signs" or proof of his presence. They at least recognized his basic claim and understood the authority behind his actions. They wanted proof through a messianic miracle, a "sign" that his status was real.

Jesus' incredible response (2:19)

Jesus intended several things when he retorted, "Destroy this temple, and I will raise it again in three days." He knew the leaders would understand it literally and that it would cause quite a reaction, especially since it hints that they could commit an act of much greater violence against the temple than he had already done. To destroy or desecrate the temple would be a capital crime to both the Romans and the Jews. In fact, this literal meaning was used in testimony at Jesus' trial in Mark 14:58, when they twisted it around and said he intended to destroy it himself.

But Jesus meant it metaphorically, with his body the temple of God that would be "destroyed" on the cross. "Three days" is an Old Testament symbol for the restoration of Israel (Hos 6:2), a perfect symbol for the resurrection of Jesus. They would do just what Jesus said: place him on the cross, and the Father would raise him up three days later. Jesus meant this as a prophecy; they took it as a warning. Jesus is giving them a far more incredible "sign" than they could ever ask for, but they failed to know it. Many think Jesus' death and resurrection is actually the "seventh" sign of this Gospel (John 2–12 only covers six miracles), and that makes good sense.

Their misunderstanding and its correction (2:20–21)

Jesus hardly expects the leaders to catch his prophetic meaning, and their reaction is perfectly reasonable: "It has taken forty-six years to build this temple, and you are going to raise it in three days?" Herod began building the temple in 20/19 BC. It actually wasn't fully completed until AD 64, so it was still in the process of construction at this time. This is an important note for dating the life of Jesus, since it means he began his public ministry about AD 27/28.

In one sense his promise relates to both temples, for there is a secondary prophecy of the destruction of the temple in AD 70. The Jewish temple will be replaced by what John states in 2:21, "the temple he had spoken of was his body." The true "temple" refers to his death and resurrection and the new life that will produce. God's own people, the Jews, have rejected his revelation in Jesus (1:11), but he still loves them completely (3:16) and has sent his Son to die on the cross so they can find forgiveness for their sins. In John this first Passover foretells the third Passover, when Jesus' "temple" will be destroyed and he will be raised three days later.

The aftermath: belief (2:22)

This is the second time the disciples "believed" (after 2:11), living out the promise of 1:12-13. Belief in John is closely linked with the reality of the resurrection, for the act of "raising him from the dead" anchors everything in the new life God has produced through the death and resurrection as a single event in salvation history. There is also total contrast with the leaders, who are turning more and more against Jesus every day.

Their belief echoes once more the centrality of faith-decision in John. The disciples believe two things: the Scriptures, with stress on the witness of the Scriptures to Christ (5:39, 46), and "the words that Jesus had spoken," also part of the witness theme in John (5:31-36; 8:14-18). The contrast with the leaders is even more evident here, for Jesus' followers were seeking truth. They were often confused, and this is part of the misunderstanding theme in John, but they were completely open for the passion events to correct them and at all times believed. In John's Gospel memory means recollecting Jesus' teaching, perplexing before but suddenly making sense in light of subsequent events. This remembrance inaugurates faith (2:22; 15:20; 16:4).

INADEQUATE FAITH BASED ON SIGNS (2:23-25)

This is a transition section, ending the clearing of the temple with people coming to Jesus and introducing the Nicodemus section. It is seemingly insignificant yet quite important for John's discipleship theme. At first these "many people" appear to become followers of Jesus, believing "in his name" because they had seen "the signs he was performing." Yet there are two difficulties here.

First, we have only seen a single sign so far. Some think this means the cleansing of the temple was a messianic sign, but this is unlikely, since John sees the second sign in 4:54. I think John is indicating that there are other sign-miracles that he did not have room to note; he had to be selective (as he says in 20:30). Nicodemus will mention these as well (3:2).

Second, there are questions about the level of faith these "many people" actually had. The "belief" (Greek: *episteusan*) "in his name" echoes 1:12 and seems genuine, but it may be spurious because we are told Jesus refused to "entrust himself to them" (2:24), which uses the same root word (*pisteuō*) but with a double meaning. They believed in him, but he at no time believed in them. Therefore he did not trust their seeming decision. The reason is that he "knew all people"; he knew that their faith-decision was incomplete. They had seen the signs, but they had not heard the teaching. John is telling us that a sign-based faith is not enough. They saw miracles but did not yet understand them or what they signified about Jesus. They "believed" in Jesus, but did they truly believe?

Jesus' actions are further explained in 2:25: "he knew what was in each person," that is, "what mankind is really like" (NLT). Faith in miracles as signs is a good first step, but it is incomplete without knowledge. These people got excited by partial truths, but theirs was not a saving faith yet. Their burgeoning faith is contrasted to the radical disbelief of the Jewish leaders (2:18–22) on the one hand and the true faith of the disciples (2:11) on the other hand. True faith centers on who Jesus is and not just on what he does; their belief was little more than astonishment at the stupendous miracles. We can see three levels of faith in John—unbelief (the leaders), partial faith (here and 6:66), and true faith.[2]

Chapter 2 begins with the public ministry of Jesus, which John organizes around seven miracles that are "signs" of the reality of Jesus' messianic and divine person and work. The first sign,

------

2. We miss an important ministry category if we take this as a total darkness of unbelief and lump these with the leaders. John sees a critical distinction—these people are interested and searching. They care. Their error is in thinking they have reached the goal and are true believers.

in 2:1–12, is a fascinating portrait of the man himself. Several scholars have pointed out how miracles can function as parables, because they center not just on the powerful work itself but on the message of the scene as well. Jesus reveals himself here, for he had come to enjoy a bit of rest and relaxation with his disciples but suddenly was asked to do what he did not want to do: perform a miracle that would both alleviate a desperate problem for the groom and his family but also launch his messianic destiny before he wanted to do so. Need outweighed personal preference, and we have here a lovely picture of Jesus giving in to his mother and performing one of the great messianic miracles, changing the water into wine. This scene provides a wonderful anticipation of the messianic wedding feast that will take place at the second coming, when again Christ will multiply the bread and the wine when we sit with him at the outset of our eternal home in heaven (Rev 19:6–9).

So Jesus here inaugurates and enters his ultimate messianic work, and in the story of the clearing of the temple (2:13–25) we see how his messianic zeal has consumed him and guided his actions. There is a critical lesson for us in this, for we too should experience righteous indignation when we see the things of God being desecrated. The chief priests had replaced worship with profit-driven commerce by selling sacrificial animals and exchanging money right in the temple precincts themselves. Jesus confronts their perfidy and purifies his Father's house, giving all of God's people a model to follow when his name is defiled.

In 2:23–25 we see a critical third category between faith and unbelief. Many, like Nicodemus in chapter 3, are quite interested in Jesus but unwilling to commit fully. The belief here is incomplete yet moving in the right direction. In spite of their seeming belief, Jesus refuses to believe in them because he knows their heart is not right. Today we would call this middle group "seekers." They are interested but uncommitted and unwilling to make a decision yet. Yet another group I call "quasi-Christians." These attend church services frequently but remain largely uninvolved and neither give to God nor work for him. That group can often constitute over half of the church.

The existence of both these middle groups means we need to do evangelism inside as well as outside our local churches. These people *seem* to believe but show no "fruit" (John 15:1–8) of it, and like Jesus we dare not trust that they are true believers.

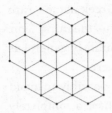

NICODEMUS AND THE NEW BIRTH
(3:1–21)

I n 2:18–22 a negative public encounter took place in which the leaders challenged Jesus' authority. Here a positive private encounter takes place as Nicodemus tries to come to grips with the reality of Jesus. Clearly Nicodemus is one of the many who "believed" in 2:23. As in 2:25, Jesus knew what was truly in the heart of Nicodemus. In fact, this establishes the tone of all the salvation encounters in the rest of the book, like Jesus' insight into the heart of the Samaritan woman in 4:15–21.

This entire dialogue centers on Jesus correcting one of those who had an inadequate faith. Nicodemus's conversion moves the length of the Fourth Gospel, as he undergoes spiritual conviction here, is seen on Jesus' side (perhaps as a secret follower) in 7:50, and is clearly a believer in 19:39.

INTRODUCTION: NICODEMUS
COMES AT NIGHT (3:1-2)

Nicodemus is "one of the Pharisees" described in 1:19, 24, and is a major leader, "a member of the Jewish ruling council." The Pharisees were lay leaders, legal experts in the Torah. By describing him this way, John is telling us he came from an aristocratic, wealthy family and was one of the Pharisees in the **Sanhedrin** (the "ruling council" of the Jews). He had a distinct Greek name—rare among Jews who lived in the Palestine region—meaning "conqueror of the people," so he may have been a military general as well. He was the perfect one to question Jesus here.

In verse 2 we are told he comes "at night," possibly to avoid being seen by his fellow leaders or perhaps to have a completely private interview. In John, however, there are symbolic overtones, with "night" used to typify spiritual darkness (1:5; 3:2; 9:4; 11:10; 13:30). As in 1:4-5, 7, 9, light is confronting darkness with the promise of salvation. Nicodemus is not yet a follower of Jesus (see below) and so is speaking from the standpoint of the dark world in which he dwells.

He begins positively, acknowledging Jesus as "rabbi" (see 1:49) and stating that he represents a group of leaders ("we know") who think Jesus is indeed "a teacher who has come from God." In the first century, rabbis were emerging as the official teachers of Judaism who explained Torah to the rest of the nation, but Nicodemus is going further and recognizing Jesus as "from God," a startling acknowledgment of his divine origin and call. He is hardly confessing Jesus' deity; rather, he is saying that God is behind everything Jesus is doing. Nicodemus's words contrast those of the Pharisees in 9:16, who say, "This man is not from God."

As in 2:23, his faith is a viable first step: "No one could perform the signs you are doing if God were not with him." This is certainly correct and would identify Jesus as more than a rabbi, as one of God's prophets, greater than the Baptist, who did not wield such powerful signs. But as in 2:24-25, Jesus will now begin to show inadequacies in Nicodemus's belief structure. Primarily, he has an inadequate, sign-based faith that needs to go the next step, namely, that of new birth.

Some scholars regard this scene as more of a duel of wits than Nicodemus's honest inquiry into the truth about Jesus. They see Nicodemus and Jesus as engaging in open conflict or debate, with Jesus emerging the clear winner. As interesting as this possibility is, I believe John pictures Nicodemus as inquiring honestly and openly; and that in John this is one of several salvation confrontations (like the Samaritan woman in chapter 4 or the blind man in chapter 10), a necessary step in Nicodemus's eventual conversion. I see it as a positive dialogue rather than negative debate.

FIRST DIALOGUE: YOU MUST BE BORN AGAIN (3:3–4)

Jesus now takes Nicodemus that next step by way of his second double-*amēn* saying (after 1:51). Yet he doesn't answer Nicodemus's implied question about Jesus as a sign-producing rabbi. Rather, he wrenches the man out of his comfortable rabbinic categories by beginning with the mind-boggling statement, "no one can see the kingdom of God unless they are born again." There is a play on words here, as "again" (*anōthen*) is both related to time ("again, anew") and space ("from above"). It carries both meanings here. In other words, Jesus is demanding a heaven-sent new birth.

He is the King of Israel (1:49) who has brought the kingdom of God with him in his coming to earth (Mark 1:15). God himself was the first true king over Israel (1 Sam 12:12; Zeph 3:15), and the people longed for a future kingdom at the day of the Lord, when they would be liberated by the messianic deliverer (Isa 9:2–7; Zech 9:9–17; Mal 4:5). Jesus is claiming that only this rebirth will enable anyone to see and experience this kingdom. Nicodemus would have thought of the Jewish national hope, but Jesus was redefining the concept. He will later tell Pilate, "My kingdom is not of this world" (John 18:36), meaning it is a heavenly reality, only available with the heaven-sent new birth. It cannot be entered only by virtue of membership in the covenant people, the Jews.

This kingdom of God is inaugurated—that is, it is both here (already) and imminent (not yet) and will be consummated at the second coming. In John, Jesus does not speak of the kingdom often; the term only appears here and in 18:36. Rather, his teaching on the subject focuses on the concept of "eternal life," itself both present and future—we have "life" now in Christ (3:16; 5:24) and will be resurrected at the last day (5:28-29; 6:39-40).

In 3:4 Nicodemus misunderstood Jesus on a literal plane; this is quite common in John and always moves the dramatic dialogue along by highlighting what Jesus is saying. His words demonstrate that he did not truly realize Jesus had come from God, for he had no clue the new birth was meant to be a heavenly reality. To him, "born again" meant a baby entering the birth canal a second time. His neat, rabbinic categories had been bypassed on the spiritual plane, and he couldn't leave the earthly plane.

SECOND DIALOGUE: YOU MUST BE BORN OF WATER AND SPIRIT (3:5-8)

THESIS: BORN OF WATER AND SPIRIT (3:5)

Jesus now introduces a second metaphor via another double-*amēn* to clear up the confusion—"no one can enter the kingdom of God unless they are born of water and the Spirit." It was traditionally thought that this meant natural birth (water) and spiritual rebirth (the Spirit), but that is unlikely. In the Greek they are interdependent, "born of water, namely, the Spirit," and in 7:38-39 John states that the "living water" is "the Spirit." The water metaphor in John refers to the Spirit.

Nicodemus should have understood this for several reasons: (1) While the theme of rebirth is not an Old Testament idiom, the idea of Israel as "the children of God" should have made the birth imagery understandable. (2) Water as signifying spiritual cleansing is part of the coming of the Spirit in Ezekiel 36:25-28, "I will sprinkle clean water on you ... and put a new spirit in you." This is linked with the dry bones in Ezekiel 37 and prepares for the image of the dead raised to life. The imagery of birth from above as a new birth from the Spirit's cleansing flows right out of Ezekiel.

CLARIFICATION: SPIRIT-CONTROLLED REBIRTH (3:6-8)

Nicodemus is clearly confused, and so Jesus explains the concept further. There are two kinds of birth—physical or "fleshly" birth and spiritual birth. Jesus contrasts the two. The NLT provides a good translation: "Humans can reproduce only human life, but the Holy Spirit gives birth to spiritual life." Nicodemus had failed to grasp this, and so long as he remained on the earthly plane he could never find eternal life. Only when he turned to the Spirit "from above" could he have spiritual life.

Nicodemus knew Ezekiel, and so Jesus says he "should not be surprised" (3:7) at this. Jesus therefore rebukes him for his astonishment. Moreover, the implication is obvious: "You must be born again"; *dei* ("must") means that spiritual rebirth is a divine necessity. Without it there is no possibility whatsoever of entering God's kingdom. The plural "you" connects Nicodemus with all humanity. He thought that as a leading teacher or rabbi, he controlled the process, but he is merely another person who needs the new birth to have life. It is completely inadequate to think any person or system of teaching controls the process of salvation. The Spirit is in control, not one school of thought or one leading authority. We are "born of the Spirit," not as a Baptist or Reformed or any other theological category.

Jesus uses a third illustration in 3:8 (after "born again" and "born of the Spirit"). We all realize no one can control the wind— "The wind blows wherever it pleases. You hear its sound, but you cannot tell where it comes from or where it is going." In other words, while you feel the wind and hear it, you know neither its origin nor its destination. This involves a play on words, with the Greek *pneuma* referring both to the wind and the Spirit. Likewise, in Ezekiel, it was "breath" from the "four winds" of God that brought life to the dry bones (Ezek 37:9).

Jesus is saying this breath is the Spirit/wind of God, and the Spirit controls it, not us: "So it is with everyone born of the Spirit."

He controls the process of salvation. We feel the presence of the Spirit and hear his voice, and we distinguish this from the flesh. We believe or accept his work (1:12), but the process is his, not ours. The power of the Spirit in us is a mysterious force, and our job is simply to open our heart to him. That is what Nicodemus cannot comprehend, a force that he does not control. Yielding to the Spirit is beyond his ken. All any of us can do is allow God and the Spirit to do their work and give us the new birth. We accept it; we do not control it.

JESUS CONFRONTS NICODEMUS'S IGNORANCE (3:9–12)

Jesus had challenged Nicodemus for his astonishment in verse 7 and now does so a second time. Nicodemus is still confused in verse 9 and asks, "How can this be?" He is asking the question for all John's readers here. We are at the heart of the salvation theme in John's Gospel. To have eternal life, it is necessary to be born of the Spirit and to surrender completely to his work in us. As Paul says, we do not save ourselves but make a faith-response to Jesus' atoning sacrifice. John echoes that here; it is a heavenly rebirth that is of the Spirit and not the flesh. In one sense his confusion is understandable, for these new-covenant truths seemingly go against the covenant privileges of Israel and the importance of faithful adherence to the Torah. Jesus has just burst these categories.

Jesus' response in verse 10 was implicit in verses 3–6: "You are Israel's teacher … and do you not understand these things?" We do not hear Nicodemus again. The rest of the dialogue is all Jesus, who does not accept Nicodemus's responses as an honest search for truth by a teacher of Israel but charges him with ignoring a truth he should have understood. Jesus takes the offensive. Since Nicodemus was a respected Jewish teacher, he should have caught what Jesus had been saying. His problem was not ignorance but unbelief.

With this introduction to the topic, Jesus now turns to the problem itself in verse 11, using another solemn double-*amēn* saying.[1] He begins with an authoritative, "we speak of what we know, and we testify to what we have seen." Some interpreters think the "we" is a plural of majesty, stressing the authoritative teacher (we know) and witness (testify) behind what Jesus has said in verses 3–10. This is correct, but I think it is more. The "we" represents the voice of the Triune Godhead. Jesus is the Living Revealer, the voice of God, and the witness is that of the Spirit also behind what Jesus is saying.

At the same time, the "you" behind "you do not accept our testimony" is also plural, referring to Nicodemus as the representative speaking for the Jewish people and the world. This goes back to 1:11, "his own did not receive him." Again, it is not an issue of ignorance or lack of understanding but of rejection of truth. Nicodemus and the Jewish people are refusing to accept the kingdom truths of Jesus. Moreover, since in 1:10–11 the Jews are part of the world, this expands to all the world outside the kingdom of God. This will be evident in 3:16, where God loves "the world" as a whole.

Jesus makes this perfectly evident in verse 12, where it is unbelief and not just ignorance that is at the heart of the problem: "I have spoken to you of earthly things and you do not believe; how then will you believe if I speak of heavenly things?" In verse 6 it was flesh versus Spirit, and here Jesus makes the same point about the earthly versus the heavenly. Jesus spoke truth from a heavenly perspective while Nicodemus understood things only from an earthly perspective. We might think Jesus is using "heavenly" to speak of the illustrations like physical birth, water, or wind, but Nicodemus was not refusing to believe in that. Jesus is speaking of the new birth as it involves the conversion of earthly beings. Heavenly truths, then, are **apocalyptic** truths about the coming kingdom and the cosmic realm. What is happening now

---

1. See the commentary on 1:51.

in this world, including the gift of salvation and the presence of
the kingdom, is the earthly. What will happen at the end of this
world—the arrival of the final heavenly reality—is the heavenly.

JESUS DEMONSTRATES HIS
HEAVENLY AUTHORITY (3:13-15)

Jesus now points to a series of apocalyptic realities that demonstrate his heavenly authority. "Apocalyptic" refers to the process
by which God reveals hidden truths (*apokalypsis* is the Greek title
of the book of Revelation). Jesus alone has the right to reveal heavenly realities, for he alone has ascended to heaven and come back
to earth. At first glance this seems wrong, for Enoch was translated to heaven (Gen 5:24), and Elijah ascended to heaven in a fiery
chariot in a whirlwind (2 Kgs 2:11). Jewish tradition also said that
Moses was caught up to heaven at his death. However, Jesus was
not denying these events.

The context provides the answer, as caught in the NLT translation: "No one has ever gone to heaven and returned." This refers
back to John 1:51, with its teaching regarding Jesus as the Son of
Man who has united heaven and earth. This actually becomes
a primary theme in the first part of John, centering on the two
Greek terms *anabainō* ("ascend") and *katabainō* ("descend"). Jesus
is the Son of Man who "descended" from heaven at his incarnation
(3:31; 6:33, 50, 51, 58) and then will "ascend" back to heaven at his
death and resurrection (6:62; 13:3; 16:5; 20:17). Moreover, he like
the angels in Jacob's ladder in 1:51 can ascend and descend between
earth and heaven at will. No one else has ever or ever will have
that access and authority to speak heavenly realities. Heaven is
his origin, and a key element of John's presentation of the Son of
Man is that he is a heavenly being who came down from heaven
and thus can speak heavenly truths.

In verse 14 Jesus turns to another apocalyptic image Nicodemus
should have known. In Numbers 21:4-9 "Moses lifted up the snake

in the wilderness." Israel had been complaining against God so God had sent poisonous snakes, which killed many Israelites. When the people repented, God had Moses place a bronze snake on a pole, and whoever looked at it lived. Jesus saw in this an illustration of the new life that people can have by turning to him in repentance and faith. Here he turns to salvation and the gospel, the new birth of 3:3–5.

Just as the bronze snake was "lifted up" on the pole, "so the Son of Man must be lifted up." Jesus saw in the Numbers incident a connection with the divine necessity (*dei*, "must") that he must be "lifted up" in the cross and resurrection. The connection between the bronze snake and Jesus is **typological**, a method of interpretation in which an Old Testament event (type) is reenacted by a contemporary fulfillment (antitype).

Jesus' theme is that when the Son of Man is lifted up on the cross, he is lifted up into glory. This verse introduces John's version of the three **Synoptic** passion predictions, found in the three "lifted up" sayings of John 3:14; 8:28; 12:32–34. Jesus is predicting his death on the cross as both his exaltation to glory and the basis of salvation for sinners. Jesus' humiliation is his exaltation and the basis for our being lifted up to God through conversion.

The purpose of his being lifted up is expressed in verse 15: "that everyone who believes may have eternal life in him." Jesus is giving himself up to the cross so that his exaltation will make possible our glorification through our salvation. Through faith-decision, repentant sinners are reconciled with God and given a new authority as his children (1:12) and see his glory (2:11). Apart from his being "lifted up" there would be no possibility of belief or of the salvation that results. "Eternal life" appears here for the first time in John, and it is found twenty-three times in John's Gospel and his letters. It not only depicts our future life in eternity but is also a present possession, a life that infuses the new child of God at the moment of the new birth.

COMMENTARY: LIFE AND LIGHT
CONFRONT THE WORLD (3:16–21)

The tone changes here and culminates the theological development of the Jesus story so far, beginning with perhaps the most
well-known verse in the Bible. Nearly all interpreters agree that
the dialogue ceases at 3:15, and this section is John's own commentary on and summary of the implications of the first three chapters. The primary theme recapitulates the prologue and its theme
of light encountering the darkness. This passage adds to the story
of the light-darkness conflict.

THESIS: THE LOVE OF GOD AND THE MISSION OF JESUS (3:16–18)

The opening words, "God so loved the world," tell us that the cross
was an act of love on the part of God. "So" translates the Greek
houtōs and indicates degree, so that many translate, "God loved
the world *so much* that …" (GNB, NCV, NIRV). Others prefer to see
it as explanatory: "God loved the world *in this way* …" (CSB). Both
are viable, but I prefer the former, stressing the incredible love of
God. As we saw in 1:10–11, the world does not love God, but God's
love is so deep that "he gave his one and only Son" to be the atoning sacrifice on the cross for the salvation of the lost. This is a central verse, for the entire mission of Jesus flows from it. Parallel
verses are found in 1 John 4:8 ("God is love") and 9 ("This is how
God showed his love among us: He sent his one and only Son into
the world that we might live through him").

The Gospel begins with the love of God, for that is the only
reason that can suffice for God creating a species he knew would
rebel and reject his love. He wanted an object for his love and so
willed that it be possible for this sin-laden species to find salvation and reconciliation with him. The only way was to send "his
one and only Son, that whoever believes in him shall not perish
but have eternal life." The mission of Jesus, the reason he was
sent, was to be "lifted up" on the cross and procure salvation for a

lost and hopeless people, who find it through faith-decision. The result then is that they "shall not perish," the certain end for a hopelessly fallen race, and that they "have eternal life," which as was said in the commentary on verse 15 means new life now and ongoing life in the future. Eternal life is a present possession as well as a future promise.

John explains this saving purpose of the love-driven mission of Jesus further in verse 17. God's loving character led to his resultant action, sending his unique Son into this sinful world to die so he could save it. The mission of the Son "sent by the Father" occurs forty-one times in John and stems from the Jewish idea of the *shaliach*, or "sent one," a representative or ambassador who is the voice and presence of the sender. This is at the heart of the mission theme in John—Jesus as the Revealer or divine envoy of the Father.[2]

Following the format of verse 16b, John highlights the negative side first. The mission of the divine envoy is not judgment; God wants no one to be destroyed (2 Pet 3:9). The purpose is to provide salvation, not condemnation, though as we will see later that will indeed take place. God sent his Son "to save the world through him." This is the first time "save" appears, and it is synonymous with "born from above" in verse 3 and "have eternal life" in verse 16.

There are two sides to the offer—salvation and judgment, developed further in verse 18. For those who come to faith-decision there is no condemnation. They stand before God justified, or declared right with him in his courtroom (Rom 3:24). Unbelievers, on the other hand, stand "condemned already because they have not believed in the name of God's one and only Son." The "already" refers to the moment they rejected Christ. This is not the final judgment at the Great White Throne of Revelation 20:11–15 but the general condemnation that rests on those who refuse to believe. Every person is drawn by the convicting presence of the Spirit

---

2. See "Major Theological Themes" in the introduction.

(John 16:8–11) to faith-decision in the "name of God's one and only Son" (1:14). As discussed in the comments on 1:12; 2:23, the "name" of Jesus refers to all he is as the God-man.

THE LIGHT-DARKNESS CONFLICT (3:19–21)

These two verses restate the basic premise of the prologue regarding light and darkness and labels it, "This is the verdict," continuing the law-court imagery of condemnation (*krinō*) from 3:18 with the term *krisis*, which refers to the verdict of judgment. The divine condemnation of unbelievers is completely just, stemming from their rejection of the light. Rather than explaining the verdict, this text explains the basis of the verdict. John recapitulates 1:4–5, 7, 9 — Jesus, the light of the world (8:12), the light that shines in the darkness (1:5), encounters every person ever born (1:9). However, as this verse states, "people loved darkness instead of light because their deeds were evil."

There is a powerful progression from verses 16 to 19. God loved the world enough to send his Son to die in order to save it, but sinful humanity loved darkness rather than God or the light he sent. The sin-sick world has made an emphatic choice to turn against God and embrace darkness. This is easily proved in our time. Movies and the media, whenever they wish to portray what they think of as "fun," always show nighttime scenes, usually in places that "come alive" when it gets dark. Evil is the action side of darkness. Darkness is what it is; evil is what it does!

It becomes clear in verse 20 that the world doesn't simply prefer darkness; it "hates the light" and refuses to go near it because light "exposes" darkness and its evil deeds. I have probably noted 3:19–20 in sermons as often as any passage in these first three chapters, for it is close to the best passage in Scripture for showing why the world will always turn against God's people. Since we are the light of Christ in a world of darkness, this world wants nothing to do with us.

The light shining in the darkness cannot be extinguished (see 1:5), so the pretense of sinners to be doing good in an ultimate sense is over.[3] Fallen humanity has always fooled itself into thinking that good would ultimately result from its deeds. However, when their self-centered nature and pleasure-seeking motives are placed into relief by the light of God in Christ, they can no longer live that lie. The darkness of the red-light district (note the term here!) is always cloaked in artificial light. When the light of Christ shines, that darkness is exposed. Those who reject the light are guilty, and God's verdict is shown to be completely just.

In contrast, "whoever lives by the truth comes into the light" (v. 21). Those who live for sin avoid the light, while truth-seekers are drawn to it. They prove that they love the light by "coming" to it and "doing" it. There is a critical reminder in this. True belief is not simply intellectual assent; it is shown in daily action. Those who believe the truth *do* it. They live it out in their daily lives. In Romans 12:2, those with a transformed and renewed mind "prove" in their lives that the will of God is "good, pleasing and perfect." They want others to see that "what they have done has been done in the sight of God." They become witnesses to the supreme value of doing the will of God. Others can see in them that the God-centered life is the only one worth living. As others watch their lives unfold, they realize not just how worthwhile the lives of these believers are, but even more importantly how glorious the light of God can be for their own lives.

———

There are two parts to this passage, the Nicodemus dialogue (3:1–15) and John's commentary on the implications of the dialogue for God's people and the world (3:16–21). In the plot development of this Gospel, Nicodemus is the representative Jewish leader coming

---

3. This does not deny Calvin's doctrine of common grace, that the unsaved have an impulse to do good as well. Rather, this means that at the heart their desire will always be to live for self.

to Jesus, one of the "many" from 2:23-25 with a half-hearted "belief" in the power of his sign-miracles. Thus he represents us as well. In 3:3-8 Jesus explodes Nicodemus's (and our) mistaken priorities by showing him that we cannot be part of God's kingdom until we are born anew of the Spirit and submit to the salvation he produces in us. Like the winds coming out of the Judean wilderness, the Spirit brings the new birth, and our part is to accept that gift (1:12).

We must not fall into Nicodemus's ignorance (3:9-12). Like him, we think on the earthly plane and diminish what Jesus is saying by reworking it on the human level. The new birth and the gift of God is not a human-centered phenomenon that can be defined as church membership or visualized by a certain lifestyle. It is a heavenly reality under the control of the Triune Godhead, and we accept it by faith, not by works.

The final part of the dialogue (3:13-15) demonstrates Jesus' heavenly authority to make such statements by highlighting his apocalyptic side. He is the only one ever born who has descended from heaven and ascended back into heaven, therefore controlling heavenly realities. Moreover, his destiny is to reenact or fulfill Moses' bronze snake of Numbers 24 by being "lifted up" to glory on our behalf, one of three predictions of Jesus' death in John. The cross is the basis of our salvation, and when we turn to the cross and find faith, we come to share in the glory of Christ through salvation.

In the commentary discussing the implications of this new birth (3:16-21), we have the Gospel in embryo. We have all grown up in darkness, and yet the love of God has reached down and raised us up to his light. Yesterday as I write was Easter service, and we heard a message on the new life God has made available to sinners through the sacrifice of his Son. It was extremely powerful. The promise of Christianity centers on the light of the gospel making eternal life available to those living in darkness and despair. God truly loves us "so much" more than we can ever comprehend.

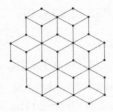

THE BAPTIST TESTIFIES TO THE GLORY OF CHRIST

(3:22–36)

In these verses, John the Baptist appears for the final time, bearing witness to Jesus (see 1:6, 15, 19, 29, 36). As with his other testimonies, this one centers on the fact that John's ministry had fulfilled its God-given purpose and was in process of being subsumed under Jesus' greater prophetic and messianic work. John is the best man (friend of the bridegroom) who happily presents the bride (the messianic community) to the groom (Jesus). Here for the final time he hands his ministry over to Jesus.

Most versions give the impression that his witness continues through verse 36, but in actuality it ends at verse 30. As in 3:16, a change in tone and perspective indicates that John the evangelist in verses 31–36 is writing another editorial summary. This one builds on two earlier emphases: first, the ascent/descent motif of 3:13, in which Jesus is the heavenly being who descended from heaven in his incarnation (vv. 31–33); and second, Jesus as God's sent one or envoy who is the Revealer and voice of God (v. 34), confronting all with the necessity of faith-decision (vv. 35–36). These two **christological** high points reverberate through this material.

THE BAPTIST GIVES HIS FINAL WITNESS (3:22-30)

THE SCENE: BOTH BAPTIZING IN JUDEA (3:22-24)

A short time after the Jerusalem ministry of 3:1-21, he took his disciples "into the Judean countryside," possibly just before his trip through Samaria (ch. 4) back to Galilee (4:43). Only here in the Gospels do we see Jesus baptizing followers, though we learn in 4:2 that only his disciples did so. Since some of them had been followers of John the Baptist (1:35-51), perhaps they wanted to continue that "baptism of repentance." Jesus wanted to "spend some time with them," probably to get to know them and mold them into a team. For Jesus, baptism for the church would begin with the Great Commission after his resurrection (Matt 28:19), so he did not participate in John's baptism.

Meanwhile, John was already in Samaria at a natural spring with "plenty of water" at Aenon near Salim, east of Shechem and Mount Gerizim. A side note in 3:24 tells us this occurred "before John was put in prison," a story not in John's Gospel but narrated in Mark 1:14; 6:14-29, and parallels in the other **Synoptics**. In fact, John the Baptist may have been forced to move north from Judea because of Herod's persecution. Jesus would have been in the northern part of Judea, not too far from him. The purpose of this note is to situate this event chronologically and to show another area in which John the Baptist prepared for Jesus, who took over after the Baptist was arrested and moved the messianic work to its God-intended conclusion.

THE CONFLICT OVER BAPTISM (3:25-26)

A controversy erupted when a certain Jew began to debate John's disciples about "ceremonial washing," or purification rites, such as the washing of hands (Mark 7:1-5) or the **Qumran** community's practice of daily washings. Included in this would perhaps be the merits of John's baptism versus that of Jesus. This is indicated by the fact that when John's disciples came to him, they didn't discuss the debate they'd just had but rather brought up the fact that "that man who was with you on the other side of the Jordan"—these are disciples who know little about Jesus and who consider John to be the "rabbi" or teacher—"look, he is baptizing, and everyone is going to him."

Baptism was a rite of ceremonial washing, and so John versus Jesus had most likely been part of the debate. The "certain Jew" may have been leaning toward Jesus and so was asking about the connection. It is important to note that there is nowhere in any of the Gospels any indication of rivalry between John and Jesus, but still his followers seem visibly upset by the diminishing of their popularity, and so there may be a hint of jealousy. Notice that they call Jesus "the one you testified about" as Messiah. They were not believers and were worried that Jesus and his growing circle of followers were about to eclipse them. They don't dispute his testimony; rather they question what it means for them.

THE BAPTIST'S FURTHER TESTIMONY (3:27–30)

John responds in verse 27 by elaborating on his earlier predictions (1:6, 15, 19, 29, 36), beginning with a general truth: "A person can receive only what is given them from heaven." This applied to both Jesus and himself, and he uses it to lead into his clarification as to the difference between his God-given ministry and that of Jesus. God had given each the calling intended for him. John was content and rejoiced that he was allowed to prepare for the Messiah, and he wants his disciples to rejoice as well. This is a relevant topic for those of us who are not content with our lot in life. We all must realize that God loves us enough to give us exactly the life that is best for us. Will we accept this or become bitter and go another way?

In verse 28 Jesus reminds his followers that the Baptist had testified earlier, "I am not the Messiah but am sent ahead of him" (1:20). John was the divine messenger and forerunner who would "make straight the way" for the Lord (1:23, from Isa 40:3). This is a remarkable testimony for one who was completely aware that his ministry was about to end, yet was perfectly content with what God had in store for him. What a lesson for all of us!

To make his point absolutely clear, John in verse 29 uses the illustration of the "friend who attends the bridegroom," or best man, whose duty in Jewish weddings was to oversee the details. His was an important part, as he took care of all the practical needs and made everything ready for the festivities. He was in charge of getting the bride ready, overseeing the purification rites and leading the procession that brought the bride to the groom's house for the ceremony. Still, all the attention was on the wedding couple, and the friend was happy just to wait and listen and to be "full of joy when he hears the bridegroom's voice." The purpose of the friend was to deflect attention to the groom and to lead all the preparatory events, then disappear when the groom arrives. John was overjoyed to have that role.

Behind this is the imagery of Israel as the bride of Yahweh (Isa 62:4–5; Hos 2:16–20) and the church as the bride of Christ (Eph 5:25–27; Rev 21:2, 9). John the Baptist has fulfilled his office, and he can testify to his disciples that "that joy is mine, and it is now complete." Jesus has arrived, his messianic ministry has begun, and so the Baptist's part is over. He is not only content, he is filled with joy that he has successfully completed his part, and as the friend of the bridegroom he can now place the hand of the bride into that of the bridegroom and know that all is well.

His concluding statement (v. 30) clarifies further his earlier witness that Jesus, the "greater" one, would surpass him (1:15, 30). John uses the Greek word *dei* ("must") to communicate that it was God's sovereign will that Jesus "must become greater; I must become less." God's plan demanded John's diminished role, but that also meant that the sovereign plan was being successfully completed, and in that John could only rejoice in his privileged role. *Dei* is a very important term in John and Revelation, showing God's predetermined will and denoting the essential parts of the divine plan of salvation. John the Baptist's part in it was now over, but his joy continued.

COMMENTARY: JOHN POINTS TO THE GLORY OF THE SON (3:31-36)

The second editorial summary on the part of John the evangelist (after 3:16-21) centers on the person and work of Jesus the Christ. It is an essential part of the theology of the whole Fourth Gospel and especially emphasizes his glory and exaltation. His purpose is to build on the Baptist's testimony and deepen our understanding of this One whose ministry is now beginning to emerge.

THE EXALTATION OF THE ONE WHO SPEAKS (3:31)

Building on the Baptist from 3:29-30, in verse 31 the evangelist makes clear that "the one who comes from above is above all." Jesus is the "greater" being because his origin is "from above" (Greek: *anōthen*), the same term as "born from above" in 3:3. The basis of the heavenly rebirth Jesus has made possible is his heavenly origin, and so he is "above all," greater than all others.

In total contrast, "the one who is from the earth belongs to the earth." The heavenly is infinite, the earthly is finite; the heavenly is eternal, the earthly is temporary. The earthly would include not only the Baptist but also Nicodemus. The earthly person "speaks as one from the earth," in a limited way and from a finite perspective. Prophets like the Baptist could prophesy but could only repeat what God told them. They had no access to heavenly secrets and no control over "birth from above." Teachers like Nicodemus could only explain what was said in the mysterious books God had inspired and were limited in their ability to interpret.

THE RECEPTION OF THE ONE WHO SPEAKS (3:32-33)

John goes on to say that Jesus, with his perspective "from above," observes our earthly situation with heavenly knowledge, implying that the Father himself speaks to the Son about all heavenly issues. What the Son hears and sees takes place within the Triune Godhead and concerns eternal truths. However, the sad fact is that though the one with the heavenly authority "testifies to what he has seen and heard"—these heavenly truths passed on to earthly, finite beings—"no one accepts his testimony." His witness centers on the most important facts ever made known to humankind, yet no one cares. As in 1:10-11, the very people of the world created by the God-man have refused to know or accept these truths. The single most important witness in all of history is greeted with unbelief.

And just as 1:10-11 (rejection by the world) is followed by 1:12-13 (acceptance by many), so here 3:32 (rejection) is followed by 3:33 (acceptance), but this time the emphasis is on the Godward aspect, as those who open themselves to these truths and "accept" the heavenly witness "certify that God is truthful." It is God who has sent his Son and worked out his plan of salvation through him, so while Christ is truth (14:6), so also God is truthful. "Certify" or "affirm" (*sphragizō*) is a legal term for sealing an official document and certifying that it is true and valid. The imagery is a seal that authenticates a legal decision, so that those who "accept his testimony" become legal witnesses to the truth-claims he states.

THE SPIRIT BEHIND THE ONE WHO SPEAKS (3:34-35)

With verse 34, John specifies who is behind every word Jesus speaks, completing the trinitarian thrust of this passage. The Son has a twofold anchor, the God who "has sent" him as his envoy and the Spirit who fills him with his empowering presence. Thus when he speaks, he "speaks the words of God." The Word (Greek: *logos*, as in the prologue) proclaims the words (*rhēma*). The words of Jesus are "Spirit and life" (6:63), for they are "the words of God" (here) and "the words of eternal life" (6:68). Jesus is the divinely sent herald, God's ambassador from heaven, and as the **shaliach**, or "sent one," he speaks with the very voice of God.

Within this authority as God's very voice, God "gives [him] the Spirit without limit." Since "him" is actually not in the text, it is possible to construe this as Jesus giving the Spirit to us. While a few take it this way, the context makes it far more viable to see God giving the Spirit to Jesus. A later rabbi said the Spirit rested on the prophets "according to the measure" of each one's calling (Leviticus Rabbah 15:2). There is no measure or limit to Jesus' calling, so the Spirit descends on him (1:32–33) with limitless power. This is the Trinity: The Father sends the Son and bestows on him the limitless Spirit.

Moreover, according to verse 35, "the Father loves the Son and has placed everything in his hands." The Father's love is limitless (5:20; 10:17; 15:9; 17:23–26) and so is both the Spirit and the authority given the Son over his creation. This returns to the Word as Creator (1:3–4), with Jesus the cosmic Lord over "everything." Christ's sovereign control is universal and eternal (see Col 1:15–20), and he knew that the Father had "placed everything in his hands." Christ is both omniscient (see 1:42, 47) and omnipotent. The point here is that this sovereign Christ with limitless authority and the limitless Spirit has brought salvation to sinful humankind.

THE CHOICE ALL HUMANKIND MUST MAKE (3:36)

There are only two responses to Christ (as in 3:19–21): unbelief (loving darkness) or belief (coming to the light). This verse, with its emphasis on the response to Christ, provides a fitting climax to all of 1:19–3:35, especially to chapter 3. The rest of the book will continue this theme, and in the "motto" at the end of the Fourth Gospel we will be told, "these are written that you may believe" (20:30–31). This is an encounter Gospel, demanding faith-decision as the only possible response to the truths revealed, a decision that will determine the reader's eternal destiny.

"Whoever believes in the Son has eternal life" as a present possession. (John uses present tense throughout this verse.) It belongs to them now as well as in the final resurrection. On the other hand, "whoever rejects the Son will not see life," neither in the present nor in the eternal future, because "God's wrath remains on them."

In 3:18 we saw that the unbeliever "stands condemned already." Their condemnation does not await them at the final judgment; God's wrath already rests on them because of their repeated rejections of Christ virtually every day of their lives. Our holy God is characterized with two interdependent aspects of his being—justice and love. To reject his love is to fall under his justice, and a just God must respond with wrath to those who reject his Son. As divine love and bestowal of life are present realities, so also are divine justice and wrath.

This is the end of John the Baptist's ministry in this Gospel, and it concludes the first major section of Jesus' ministry. He will now begin to branch out from those in 1:11 (ministry to "his own," the Jews) to those in 1:10 (ministry to the world). He will begin with the Samaritans in chapter 4, being identified as "the Savior of the world" (4:42).

The first section (3:22–30) is all about the Baptist's realization and joy at his now-finished part in salvation history. As the best man at the wedding between Jesus and the church, his task was to prepare the way for the messianic era. He has now successfully completed that task and so happily steps aside, content at a job well done. This is an important lesson, as most of us have subordinate parts to play in the kingdom, yet all have important roles. We need to realize that God loved us enough to give us exactly the right place in his plan. We, like John, must be content to accept our God-given ministry and place.

The second half is John's editorial summary (3:31–36) of the truths that have just been enunciated, centering on the authority of the one who is "from above" and so has heavenly authority behind what he reveals. His witness is authenticated first by those who accept it and certify the divine truths, and second by the Spirit, who undergirds these truths and provides limitless power to the divine speaker. The trinitarian thrust is unmistakable; the whole Godhead is behind the gospel truths. The omnipotent Christ, the one in sovereign control of his creation, has brought salvation to humankind. Therefore, every person is brought by the convicting power of the Spirit (see 16:8–11) to faith-decision and must choose between belief and rejection of the Son, the Savior of humankind. This will determine whether they have eternal life or remain under the wrath of God. That is the point of the Fourth Gospel, and points to our task—we have a mission to take God's salvation to a lost world.

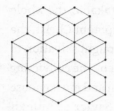

THE SAMARITAN WOMAN
AND RETURN TO CANA
(4:1–54)

John has concluded the first part of Jesus' ministry as framed by the witness of John the Baptist (1:19–34; 3:21–36). Jesus now heads to Galilee for the second time (the first was in 2:1) and in obedience to the Father goes through Samaria, engaging in the first mission outside Jewish territory recorded in the Bible since Jonah and initiating the prophetic launch of God's mission to the world.

This is the third salvation drama, after 1:35–51 and 3:1–15, and once more Jesus takes the initiative (see 1:43). In 3:1–15 he reached out to a Jewish leader, here to a despised woman from the wrong side of the tracks (a Samaritan, a woman, an immoral person). This becomes a perfect model of mission, for none of Jesus' disciples would ever have conceived of her as Jesus' choice for the first non-Jewish convert. The message here is that every single person is an object for mission. Christ died for all, and there is no place for prejudice in the church. My commentary below will be somewhat detailed, for I want to use the various "encounters" between Jesus and the Samaritan woman to show the narrative progress of the Gospel as Jesus confronts her and leads her to faith-decision.

In recent years several interpreters have seen this drama as an ironic twist on the typical hospitality story.[1] Jesus visits a Samaritan village, where as a stranger he should be welcomed and offered hospitality, but the fact that it is a Samaritan village and that he encounters a woman is highly unusual. Even more so is the fact that very quickly the scene is reversed and Jesus becomes the host, offering the woman "living water." Her positive reaction to Christ is the direct opposite of the absence of any reaction on the part of Nicodemus. This becomes a central section for John's mission theme, for it contains the first discourse on mission (4:31–38), and therefore Christ's mission to the despised Samaritans launches God's mission to the world.

JESUS RETURNS TO GALILEE
THROUGH SAMARIA (4:1–6A)

In verse 1 John explains the reason Jesus decided to leave Judea and return to Galilee—a controversy brewing when the Pharisees, the enemies of the Baptist and Jesus, "heard that he was gaining and baptizing more disciples than John." The opposition in Judea was starting to get organized, so Jesus probably decided to leave. John clarifies in verse 2 that in reality it wasn't Jesus but his disciples who did the baptizing. It appears to be more of a historical note, and Jesus' leaving Judea was not due to tensions with John the Baptist but to the situation with growing opposition from the Pharisees.

The critical term in verse 4 is that Jesus *"had to"* (Greek: *edei*, "must") "go through Samaria." Some have thought this means simply that Jesus, possibly in a hurry, felt he had to take the shorter route through Samaria rather than the longer route on the other side of the Jordan through the Gentile lands. Josephus

---

1. Others have seen it as a takeoff on betrothal rites, since Abraham/Rebekah (Gen 24:1–27), and Jacob/Rachel (Gen 29:1–12) both met at wells. However, the imagery of hospitality fits much better.

even said this was the normal route to travel from Judea to Galilee (*Antiquities* 20.118). However, this is unlikely, for Samaritans were enemies of the Jews, and the Pharisees and other conservative Jews avoided it. Most likely when Joseph and Mary went to Judea for the festivals, they took the outside route.

So "had" has its usual force in John of portraying divine necessity (3:7, 14, 30), in particular the God-destined importance of beginning the universal mission of Jesus and the church with Samaria. Jesus was following the Father's designated path. Everything in John takes place as part of God's plan, and the mission to the world is initiated at just the right time. God's will led Jesus into Samaria to the village of Sychar, and he had prepared the woman to be at the appointed spot at the appointed time.

As he passed through Samaria, Jesus came to the village of Sychar near Jacob's well (v. 5). This would probably be just east of Mounts Gerizim and Ebal, in the heart of Samaritan territory, but we don't know for certain. The animosity between Jews and Samaritans derived from the Jews' demand that these half-Jews (the Assyrians forced them to marry pagans) divorce their pagan wives at the return from exile. They refused, and the enmity continued for the next several centuries.[2] The dislike of one another was still strong during the time of Christ.

Jacob's well (v. 6) is not mentioned in the Old Testament, but the tradition exists clear up to the present and is probably correct. This well is about a hundred feet deep, seven feet in diameter, and is fed by an underground bubbling spring, which fits the story here with the "living water." "The plot of ground Jacob had given to his son Joseph" is mentioned in Genesis 48:22, when Jacob on his deathbed bequeathed it to Joseph. It lies just a short distance from the well.

---

2. For this background see Ezra 4; 2 Kings 17:29–41.

INITIAL ENCOUNTER: JESUS
ASKS FOR WATER (4:6B-9)

Here the subnarrative on hospitality begins. Jesus arrived there at noon, one of the hottest times of the day, and tired from the long walk, he sat beside the well to rest. The Light of God was about to shine forth on the Samaritan world. At this time a Samaritan woman came to draw water, and the scene was set. Jesus was there alone, for "his disciples had gone into the town to buy food" (v. 8). One might think this unusual, since the Samaritans were considered unclean, but Galilean Jews were not as legalistic as the Judeans, and travelers in Samaria either had to carry a lot of provisions or buy food there. Jesus was waiting for them to return.

As he was waiting, a Samaritan woman came to the well, also for water. This was unusual for two reasons: first, women generally came in groups rather than singly; and second, they came in the morning rather than the heat of the day. Likely (as we will see) this was because she was considered an immoral woman and so was not welcome in the company of the others. She came when she could be alone.

Jesus' request in verse 7, "Will you give me a drink?" would have startled the woman. In speaking to her, he broke several taboos: (1) a religious taboo, with the Samaritans accepting only the Pentateuch as canon and Mount Gerizim rather than Mount Zion as the holy mount; (2) a sexual taboo, with men not associating with women socially; they would never initiate a conversation with a woman who is a stranger; (3) an ethnic taboo, with Jews staying away from Samaritans and vice versa. Jesus freely ignored such things when the gospel was at stake, providing an important model for ministry today among the homeless and marginalized.

Jesus' request for water was carefully calculated. Her reply in verse 9 ("You are a Jew and I am a Samaritan woman") shows the distance between the two groups, centering on the inappropriateness of this, as John explains ("Jews do not associate with Samaritans"). The verb indicates not only association but also using the same utensils, which may be unclean. The Jews were normally very careful about such things and would never drink from the same bowl, so she is shocked.

Still, Jesus often got into trouble for eating with disreputable people (Matt 9:11; 11:19; Luke 15:2; 19:7), so this was an extension of his normal practice. He had a higher purpose in his request, preparing her for his next offer. The gospel rises above all taboos, for the salvation of souls has priority over religious concerns.

SECOND ENCOUNTER: JESUS OFFERS LIVING WATER (4:10-12)

The first request set the stage for this rejoinder, as Jesus turns the tables on the hospitality narrative and assumes the place of the host offering a new kind of water. The woman is shocked by who she perceives him to be, a Jewish male addressing a Samaritan woman. Yet he is so much more, and he moves her step by step in that direction, challenging in verse 10, "If you knew the gift of God and who it is that asks you for a drink. ..." The "gift of God" means that God is extending to her through Jesus the gift of eternal life and of the Holy Spirit, as we will see below. She is not speaking just to a Jewish male or even a prophet, as she thinks, but to the One who extends the gift of salvation from God to her.

Jesus offers her "living water," which to her refers to the spring water (from fresh bubbling springs like the pool of Bethesda or this well), but in its intended metaphorical sense refers to the "water of life" from God. In the Old Testament this term was often used of the Torah or wisdom or the Spirit of God, since God is the fountain of life and of knowledge (Isa 12:3; Jer 2:13; Zech 14:8). It typifies the life-giving power of God and the presence of the Holy Spirit. This can only come from Jesus, God's Son and the bestower of the Spirit, culminating in Revelation 22:1-5 and the river of the water of life flowing to God's people. We see here a trinitarian thrust, as every member of the Godhead is the source of this life.

The woman, like Nicodemus, understands this on the earthly plane and so says in verse 11, "Sir, you have nothing to draw with and the well is deep," for this well was a hundred feet deep. She adds, "Where can you get this living water?" There would undoubtedly have been at least a rope, with each villager bringing their own bucket (due to the laws of purity). She is confused by a promise Jesus seemingly cannot keep.

So she goes on the offensive in verse 12, "Are you greater than our father Jacob, who gave us the well?" She is not mocking him, but she is incredulous and skeptical about his implicit claims. He seemed an average-looking Jewish male, so why such outrageous statements? Jacob had originally dug the well, and it had been used ever since by his progeny. Did Jesus think himself better than one of the patriarchs? She might be thinking of the prophet like Moses (Deut 18:15), who drew water from the rock (Num 20:2–13); surely he didn't seem superior to that figure.

THIRD ENCOUNTER: JESUS OFFERS
THE WATER OF LIFE (4:13–15)

Jesus is drawing the stakes higher and higher and offering it all to this Samaritan woman, moving from water to living water to the water of eternal life. Now she cannot miss his spiritual meaning. He begins at her earthly perspective in verse 13: "Everyone who drinks this water will be thirsty again." As important as the well was, it could only provide temporary satisfaction.

But Jesus does not have this water in mind. "Whoever drinks the water I give them will never thirst." The well water had to be drawn up with a bucket, but the heavenly water Jesus is offering "will become ... a spring of water welling up to eternal life." The Greek word behind "welling" or "bubbling" is a strong one, picturing a geyser leaping up, a picture often found in the Old Testament (Isa 49:10; 55:1–3). Those who partake of this water "never thirst" again, with the Greek meaning "never again for eternity," for new life will literally explode out of this messianic spring. The result is not just a prolonged earthly life but "eternal life."

She does not fully understand but cannot miss the basic nuance, so she responds in verse 15: "Sir, give me this water so that I won't get thirsty and have to keep coming here to draw water." She understands that he has access to a supernatural supply of water, but she is still thinking of literal water. She asks him to fill her bucket with this new water. Still she exhibits no awareness of the spiritual reality Jesus is addressing. We cannot know whether she actually believes what he is saying at a basic level or is slightly mocking, but she wants a part in the action if there is any truth to it at all.

FOURTH ENCOUNTER: JESUS IS AWARE OF HER MARITAL SITUATION (4:16-18)

The Samaritan woman is clearly thinking only of the earthly situation, so Jesus changes tack and addresses her past and present, showing the same supernatural awareness he did with Simon (1:42) and Nathanael (1:47). His intention is to force her to come face to face with not only who she is (which she knows) but with who Jesus himself is. He begins in verse 16 by asking her to fetch her husband, leading her to admit she was currently unmarried (v. 17). She likely thought this would end the discussion, but his purpose was to uncover her true spiritual condition. Before she could partake of the living water, she must come to grips with her moral condition.

Needless to say, his omniscient response shocks her. As in 1:5, the light of Christ is shining in her dark places and confronting her with her true situation. Her five marriages (4:18) likely included several divorces. In Judaism, the school that followed the rabbi Shammai was strict, but the school that followed the rabbi Hillel (the predominant approach) allowed divorce for nearly any reason whatsoever (like our society today). Still, more than two or three divorces were considered shameful, and the Samaritans were undoubtedly similar. This is why she was forced to get water by herself at noon; she was probably shunned by the other women. Her current living arrangement (with a man who was not her husband) would have added to her shame. She would have been considered immoral for her number of husbands as well as for her current living arrangement, and Jesus is confronting her with the problem that is keeping her from being able to partake of the living water.

FIFTH ENCOUNTER: THE WOMAN INCREASES IN AWARENESS AND WORSHIP (4:19–22)

Jesus' knowledge and revelation of her true situation force her to rethink who he actually is, so she says in verse 19, "Sir, I can see that you are a prophet." She might mean that he is an inspired prophet like those of the Old Testament with special insight from God (see Luke 7:39). Alternatively, perhaps she wonders if he might be "the prophet," the "prophet like Moses" of Deuteronomy 18:15 (as in John 1:21), called the *Taheb* by the Samaritans, which was their equivalent to the Jewish Messiah. Likely there is further double meaning, with the woman thinking the first and the author hinting at the second.

If he is a prophet, she is hoping he can settle a major debate between the Jews and Samaritans regarding the proper place of worship. In verse 20 she asks whether Jerusalem or "this mountain" (Mount Gerizim in Samaria, where "our ancestors worshiped") is the proper place for worship of God. The Samaritans had built their own temple there and rejected worship at the Jerusalem temple. They believed the command to build an altar upon entering the land in Deuteronomy 27:4–8 referred to Mount Gerizim (rather than Mount Ebal, as the text says), and that Gerizim had priority of place over Jerusalem, which they argued did not arise until after the period when the Pentateuch was written.

This is a turning point in the dialogue, for she is now thinking on the spiritual plane, and the discussion turns to worship.

Jesus' answer in verse 21 certainly shocks her, beginning with the same "woman" he used with his mother in 2:4. He calls on an initial "belief" in what he is about to say, clearly as prelude to a deeper faith-decision to come.

Then he makes a prophetic claim regarding a coming "time" or "hour," pointing to an **apocalyptic** event in the future when Jewish worship in Jerusalem or Samaritan worship on Mount Gerizim will be no more. Some interpreters think this is a reference to the destruction of the temple in AD 70 and the decentering of Jewish worship in the aftermath. However, it is better to see it as pointing to the arrival of the new kingdom of God. Yet this is not the **eschaton**, or end of all things, but the new era of salvation inaugurated by Jesus' death and resurrection. Access to the Father will be direct (see Heb 8:10–11), and neither Mount Gerizim nor Jerusalem will be important. Moreover, he hints that Jews and Samaritans will worship together, not separately and in conflict with one another.

In 4:22 he answers her question more directly, stating that the Samaritans "do not know" the true object of worship, God, while the Jews "worship what we [Jesus includes himself] do know," namely, the God of the Old Testament whose true temple is in Jerusalem. The reason for this (Greek: *hoti*, "because, for") is that "salvation is from the Jews," with "from" (*ek*) referring to source. This hardly means that all Jews will be saved or that there is no salvation without becoming Jewish (that will be debated in Paul's letters to the Galatians and Romans), but that Christ and his salvation come from within the Jewish matrix. So Jesus clearly sides with his Jewish background in answering the Samaritan woman.

SIXTH ENCOUNTER: TRUE WORSHIP IS IN SPIRIT AND TRUTH (4:23–24)

For the second time Jesus tells her, "a time is coming," but in verse 23 he adds "and has now come." The hour of destiny in John (see 2:4; 4:21) always refers to the God-appointed time of Jesus' passion.

The point here is that the new age of salvation has now arrived in Jesus. There is an already/not yet tension in this, as the kingdom has already come but has not yet been consummated, which "time" will come with Jesus' passion and death on the cross. There are three stages of salvation history in John—the incarnation, the life and death of Jesus the Christ, and the second coming. John stresses the first two here.

The "now-ness" of salvation is defined by worship: "True worshipers will worship the Father in the Spirit and in truth, for they are the kind of worshipers the Father seeks." There is an A-B-A pattern in verses 23–24, with "worship in Spirit and truth" framing "God is Spirit." Jesus begins with "true worshipers" for two reasons: (1) neither Jewish nor Samaritan worship will suffice any longer (v. 21, "neither on this mountain nor in Jerusalem," each with their own material temple), for a new worship has been introduced in the new age of salvation; and (2) proper worship now centers on Christ and the new life he has brought. The image of God "seeking" such worshipers is a strong one. The Father wants only those whose heartfelt worship is Spirit-driven and Spirit-centered. This worship is trinitarian, as all three members of the Godhead are involved in such true worship.

Jesus defines this true worship in verse 24. It centers on the Father-child relationship. The new family of God has been instituted by Christ. We respond to the Father's love with worship. The basis of this is in the fact that God the Father "is spirit."[3] John defines God three ways in his writings: "God is spirit" (here), "God is light" (1 John 1:5), and "God is love" (1 John 4:8). At one level, saying that God is spirit means that he is not a corporeal being but a spirit being. He is not material and should not be worshiped in a material way, whether in Jerusalem or on Mount Gerizim, in this new age of salvation. At the deeper level, he is totally transcendent

---

3. The NIV prefers to use small s here to designate the spirit-form God takes and capital S elsewhere to designate God's essence as Spirit.

and beyond our understanding, yet he has revealed himself to us and allowed us into his family. That is one of the great mysteries. As Spirit he gives life and lifts us above our own creaturely finiteness to experience him.

Since God is spirit in form and essence, worship cannot be material but "must" (Greek: *dei*)[4] take place "in the Spirit and in truth." In Greek, these are both governed by a single *en* ("in") and form a single idea, "truly in the Spirit." There is a double meaning here. In one sense, this worship is "in the spirit"; worship centers on the whole inner being of the worshiper, and is deeply spiritual and wholehearted. In another sense, this worship is only possible "in the Spirit" due to the enabling presence and power of the Holy Spirit. He is "the Spirit of truth" (14:17; 15:26; 16:13). The new birth is "from above" (3:3), and Jesus is "from above" (3:31), so true worship is heaven-enabled and heaven-centered, taking place when we are seeking and thinking "on things above" (Col 3:1-2). Those in the Spirit worship with all their soul, heart, mind, and strength.

SEVENTH ENCOUNTER: JESUS IDENTIFIES HIMSELF AS THE CHRIST (4:25-26)

Here is the culmination of this salvation drama and faith-encounter, as the woman realizes that Jesus is more than a prophet. His incredible explanation of true worship triggers a thought regarding the Samaritan *Taheb*[5] and Jewish Messiah, so she asks him to explore this in verse 25: "'I know that Messiah' (called Christ) 'is coming. When he comes, he will explain everything to us.'" She is still confused and has a vague idea that something extraordinary has happened, but she cannot yet define what it is. So she asks Jesus about the Messiah, the Jewish equivalent of the *Taheb*, who

---

4. Another instance of the *dei* of divine necessity; see comments on 4:4.

5. *Taheb* means "restorer" and was the Samaritan equivalent of the Jewish Messiah, the "prophet like Moses" of Deuteronomy 18:15, as noted in the comments on John 4:19.

would teach and reveal "everything." As several interpreters have pointed out, this idea of the *Taheb* as teacher is more a Samaritan idea than a Jewish one, and she is bringing the two figures together.

Jesus does not bother to correct her but uses her partial understanding to identify himself to her in verse 26: "I, the one speaking to you—I am he." He begins with the very important Greek phrase *egō eimi*, building on the self-revelation of God at the burning bush in Exodus 3:14, "I AM WHO I AM." This is God's true covenant name as Yahweh, reflected also in Isaiah 41:4; 43:10–13; 48:12; 52:6 and seen in John again in 8:24, 28, 58, and in the seven "I am" sayings.[6] He is hardly revealing his deity to her, but the evangelist wants the reader to pick it up. He is revealing to her that he is the true *Taheb* who alone can "explain everything" and provide the living water.

THE DISCIPLES RETURN AND THE WOMAN WITNESSES (4:27–30)

The disciples finally return with the food they purchased (see 4:8), and their return comes right at the conclusion of Jesus' self-revelation, sending the drama to the next level—that of witness. There is a clear contrast between the woman's excited sharing with the townspeople and the disciples' surprise at Jesus' speaking to her. What's more, they are unwilling to enter the dialogue, reflecting their bias against speaking with both women and Samaritans. John tells us in verse 27 that "no one" was willing to address either the woman (to ask her, "What do you want?") or Jesus (to ask him, "Why are you talking with her?"). The **Mishnah**, an ancient Jewish source, tells us that Jews generally thought that men should not talk publicly with a woman, and it was even worse for a rabbi to waste his time doing so (m. Abot 1:5). Jesus had none of those misogynistic tendencies, but clearly his disciples did.

---

6. John 6:35; 8:12; 10:7, 11; 11:25; 14:6; 15:1–5.

The woman was just the opposite. There is no doubt that Jesus had touched her deeply, for in verse 28 she leaves her water pot and runs back to the village to tell everyone what had transpired. Three things show her state of mind: (1) Water jars are important utensils and would only be left if she was completely consumed by the task before her.[7] (2) As we saw just now, women did not speak publicly, especially to men. They could not be official witnesses of anything. If a robbery was witnessed just by several women, the thief could not be brought to justice, for none of the women could testify. (3) She was vilified by the village as an immoral person and had to come to get water at noon so she wouldn't have to face the other women. In her excitement and haste to tell the village the exciting news about Jesus, she ignored every one of these barriers.

Her invitation to "Come see" (v. 29) reflects the invitation of Jesus in 1:39 and of Philip in 1:46. Like those, her invitation is sal-vific in intent and in fact leads to faith-decision on the part of many of the townspeople. Her testimony that he had told her "everything I ever did" stems from 4:17–18 and would be seen as the vision and insight of a prophet. Her concluding question shows that she too is near conversion, with "could" (Greek: *mēti*) indicating the ten-tative nature of it: "Could this be the Messiah?"

The whole village is asking this with her, and we move directly into the mission of Jesus to the world; she, like Andrew and Philip in 1:35–50, takes the messianic invitation to others. The villagers' response is immediate. They exited the town and "came out" (it is imperfect tense, so "began coming" would be better) to Jesus. Think of it this way: While Jesus is delivering his mission address in verses 31–38, these villagers are on the way to him to exemplify the harvest. Her witness is successful. As before, her conversion

---

7. Some see symbolic significance in this, as she leaves behind the earthly well water in her excitement to have the living water and share it with her fellow townspeople. There is no indication of this in the text, but in light of the strong use of symbolism throughout, it is definitely possible this is part of the meaning.

is not narrated but is implicit in her actions. She is very likely among those who "believe" in 4:39, 41.

JESUS DISCOURSES ON MISSION (4:31–38)

This mission sermon progresses similar to the encounters with the woman, so I will outline it as a series of interactions with the disciples. Many consider this an excursus or interlude, but it is actually integral to the message of the whole chapter, showing that all along Jesus' purpose was to have a "harvest" in Samaria. He believed it was time to go to the next level and reach not just the Jews but also the world with the gospel of salvation.

FIRST INTERACTION: A NEW KIND OF FOOD (4:31–33)

The scene begins on the earthly plane, with the disciples urging in verse 31, "Rabbi, eat something." They have missed the meaning of every single thing they have seen, centering on food for the stomach instead of the eternal food Jesus has been feeding the woman. To them Jesus was a hungry rabbi; to the woman he was a prophet, possibly the Messiah. At this time Jesus alone knew he was Son of God, living Word, and Savior.

Jesus has prepared a vastly superior meal and so responds in verse 32, "I have food to eat that you know nothing about." The living water he had offered the woman and the spiritual food he was offering them now were the furthest things from their minds. So they interpret what he says with the same kind of materialistic ignorance Nicodemus and the Samaritan woman displayed, saying to each other, "Could someone have brought him food?" (v. 33). They were spiritually challenged at this stage, still in their spiritual infancy. Sadly, this continued virtually until their receiving of the Spirit at Pentecost.

SECOND INTERACTION: GOD'S WILL AND WORK (4:34)

Jesus now makes clear that he is not speaking of earthly but spiritual food, defining it properly: "My food ... is to do the will of him

who sent me and to finish his work." Jesus' true nourishment is
to respond to the *dei* (divine leading; see comments on 4:4) of his
Father and act on it. His food is to complete his divinely given mission ("him who sent me") as God's envoy, bringing salvation to the
world. The mission to Samaria is essential to that divine will, and
he must "finish [God's] work" in Samaria and the world. It is the
Father's will and work that nourishes and drives Jesus, and he is
inviting his disciples to consume that heaven-sent meal with him.

Behind this is Deuteronomy 8:3: "Man does not live on bread
alone but on every word that comes from the mouth of the LORD."
The Israelites had grumbled about the manna, but Moses pointed
to what really matters. Jesus had a similar lesson for his disciples.
He is thinking similarly to Paul in Romans 12:2, where transformed
Christians prove with their lives how "good, pleasing and perfect"
the will of God is for them. In John a major purpose of Jesus is to
"do the will of God" (5:30; 6:38), and those who follow his example
have the guarantee of eternal life (6:39, 40). Finishing God's work
is closely aligned with the hour of destiny in Jesus' passion, and
the evangelization of the Samaritans was to be one of the results
of Jesus' making salvation possible for the world on the cross.

THIRD INTERACTION: THE HARVEST (4:35-38)

The will and work of God center especially on the harvest, and
once more Jesus uses an earthly metaphor to picture a spiritual
reality. He begins in verse 35 with an observation taken from the
world of agriculture: "It's still four months until harvest." Farmers
normally waited four months from planting to harvesting. Jesus
declares the time of waiting over for God's harvest of souls. "Open
your eyes and look at the fields! They are ripe for harvest." God's
harvest is not like the earthly harvest. There is no gap between
planting and harvest. When the gospel seed is planted, harvest
begins immediately.

He is referring generally to the mission of his team and specifically to the villagers of Sychar, who at that very moment are on

their way to Jesus (4:30). The disciples lack vision. They need to look up and see Samaria as a field ripe for harvest. This is a very important metaphor for our day as well. All of us need to look up and see how God has readied people around us for the harvest, and it is up to us to pluck the crops he has prepared.

In verses 36–38 John develops further this theme of the immediacy of the harvest. In the soils of Galilee, the planters are busy, but the harvesters have not yet begun. In the kingdom mission, "*Even now* the one who reaps draws a wage and harvests a crop for eternal life." There is some debate as to the identities of the planter and the harvester. The planters are variously seen as the Old Testament prophets or John the Baptist, Jesus himself, or even the woman planting the seed in her fellow townspeople. The harvesters could be Jesus and the disciples, but some have said the Father plants, Jesus and his disciples harvest; others, that Jesus is both planter and reaper. I agree with those who say that Jesus deliberately does not specify the two because this is a seminal story indicating the mission of God and his people as a whole. Therefore all the options are part of the drama. We could say that we ourselves are both planter (as we spread the gospel) and harvester (as we bring people to Christ).

The main point is seen in the "true" proverb of verse 37 ("one plants and another reaps") and the result that awaits them (v. 36b), "so that the sower and the reaper may be glad together." Jesus is probably echoing Amos 9:13, which alludes to the restoration of Israel: "The days are coming … when the reaper will be overtaken by the plowman and the planter by the one treading grapes." Amos (and Jesus here) speaks of the incredible plenty that defines God's harvest, a harvest yield so great that both sower and reaper function together. This is the **eschatological** harvest of souls into the kingdom, so the disciples (and we) are promised an incredible future for the kingdom and the church. According to Isaiah 65:21–22, God's people will "eat the fruit of their own vineyards" and "have time to enjoy their hard-won gains" (NLT). The task of

God's people is clear: proclaim the gospel (plant) and win people for Christ (harvest), and this joyous task will dominate the church age.

Jesus is saying that the messianic age has arrived, a time of wondrous harvest. The mission of the church is a kind of **parousia**, a preliminary second coming as Jesus precedes his followers in drawing the world to himself. The Samaritans were the first crop to be harvested, and the disciples are invited to participate at both ends of the task, proclaiming and integrating the fruit harvested into the Messiah's community.

In verse 38 Jesus expands on the part the disciples are to play in this new thrilling task. They, like Jesus, are to become sent ones, divinely sent envoys of the new kingdom reality. The seed has already been sown, so they get to "reap what [they] have not worked for." Some have tried to read this in light of the later mission to the Samaritans in Acts 8, but that is unnecessary and unlikely. Jesus is referring to what is happening here in John 4. Those who have already "worked" or "planted" would be the Old Testament prophets and especially John the Baptist, who had ministered in that region (see 3:23). These have "already done the hard work," and the disciples "have reaped the benefits of their labor." Theirs is the great privilege of seeing the fruits of the harvest come into the new community. Yet Jesus had more in mind than this single event. This is a promise to the future church as well. We all get to participate in God's harvest and see people enter the kingdom through our labor. There is nothing better than that!

THE HARVEST: JESUS IS SAVIOR
OF THE WORLD (4:39–42)

The mission discourse of verses 31–38 is now acted out in the fields of history. The woman had given her testimony in verses 28–29, and the townspeople had started out to see Jesus in verse 30. Now they arrive, and many of them "believed in him" as a direct result of her testimony. So she is another (after Andrew and Philip in chapter 1) in a long line of planters, and God uses her witness to

Jesus' divine omniscience ("told me everything I ever did") to produce a great harvest of souls.

In verse 40 the villagers beg Jesus to stay, a highly unusual gesture in light of four centuries of animosity between Jews and Samaritans. But these people are no longer estranged, for they have become followers who are asking for their "rabbi" or teacher to remain with them awhile. Now the woman's witness is not enough, and they want more. So Jesus stays two more days, and their response is much greater than that of Nicodemus. Even more of them become believers (v. 41), and their response is not merely sign-based (as was Nicodemus's) but "because of his words." No longer are they secondhand followers anchored in her witness; they say, "now we have heard for ourselves, and we know" Jesus.

This culminates in their confession in verse 42 that Jesus is "Savior of the world," another astounding affirmation like those in 1:41, 49. It concludes not just the Samaritan episode but the whole of 1:35–4:42. The "one and only Son" sent by God to provide salvation for sinful humankind (3:16–17) can alone remove sin from the world (1:29). He is the one who has come as the Living Revealer and provided the living water (4:10) and shed the light of God on every person (1:4, 7, 9). Thus he is "Savior of the world" (see also 1 John 4:14). These Samaritans in becoming believers have realized that their *Taheb* was actually the Jewish Messiah, indeed the Messiah for the whole world. In so doing they are the first proof that Jesus has come not just for the Jews but for the world, with themselves the first harvest in this new age of salvation for all peoples.

JESUS PERFORMS A SECOND SIGN AT CANA (4:43–54)

Jesus' movement north once more brings him to Galilee, and to the very town where he had earlier changed the water into wine, Cana. Here will end the initial phase of Jesus' public ministry, and again the gospel will triumph. While Jesus does indeed perform a powerful healing miracle, the central theme continues the mission emphasis of the Samaritan episode, and the result of the miracle is the belief and conversion of the official's whole household.

THE IRONIC "WELCOME" IN GALILEE (4:43–46A)

At the end of his two days with his Samaritan followers, Jesus returned to Galilee. This had been his intended destination all along (4:3), and John is connecting Jesus' Samaritan ministry with his Galilean ministry as a single mission to the world. In 1:10–11 the Jewish people are part of the world, so Jesus as Savior of the world combines the Jews with the Samaritans into a single world mission. In this Gospel, the God-led mission began with Jesus' choice of disciples to form his mission team, proceeded to Nicodemus (the religious elite), then the Samaritan woman (the outcasts), and now to Galilee, where his mission will begin in earnest.

There seems to be a contradiction at the outset. In 4:44 Jesus "testifies" (continuing the witness theme) that "a prophet has no honor in his own country," yet verse 45 says the Galileans "welcomed him." Several solutions have been suggested: (1) His "country" or "homeland" (*patris*) is Judea, so he is dishonored in Judea but welcomed in Galilee. The problem is that John stresses Jesus' Galilean origins and never mentions his Judean birth in Bethlehem. (2) The dishonor is from the world as a whole, but John makes the Jewish people part of the world in 1:10–11. (3) His "own country" is the Jewish lands as a whole, including both Judea and Galilee, with the welcome reception here an ironic, apparent thing based, as in 2:23, on excitement generated by the sign-miracles rather than who he is in reality. This, as we will see, fits the context best. So verse 44 establishes the true atmosphere, while the welcome of verse 45 is pure irony and will be short-lived.

When we look carefully at the basis of the Galilean "welcome" in verse 45, this view is corroborated. Their welcome was due to the fact that "they had seen all that he had done in Jerusalem at the Passover Festival," namely, the miracles. Jesus had become their "flavor of the month," and they wanted their equivalent of a rock festival to take place. Their interest was not religious in the least. It was not the Messiah they were focused on but a wonder-working figure who would bring excitement into their lives. The "life" they wanted was earthly, centering on powerful wonders, rather than spiritual, centering on faith-decision. This earth-centered focus will dominate the next several chapters.

Cana Revisited: The Royal Official's Son (4:46b–47)

Jesus returns to Cana, where he had turned the water into wine, and there he meets a government official from Capernaum. As a "royal official" (*basilikos*), undoubtedly under Herod Antipas— who was not a king but a member of a royal family—he was an important personage. He could have been Chuza, Herod's "business manager" of Luke 8:3, or Menaen, Herod's "childhood companion" (NLT) of Acts 13:1.

He had likely heard of Jesus' earlier Cana miracle and so traveled to Cana (a distance of about sixteen miles) to ask Jesus to return to Capernaum with him and heal his son, who was close to death (v. 47). We don't know whether the man was Jewish or Gentile. Jesus' response in verse 48 ("you people") makes it likely he is Jewish. There is no hint at this point that he was a true follower. Rather, he was a believer only in Jesus' miraculous powers.

Jesus' Harsh Response (4:48)

In the story Jesus' response is to the royal official, but in the statement he addresses the crowd as a whole (using the plural "you people"), deriding the fact that "unless you people see signs and wonders, you will never believe." This links them with the shallow followers of 2:23–25. There the people "believed" only in the sign-miracles, and Jesus refused to believe or trust in them. The same is true of these Galileans, whose welcome of verse 45 is now tainted with shallow belief and demand for the spectacular. This royal official is being accused of being one of them, for he so far had demonstrated only a desperate hope that a miracle might heal his son rather than true faith in Jesus. This will change, but at the outset his faith is incomplete.

Unlike the centurion in Matthew 8:8,[8] this man thought Jesus could only heal the child if he was physically present. There was no real faith in the power of Jesus' word of healing. This is why Jesus rebukes the man and his belief in only the "signs and wonders" rather than in Jesus himself. Astonishment that is anchored only in the sensational will never suffice for genuine faith in the Savior of the world. This statement ("you will never believe") is also an implicit challenge for the official to find faith.

THE OFFICIAL'S DEVELOPING FAITH (4:49–50)

The official has a single focus with one concern, the life-threatening situation with his son, and so responds simply, "Sir, come down before my child dies." The time is short, and his desperation gets greater and greater. This important official with all his authority humbles himself and speaks to Jesus as a servant to his "lord" (Greek: *kyrie*, "sir"). He is no longer a powerful government figure but a scared father.

Jesus honors the father's loving cry and calls for him to have faith. He refuses to go to Capernaum because there is no need for him to do so. The key is the present-tense command in verse 50, "Go [on your way]," followed by a promise demanding faith, "Your son will live." The father/official must have faith that Jesus' words have healing powers and trust that his son has been healed from a distance. He is asked to put feet to his faith and go on his way, trusting that Jesus has indeed healed his boy.

---

8. Many have thought that the Matthew 8:5–13 story of the healing of the centurion's servant is the same story retold by John here, but the details in that story are clearly different (a centurion, his servant, and his clear faith in Jesus). These are certainly two different miracle stories.

The man's faith finally shifts from the earthly miracle to the heavenly miracle worker. "The man took Jesus at his word and departed," with his faith properly centered on the power of Jesus' words. So he started home, as Jesus had commanded. It took an immense amount of faith to do this while he still knew nothing, but he had turned the corner. The key to a burgeoning faith is this very combination of belief with response.

HEALING AND FAITH (4:51–54)

In verse 51 the man proves the reality of his faith in Jesus by "going down" (omitted by NIV) to Capernaum. The Sea of Galilee was 700 feet below sea level, so the trip would have been downhill all the way. Before the entourage arrived back in Capernaum, the good news came. Servants from home met him with the momentous report "that his boy was living."

The most amazing thing occurred when he "inquired as to the time when his son got better" and learned it was at one in the afternoon (the "seventh hour" from dawn, or six in the morning) when the fever had abated. The father then realized "that this was the exact time" when Jesus had told him, "Your son will live." The result was completely natural: "He and his whole household believed" (v. 53).

Note the progression of faith: the royal official originally had an inadequate faith based entirely on reports about the wondrous signs (4:48). After he encountered Jesus, he found a preliminary faith and obeyed him, heading for Capernaum (4:50). Finally, after the report that his son had been healed and his life spared, he and his entire family experienced a full-fledged faith in Jesus' person as well as his powerful works. Jesus' power came from within and resided in his words, for he had power over life, spiritual as well as physical (5:21; 11:25).

John the evangelist tells us that "this was the second sign" (v. 54) Jesus had performed in his Galilee ministry. He wants to make certain we understand that it pointed to Jesus' character as Son of

God and Savior of the world. Jesus had fully taken his life-giving ministry, both physical and spiritual, to Galilee. Of course, he had performed several miracles in Judea (2:23), but these were the two thus far in Galilee, and they proved who he was. The power of God in Jesus was on the move, from Judea (chs. 2–3) to Samaria (ch. 4) to Galilee (here) and on to encompass the whole world.

———

This chapter plays a critical role in the development of John's Gospel. Here John's mission theme takes an important turn, leaving the mission to the Jews and inaugurating God's mission (seen in the divine "must" of v. 4) to the world, culminating in the Samaritan confession of Jesus as the "Savior of the world" (v. 42).

The progress of Jesus' dialogue with the Samaritan woman is a perfect model for an evangelistic encounter of any kind. In Jesus' presentation, he takes an everyday item (the drinking water from the well) and turns it into an offer of salvation in three steps. He responds to the request for water by offering not just well water but living water, which he further explains is the water of life. When the Samaritan woman doesn't get it, he reveals his true nature as Messiah and transcendent figure to her, unveiling the living water as part of the new age of salvation with a new way of worship "in Spirit and truth."

When she begins to glimpse the reality of what he is saying, she becomes a witness along the lines of Andrew and Philip in 1:35–50, inviting her fellow townspeople to "come and see" this Jesus. At this point (4:31–38) the evangelist recalls Jesus' mission discourse as he invites the disciples to partake of his greater "food": doing the will of the Father and becoming part of God's great harvest in the surrounding world. This is also an invitation to us, the readers, to enter this harvest as well. We, even more than the disciples, get to reap what we have not worked for (v. 38). The harvest has been made ready, and it is our privilege and joy to see the miraculous fruit and be part of the reapers who bring these souls to the eternal harvest.

The healing story of 4:43–54 demonstrates several things, primarily Jesus as Savior and healer of the world. Miracles in John are "signs" because they signify who Jesus is and center on Christ more than on the supernatural healing. This story culminates the movement of the opening stages of Jesus' public ministry with the salvation of the royal official and his entire family. John's interest is in the conversion of this powerful public figure more than in the healing of his son. The progression of the subjects of these salvation dramas so far in this Gospel—from the disciples of John to Nicodemus to the Samaritan woman to the royal official—shows that John wants each of us to get involved in spreading the light of Christ "to everyone" in the world (1:9), from the least to the greatest.

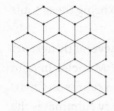

CONFLICT AFTER A HEALING
(5:1–47)

The healing of the royal official's son closed the previous section of John. That healing was the second Cana miracle, which frames 2:1–4:54 with Cana miracles and concludes the series of episodes that contain the mission of Jesus to the world. That section moved from the Jewish official Nicodemus to the Samaritan woman to the official, and geographically from Judea to Samaria to Galilee.

Another miracle now begins a long section of the Gospel that focuses on Jesus and the Jewish festivals (5:1–10:42). Scholars divide this section in many different ways, and there are almost as many different plots as there are commentaries. The only divisions of the Gospel of John on which there are general agreement are the beginning section of 2:1–4:54 and the fact that the coverage of Jesus' public ministry ends at 12:50. The basis for my outline is the fact that in this section John centers on Jesus' fulfilling the imagery of the feasts of the Jews, moving from Sabbath (ch. 5) to Passover (ch. 6) to Tabernacles (chs. 7–9) to Dedication/Hanukkah (ch. 10). The other primary theme in this section is the growing opposition and conflict between Jesus and the Jews. These two themes will dominate this section. In these chapters, the opposition increases progressively in intensity.

JESUS HEALS A LAME MAN ON
THE SABBATH (5:1–15)

This sign-miracle begins a series on Jesus as God's envoy and source of life in the midst of rejection and opposition. In the next few chapters we will see a series of **christological** affirmations presenting Jesus as Bread of Life (ch. 6), Giver of the Spirit (ch. 7), Light of the World (ch. 8), Giver of Sight (ch. 9), the Gate (ch. 10), and the Good Shepherd (ch. 10), several of them presented as "I am" sayings.[1]

The geography of this section is difficult to follow, as Jesus returns to Jerusalem (5:1), heads back to Galilee (6:1), then back once more to Jerusalem (7:10), where he seemingly remains until his death. This is radically different from the **Synoptics**, in which Jesus' first trip to Jerusalem occurs just before his death. The best explanation for this and the numerous Jerusalem trips (2:13; 5:1; 7:10) is John's decision to deliberately supplement the Synoptics and portray Jesus' extensive ministry in Judea. I think that John has the more chronological order of events among the Gospels. The old view that John is less historical than the others is being reversed by many recent studies.

JESUS AND THE MAN AT THE POOL (5:1–5)

As the scene opens we see Jesus going "up to Jerusalem for one of the Jewish festivals." Scholars have posited virtually every festival at one time or another, but the anarthrous (without a definite article) "a festival" means that John does not want us to think of any particular one. Rather, this introduces the whole section, which will feature four of the seven festivals (see above). Jesus has been in Cana of Galilee, and he goes "up" to Jerusalem because he will be traveling from the Jordan River up to Jerusalem, which is 2,500 feet above sea level. The route takes him through Jericho near the

---

1. See commentary on 6:35.

Jordan, and the fifteen-mile walk from there west to Jerusalem was quite rugged, ascending 3,500 feet "up" to the city.

Upon arrival Jesus went to the pool of Bethesda near the "Sheep Gate," a small opening on the north wall of the city, northeast of the temple, through which the sacrificial animals were brought. "Bethesda" is transliterated from Hebrew and means "house of outpouring." Archaeological excavations near the Church of Saint Anne have uncovered large twin pools, surrounded by four colonnades or covered porches, with a fifth one between the pools. When Jesus arrived there were "a great number of disabled people" lying around on the porches, and John specifies them as "the blind, the lame, the paralyzed" (v. 3).

Some manuscripts include quite a bit of material, constituting 5:3b–4, describing an angel stirring up the waters (see the KJV, the NASB, or the textual notes of any other Bible). It is missing in the oldest manuscripts, and most scholars agree that it likely was an ancient tradition about the pool that was not originally in John's text. At any rate, this tradition does explain why all the sick and disabled were gathered by the pool, with each one hoping to be the first into the pool when it bubbled up.

When Jesus arrived he met a man who had been "an invalid for thirty-eight years" (v. 5). This doesn't mean he had been coming to the pool for that long a time, but it probably does indicate he had been doing this for many years. He is unable to walk and is desperate to find healing. Several interpreters think this is an allusion to the thirty-eight years Israel wandered in the wilderness because of their sin (Deut 2:14), but there is no real hint of such a link here. It is probably a historical note to stress how hopeless his situation was.

HEALING ON THE SABBATH (5:6–9A)

There is some difference of opinion regarding how Jesus discovered the man's plight when he "saw him lying there" (v. 6).

Several translations have Jesus "learning" about the situation from others (NIV, NET), but others have him supernaturally "knowing" about his illness (NLT, NASB, ESV—the verb is ginōskō, the basic verb for "knowing"). Since omniscience is a frequent motif in John, seen regarding Simon (1:42), Nathanael (1:47), "all people" (2:24–25), and the Samaritan woman (4:18), I think this likely also portrays Jesus' divine knowledge. As before, Jesus with this knowledge elicits a response, "Do you want to get well?" At first glance it seems a silly question—of course he does! But Jesus wants the man to get involved in the process, not to remain passive throughout.

The lame man considers Jesus just another bystander and begs for help (v. 7). He had no one to help him get to the water when it was stirred up, and he earnestly believed the tradition to such an extent that he came regularly to the pool. This is an example of Jewish folk religion, not that different in kind from pagan folk beliefs in an impersonal god who gave power to the water. Someone always beat him to the pool, so he had years of frustration behind his plea that Jesus help him get there first. Indeed, help had arrived, but not the kind he expected.

Jesus' command in verse 8 must have shocked him, for it bypassed the waters entirely: "Get up! Pick up your mat and walk." One can only imagine his feelings as he felt the healing power of God flow through his emaciated body. He could have visibly watched the muscles in his legs grow as he lay there. His crippling disease was not just taken away; his muscles were given a strength they had never before possessed, a holistic healing process in seconds. The "mat" would have been a light, straw-filled sleeping mattress used by the poor. Clearly he was enabled to get up that instant, given the balance to stand possibly for the first time, roll up his mattress, and take a few steps. What excitement there must have been! This was not an angel but the Son of God who was at work.

THE SABBATH CONTROVERSY (5:9B)

However, the healing caused a problem. It was the Sabbath, and the religious establishment was scandalized that Jesus had breached their oral traditions. The Torah said simply that a person should not work on the Sabbath, but the Pharisees had developed in their oral tradition an elaborate classification of thirty-nine types of "work" that were prohibited. Such work would only be allowed in life-threatening situations. Jesus was breaking the law because the man's life was not in danger, so they expected Jesus to heal the man the following day. Moreover, the man carrying his mat also constituted work, for moving things from one place to another was one of the thirty-nine categories.[2] So he was in trouble too.

INTERACTION WITH THE LEADERS (5:10-13)

A series of challenges from the leaders cause the healed man to rethink his gratitude to Jesus. He is in a bind, and three things in the developing situation demonstrate his insensitivity to the spiritual realities in the scene:

1. When the leaders accuse him of breaking the Sabbath laws by carrying his mat (v. 10), he shifts the blame from himself to Jesus, who told him to take up his mat and walk (v. 11). He shows little or no gratitude but cares only for himself.

2. When these authorities ask for the identity of the individual who had done such a thing (v. 12), the man shows he had not even bothered to learn the name of the healer. He was so self-centered that he was not even interested in getting to know who could have performed such an astounding miracle. In the meantime, Jesus had "slipped away into the crowd that was there" (v. 13), and the man had not even noticed he was gone.

3. When the man learns Jesus' identity, he reports Jesus to the leaders (next section). Step by step, the man turns

---

2. As recorded in the later Mishnah; see m. Shabbat 7:2; 10:5.

away from following Jesus and joins the Jewish authorities against Jesus. This is highly unusual in miracle stories, but John wants to show how many of those surrounding Jesus were half-hearted followers (2:23–25) or even became his enemies (here).

REACTION TO JESUS (5:14–15)

The healed man never searches for Jesus. Rather, Jesus finds him in the temple, the natural place for a healed person to go to thank God. He gives him a chance to repent, warning him, "See, you are well again. Stop sinning or something worse may happen to you" (v. 14). Throughout the miracle stories physical healing is accompanied by spiritual healing. Often the verb *sōzō* is used with a double meaning, "heal" and "save" (Mark 5:34; 6:56; 10:52). Now that the man has been transformed physically, it is time to be transformed spiritually, to get right with God lest he face "something worse," divine judgment for sin.

There are differences of opinion regarding the relation of the man's sin to his illness and whether Jesus' command to "stop sinning" is meant generally of the sin condition or specifically of a particular set of sins that might have caused the illness. I find it doubtful Jesus has a specific sin in mind behind the illness (see Luke 13:1–5; John 9:3) and believe it better to see this as general repentance, especially in light of the man's shallow spiritual condition demonstrated in verses 10–13 above.

His reaction in verse 15 shows how obdurate he has become. Instead of repenting he goes and reports Jesus to the authorities. He is more interested in getting right with the Jewish leaders than he is in getting right with God. He had shown a glimmer of faith when he obeyed Jesus by getting up with his mat in verse 9, and that had led to physical healing. Now he is challenged to go the second step and turn from sin to God, to choose between life and eternal judgment. He fails in this far more important area. To save his own hide, he turns Jesus over to his Jewish enemies.

This is the key message of the Fourth Gospel—light versus darkness, life versus judgment. We are making the same choice as this man, and it will determine whether we possess eternal life or face eternal judgment. This man symbolizes "his own" in 1:11 who refuse to "receive" Jesus and become part of the unbelieving world. There is an intended contrast between this man, who never came to faith and reacted to healing with disbelief, and the man born blind of chapter 10, who accepted the Jewish ban out of his true faith in Jesus.

JEWISH LEADERS QUESTION JESUS' CLAIM TO BE SON OF GOD (5:16-47)

The problem with the lame man was that he didn't care who Jesus was. The problem with the Jewish leaders was that they opposed who Jesus was. In this section Jesus will confront them with the reality of who he truly is: the Son of God and God of very God. As he does, they will come face to face with the necessity of committing themselves not only to Jesus but also to who he is. Moreover, one cannot know God apart from Jesus, for he is the Living Revealer of his Father, the only path God has provided for knowing him. Here we see the oneness between Father and Son in all its glory.

THESIS: SHARING THE FATHER'S WORK (5:16-18)

Two facts highlight this transition paragraph: The opposition increases against Jesus as a result of the lame man's betrayal, and Jesus reveals to all his true relationship with his Father. Some interpreters group this passage with the preceding miracle story due to this opposition, but the revelation of verse 17 is central to the discourse of verses 19-30, so it belongs here.

John puts the situation strongly, calling the reaction of the Jews "persecution" in verse 16. This is emphasized by the imperfect tense, describing an ongoing string of hostile reactions ("kept on persecuting"). This serious opposition will become commonplace in the rest of the Gospel, culminating in the cross.

Jesus' response in verse 17 may seem moderate to us: "My Father is always at his work to this very day, and I too am working." To modern readers this says simply that Jesus is busy doing God's work, but the Jewish people here rightly see that it implies a great deal more, revealing both who the Father is and how Jesus related to him. The Sabbath issue in this controversy will effectively disappear and be replaced by Christology, for Jesus is actually stressing his equality with God.

The rabbis taught that only God can work on the Sabbath, alluding to creation and the creative nature of God as part of his ceaseless activity in the world (Exodus Rabbah 30:6). If God ceases to work on the Sabbath (Gen 2:2), they asked, how does the universe keep running? But then does he himself become a Sabbath breaker? No, because as God he is exempt, and his breaking the Sabbath is necessary to keep the world functioning. Within this logic, Jesus' claim to work alongside his Father is tantamount to declaring that he is equal with God, and he makes this all the stronger by calling God his Father (he does so nine times in 5:17–26).[3] He is claiming God as his Father in an exclusive sense, so to them this constitutes blasphemy.

As a result, "they tried all the more to kill him" (v. 18). This is the first time John mentions the Jewish leaders' intention to kill Jesus, but the expression *all the more* shows that they had decided earlier that Jesus must die. In the Synoptics this occurred near the beginning of Jesus' ministry (in Mark 3:6 and parallels) after a series of encounters between Jesus and the leaders.

THE PRESENT: SHARING LIFE AND JUDGMENT WITH THE FATHER (5:19–24)

Jesus responds to their charges in 5:19–30 with a lengthy discourse defending his right to make himself equal with the Father. He

---

3. Of the 414 times *patēr* ("father") is used in the New Testament, John contains 136 of them, stressing the unique unity and love between the Father and Jesus.

shows that he shares his Father's power in life and judgment in two parts. In the first (vv. 19–24), he describes this power in terms of realized **eschatology**, saying that these powers are his *now*; in the second (vv. 25–30), he describes it in terms of final eschatology, saying that he is in charge of the final judgment in the future. This first half is organized around four "for" (Greek: *gar*) clauses, stating the reason why Jesus can claim this special relationship with his Father.

The center point: dependence on the Father (5:19)

This passage is incredibly important, for it combines two essential christological points: Jesus' equality with the Father and his subordination to the Father. Everything in verses 20–30 flows out of this claim, and that is why this is an important double *amēn* ("truly, truly," see 1:51; 3:3, 5, 11) saying. The first *gar* clause here explains that sonship demands unity of action: "The Son can do nothing by himself; he can do only what he sees his Father doing, because [*gar*] whatever the Father does the Son also does." John is emphasizing the unity of the Father and the Son in terms of action.

Note that the Son is at the same time both one with the Father in his nature and dependent on the Father in his action. There is a unity in being and at the same time a functional subordination between Father and Son. This says three things about the Father-Son relationship: the Son does nothing apart from his Father; the Son sees and knows his Father intimately; and the Son is completely obedient to the Father, so that he reveals the Father perfectly in everything he does. This means that the "work" of the Son is as limitless as that of the Father.

The love of the Father (5:20)

The basis (*gar*, "for") of the total sharing between Father and Son is that "the Father loves the Son and shows him all he does." All Jesus does is anchored in the love of the Father, and love is the binding

force of the unity of the Godhead in the Trinity.⁴ The present tense
of "loves" and "shows" demonstrates the ongoing love between the
two. The sharing is absolute; nothing is held back. The previous
verse stresses that the Son "sees" the Father, and here the flip side
is found, as the Father "shows" everything to the Son. This reciprocal knowledge is grounded in reciprocal love, and here we are
told the basis of the omniscience Jesus has frequently possessed
(1:42, 47–48; 4:18; 5:6), as all truth and knowledge is available to
Jesus from the Father.

In fact, this revelation of the Father to the Son and through the
Son to us will enable the Son to perform "even greater works than
these," meaning greater even than the sign-miracles like the healing of the lame man. This most likely points to the next two verses,
describing how the Father gives to the Son authority over life and
judgment. The greatest miracle of all is the gift of eternal life, as
we will see again in 14:12. The purpose of this is "so that you will
be amazed," pointing to the many times the people marvel at the
knowledge and power of God in Jesus (3:7; 4:27; 5:28; 7:15, 21). This
shocked wonder they feel is a first step toward faith, the result of
encountering God in Jesus as the Son makes known the Father in
himself (see 1:18).

Authority over life and judgment (5:21–22)

Here Jesus proves the validity of his claim to equality with the
Father from the standpoint of the essential work he shares with
the Father in giving life and in judgment. In this too, the Father
shows the Son all things, which the Son then sees and does.

In this passage, the Father "raises the dead and gives them
life," and in union with the Father, the Son "gives life to whom
he is pleased to give it." Jews understood the raising of the dead

---

4. Interestingly, the "love" of the Father in 3:35 translates the Greek *agapaō*,
while here it is another word for "love": *phileō*. In John, however, the two
terms are synonymous.

to be the special provenance of God (1 Sam 2:6; 2 Kgs 5:7), and later rabbis thought that not even the Messiah would possess it (b. Ta'anit). Elijah's raising of the widow's son in 1 Kings 17:17-24 occurred only because God did the work through him. Jesus disproves that theory and transcends Elijah. He shares the divine power of life and bestows it on anyone he wishes. Jesus, with the Father, is sovereign over life—including the ability to grant eternal life now and final resurrection later.

The fourth and final *gar* clause (v. 22) turns to the opposite eschatological reality: divine judgment. This is another startling statement: "The Father judges no one, but has entrusted all judgment to the Son." In the Old Testament and Judaism, Yahweh alone is the final judge, yet Jesus is claiming that the power to judge has now been entrusted to him. This hardly means that God ceases to be the final Judge, for according to Revelation 20:11-15 God is on the throne of judgment. So this means Jesus shares that authority with his Father.

There is a seeming contradiction with 3:17, in which the evangelist says Jesus was not sent "to condemn [*krinō*, judge] the world." Yet here, in 5:30 and 9:39 it says he came to judge. The solution is in 8:15-16, in which Jesus states, "I pass judgment on no one. But if I do judge, my decisions are true." Jesus did not enter this world to judge, but he encounters every person, and to those who reject his offer, he becomes judge.

The purpose: honoring the Son (5:23)

One primary purpose (Greek: *hina*, "so that") is "that all may honor the Son just as they honor the Father." Father and Son are equal in authority and so deserve equal honor. The Son is subordinate and obedient to the Father, but he is also equal in authority and power. Not only that, but the way they treat the Son is the way they are treating the Father. So the reverse is true: "Whoever does not honor the Son does not honor the Father, who sent him."

This is a major facet of John's theology as reflected in Jesus' teaching: one cannot believe or honor God without believing and honoring Jesus (5:38, 43–44; 7:16–27; 8:19, 28, 42, 47; 10:38; 14:1), and the Son is the only path to God (14:6). Those Jews who thought they could be God's people while they rejected Jesus were utterly mistaken. Jesus is the Sent One, the envoy of God, and as such he is both the revealer of the Father and the recipient of the Father's honor. There is no other way to God (14:6).

The necessity of hearing and believing (5:24)

We are now at the heart of everything, bringing Christology (the doctrine of Christ) and **soteriology** (the doctrine of salvation) into wondrous unity. This is introduced by another double *amēn*, pointing to a solemn truth (see 1:51; 5:19). If Jesus is indeed one with God (5:19–23), then we can experience eternal life only by hearing and believing in him. This is John's gospel in embryo, and it culminates the last five verses. Jesus as the Sent One is God's agent and revealer, with divine authority over life and judgment. Therefore we can participate in the eternal life he offers and avoid the judgment that comes from refusing that offer only by listening to his divine truths and believing in his divine Person.

Hearing in John is the preliminary step to believing, and true hearing demands response. In both Hebrew and Greek the verb for hearing connotes obeying; we have not listened until we have responded. At the same time, when we hear Jesus we also hear the Father. Conversion is a trinitarian act and results in eternal life bestowed by the Triune Godhead.

As I have stated several times, this eternal life is a present possession as well as a future gift, as seen in the fact that the verbs ("hearing," "believing," "has," "comes") are present tense, referring to the continuous possession of salvation throughout one's earthly and heavenly existence. The perfect tense phrase "has crossed over from death to life" emphasizes the state of being resulting from this possession, so enjoys much the same force. Life describes our state of existence from the moment of faith-decision. Believers have already "passed from death to life" (1 John 3:14), and for them physical death is a step upward to claim what is already theirs. Death is personified in John and Paul as an evil force that reigns over sinful humankind, but for the saints "death has been swallowed up in victory" (1 Cor 15:54, from Isa 25:8).

THE FUTURE: SHARING FINAL LIFE AND JUDGMENT (5:25-30)

The dead hear and live (5:25)

There is an already/not yet tension in the phrase "a time is coming and has now come," repeating 4:23. The final kingdom age has now arrived in Christ, a time "when the dead will hear the voice of the Son of God and those who hear will live." The afterlife anticipated by the Old Testament saints has already become a reality, and eternal life, as I have been saying, is both a present possession and a future certainty for those who believe. Apart from Christ, all people already constitute "the dead" in sin, and the only hope is the life-giving word of Christ who is the Word (1:1-18; 6:63, 6:68; 10:3, 16, 27; 11:43). The life of final resurrection is available in the here and now for those who listen and come to faith.

Authority to give life and to judge (5:26-27)

In these verses, Jesus restates and builds on the proclamation of this authority earlier in 5:21-22. It is the Father who "has life in himself," meaning he is the source and the repository of all life (so Gen 2:7; Deut 30:20; Job 33:4; Ps 16:11). The life the Son possesses stems from the Father, who "grants the Son also to have life in himself." This transcends life-giving power. The Father and Son possess life; it is integral to their being and inherent in who they are. The functional (the power to give life) flows out of the ontological (they are life). Once more, we see the subordination of the Son, who receives life from the Father as integrated into the equality with the Father, both of whom are personified by life.

In the same way "authority to judge" has passed to the Son from the Father (5:27). The positive (giving life) and the negative (pronouncing judgment) aspects of this authority are intertwined and depend on each individual's faith-decision. Jesus came to save, not bring judgment (3:17), but his coming forces encounter with the light of God (1:4–5, 7, 9) and demands decision. That decision determines one's destiny, whether they are given eternal life or face final judgment.

The power to judge belongs to the Father but has been passed to the Son "because he is the Son of Man." "Son of Man" is anarthrous (lacking the definite article), and the absence of the article makes some think this has minimal force here: "a son of man." But there is a better explanation. In the Greek a predicate noun coming before the verb "to be" lacks a definite article, and that is the case here. So it should be translated, "because he is *the Son of Man*." The title first appeared at 1:51 and is **apocalyptic** in force, echoing Daniel 7:13–14, where the Son of Man is a glorified figure who is given dominion over this world. As the God-man, Sovereign over creation and the glorified Word of God, he has the power and right to judge.

Life and judgment in the final future (5:28–29)

Like Nicodemus in 3:7, those present for this teaching are "amazed" and shocked at such bold proclamations. Such divine truths are incredibly hard to comprehend, let alone accept, yet at the same time they are simply introducing even more difficult truths and prove preliminary to Jesus' next pronouncement. He wants them to know that a future reality will help them to understand the present truths they are struggling with: "A time is coming when all who are in their graves will hear his voice." Once more, he is "the Word of God," the Living Revealer, so his is the very voice of God. He is the Son of Man from Daniel 7, so his voice will enact Daniel

12:1-2: "Multitudes who sleep in the dust of the earth will awake: some to everlasting life, others to shame and everlasting contempt."

Here the fulfillment of Daniel 12 takes the form of Christ's authority over life and judgment, as seen in 5:29: "and come out—those who have done what is good will rise to live, and those who have done what is evil will rise to be condemned." This is clearly a reference to the **parousia**, the second coming, when he "will come down from heaven with a loud command" (1 Thess 4:16). All humankind will be divided into two groups, the only division in all of history that truly matters—the good who inherit eternal life, and the evil who face eternal punishment. In the New Testament we know that the moment believers die their souls go to be with Christ in heaven (2 Cor 5:1-10), while their bodies lie in the grave awaiting the final resurrection. That resurrection takes place here, as their bodies in the grave hear the commanding shout from Christ and rise to meet the Lord (1 Thess 4:14-16) and to be reunited with their souls, which have been in heaven and have returned with Christ.

The unsaved do not rise at that time but rise at the final judgment of Revelation 20:12-13, when the sea along with death and Hades "[give] up the dead ... and each person [is] judged according to what they had done." Here this is described as "rise to be condemned," literally "a resurrection of judgment" (*krisis*). Their belief or unbelief, as the case may be, accompanied by the deeds that result from that decision, determine their destiny. In 3:21 "whoever lives by the truth comes into the light," and here these people inherit eternal life. These light-bearers have resurrection life now (compare Rom 6:4-5) as well as the promise of everlasting life in the future. Those who choose evil are under indictment now (5:22-24) and will rise to everlasting judgment (here).

The righteous judgment of Christ (5:30)

John recapitulates 5:19-20 in order to show how righteous and just the judgments of Jesus really are. If he made such decisions "by himself" they would be "nothing," of no value. But he makes no decisions on his own: "I judge only as I hear." It is God who directs him. Switching to the first-person "I" for emphasis, he testifies to his complete dependence on his Father in every judgment he makes. In verses 19–20 he sees the Father; here he hears the Father. So he doubly submits to the Father's will. Therefore all his judgments are completely righteous and just (*dikaia*, meaning both here).

These are the Father's decisions, the result of God's will and voice passed on to his Son. Jesus is the divine herald and envoy and does not act on his own. Since he conveys the decisions of God and does so "not to please myself but him who sent me," every judgment can be completely trusted as from God. His judgments are "righteous" in the sense that they stem from the very character of God and "just" in the sense that they reflect divine justice in this world.

WITNESS AND UNBELIEF (5:31–40)

Witness is a major theme in John, with forty-seven of seventy-seven New Testament occurrences of "testify/witness" found in his writings (thirty-three in his Gospel). The word "witness" looks to objective testimony to the truthfulness of Jesus as the Living Revealer of God and of the revelations he makes. It is the antithesis of the falsehoods the Jewish leaders spread about Jesus. He claims here that even if they do not wish to accept his own self-witness to the truth of what he is saying, there are several other sources of witness to corroborate the truthfulness of what he says. In this passage, Jesus first presents four sets of witnesses to the validity of his claims (vv. 31–40), and then the Jews are guilty of unbelief and reject the witnesses (vv. 41–47).

The true witness (5:31–32)

Jesus starts this section by agreeing with his detractors and admitting, "If I testify about myself, my testimony is not true" (in 8:14, he says it is actually valid). The term Jesus uses is *alēthēs*, "true, valid," and looks at the issue from a legal standpoint. The idea that a person cannot testify for themselves is a rabbinic principle (m. Ketubbot 2:9). This is pure common sense, for a court of law could never trust a biased self-witness. Deuteronomy 17:6 and 19:15 say that in a legal case, two or three witnesses are needed to convict a person. While Roman law was based on interrogation of the accused (as in Jesus' trial before Pilate), Jewish law was based on eyewitness testimony. So Jesus is not saying his self-witness is wrong, only that in a legal sense it is insufficient.

Jesus' point is that if they do not wish to accept his own testimony regarding his relationship with God his Father, there are other "valid" witnesses. So in 5:32 he adds, "There is another who testifies in my favor, and I know that his testimony about me is true." It is interesting that Jesus does not name that "other witness." Virtually everyone agrees this must be the Father himself, but he is not named until verse 37, probably because Jesus believes this "other" voice is behind all four sets of witnesses in 5:33-39. All are variations of the Father's witness.

The witness of John the Baptist (5:33-35)

With the words "you have sent to John," Jesus refers to that earlier Sanhedrin-sent investigation recorded in 1:19-28, when priests and Levites interrogated John the Baptist. Jesus' point is that "he has testified to the truth" in his witness of 1:23 that he was tasked by God to "make straight the way for the Lord" (from Isa 40:3), that he was "unworthy" even to loose Jesus' sandals in 1:27, and that Jesus is "the Lamb of God, who takes away the sin of the world" in 1:29 and "God's Chosen One" in 1:34. Later, in 3:27-30 the Baptist said that he rejoiced at the privilege of preparing for the Messiah, Jesus.

In 5:34 Jesus clarifies that he himself does not "accept human testimony" in order to anchor his own self-awareness. Neither he nor the Father needs human confirmation to establish their identity. They are "from above" rather than of earth and exist at a higher plane. He and the Father are one (5:17, 19; 10:30), and so he has power over life and judgment. The witness is for the benefit of those on earth, to prove the reality of Jesus to them "so that [hina] you might be saved" (my translation). The witness is to enable the hearers to realize the truth about Jesus, believe, and be saved from sin and death. This is in keeping with 1:7, where God's purpose in sending John was "to testify concerning that light, so that through him all might believe."

Now in 5:35 Jesus turns and gives his testimony as to the worth and purpose of John. In 1:6–8 John says that the Baptist is "not the light" but came "as a witness" to the light. Yet here Jesus says he "was a lamp that burned and gave light." However, this is not a contradiction, for when you combine the two, he is a lamp that contains the light of Christ and bears witness to it. The idea behind "burned and gave light" depicts his meteoric rise and powerful ministry as the messianic forerunner. This may well allude to Psalm 132:17, "Here I will make a horn grow for David and set up a lamp for my anointed one."

The second half may well indicate that John was in prison under Herod at this time: "You chose for a time to enjoy his light." The emphatic "you yourselves [hymeis] chose [only] for a time" stresses the fickle extent of commitment on the part of the Jewish people. As in 2:23–25, the level of their allegiance to both John and Jesus was quite shallow, and it waned almost before it had time to develop. Their excitement was quite short-lived and did not meet John's true purpose of producing faith in Jesus as the Messiah.

The witness of Jesus' works (5:36)

In and of itself the witness of the Baptist is not enough, and Jesus has a "testimony weightier [greater] than that of John": he has to accomplish "the works that the Father has given me to finish." The reason they are "greater" is that the Father is producing them in Jesus as opposed to the Baptist's deeds. John's accomplishments, as great as they are, cannot match what God is doing in and through

his Son. John was "sent" as a witness in 1:6–8, but the sending
of the Son as the divine envoy is infinitely greater. These works
center on the sign-miracles that demonstrate the divine reality
behind them but also include his teaching. The point here is the
apologetic value of these signs and wonders as they prove who
Jesus is, not only the One who is greater than John but also who
at the same time is greater than Moses and Elijah, the wonder-
working prophets.

The witness of God himself (5:37–38)

Jesus has come full circle and reintroduces from verse 32 the witness of "the Father who sent me." This witness undergirds all the
others and provides the culminating testimony. Some think this
is specifically a reference to the Father's witness at Jesus' baptism,
but that is recorded in the Synoptics rather than in John's Gospel
(see 1:32–33), so that interpretation is unlikely. Jesus' words more
generally refer to the Father's underscoring all the other witnesses
to Jesus.

However, they had never "heard his voice" like Moses did at
Sinai (Exod 33:11) or like the prophets and especially Jesus had.
The Greek is emphatic: "never at any time" (pōpete), meaning the
Jewish people rejected Moses and the prophets and Jesus. Nor had
they ever "seen his form" (eidos, true appearance), referring especially to the image of God in Jesus (1:18; 14:9). God has revealed both
himself and Jesus, utilizing both hearing and sight, and his people
have rejected it all (1:11).

In verse 38 there is a third level of witness and revelation:
his word dwelling in them. Jesus is the Word of God, the Living
Revealer of the Father (1:1–18). The true people of God will center
their lives on God's Word (Josh 1:8; Pss 1:2; 119:15, 23), but these are
false followers of God, under a threefold condemnation here for
rejecting God's revelation of himself through hearing, sight, and
thinking. Their minds were closed to the truth, for they refused
to believe in the One God sent.

The witness of the Scriptures (5:39-40)

This would have been a particularly strong witness, for the scribes and the rabbis went to great lengths to gain a deep understanding of the Scriptures and had developed an extensive oral tradition to help the people remain faithful to the Torah/law. The verb behind "search" (*eraunate*) connotes a careful inquiry and is a semi-technical rabbinic term for professional exposition of the Word of God.

Moreover, they did so thinking that "in them you have eternal life." They are definitely right about that, but at the same time they do not find that life because they "refuse to come to me to have life" (5:40) and accept the fact that they "testify about me." They sought eternal life in the wrong place, because the Messiah—the only basis for life—had come in fulfillment of the Scriptures. Since they have rejected Jesus Messiah, there is no hope for life.

New Testament writers developed a vast number of fulfillment passages, proving that all the messianic prophecies of the Old Testament pointed to Jesus. The basic problem was that while they accepted the prophecies, they refused to consider that they were fulfilled in Jesus. They preferred the minute details of Torah to the broad sweep of scriptural witness for Jesus.

THE UNBELIEF OF THE JEWS (5:41-47)

In this section on witness, Jesus is defensive, answering Jewish charges regarding the validity of Jesus as Messiah and Son of God. Here Christ goes on the offensive, charging the Jewish leaders and people with unbelief.

The contrast between Christ and them (5:41-42)

Jesus begins by separating himself from human praise: "I do not accept glory from human beings." He has no need of human witnesses or of human approval, no need of praise or esteem from the people around him. He has all the approval he needs from the Father; as Romans 8:31 states, "If God is for us, who can be against us?"

This is especially true because "I know you," a thought that goes back to 2:24–25, where the evangelist first stated that Jesus "knew all people" and their poor commitment to God and truth. With this deep knowledge, he knew that "you do not have the love of God in your hearts." Certainly these Jewish leaders believed that they loved God; in fact, their oral tradition had been devised to ensure a right relationship with God. However, their rejection of God's Son proved they didn't truly love God. Their "God" was no longer the God of the Scriptures, for that God sent his Son Jesus as the basis and ground of their salvation.

Their receptivity toward Christ (5:43–44)

The contrasts continue. Jesus has "come in my Father's name," while the messianic pretenders[5] have come in their own name, yet the Jews reject Jesus and follow the false claims. Jesus had extensively developed the reality of his equality and subordination to the Father in the first part of this address (5:19–30), but his listeners turned a deaf ear to the truths he proclaimed. They have refused to accept God's envoy, and that will have serious repercussions.

On the flip side, they are completely naive toward these counterfeit messiahs. Jesus comes with the authority of God while the liars appeal only to their own authority. And these foolish Jews fall right into their trap. Sinful humanity cannot understand Jesus' appeal to God since they don't know God. Sin accepts the lies because they appeal to the sinner's own ego. Flattery can get you far in a self-centered world.

This thought continues in verse 44. Jesus is incredulous at the illogicality of it all. They "accept glory from one another" and at the same time refuse to accept "the glory that comes from the only God." That is the exact reverse of any thinking person, so Jesus asks, "How can you believe" on such a basis? The worldly self-centeredness of

---

5. It has been estimated that as many as sixty-four false messiahs came forth in the first century.

these claimants struck a responsive chord in their hearts, so they flocked after the lies. Their whole life was given over to striving for human praise rather than pleasing God. This is a question we all must ask ourselves: To what extent do we want attention from those around us rather than seeking glory and praise "from the only God"? Our answer to that will tell us how easily we can be manipulated by those who appeal to our self-interests.

Their true accuser: Moses (5:45–47)

Jesus has labeled the official witnesses at the trial, but the scene has changed. In 5:31–40 Jesus was on trial answering the charges of the Jews and calling forth witnesses, but here the accused has become the Jews, answering charges regarding their unbelief. Moses becomes the prosecuting attorney here, "accusing" them of unbelief at the *bēma* (judgment seat) of the Father. Jesus is the Judge (5:22, 30; 9:39). He does not need to bring the charges; Moses will perfectly suffice, for it is his prophecy of the prophet like Moses (fulfilled in Jesus) that the leaders have denied. It is Moses who gave Israel the Torah and was the deliverer or savior of the nation. Jesus is saying that the Jewish leaders have actually fooled themselves, for it is Moses who will produce the evidence against them. If they were truly followers of Moses, they would be followers of Jesus, for Moses prophesied of him.

Salvation under the old covenant centered on four things: the law, the land, the temple, and the covenants. Moses had been the channel through whom God gave the law, Israel was brought into the land, and worship was established in the tabernacle (predecessor of the temple). Moses had been involved in all four instruments of salvation, so it is easy to see why Jesus called him the one "on whom your hopes are set." For the Old Testament people of God, their faith and hope would be in Abraham and Moses, the two who initiated them as a nation and as a covenant people. Yet in 5:44 Jesus tells them they have rejected "the only God," the One who sent Moses.

Their faith and belief was supposed to be in Moses, yet "if you believed Moses, you would believe me, for he wrote about me" (5:46) in Deuteronomy 18:15 (the prophet like Moses). In fact, Jesus (and Paul) would say that all of Moses' writings had Jesus in mind, for he as the Messiah fulfilled the law itself since "Christ is the culmination of the law" (Rom 10:4). So their unbelief regarding Christ constitutes unbelief in Moses, for they have rejected all he wrote since it all ultimately had Christ in mind. The Jewish people prided themselves on their faithfulness to Scripture, yet they are denying the very one Moses had prophesied about. Their guilt is proven.

So Jesus concludes (5:47) that their refusal "to believe what I say" was made necessary by the very fact that they "do not believe what he wrote." Since Moses do not believe Moses, it is only logical that they will not believe Jesus. They have rejected the only source for truth, so their disbelief is the natural result, and their condemnation is certain. No wonder Moses will stand up against them in the final judgment.

———

The healing at the pool of Bethesda (5:1-15) initiates the primary section on Jesus' public ministry (5:1-10:42) and centers on an unusual figure, a lame man who is self-centered rather than filled with faith and who never shows any spiritual awareness. In telling this story, John wants to show us two things: First, Jesus came for and cares about all people, the spiritually hardened as well as those who open up to the gospel. He loves and heals even those who reject him. Second, ministry is not always successful. We, like Jesus, will often spend our time and effort on those who do not return our love and concern for them. We are called to minister, not just to be successful. Jesus exemplifies the unfruitful ministry effort here.

The increasing opposition against Jesus begins in 5:16-47, and it will be consistent throughout the rest of this Gospel, culminating in

Jesus' passion. It begins here as Jesus affirms his equality and union with his Father, seen as blasphemous by the Jews. Jesus responds with the powerful discourse of 5:19–30, showing that in both the present and the future he shares the authority of his Father in the giving of life and the proclamation of judgment. This is a clear affirmation of his deity. Yet at the same time this clearly states his subordination to the Father, for it is God who "shows" and "gives" these powers to Jesus, and his work clearly flows out of the Father's work. The Father and Son constitute life; it is inherent in their being. Hence they alone have the power to give life, and this gift is both a present possession and a future certainty for believers.

The rest of this chapter addresses how the Jewish people (and we today) should respond to Jesus' claim that he is one with the Father. In a Jewish trial two to three witnesses are needed to prove a case. Jesus admits that his own witness in a trial is not valid and so gives four other eyewitnesses: the Baptist, Jesus' works, the Father himself, and the Scriptures (5:31–40). There is more than enough earthly evidence to prove the case of his claim to equality with the Father. The implications are as profound for us today as they were for Jesus' Jewish audience. He is indeed the Son of the Father, and salvation can be found only in him. Those who waffle on their commitment to Christ are playing games with their eternal destiny.

In fact, the Jewish people are proof positive of what happens, for these witnesses, especially Moses, are proving them guilty of unbelief (5:41–47). It is amazing that those who reject Jesus and his relationship with God his Father are so easily fooled by those counterfeit messiahs who appeal to our own self-interest. We look beyond their lies because we like what they say. Since everything Moses wrote, direct prophecy like Deuteronomy 18:15 and the Torah material that pointed forward to and was fulfilled in Jesus (Matt 5:17–20), these Jews could not believe in Moses without believing in Jesus. For us as well the truth is certain: only belief in Jesus can make it possible to be a child of God and a member of his people.

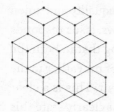

TWO SIGN-MIRACLES
(6:1–21)

This chapter is the famous "bread from heaven" passage, which centers on the "I am" saying in verse 35, "I am the bread of life." John chooses to present these two sign-miracles here because they signify the two aspects of that saying, with the feeding of the five thousand undergirding the "bread of life" part and the walking on water undergirding the "I am" part (see v. 20, "But he said to them, 'I am [*egō eimi*]; don't be afraid'" [my translation]).

The chapter breaks down into three parts: the two sign-miracles pointing to the "I am the bread of life" saying (vv. 1–21); the theology flowing out of the saying presenting Jesus as the Bread of Life (vv. 22–58); and the divisions this caused among Jesus' followers (vv. 59–71).

JESUS FEEDS THE FIVE THOUSAND (6:1–15)

This is the fourth sign-miracle in John and the only one found in all four Gospels, probably because of the depth of its theology. It looks backward and reproduces the manna in the wilderness (Exod 16) and the multiplication of loaves when Elisha fed a hundred with twenty loaves of bread in 2 Kings 4:42–44.[1] Moreover, along with the Cana miracle of 2:1–11, it also looks forward to the provision of food and wine at the messianic banquet (Isa 25:6–9). The theme it presents is God taking care of his people and providing for their needs. In this sense there is a theology of community here, with Jesus and his Father caring for their family.

THE SCENE: A MOUNTAINSIDE AT PASSOVER (6:1–4)

Jesus continues his globe-trotting ways and has already left Galilee (ch. 5) and returned to Jerusalem for Passover. In verse 1 he crosses to "the far shore of the Sea of Galilee," opposite Capernaum and the seaside Jewish villages, into what is called today the Golan Heights, the hill country of the region. The lake was popularly called the Sea of Galilee, but Herod Antipas had renamed it Sea of Tiberias in honor of the Roman emperor. It is hard to know why John gives us that tidbit here. Perhaps he felt he should use the official name in this instance.

As with most places Jesus went, a "great crowd" followed (v. 2), undoubtedly hoping to see another of the signs like Jesus' healing the sick, like the lame man recounted in chapter 5. It is clear that, like those mentioned in 2:23–25, theirs is an inadequate faith centered entirely on the miracles rather than on the person. When Jesus got there, he climbed up a mountainside (v. 3), probably to be alone with his disciples. Several interpreters think John's purpose here is to liken the scene to Moses on Mount Sinai (see the manna connection in 6:31–33).

John tells us this took place when "the Jewish Passover Festival was near" (v. 4). This is the second of three Passovers in John (with 2:13; 13:1) and is mentioned to add a theological aspect to the scene. The Passover celebrated the death of the sacrificial lamb for the people, and Jesus in 1:29 is "the Lamb of God, who takes away the

---

1. Note that Elijah multiplied the loaves fivefold while Jesus (five thousand with five loaves) multiplies it a thousandfold.

sin of the world." The Passover involved the eating of a lamb and of bread, and this is one of the central ideas in the chapter.

THE DILEMMA: INSUFFICIENT BREAD (6:5–7)

Jesus' attempt to get away by himself with his disciples failed to work. When Jesus looks up, the crowd has followed them onto the mountain. He decides that this is a good opportunity to "test" (v. 6) his disciples' faith (see Jas 1:3, "the testing of your faith") and see their level of trust in him and in God. He asks Philip (who comes from Bethsaida nearby and knows the area), "Where shall we buy bread for these people to eat?" He was not asking where a general store might be found, since we are told in verse 6 that "he already had in mind what he was going to do." His purpose was to involve his disciples in this miracle and get them to react. In the **Synoptic** version, this is even more emphasized, and the disciples are involved in every part of the miracle.

Like Nicodemus and the Samaritan woman before him, Philip was thinking entirely on the earthly plane and so opined, "It would take more than half a year's wages to buy enough bread for each one to have a bite" (v. 7). Actually, two hundred denarii (a denarius was a day's wage for the average worker) would be close to eight months' wages, a small fortune. They didn't have caterers back then, so this would have been impossible to pull off on the spot.

THE SOLUTION: A MIRACULOUS FEEDING (6:8–11)

Andrew speaks up in verse 8, pointing out a young boy in the crowd with "five small barley loaves and two small fish." Barley loaves were coarse, the food of the poor, and the fish were either dried or pickled fish or perhaps a fish paste to give the bread some flavor. Apparently, few others had brought much food, for he added, "How far will they go among so many?" The detail of the barley loaves may well echo the Elisha miracle, with its multiplication of twenty barley loaves. If so, Jesus is being depicted as the greater Elisha.

The disciples have no answer to the dilemma, so Jesus takes matters into his own hands and shows them the solution he had planned all along. He has them seat the crowd. John echoes Mark 6:39, who stresses the "green grass," telling us it was still spring before the summer heat had taken over and burned the grass brown. This was an unbelievably large crowd. In verse 10 we are told there were five thousand men in it, so with women and children there could have been ten to twenty thousand people there. Jesus is unfazed by the size of the crowd and tells everyone to sit down for a meal as if it is just a family gathering. The disciples had to have been astounded, looking around to see where the food might be coming from. The dining table is to be a large field, probably a plateau on the mountain.

Jesus then in verse 11 becomes the head of the family and "gave thanks" for the food. His prayer would have been like the common Jewish blessing, "Blessed art thou, O Lord our God, King of the Universe, who bringest forth bread from the earth." In the Synoptics, the disciples distribute the bread, while here it is Jesus. He remains in total charge. The miracle itself is extravagant, and the people ate "as much as they wanted" of the bread and the fish. The common food for the poor turned into a lavish banquet, and they stuffed themselves. God's supply is boundless, and he provides far beyond everyone's expectations.

The Aftermath (6:12–13)

John continues to stress the incredible bounty in the gathering of the leftovers after everyone is stuffed. Jesus finally includes the disciples in this and tells them in verse 12, "Let nothing be wasted" (this can also be translated, "so that nothing might be lost"). This is a Jewish custom and emphasizes not so much cleaning up after the meal as making sure nothing useful is thrown away. It is common to see symbolic significance in this, perhaps fulfilling Jeremiah 31:14, "My people will be filled with my bounty," or an allusion to

Jesus' mission as in John 6:39, "that I shall lose none of all those he has given me." Both fit this passage well.

The primary emphasis comes in verse 13, where we are told they "filled twelve baskets with the pieces of the five barley loaves left over." The basket would have been a small wicker basket of the type used for provisions when traveling. There is far more left after everyone has been filled than before they started.

Various meanings have been given to the twelve baskets. Combined with the seven baskets left after the feeding of the four thousand in Mark 8:8 and parallels, the number itself is likely significant. Probably the best interpretation is the restoration of the twelve tribes in Jesus' choice of twelve disciples to form the nucleus of the new Israel. God is pouring out his generous provision into his new community centered on the Messiah.

THE ATTEMPT TO MAKE HIM KING (6:14–15)

The crowd, seeing his miraculous power and thinking it constituted a reenactment of Moses and the manna in the wilderness (Exod 16), concluded, "Surely this is the Prophet who is to come into the world," thinking Jesus is the prophet like Moses of Deuteronomy 18:15. John the evangelist agrees with this, since Judaism regularly saw this figure as the coming Messiah, but he did not agree with the political overtones it was given, as we see in verse 15.

Jesus, using the same omniscient insight as in 1:34, 47; 4:17–18, realized that their comment was not religious but political and that they "intended to come and make him king by force." This does not mean that they were going to hold a sword to his throat or kidnap him away from his disciples, but that they would forcefully take up swords, declare him king, and go to war against Rome. This kind of thing took place more than once. Even a hundred years after this, Simon Bar Kokhba tried to establish an independent Jewish nation from AD 132 to 135.

The Jewish people, including the Twelve, had no understanding of a suffering Messiah as in Isaiah 53–54. To them, Isaiah 53–54 portrayed Israel's suffering, not the coming Messiah. They thought only of the Messiah as the King who would repeat Moses' deliverance of Israel from the Egyptians by defeating the Romans. They saw in Jesus the warrior-Messiah who offered them the opportunity for liberation, and they were perfectly willing to force him to go along if necessary.

Jesus' response was immediate. He refused to stay around and play their game. He "withdrew again to a mountain by himself," sending the disciples back across the lake to the Jewish side. In Mark 6:46 he went further up the mountain to pray, and in the historical event both are true. He wished to be alone with his Father and get away from the false expectations of the crowd.

JESUS WALKS ON THE WATER (6:16-21)

This story seems out of place, interrupting the movement from the multiplication of the loaves to Jesus as the Bread of Life. However, it actually fits well, identifying him as the divine provider and as the "I am." Jesus has gone up into the hills to be by himself, and the disciples at this stage are on their own. This becomes quite significant.

THE DEPARTURE OF THE DISCIPLES BY THEMSELVES (6:16–17)

John doesn't tell us that Jesus sent them across the lake as in Mark 6:45, where Jesus made his disciples get into the boats and head across. Here they themselves go down to the lake, and when he didn't come by the time it was dark, they headed across. Likely John wants to stress that the disciples are alone, facing the darkness by themselves (see 1:5; 3:2). The darkness and Jesus' absence are interrelated, and the crisis that follows is linked to these facts.

THE WALKING ON THE WATER (6:18–19)

The lake is thirteen miles north-south and seven miles east-west at its widest part. The disciples were headed across at the northern tip, probably a five-mile journey. On the eastern shore where they were, the lake is ringed by mountains, and often the wind whips through the mountain passes, causing terrible storms and waves on the lake. One of these storms caught the disciples on the way across, and it was a particularly violent one.

The disciples embarked in the boats about dusk, and Mark tells us that Jesus came to them about three in the morning. When they started, "a strong wind was blowing," and very soon "the waters grew rough" (v. 18). When Jesus arrived, they had probably been rowing for their lives about seven to eight hours, and John here tells us they had only "rowed about three or four miles" to that point. In normal conditions it would take experienced rowers only an hour or so to row that far.

They were naturally at the end of their strength and filled with terror when they saw this apparition coming out of the driving rain. It was "Jesus approaching the boat, walking on the water" (v. 19). There are several miracles here. Much of that time, Jesus had been on the mountain praying to his Father, and from that vantage point he "saw the disciples straining ... because the wind was against them" (Mark 6:48). He saw them several miles away through the pounding rain! Then he walked straight to them through that same rain, stepping from one huge wave to another for four miles. Stilling the storm may actually have been one of the lesser miracles.

The picture depicts the disciples watching Jesus approach their boat step by terrifying step. Those who have rewritten this story as Jesus walking on the shore go to ridiculous lengths to avoid admitting a miracle occurred. This story would never have been remembered if that was all it was. In actuality this is an allusion to "the Spirit of God ... hovering over the waters" in Genesis 1:2. As in John 1:1-4, Jesus takes control of his new creation.

Needless to say, the disciples are filled with fright, and Mark 6:49 tells us they "thought he was a ghost." Likely what they thought was, "He is what we are going to be soon—ghosts." Christ in his feeding miracle had just proved to them that God would provide for his people, but they in their terror had forgotten all that.

They thought that God and Jesus had abandoned them, and they were about to be drowned. As this phantom approached, their consternation as well as their fear grew exponentially.

JESUS CALMS THEIR FEARS (6:20–21)

Jesus immediately turned the situation around with two little words, *egō eimi*, "I am." They hardly caught this at that moment, as they were focused only on their coming death. The NIV translates, "It is I," and while that is correct, it is probably better to see it as John did, saying "The I Am is here," or "I, Yahweh, am here." In several places in his Gospel, John has Jesus saying "I am" with no predicate (8:24, 28, 58; 13:19; 18:5), and in several other places he uses predicated forms like "I am the bread of life" (6:35).

These "I am" sayings reflect God's revelation of himself to Moses at the burning bush—"I AM WHO I AM" (Exod 3:13–15)—as well as its use in Isaiah 43:10, 25; 47:8, 10; 51:12; Hosea 13:4. Jesus is identifying himself as "very God of very God," as the Nicene Creed would later put it, as he also does in the "I am" passages listed above. Needless to say, the only proper conclusion is his command, "Don't be afraid." There is no place for fear when Jesus takes charge of the elements, for they are part of his creation.

At that moment, the disciples recognized Jesus, stopped being terrified, and "were willing to take him into the boat" (v. 21). The stilling of the storm, emphasized in Mark 6:51, is not actually mentioned here. Instead, we are told, "Immediately the boat reached the shore where they were heading." Some think that no new miracle is intended, but I think there is an allusion to Psalm 107:29–30, where it says that God "stilled the storm to a whisper" and "guided them to their desired haven." Christ has seen their plight, taken extraordinary steps to watch over them and keep them safe, and then got them to their God-ordained destination. His vigilance over his chosen people is indeed miraculous.

———

These two side-by-side miracles are together in three of the four Gospels (Luke omits the walking on the water episode) and build on each other. This is especially true here in John, for they form the prologue to the Bread of Life discourse and introduce its themes. The feeding episode prepares for Jesus' emphasis on himself as the Bread of Life, and the walking on the water episode prepares for Jesus' "I am" saying. The message is Christ's provision and care for his followers.

Jesus' feeding of the five thousand echoes God's provision of manna in the wilderness, and Jesus is the new Moses meeting the needs of God's people. This parallel highlights both his sovereign control of his creation and his bountiful, even lavish supply in meeting the needs of his followers. The choice of the Twelve has initiated the new people gathered around the Messiah, and Jesus is watching over them and filling their lives with God's plenty.

The second sign-miracle, the walking on the water, shows how poorly prepared the disciples were for the events to come. Several of them were professional fishermen and had grown up on this lake with its sudden squalls. Yet when this especially severe one hit, they were not ready and forgot all about the message of the feeding miracle, that Jesus and his Father would take care of them. When he miraculously walked across the storm-driven waters to them, they thought he was a ghost come to gather them home (Mark 6:52 says "their hearts were hardened"). In the midst of all this, Jesus comes to them, stills the storm, and gets them to shore. The message to us is clear: God and Jesus are indeed watching out for us and can see a lot farther than we think!

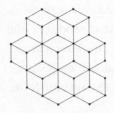

THE BREAD OF LIFE DISCOURSE
(6:22–59)

John's Gospel is completely opposed to shallow followers who give Jesus only a portion of their lives. This great discourse centers on Jesus' demand that since he is the Bread of Life, everyone who believes on him must surrender all to follow him. There is strong exodus **typology** in this passage. The event takes place at Passover (6:4) and is introduced with the two sign-miracles of 6:1–21: God supplies manna for the needs of his people and leads the disciples to safety across the dangerous waters of the sea. Jesus presents himself as the divine manna or bread, and this prepares for his demand that he be consumed completely as the Passover Lamb by those who want eternal life (6:53–58).

In 5:21–29 Jesus described himself as the life-giver, and this passage expands on that theme. He gives life because he is the Bread of Life, and so he must be consumed utterly. Many have thought this is an artificial sermon constructed in several stages, but it is clearly a well-constructed unity and is likely a Jewish **midrashic** sermon on the theme of God's provision of life, a homily Christ himself devised and preached in the Capernaum synagogue (6:59). No wonder it is so brilliantly done! How would you like to sit in a church and hear a sermon preached by Jesus himself?

As for the organization of the discourse, I see verses 25–29 as introductory material centering on the work that produces life, verses 30–34 as providing the key Pentateuchal citation on bread from heaven (Exod 16:4), verses 35–50 as a midrash on Jesus as the Bread of Life, and verses 51–58 on the need to consume Jesus utterly as this life-giving bread.

JOHN SETS THE SCENE FOR THE DISCOURSE (6:22–24)

This scene intimately relates the discourse to the sign-miracles, for this introduction to Jesus' teaching relates the aftermath to the miracles on the other side of the lake, focusing once more on the crowds. The morning after Jesus and his disciples had returned to Capernaum, the crowd, who had "stayed on the opposite shore [opposite to Capernaum] of the lake" throughout the stormy night, suddenly realized "that only one boat" that had brought Jesus and his band of disciples remained. This was certainly a small boat that had brought Jesus, for they also deduced that Jesus did not go with the disciples and yet was also gone. John does not explain their intentions, but we assume they still wanted to force him to join them as king of their guerrilla force against Rome (see 6:15).

They would have had to walk around the lake, but just then some boats arrived from the town of Tiberias on the northwestern side of the lake near Capernaum, perhaps to pick up some of the crowd. They landed near the site of the feeding miracle, so as many as were able could get into the boats and hitch a ride across to Capernaum, which had become the home of Jesus and his disciples for the Galilean ministry.

INTRODUCTION: JESUS EXPLAINS THE WORK THAT PRODUCES LIFE (6:25–29)

It does not take the crowd long to find Jesus. They are curious about what had happened the previous night and so ask in verse 25, "Rabbi, when did you get here?" This was a far cry from their

earlier demand for him to become king (6:15), and he was generally known as a rabbi (1:38, 49; 3:2, 26; 4:31), an official, respected
teacher.[1] Their question implies that they are unhappy he left them
there overnight.

Jesus does not respond but instead goes on the offensive (v. 26),
returning to the theme of 2:24–25 (he did not believe in them
because he knew their hearts), challenging them with another
solemn double *amēn* saying, "Very truly I tell you" (see 1:51). He
charges them with having only an earthly rather than heavenly
interest, focusing only on being fed rather than on the meaning of
the signs. They certainly saw the miracle and even tried to make
him the messianic prophet and royal Messiah (6:14–15), but they
missed that the true significance of the "sign" (see comments on
2:11) pointed to Jesus as the Bread of Life, not just as a miracle
worker. A true sign demands an encounter with Jesus, and that
will be the theme of 6:35–50.

The crowd's consuming (pun intended) interest in perishable
food (v. 27) is similar to Jesus' challenge to the Samaritan woman
that her water would only make her thirst again, while the "living
water" would become a "spring of water welling up to eternal life"
(4:13–14). In the same way, he now tells the crowd to stop seeking
food that spoils and go after "food that endures to eternal life,"
which alone is worthy of their hard work.

It is interesting that eternal life is both work (our part) and gift
(Christ's part); the two aspects function together in our lives. In a
similar paradox, faith is not a work (Eph 2:8–9), but the only work
God allows is the act of faith (John 6:29). In our time as well, too
many Christians spend their time pursuing temporary "treasures
on earth" and virtually no time building up "treasures in heaven"
(Matt 6:19–21). The only way we can achieve eternal life is through

---

1. "Rabbi" was a title of respect for a "teacher" and did not become a technical
religious term for an ordained office (demanding that they had studied under
a recognized rabbi) until the end of the first century.

the Son of Man, who united heaven and earth (John 1:51) and was appointed by God as Savior (3:17; 4:42) and Judge (5:27; 8:15-16).

The reason Christ can do this is that God has placed "his seal of approval" on him, which might refer to his incarnation or baptism but is probably meant generally of his ministry as a whole. He is the Sent One (3:17, 34; 5:23-24), the agent or envoy certified by God with authority over his creation.

The crowd asks in verse 28, "What must we do to do the works God requires? They want to know the deeds they can perform that will bring salvation. As usual they are thinking on the earthly plane, hoping to earn something from God and receive eternal life for their effort. They have completely missed Jesus' central point, repeated again here, that "the work of God is this: to believe in the one he has sent" (v. 29). Eternal life is a free gift from God and comes only through faith in Jesus. They wanted a grocery list of things they could do.

This is a common error today as well, with people attending church and doing good works to gain favor with God. The only work God allows is faith; life does not come by works. Jesus is the heaven-sent envoy from God, the only source of salvation (John 14:6). Eternal life comes only by believing in him. Paul in Romans and Galatians centers on this truth: we can be right with God only by faith and not by works (Rom 3:21-4:17; Gal 3:1-4:7).

JESUS PRESENTS HIS THEME: BREAD
FROM HEAVEN (6:30-34)

The authority Jesus was claiming went way beyond anything these people had ever encountered, so in verse 30 they ask him for an authenticating sign "that we may see it and believe you," as they did earlier in 2:18. He declared himself greater than Moses in the feeding miracle, certified as the Son of Man by God (6:27). They wondered earlier whether he was the messianic prophet; now they desire further proof. The two sign-miracles Jesus just performed should have sufficed, but they failed to understand the signs (6:26–27) and so needed more. They were probably looking for a heavenly portent like that in Matthew 12:38 and 16:1.

In verse 31 they cite the manna in the wilderness as an example of what they are looking for, probably hoping Jesus will show himself as the prophet like Moses from Deuteronomy 18:15. This is strange considering that Jesus had just performed the feeding of the five thousand, but they had failed to understand it as a sign and wanted something more decisive, another manna miracle. They quote Exodus 16:4 (probably amalgamated with Ps 78:24 and Neh 9:15): "He gave them bread from heaven to eat." What was missing from Jesus' miracle was the "from heaven" aspect, so they considered it insufficient. The Jews centered on this, as exemplified in the Midrash Rabbah on Ecclesiastes 1:9, "As the former redeemer caused manna to descend … so will that later Redeemer [the Messiah] cause manna to descend." They wanted bread *from heaven*.

With another solemn double *amēn* saying ("Very truly I tell you"), Jesus responds in 6:32–33. The "bread from heaven" has a double meaning, referring to both the manna from heaven in Exodus and the new heavenly reality Jesus has introduced (1:51; 3:13, 31). The crowd understood only the former, but Jesus intends both in his response here. He begins by correcting their erroneous interpretation of the manna episode: "It is not Moses who has given you the bread from heaven, but it is my Father who gives you the true bread from heaven." The present-tense "gives" means that the heavenly manna is an ongoing gift, provided through the Son (as in the feeding of the five thousand). This becomes clear in the next verse. The earthly manna is perishable like the food of verse 27. The Father's gift is the "true bread from heaven" that will never cease. It is not temporary but eternal.

This is clarified in verse 33, which takes us to the next level and provides the theme behind the discourse: "For the bread of God is the bread that comes down from heaven and gives life to the world." It is now clear that the "true bread of heaven" from verse

32 is Jesus himself. These are the two emphases: Jesus provides the bread (vv. 27, 33), and he is the bread (vv. 33, 35). The manna in the wilderness is typologically fulfilled in Jesus, the Word, the Living Revealer of the Father. This sums up several themes in John:

1. Christ is the true bread who "descends" (Greek: *katabainō*) from heaven, implied in 1:1–2, 14, in Jesus' incarnation and stated explicitly in 1:51; 3:13, 31 (see the discussion of the ascent/descent motif in the commentary there). It becomes a major emphasis in this discourse (6:35, 38, 41, 42, 50, 51, 58). Jesus' true origin is heaven, and God has sent him to earth as his representative or agent.

2. Jesus is the provider of life, also in the prologue (1:4) and often elsewhere (3:15, 16, 36; 4:14; 5:21, 24, 26, 29, 39–40; 6:27). This theme will also dominate this discourse (6:35, 40, 47, 48, 51, 53, 54).

3. The focus shifts from the Jews to "the world," stressed also in the prologue (1:9–10) and later (1:29; 3:16–17, 19; 4:42; 6:14), and stressed here in 6:51. The message of the Fourth Gospel is that the world, consisting of Jew and Gentile alike, is filled with sin and yet is the focus of God's salvific love (3:16). Salvation is for both Jew and Gentile God's free gift received through faith.

Like Nicodemus and the Samaritan woman, the crowd only catches Jesus' meaning at the earthly level and so answers in verse 34, "always give us this bread." The woman in chapter 4 wanted "a spring of water welling up" (4:14–15), and the crowd wants the same with the eternal bread, probably thinking he was granting their request from 6:30–31.

JESUS IS THE BREAD OF LIFE (6:35–50)

There is considerable debate over the possible sacramental overtones of this passage. Many, especially those from high-church traditions (those with a very high view of baptism and the Eucharist), see the language of verses 51–58 as portraying a sacramental view of the Eucharist, according to which taking the bread and the wine is consuming the body and blood of Christ. Since John does not have an account of the Lord's Supper, they believe this is provided in its place as a theology of the Eucharist. Others see no such connotation but believe Jesus rather was using Passover imagery to demand that those who come to him surrender themselves completely to him. As I will argue in the discussion below, I agree with those who take a mediating position, with Christ's primary intention the latter but recognizing that later followers could not fail but see eucharistic connotations when reading this material.

FOUNDATION STATEMENT (6:35–36)

"I am the bread of life" in verse 35 is the first of seven well-known "I am" statements in this Gospel.[2] This one culminates 6:25–34 and dominates all that follows. Together, these seven statements fill out the significance of Christ as Yahweh. They also define the person and mission of the divine Son. This saying presents Jesus as the only food that can provide eternal life. (The genitive "of life" is objective, meaning "the bread that produces life.") Moses and the manna from heaven could never provide this, as that miracle was earthly and temporary by its nature.

The two statements that follow tell how seekers can find this life; they must both come and believe. They are two sides of the same coin—coming is the prelude to believing, and together they constitute the process of conversion. Jesus makes this life possible, but true disciples must come and avail themselves of it by faith/belief. Coming and believing thus combine the bread metaphor ("never go hungry") with the living water metaphor of 4:14 ("never be thirsty"), and together they prepare for the later image

---

2. The bread of life (6:35); the light of the world (8:12); the gate (10:7, 9); the Good Shepherd (10:11, 14); the resurrection and the life (11:25); the way, the truth, and the life, (14:6); and the true vine (15:5).

of eating Jesus' flesh and drinking his blood in 6:53-56 (see also 7:37, where the thirsty "come to me and drink").

In verse 36 Jesus defines the divine and human sides of coming to salvation, and in this sense brings together the Calvinist and Arminian perspectives on divine sovereignty and human responsibility. Both are actually needed for the full effects of salvation to be experienced. The human side is to come and believe, and the divine side occurs when God knows and "draws" people to Christ (vv. 40, 44), gives them to him (vv. 37, 39), and keeps them secure in him (vv. 40, 44). The crowd refused to believe even though they had seen what Jesus said and did (v. 36), demonstrating the same unbelief as that in 1:11; 3:19-20; 5:38, 46-47. They had seen the sign and asked for more (v. 30) but failed to understand or accept what he said. They made their decision, but it was to come and *not* believe. Here we see both the proclamation of the loving Lord and the unreceptive nature and response of the crowd, and their guilt is front and center.

FAITH AND SOVEREIGNTY (6:37-40)

Jesus' point in these verses is that the unbelief of the crowd does no damage to God's plan, for the elect will come. They had not found faith because they were not of God. This is one of the great Scripture passages on the sovereignty of God in salvation. The crowd's rejection of Christ is of little significance, for they are merely acting out the results of the fact that God had already rejected them.

Note the progression of predestination in verse 37: "all those the Father gives" is the divine choice, and "will come to me" is the human response.[3] There is a two-way street here: Jesus brings people to God, but they already belong to God and are God's gift to his Son. God has chosen them from before the foundation of the world, and they *will* come to Jesus. So God is aware of those who

---

3. See also the comments on 8:28-30 below on the question of foreknowledge.

refuse to come and believe, and their refusal is indeed part of his plan. The elect will come, and "whoever comes" Jesus will "never drive away" and keep secure (see John 10:27–29; 1 Pet 1:5). They belong to God and are given to Jesus, so Jesus not only accepts them but also watches over them. The balance between divine sovereignty and human responsibility in verse 35 is on full display also in verse 37.

This sovereign power in salvation is anchored in the will of God (vv. 38–40). Jesus has "come down from heaven" ("come down" is Greek *katabainō*; see v. 33) to fulfill the mission given by his Father, and thus his entire purpose is "not to do my will but to do the will of him who sent me." This repeats 4:34, where Jesus' "food" consisted of "doing the will of God" by gathering souls for the kingdom. He was "sent" as God's sovereignly appointed envoy (stressed in 6:27, 29, 39, 44, 57). His origin is heavenly, and he has descended to earth for the sole purpose of obeying his Father's will rather than doing it his way (see also 5:30).

In verse 39 Jesus defines the will of the sender from verse 38: that he, Jesus, "lose none of all those he has given me, but raise them up at the last day." The progression continues—God gives them (v. 37), then Christ protects them (vv. 39a, 44), and then together the Godhead raises them up at the final day (v. 39b). Scholars describe this progression with the phrase "realized **eschatology**," meaning that God through Christ ensures in the present the future security of all true followers. The final eschatology here is seen in the future promise of resurrection (6:39, 40, 44, 54). We have already seen this promise in 5:28–29, and it is clear that John's Gospel contains both realized (present) and final (future) aspects of God's salvation for believers.

These themes culminate in verse 40, where Jesus elaborates on "my Father's will" in even more detail: "Everyone who looks to the Son and believes in him shall have eternal life, and I will raise them up at the last day." Jesus now interprets the "coming" of verse 35 as turning to the Son and visualizing all he has done. This then produces faith-decision, which results in the present possession of eternal life and the future promise of final resurrection, both of which are frequent emphases in this Gospel.

Once again the two sides of salvation, human decision ("looks/believes") and divine sovereignty ("my Father's will"), flow together. Yet there is still the question of what it means that Jesus will "lose none." After all, there seem to be exceptions to this in John 6:60–66 (the apostasy of "many of his disciples") and 17:12 ("none has been lost except the one doomed to destruction" [Judas]). But were these true followers? Judas was not; he was a "devil" from the beginning (6:70–71), but the disciples of 6:60–66 may have been (see below).

The final balance between security and responsibility is a mystery and will never be truly solved until eternity arrives. In the meantime, John's Gospel is a perfect book for working on the issue, since both sides are clearly present and held in proper tension. John does not seem nearly as confused or concerned about the issue as we are, but then he did not have to write with the last five hundred years of debate in mind and interact with both Calvin and Arminius.

DEBATE WITH THE JEWS (6:41–46)

The unbelief of the crowd now becomes quite apparent as they begin to "grumble" about Jesus' claim to be "the bread that came down from heaven." John shifts for the first time to their identity as "the Jews" in order to align their hostility and opposition with the earlier portions of this Gospel, where the phrase "the Jews" serves as shorthand for the Jewish leaders who are opposed to Jesus. Thus the use of "grumble" or "murmur" (*egongyzon*) is aligned with the wilderness grumbling against God (Exod 15:24; 16:2, 7), seen later as unbelief (Ps 106:24–25) and disobedience (Isa 30:12). These Jews ignored his claim to be life-giver and focused on his claim to have descended from heaven (similar to 5:17–18).

Their opposition centered on their knowledge of his humble origins as the son of Joseph (6:42), a lowly carpenter many of them knew. From this they justify their rejection of his claim to have come from heaven. This was a common objection to Jesus' claims (Mark 6:3; Luke 4:22). His opponents focused only on the earthly and willingly ignored the hand of God and the heavenly realities on these things, much like people do today. Jesus may have been the earthly (adopted) son of Joseph, but he was the eternal Son of God, and their refusal to consider the deeper realities would cost them for eternity.

Jesus responded like Moses in Exodus 16:7–8, who pointed out that Israel's grumbling was against the Lord and would have lasting consequences. Jesus then responded to their complaints by repeating what he had just said in verse 37 but with one significant difference. There they are "given" to Jesus, but here they are "drawn" by God (v. 44). Only then can a person "come." Once more God sovereignly controls salvation, and only those he brings to faith can come. The verb for "draw" (helkusē) implies the inability of the people to perform the act by themselves and the drawing power of the one bringing them to the action.

Theologians debate how far this should be taken. Is this "irresistible grace," the doctrine that those who are drawn will come, and that this drawing is restricted to the elect? Many assert that this drawing power of God is always successful. I believe this interpretation goes too far, for in 12:32 Jesus claims to "draw all people" to himself, and he is hardly teaching universalism. I believe that 6:44 refers to God's control of salvation and to the security of the believer. Jesus is saying that rejection of him is a rejection of God's drawing power, an act that leads to eternal rejection and judgment by God. God drawing people to himself refers to the convicting work of the Spirit (16:8–11), which I think is universal, like the illumination of every person by the light of God (1:4, 7, 9). All are drawn by God, but their response determines who among those

drawn find life. The Spirit convicts, overcomes the total depravity of each person, and makes faith-decision possible.

Jesus anchors his assertion regarding God's choosing and drawing in a free translation of Isaiah 54:13: "They will all be taught by
God" (v. 45).[4] This passage speaks of the coming of the new covenant (see Isa 42:6; 54:10; Jer 31:31–34), in which God promises a new
and glorious future for Zion, with his people enjoying a new, direct,
internal relationship and access to him. Jesus is saying this now
characterizes his followers. The "all" in the quotation includes the
world (see 6:14, 33), Jew and Gentile together. Again, "all people"
are illuminated by the light of God and convicted by the Spirit, and
are thereby brought to faith-decision.

In the second half of the verse, it is only those who have "heard
the Father and learned from him" who "come to" Jesus. This is a further definition of God's "drawing" and "giving" those he has chosen
(vv. 37, 44). Jesus has now used four metaphors for conversion in
this discourse: "see" and "believe" in verse 40 and "heard" and
"learned" here. Conversion involves eyes, heart, ears, and mind, a
total process in which God captures and involves one's entire being
in a holistic change from the earthly to the heavenly.

The Jewish people rejected God's call at every level. They had
been drawn but refused it vehemently. To clarify the means by
which God teaches, Jesus adds that he is the only path to knowing God, saying in verse 46, "No one has seen the Father except
the one who is from God; only he has seen the Father." In other
words, how will these people hear and be taught by God? Only by
listening to and heeding his Son, Jesus. Repeating 1:18; 5:37, Jesus
states that no one but him has ever seen his Father. He is the only
revelatory instrument through which God can be revealed and the
only Savior through whom anyone can ever be saved (14:6–7). To
turn your back on him is to ensure that you will never know God.

---

4. The passage reads, "All your children will be taught by the LORD, and great
will be their peace."

SUMMARY ON THE BREAD OF LIFE (6:47–50)

This is the concluding section of the Bread of Life discourse, so Jesus wants to bring together the primary points. Verse 47 is the eleventh solemn double *amēn* saying so far and repeats a primary theme found in 3:15, 16, 36; 5:24; 6:35, 40, inviting Jesus' listeners (and John's readers) to believe. John doesn't add the "in him" (found in nearly all the other invitations to belief) because that is obvious from everything Jesus has said so far. Jesus provides the only path to salvation. This is also the eleventh time "eternal life" has appeared thus far. The true final goal of this Gospel is to bring all readers to life through faith-decision (as stated in 20:31). Faith in Christ is clearly the only way, for Jesus is the only "bread" given by God "by which we must be saved" (Acts 4:12).

The primary focus of this chapter is found in the next verse (v. 48), which repeats the "I am" saying of 6:35: "I am the bread of life." Everything has led again to this point, which frames the entire discussion. The Jewish listeners here had no access to God because they had no faith. Salvation is not based on one's pedigree or good works or relation to the law of Moses. It stems entirely from one's relation to the "bread of life." Jesus here returns to the theme of manna in the wilderness that has dominated the chapter (and will do so again in 6:51–58).

With logical precision, Jesus concludes the discourse with the death-life antithesis of verses 49–50. Their ancestors who had only manna perished (v. 49), while those in Jesus' time who eat the bread that "comes down from heaven" will not die (v. 50). Like all perishable things (see 6:27), manna kept the Israelites alive for a while but was unable to sustain them long term. All who ate it eventually died. There is only one path to everlasting life, to eat "the bread that comes down from heaven." God is the true and only source of this new everlasting life, and the Jews of Jesus' day missed it because of their opposition to Jesus. He is the only bread that one can "eat and not die."

JESUS TELLS HIS FOLLOWERS TO EAT HIS
FLESH AND DRINK HIS BLOOD (6:51–59)

This passage is not an isolated, sacramental exposition of the theme but is a natural extension of what Christ has been saying all along. He has now anchored his discussion of salvation thoroughly in the bread metaphor and shown that he indeed is the bread that produces life. The logical next step is the invitation to the reader to partake of this bread and find salvation, so Jesus does this with the metaphor of eating the bread. But he wants to get across the importance of experiencing him with total surrender, so he brings in the imagery of the Passover lamb, which must be utterly consumed by the family.

Christ insists on a total encounter with him as God's envoy. There are three emphases in the passage:

1. The thrust of the whole chapter lands here with the demand that people consume Jesus entirely as the Bread of Life in order to be true followers. Half-hearted followers fall away in 6:60–66. This is so important today with the high percentage of people in our churches who surrender little of the world in order to follow Christ, who want to have their cake and eat it too.

2. This imagery points forward to Jesus' death, when he would surrender his "flesh" for "the life of the world" (v. 51) and become "the Lamb of God, who takes away the sin of the world" (1:29). The bread produces life through the death of the One who at the same time is the manna and the Lamb.

3. Jesus was not preparing here for his sacramental Last Supper, but John and his readers would likely see sacramental influence in the language and imagery of this material, so it is likely present but secondary to the message of a total encounter with Christ.

THESIS: THE LIVING BREAD (6:51)

In verse 48 Jesus provided a restatement of the main theme of himself as the Bread of Life, and here he addresses two further critical aspects in verse 51. He further develops the basic point by saying he is "the living bread that came down from heaven," turning it into a description of his essence as the Living One. In 4:10 he offered the Samaritan woman "living water" to drink, and now he is "living bread" to eat. This is the sixth of seven times in this chapter Jesus describes himself as descended from heaven (see 6:33, 38, 41, 42, 50, 51, 58), further stressing his true origin from God.

The salvation he brought is also "from above" (see 3:3), and what is at stake is not earthly nourishment or success but eternal life. The bread from heaven is heavenly rather than earthly and provides everlasting rather than temporary life. Only those partaking of this bread will "live forever," an incredible promise. This becomes the major image of this last part of the extended discourse, and it culminates in the startling final part of this opening statement: "This bread is my flesh, which I will give for the life of the world," an obvious reference to Jesus' passion.

The "Word [that] became flesh" (1:14) will surrender his flesh on the cross so the world may live. Jesus stated in 6:33 that "the bread of God ... gives life to the world," and here that bread is Jesus himself. The great paradox of Christianity is that life comes through death. Jesus died that we may live, and we die to the things of the world so that we may live for God (Rom 6:4–6). Here Jesus dies "for [Greek: *hyper*] the life of the world." The preposition signifies substitutionary atonement—that Jesus is the vicarious sacrifice substituting himself for sinful humanity. John often uses it in sacrificial contexts in his Gospel (10:11, 15; 11:50–52; 15:13; 17:19) to point to the fact that our life has its basis in Jesus' atoning sacrifice. We appropriate this life by faith, eating this bread and trusting in his fleshly sacrifice that atones for our sin.

EXPLANATION OF THIS IMAGERY (6:52–57)

This starts an argument among the Jewish listeners who are living on the same earthly plane as Nicodemus and the Samaritan woman: "How can this man give us his flesh to eat?" They wonder if he is encouraging cannibalism. "Argue sharply" (v. 52) is a strong term that intensifies the grumbling of verse 41. John likely is echoing Israel's striving with Moses in Exodus 15:24; 16:2; 17:2. They are certainly not actually wondering but are mocking Jesus here, showing the depth of their unbelief.

Jesus' response in verses 53–54 forms the climax of this narrative. It must shock them to the core when he becomes even more explicit and says with another double *amēn*, the most solemn one thus far, "Unless you eat the flesh of the Son of Man and drink his blood, you have no life in you." The first half goes back to 1:29, where John the Baptist called Jesus "the Lamb of God." The Torah said that after the Passover sacrifice, the lamb was to be wholly consumed, every part (Exod 12:9–10). "Flesh" became a Jewish idiom for the whole person, so the point here is that the encounter with Jesus (eating his flesh) must be total, involving the complete surrender of one's entire being.

The second half is even more striking. By adding "drink his blood," Jesus was invoking a strange and scandalous (even repulsive) element that deepened the metaphor considerably. God forbade the Jews from drinking blood (Gen 9:4; Lev 7:26–27). Even in the early church, this was important enough that the Jerusalem Council asked Gentile Christians (who knew no such rule) to respect Jewish sensitivities and not drink blood (Acts 15:28–29).[5] Blood symbolized life in the sacrificial system and signified violent death in the ancient world, so Jesus was going way beyond normal bounds to make his point that it is to be a complete consumption and a total encounter.

---

5. Obviously this was not a vampire-type rite but referred to something like British blood pudding today.

He adds to this in verse 54, "Whoever eats my flesh and drinks my blood has eternal life, and I will raise them up at the last day," returning to the emphases of 6:39-40, 44. Here he shows more deeply that the meaning of "life" from verse 53 is both everlasting and involves the promised resurrection of the saints.

This statement was also a clear forward-looking prophecy of his death on the cross. Only the one who utterly surrenders to Jesus and his atoning death has life. So while all of us reading this today, as well as John's original audience, hear the sacramental overtones when we read this, there is no evidence or language here to indicate Jesus was thinking ahead to the Lords' Supper. He had in mind, rather, the necessity and significance of his death.

In light of the fact that earthly sustenance is temporary and "spoils" (6:27), and the even more critical fact that the bread Jesus gives himself as the Bread of Life yields everlasting life, he can now conclude that "my flesh is real food and my blood is real drink" (v. 55). It is "real" or "true" (Greek: *alēthēs*) because it lasts forever, while all earthly provision perishes. He said this same thing to the woman at the well in 4:13-14 when he told her he could give her living water that "wells up to eternal life."

This means that anyone eating and drinking this Bread of Life "remains in me, and I in them" (v. 56), for they will be in union with him. This union with Christ has been labeled "mutual indwelling" and is a major theme of John's writings, appearing in 14:20; 15:4-7; as well as 1 John 2:24; 3:24; 4:15. The Father and the Son are one (John 10:38; 14:20; 17:11, 21), and when we become one with the Son, we share in that union. Moreover, when we are one with the Godhead, we are one with one another (17:20-26).

CONCLUSION (6:58-59)

To bring the discourse to a conclusion, Jesus repeats two items—the temporary efficacy of the manna from verses 49-50 and the ascent/descent theme from verses 16, 33, 38, 41, 42, 50, 51. Jesus is the true "bread that came down from heaven" (v. 58), the only means to God's gift of eternal life. All other human-generated methods for attaining salvation, including the law of Moses, are temporary and like the manna that fell in the wilderness, for that manna saved their lives and was indeed a gift from God, but still "your ancestors ate [that] manna and died." In complete contrast, "whoever feeds on this bread will live forever." So Jesus alone is "the bread of life" (vv. 35, 48), and only he has his true origins in heaven. Therefore, he and he alone can provide everlasting life.

The final point is the setting for this great discourse (v. 59), his "teaching in the synagogue in Capernaum." This passage highlights the significance of this Passover imagery in Jewish worship. Some have wondered if the dialogue form actually characterized synagogue worship, but there is some evidence that it did at times take place, and the presence of a controversial rabbi like Jesus and the crowds who poured in with him would make such a thing understandable.

The more I study this incredible Gospel, the more convinced I become that John is one of the great narrators of history. This may well be the best-written book in Scripture. The way John tells a story, the dramatic portrayals he weaves into his narratives, and the theological depth of his presentations all demonstrate the wonderful writing gifts God has given him. All Scripture of course is "God-breathed" or inspired (2 Tim 3:16), but all discussions of inspiration recognize that God uses the mind and personal abilities of the individual writers, and John's are extraordinary. This chapter is expertly put together and brings out Jesus' genius for weaving metaphors into exciting tapestries of truth.

This passage begins with Jesus, in typical fashion, challenging the crowd to quit working merely for the earthly and start working for the heavenly, eternal life that God has made available (vv. 25–29). He then turns to the imagery of the manna in the wilderness, presenting himself as the bread that produces ever-lasting rather than temporary earthly life (vv. 30–34). The same message is relevant for our day as well, to start building for our retirement in heaven and not just for our retirement on earth. Many Christians are confused about heaven, some even thinking of it as a disembodied state or perhaps thinking of ourselves as little cherub angels with harps. But the biblical picture is that when Christ returns we receive our glorified, completely physical and perfect bodies, and in heaven we will exist for eternity in the joyous presence of our Lord and with each other.

The discourse proper (vv. 35–50) takes us right into the middle of the debate over sovereignty and responsibility in salvation. The basic truths (vv. 37–40, 44) are clear. All who find salvation come because God has chosen them, and when they come they are secure in their salvation and will be raised in the final resurrection. This truth comforts those who are inclined to doubt their salvation, and it explains those like the Jews in this scene who turn away from God's offer of salvation. God is absolutely in charge. At the same time, "all" are "taught by God" (v. 45) through conviction by the Spirit and are brought to faith-decision, and so all are responsible for their walk with God. Sovereignty and responsibility in salvation are thus balanced. The key is that Christ is the bread that alone brings true life, offered by God and either accepted or refused by every person ever born.

The primary message comes in verses 51–58, where we see that Jesus as the bread given by God produces true life by becoming the Passover Lamb of God who sacrifices himself on the cross to bring about forgiveness of sins. Like the lamb at Passover, all participants in the life God offers must consume him utterly to have that life by surrendering themselves utterly to God and making Christ Lord over them.

Jesus uses a startling image to anchor this, saying they must not only "eat his flesh" but also "drink his blood," shocking his listeners and thereby making even more explicit his demand to be consumed utterly by his followers. John as he wrote this much later would have realized the sacramental overtones readers around AD 80 would see in this, but these overtones are not primary. They do remind us that as we partake of the bread and wine we are symbolizing the body and blood of our Lord, but the main intention here is the demand to give our entire being over to Christ in following him.

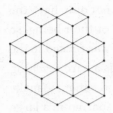

THE LOSS OF SOME DISCIPLES
(6:60–71)

This passage contrasts shallow disciples who lose heart and fall away and desert Jesus (vv. 60–66) with those faithful who are the chosen (vv. 67–71). As we have seen throughout John, Jesus' ministry fomented division, for while he did spectacular sign-miracles, he said things that were both confusing and extremely unsettling. As the Living Revealer of God (the Word, see 1:1), he shone on every person with the light of God (1:4, 7, 9) and overcame the darkness of the world (1:5). However, those of darkness did not want the light and opposed it (3:19–20), and so there could be no neutrality. One embraces either light or darkness, and those who prefer the latter must turn away from him. So all half-hearted disciples (2:23–25) must eventually make a choice, and that is what happens in this passage. Both are found, those who say no (vv. 60–66) and those who say yes (vv. 67–71). The hard sayings of 6:35–58 force final choices, so many of his so-called disciples departed.

SOME GRUMBLE AND FALL AWAY (6:60–66)

First Interaction: Life in the Spirit (6:60–63)

As John states in 1:5, when the light shines in the darkness, the darkness cannot "overcome" it. The light of God in Christ has shone in amazing ways in this discourse, and not only have the unsaved been encountered at the deepest part of their being, so have the disciples. The world of many of them was rocked to the extent that they murmured in verse 60, "This is a hard teaching. Who can accept it?" The hard sayings of Jesus force them to make difficult choices, and so at the synagogue in Capernaum a large group gathers and expresses their consternation.

This was undoubtedly a wider circle of followers, perhaps with some of the Twelve and the fully committed but also many like those in 2:23-25 with only a partial commitment. These were like the rocky soil and thorny ground in the parable of the sower (Mark 4:5-7, 16-19) that wilted as soon as troubles arrived. "Hard" (*skleros*) refers to something that is so harsh that it offends people. As a result, they were unwilling to "hear" or "accept" (*akouō*) it. They found his challenge to eat his flesh and drink his blood offensive, as would most Jews, and had a difficult decision whether to continue to follow him.

Jesus' supernatural insight (NIV: "aware," but literally he "knew in himself") leads him to interpret their murmuring correctly as "grumbling" in verse 61, and so he challenges them regarding the affront they felt at his teaching. Their reaction parallels the Jews in 6:41-42 and the Israelites in the wilderness, so they are acting like unbelievers. Jesus is confronting the darkness that lies within them and exposing it for what it is. If this bothers them, what will they do when (*ean*, "if") they see "the Son of Man ascend to" heaven?

Throughout this chapter Jesus has been depicted as descended from the Father (6:33, 38, 41, 42, 50, 51, 58), so this is not pointing to the future ascension (which is in Luke rather than John) but rather to his return to the Father and his exaltation in his cross and resurrection. In John, the cross is his destiny of being "lifted up" or exalted (3:14; 8:28; 12:32), and the cross is the ultimate scandal for the Jews in John. The theme in the three "lifted up" passages is that when Jesus is lifted up on the cross he is actually being lifted up into glory. Thus the cross is at one and the same time his deepest offense and his greatest glory. The way these disciples react to this crowning moment will determine their eternal destiny.

These disciples, like the Jewish crowds, have understood everything Jesus has been saying at the "fleshly" or earthly level, so Jesus wants them to know in verse 63 that "the flesh counts for nothing," yielding only temporary life, and cannot produce God's salvation. So Jesus turns to the Spirit and completes the trinitarian emphasis in this discourse. Salvation is the work of the Triune Godhead, and within this matrix, "the Spirit gives life."

God controls the gift of eternal life (see 3:16, 36; 5:21a, 24) and has passed that authority on to his Son (see 5:21b, 28–29; 6:27, 33, 35, 39, 40, 48, 50–51, 54, 57). The Father and Son work through the Spirit, for the power to give life is inherent in the Spirit. This is a frequent Old Testament theme (Gen 1:2; Isa 11:2, 44:3, 61:1; Ezek 37:5–6, 9–10; Joel 2:28; Zech 4:6). It is also a New Testament emphasis (Rom 8:4; 1 Cor 15:45; 2 Cor 3:6; Gal 5:16; 6:8) and is central to John's **soteriology** (3:5, 8; 7:37–39; 14:17). It is the Spirit, not human effort (i.e., "flesh"), that brings about eternal life.

Not only is the Spirit the final source of life, but at the same time "the words I have spoken to you—they are full of the Spirit and life." This is inherent in the earlier Bread of Life discourse. Jesus' teaching is filled with the power of the Spirit and produces true life in those who believe and follow them. In the Greek the verb "to be" is repeated before each term, so they have individual emphasis. As the Living Revealer and the very voice of God (see 1:18), his very words contain divine power to bring the Spirit and to give life.

SECOND INTERACTION: DISBELIEF AND THE SOVEREIGNTY OF GOD (6:64–66)

Addressing the disciples and not the crowds, Jesus cuts to the quick: "Yet there are some of you who do not believe" (v. 64). He knows that the reaction of many is not just doubt but actual unbelief, and he wants them to be aware that he knows. His omniscient insight, so much a part of this Gospel (1:38, 47; 4:17-18), is on full display, as John tells us he knew their hearts "from the beginning." Then in keeping with the central theme of the cross in these verses, John adds "and who would betray him." The present desertion of these several quasi-disciples is merely a foretaste of the greater betrayal to come by one of the Twelve, Judas.

Every pastor of a church knows people like these half-hearted participants. Many attend church regularly and seem concerned about spiritual things yet maintain a firm hold on the things of the world, and for many of them following Christ is little more than a guarantee that their life of plenty continues into eternity. There is little true commitment, and they will face the indictment of Matthew 7:21-23 and hear Jesus say in the end, "I never knew you. Away from me, you evildoers!"

Jesus' response in verse 65 is to remind them of what he had said to the unbelieving Jews in 6:37, 44, that "no one can come to me unless the Father has enabled them." In other words, God knew their hearts all along, and they were not among the elect. Clearly we do not save ourselves. Faith itself is a gift from God; "unless the Father has enabled them" is literally, "unless it has been given them by the Father." Salvation is nothing we earn but is entirely a gift from above.

It is at this point that "many of his disciples turned back and no longer followed him" (v. 66). They obviously found his teaching intolerable and were unwilling to take the next step and come to faith in him. We know nothing of how many of this second tier of followers deserted and how many turned with the Twelve back to Jesus. This was a watershed moment for the apostolic band, for Jesus' movement is now to the cross and there is no more playing around with their faith commitment. Nor is it likely that the "seventy-two other disciples" of Luke 10:1 or the 120 in the upper room in Acts 1:15 represented all the followers—almost certainly not. Still, there was never a huge number, so this was a significant event.

THE TWELVE REMAIN FAITHFUL (6:67–71)

With the unfaithful followers leaving, Jesus turns to the Twelve and asks (probably in a hurt voice), "You do not want to leave too, do you?" He knew their hearts (2:24–25; 6:64b) but wanted to challenge them regarding the level of their commitment. Are they willing to go all the way and consume Jesus entirely? As usual, Peter speaks up for all of them. His response becomes a pledge of allegiance to Jesus and the new kingdom he is inaugurating. This is the Fourth Gospel's equivalent to the Caesarea Philippi episode of the **Synoptics** (Mark 8:27–33 and parallels) when Jesus' disciples declare their final commitment to him.

Peter begins with the heart of the issue in verse 68: "Lord, to whom shall we go?" It is the polar opposite to the quasi-disciples who left, for they were wondering, "Why should we stay?" In contrast, Peter starts with the assumption of their belief in Jesus. They follow only him and cannot conceive of turning aside. The other religious options simply fell into nothingness in comparison with Jesus. They had indeed consumed Jesus the Bread of Life and so had the faith to accept the difficult teachings of 6:22–58. They did not want to follow anyone or anything else, for they realized only his teachings consisted of "Spirit and life."

Peter goes on, "You have the words of eternal life." The issue was "life," and neither Judaism nor any other religious option could provide everlasting life in heaven with God. In the process of coming to commitment, he adds (v. 69), "We have come to believe and to know," with the verbs in the perfect tense describing their spiritual state in Christ. This is where they are in life, existing in the state of believing and knowing the reality that Christ is "the Holy One of God." These two verbs, "believe" and "know," are the most frequent and important verbs in this book, describing faith commitment to Jesus and the knowledge that results from it. Christianity is a highly intellectual religion, demanding constant inquiry into the divine truths made known to us in God's revealed word.

This title, "Holy One of God," must be added to those we have already seen—the Word (1:1–18), the one and only Son/God (1:14, 18), Messiah (1:41), Son of God (1:49), King of Israel (1:49), Son of Man (1:51), Bread of Life (6:35). The title here is found elsewhere only in Mark 1:24 and Luke 4:34, when a demon is forced to confess this of Jesus. In the Old Testament, God is labeled the Holy One, indicating that he is set apart from all other gods. It is also used of God's chosen leaders (Judg 13:7; Ps 106:16) or priests (Lev 21:6–7). Here in John the "holy Father" sets Jesus apart as his own (10:36). Peter is recognizing Jesus as set apart by God to be his chosen Messiah.

Jesus links the Twelve with himself as set apart by confessing, "Have I not chosen you, the Twelve?" (v. 70). They too are set apart as chosen ones and belong to God. It is hard to know whether in this Jesus detected a note of pride in Peter and the others, as if they had selected him (as indeed, disciples of rabbis normally did). He lets them know that he, not they, is sovereign over salvation and chose them.

He also tells them that as a group they are not truly committed all the way: "Yet one of you is a devil." In 6:64 we were told of Jesus' supernatural knowledge that one of them "would betray him," and here he imparts that knowledge to the disciples themselves. He labels him a minion of Satan in verse 70, and then John explains to his readers in verse 71 which one of the Twelve Jesus was referring to: "Judas, the Son of Simon Iscariot."[1] In 17:12 Jesus will call him "the one doomed to destruction." Here he calls him "a devil," meaning he is under the control of Satan, who will use him to send Jesus to his death. In 13:2, 27, Satan first prompts Judas and then enters into him, possessing him for that final terrible betrayal. Jesus knew Judas from the start for what he was, but Jesus was in complete control even of this. He chose Judas for the

---

1. The second term in ancient names is always the place of origin, so this means "Simon from the village of Kerioth," either the one in Judea or the one in Moab (we cannot know).

Twelve knowing what he would do, probably because it was God's will that he fulfill the prophecies of betrayal.

————

In this section, we move from the strong image of the security of the believer (6:37–40, 44) to the question of apostasy on the part of some. It is hard to imagine the impact this discourse had on these followers, who had never heard anything like it. In the larger group of those who adhered to Jesus were undoubtedly people at various depths of commitment, and quite a few had barely come to grips with the fact that he was the expected Messiah and were not ready for this Bread of Life and Lamb of God imagery. So when he said they must be willing to eat his flesh and drink his blood, they too understood it literally and were offended. His answer to them in verses 62–63 is that they were not just responding to him but to the Spirit as well, for the Spirit of God gives life.

Jesus reminds them in verses 64–66 that only God "enables" salvation, and so their quasi-allegiance in Jesus is in his hands, and they will answer to God. We are reminded that when people play games with God and stumble around in their spiritual walk, they will answer to God for their half-hearted faith. In this episode, these quasi-disciples made a final decision to turn back and quit following Jesus. They would spend eternity in hellfire as a result. We must remember that "our 'God is a consuming fire'" (Heb 12:29), and he is not to be trifled with.

We must respond with Peter in verse 68 and make our pledge of allegiance to him. There is nowhere else to go or turn, for eternal life can only be found in Jesus. Shallow Christians must be made to realize the folly of placing earthly pleasure above heavenly reward. We cannot live for this world and have eternity as well. We can enjoy the gifts God gives us in our earthly existence, but we dare not dwell and depend on them. There must be balance, and our commitment must be entirely in Jesus. Our eternal destiny is at stake.

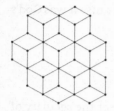

JESUS AT THE FEAST
OF TABERNACLES

(7:1–52)

The text says "after this," but we are not meant to understand that this happened immediately after; the Feast of Tabernacles took place about six months after Passover, in September-October. John's interest here is not in chronology but in showing how Jesus culminates the meaning of the Jewish feasts in himself. Tabernacles was the harvest festival and one of the better-attended of the festivals (see below). Some question whether the fulfillment of the feasts is central enough to serve as a marker in outlining John. In and of itself it isn't (the theme of conflict with the Jews is even more central in these chapters), but chapters 5–10 are organized around four of the seven feasts (Sabbath, Passover, Tabernacles, Dedication), and the theme of Jesus fulfilling the Jewish festivals in himself is well worthy of being featured.

This is the third feast Jesus has attended (Sabbath, ch. 5; Passover, ch. 6), and as before the two primary things are **christological** revelation and the conflict it engendered between the Jewish people and Jesus. The opposition intensifies, and in chapters 7 and 8 four scenes involve attempts to arrest Jesus. This is occasioned by the deep teaching of Jesus regarding himself, as he once more reveals he is the God-sent envoy and teacher (7:16–19) who has come from God (7:28–30). He adds that he will be the source of the Holy Spirit (7:37–39) and the light of the world (8:12). This led to increased opposition to his revelation that even though they thought of Abraham as their father (8:39), in reality their true father was the devil (8:44). He fulfills the imagery of this Feast of Tabernacles, both the water ceremony, which occurs in the morning (7:37–39), and the light ceremony, which occurs at night (8:12).

JESUS' BROTHERS ATTEMPT TO
GET HIM TO GO (7:1–13)

THE FESTIVAL DRAWS NEAR (7:1–2)

At the outset, we learn why Jesus was reluctant to go to Judea. The people of Judea were much more strict and conservative than those in Galilee, with the result that there were many there who wished to execute Jesus for blasphemy (see John 5:18; Mark 3:6). He remained in Galilee for a time, perhaps as long as a year. This time dominates the portrayal of Jesus' ministry in the **Synoptics**, in which Jesus did not go back to Jerusalem until passion week. It says in verse 1 that Jesus "did not want to go," showing that he is in charge. This begins a critical theme of this section: Jesus' sovereignty over the events that are to transpire. He chooses what to do and does not allow events to control him.

But verse 2 tells us that it was fall, and the Feast of Tabernacles was drawing near. It was a harvest festival, celebrating the gathering of grapes and olives (wheat and barley were in May and June). It was also an **eschatological** feast, a time of special joy because it represented the future hopes regarding the coming of the Messiah with his final kingdom. The Jewish historian Josephus called it the most joyous of the festivals (*Antiquities* 8.100). During the festival, the people built tents or "booths" to live in out of leaves and branches, and there was spontaneous breaking out of singing and dancing by groups everywhere. The name is associated with the wilderness wanderings, when the people of Israel lived in tents, and God dwelt among them in his own tent or tabernacle. As one of three pilgrimage festivals where all adult Jewish males were expected to attend (with Passover and Pentecost), there would have been huge throngs of people in the vicinity of Jerusalem.

THE TEMPTATION TO PROVE HIMSELF (7:3–5)

It is natural that Jesus' brothers would want him to go with them to attend the festival. His brothers (see 2:12) were unbelievers during his life and were probably not converted until his resurrection appearances (1 Cor 15:7). Two of them later became leaders in the church and wrote letters that were later included in the New Testament (James and Jude). At this time they had seen some of his miracles but still did not believe his claims. Partly so that he could prove himself to them, they wanted him to go with them for the festival "so that your disciples there may see the works you do" (v. 3). When they ask him to "leave Galilee and go to Judea," this may imply more than just a pilgrimage but involve a semi-permanent move. It is hard to know.

Either way, they assume Jesus wants to be a "public figure," and this means he would stop acting "in secret" and to do so he would have to openly "show [himself] to the world" (v. 4). They are hardly stating that his disciples didn't yet believe and needed to see more works. Their question is from their own standpoint and probably assumes that there are disciples in Judea who need to see miraculous works similar to those shown to his followers in Galilee. The miracles they want would be those that would glorify Jesus himself rather than God.

Their reasoning is logical. Jesus wanted a public ministry so needed to publicly "show himself to the world" via miracles. This urging is similar to Satan's temptation in the wilderness in Matthew 4:1–11, saying in effect, "You've got it, now flaunt it." In essence they were daring him to prove himself first to them and then to the "world," Jew and Gentile alike (as in 1:10; 3:16; 4:42; 6:51). They were tempting him to perform self-centered miracles purely to garner fame and fortune. Jesus would indeed prove himself to be Son of God and Savior, but not in the way they wanted. His demonstration would involve a cross and an empty tomb. The false nature of their challenge to Jesus is seen in the added comment in verse 5 that at this time they "did not believe in him," which shows that their requests did not proceed from a pure heart.

Jesus' Rejoinder to His Brothers (7:6–9)

Jesus recognizes the nature of their challenge and so responds, "My time is not yet here," referring to his time of destiny established by his Father (see 2:4; 7:30; 8:20; 13:1; 17:1).[1] They want him to fit their sense of the right time, and for them, as Jesus says, "any time will do." They saw this as the time or opportunity when Jesus could act in such a way to become famous, and any time is the right time if that is all you want. In reality, God's time is not their time; it is "not yet here" and won't be until the God-appointed "hour" of Jesus' passion.

Interestingly, in 2:4 he separated himself from a similar request on the part of his mother, saying "My hour has not yet come." Now he does the same with his brothers. In both cases he is following the true "hour" set by his Father. The right time would involve the radically different sign of the cross. Then the public manifestation would not be an act of power but a time of suffering. Their hour could take place any time, but his hour depended on his Father's will.

His brothers and their perspective are aligned not with God but with the world, so Jesus says, "The world cannot hate you, but it hates me" (v. 7). Theirs was a worldly sense of time with a worldly purpose, so what they asked would be lauded by the world. Jesus accuses the world of doing evil. The world, filled with darkness, hates the light (3:19–20), and when Jesus exposes it for what it is,

---

1. Normally the term for this in John is *hora* (2:4; 7:20), but here it is *kairos*, normally used for qualitative "time" or "season." However, in John the two are synonyms, and this too speaks of his time of destiny.

it turns against him (3:20). It hates Jesus because, as he says, "I testify that its works are evil," which is a legal metaphor picturing Jesus both proving the world's guilt before the divine law court and proving to evildoers themselves that they are guilty (compare the Spirit "convicting the world" in 16:8–11). In all of this his brothers are part of the world and are convicted regarding their own guilt before God.

In verse 8 Jesus tells his brothers to "go to the festival" by themselves, repeating what he has just said: "I am not going up to this festival, because my time has not yet fully come."[2] In saying this, he is rebuking his brothers for their false demands and their worldly desire for him to seek fame and fortune for himself. He would not go the way they wanted—providing public proof to gain attention. Rather, as we will see in verse 10, he would go in the way his Father wanted—in private, to worship God. His time of destiny would not come for a while, but he would bask in the messianic hope of the festival as another pilgrim.

As a result, for a time Jesus "stayed in Galilee" and did not go to Jerusalem with his brothers, refusing to go with their false purpose in mind. He bided his time for a few days and waited on his Father's timing. He had not refused to attend the festival; he refused to attend it with his brothers' sinful expectations in mind.

Jesus' Secret Attendance at the Festival (7:10–13)

Some interpreters have disparaged Jesus for changing his mind, but the truth is exactly the opposite. Jesus' mind is firmly fixed on his Father, and he is determined to do his will. It is mandatory not to go to the feast in the public way his brothers wanted. That would constitute self-centered thinking. It was equally necessary to go the way his Father wished—to worship and celebrate the

---

2. "Fully come" is literally "fulfilled" (plēroō), implying the fulfillment of the messianic hopes of this feast when the Messiah surrenders himself to his God-appointed destiny on the cross.

messianic hope. Against his brothers' request in verse 4, he goes "in secret" in verse 10, determined not to flaunt himself publicly but to be with his Father privately.

In the meantime, the leaders are also wondering about Jesus (v. 11), for his increasing fame has preceded him from Galilee, and they expect him to come. The implications of John's narrative are that they still want to arrest him and see him killed (5:18).

In contrast, the crowds are "murmuring" (NIV: "widespread whispering," but it is the same term as "grumbling," *gongysmos*, in 6:41, 43),[3] with some for Jesus and some against. Many think "he is a good man" (v. 11), undoubtedly due to the good effects of his miracles and of all he was accomplishing in Galilee. Others, in agreement with the leaders, think him a charlatan who "deceives the people." The power of the leaders is seen in verse 13: the crowds are afraid to take part in an open discussion "for fear of the leaders." We will see this again in 9:22, 34–35, when the officials cast anyone supporting Jesus out of the synagogue, in effect excommunicating them. They are now forcing the public to agree with them, using the threat of religious and social ostracism as a weapon to get their way.

JESUS HAS AUTHORITY TO TEACH
AT THE FESTIVAL (7:14-24)

In what follows, I along with several other interpreters see two cycles, each with three parts:

	Cycle 1	Cycle 2
Jesus teaches	14–24	37–39
Debate and speculation	25–32	40–44
Attempts to arrest	33–36	45–52

---

3. This is not as negative as in 6:41, 43, and depicts discussion behind the scenes.

FIRST INTERCHANGE: HIS ORIGINS (7:14–18)

In verse 14 John tells us that Jesus did not go until "halfway through the festival" in order to separate himself completely from his brothers. He likely spent those early days in private worship (7:10). They had wanted him to go and show off his sign-miracles at the feast, which Jesus refused because it would be at cross-purposes with his God-sent purpose as the Divine Revealer. However, he did "begin to teach," because that would fulfill his Father's will for him to be the voice of God to the people. In the midst of the tensions aroused by the leaders, he could no longer keep quiet. He was indeed showing himself to the world (7:4) but not in the way his brothers or the leaders wanted. He came with words, not works.

As a result, the Jewish people there are "amazed" (v. 15) by the depth of his knowledge and say, "How did this man get such learning without having been taught?" It was pretty much demanded at the time that someone speaking like a rabbi have training under a rabbi. One passage from the Talmud (b. Sotah 22b) says that a person who studies Torah without formal rabbinic training is no better than a common person who knows nothing. Such comments were often made about Jesus (Matt 13:54–56; Mark 1:22; Luke 2:47; 4:22) and the apostles (Acts 4:13). In our day, this would be like asking, "How could you know anything without going to one of the major seminaries?" Yet I know of PhDs who are shallow in their preaching and unschooled preachers who have incredible depth. It is the heart even more than the head that counts. The truth is that with the incredible commentaries available today, a wealth of knowledge is available to us all, and it is actually a question of our motivation to feed the flock that matters most.

In verses 16–18 Jesus reveals the true source of his insights. Their idea of authority was merely education in the right environment (like today), but Jesus' knowledge came from the God who sent him. He was not self-taught, nor was he dependent on the interpretation of others—rabbis, like most scholars today, anchored everything they said in the opinions of those who came before them.

His message came directly from God and thus was divine truth. The prophets always began, "Thus says the Lord," but Jesus did not need to do this. He was the heaven-sent envoy, the Word, the Living Revealer of God's truth. His authority is anchored in who he is.

In fact, Jesus goes on to say the truth of what he is saying is available to anyone who "chooses to do the will of God" (v. 17). Jesus has developed this in more depth at 5:37-38, 41-44, where recognizing Jesus is tied to receiving God's truths, seeking his glory, and being indwelt by his love. Jesus lived entirely on the basis of doing God's will. Those who walk as Jesus walked will know he came from God. The criterion for truth is not so much intellectual as it is ethical. It is a way of living that makes the difference, as in 3:21: "Whoever lives by the truth comes into the light." When it comes to knowing the truth, academic degrees matter less than we often think; I don't even know where any of my diplomas are. My authority comes from the Word of God and the faithfulness with which I study and teach it. My degrees are one of the least important things about me.

If Jesus went by his own ideas, he would be self-seeking. As he says in verse 18, "Whoever speaks on their own does so to gain personal glory." Those who find their own brand of truth and continually come up with new things do so for fame rather than to serve others. This is as true today as it was in Jesus' time, but everything he said and did had one goal—honoring the One who sent him. Thus he is what he commends in verse 18: "a man of truth; there is nothing false about him."

Pride is one of the greatest sins of the average Christian leader. A person who had ministered at several megachurches told me a while ago that narcissism was a given among virtually all the famous pastors. I hope that is an overstatement, but I have seen it all too often. In contrast, Jesus did not just speak truth, he was truth (14:6) and personified the true servant leader of God. As he said in Mark 10:45, "The Son of Man did not come to be served, but to serve."

SECOND INTERCHANGE: MOSES AND AUTHORITY (7:19–24)

In verse 19 Jesus challenges the authority of the leaders on the basis of their lack of obedience to the law of Moses. Their lack of righteousness is proved by their willing transgression of the Torah. He shows that while Moses has "given [them] the law," none of them "keeps the law." On a previous visit to Jerusalem, the authorities had tried to arrest him on capital charges (5:18; 7:1), and they would do so again (7:32, 45; 8:59). So he asks, "Why are you trying to kill me?" In this way they were transgressing the most serious of the laws and guilty of attempting to murder a righteous, innocent man. Moses had written a testimony to Jesus' ministry and status before God (5:45–47), and now he was a further witness to their violation of the law.

In verse 20 the crowd joins the leaders in the response to Jesus' charges, erupting and saying, "You are demon-possessed," which in the first century was equivalent to saying, "You're crazy" (as in 10:20, "He is demon-possessed and raving mad"). Few in the crowd felt any animosity to Jesus, and none were aware of the leaders' plans, so to them he was simply delusional and paranoid. As a result they rose up in defense of the leaders.

Christ responds to the crowds in 7:21–22 by continuing the theme regarding the Jewish observance of the law. He returns to the event that led to the charge against him: the healing of the lame man on the Sabbath (5:1–15). They were "amazed" at the miracle, but they reacted more to the fact that he broke the oral tradition by healing on the Sabbath. Jesus responds by reminding them that they too broke that tradition when they obeyed Moses' law of circumcision, referring to the rule that a male child be circumcised on the eighth day after birth, even if that day fell on the Sabbath (Lev 12:3).[4]

As Jesus explains in verse 23, he is making two points, both based on the principle of reasoning from the greater to the lesser:

---

4. This is further developed in the **Mishnah**: m. Shabbat 18:3; 19:1–3.

(1) Since circumcision came through the patriarchs, it had priority over the laws of Moses, especially oral traditions. (2) This established a legal precedent followed by Jesus when he healed on the Sabbath. The "work" of circumcision is the higher good and valid as a Sabbath activity, and as such it does not violate the Sabbath laws. If that is true of circumcision, which affects only a small part of the body, how much more is it true of healing, which affects the whole body. Moreover, Jesus is doing the work of God in bringing God's saving presence to bear on the lame man and healing him.

Since Jesus' healing on the Sabbath, like circumcision, is the greater good, these leaders and crowds must "stop judging by mere appearances" (v. 24). Jesus is accusing them of judging wrongly on the basis of a superficial use of the law. Theirs was an earthly perspective on the law, ignoring the divine or heavenly perspective, and they needed to see the situation of healing on the Sabbath from God's viewpoint. Then they would realize that Jesus was not breaking the Sabbath but was actually upholding its true purpose. He was a law-keeper, not a lawbreaker.

THE PEOPLE DEBATE OVER WHETHER JESUS IS THE MESSIAH (7:25-32)

His Earthly Origins (7:25-27)

The scene changes from the previous dialogue of verses 19-24, centered on pilgrims to Jerusalem from Galilee and the diaspora (the lands outside Palestine) who were not aware of the authorities' desire to arrest and kill Jesus (7:20). Now "some of the people of Jerusalem" enter the debate and start challenging him. They know the situation and so now ask, "Isn't this the man they are trying to kill?" They are surprised that a "wanted man" so bold as to challenge the leaders could have such a public persona without being arrested (7:26). The authorities had never been so tentative in handling others. Could they have studied the evidence and "concluded that he is the Messiah?" That would be a remarkable switch given the severity of their opposition to this point.

They consider this possibility only for a moment. Very quickly they change their minds, saying in verse 27, "But we know where this man is from": he is from the insignificant town of Nazareth (1:45–46) and is the village carpenter (Mark 6:3). Jesus' current home with his disciples is Capernaum. However, they reason, "when the Messiah comes, no one will know where he is from." They assume that if they know he cannot be the Messiah, the leaders would be aware of that fact as well.

This doesn't mean they were ignorant of Micah 5:2 and the prophecy of the Messiah's birth in Bethlehem. Rather, it fits a popular belief of the time either that the Messiah would be hidden by God until the divinely appointed hour for his manifestation (see 1 Enoch 48:6; 4 Ezra 7:28, 13:51–52; 2 Baruch 29:3) or, perhaps more likely, that he would be born normally but not recognized until he was made known by God (see Justin Martyr, *Dialogue with Trypho* 8). They figured that since the local Jews had known about Jesus, he could not be the Messiah.

His True Origins (7:28–29)

Jesus speaks out publicly while he is teaching in the "temple courts" and admits that they were partly correct and "know where I am from," but they are only aware of his earthly origins. Jesus' words are laced with irony; this sentence could be paraphrased, "You really think you know where I come from?" They were completely unaware of his true origins, that he actually came from God ("he who sent me"). He is "not here on my own" but is rather carrying out the mission assigned him by his Father.

In this Jesus is accusing the Jewish people of spiritual blindness and ignorance. They know neither God the Father nor Jesus the Son and Christ/Messiah. Moreover, it is the Father and not them who is "true." Jesus is "a man of truth" (7:18) and is "the way and the truth and the life" (14:6) because his Father is "true." He is truly the sovereign God of Scripture, the One who alone can bring salvation and life to his people. This God is unknown to these opponents of Jesus because they have turned away from his only Revealer and rejected his message of salvation.

Only Jesus truly knows God, for two reasons: (1) His origins are from God; and (2) his mission stems from "the one who sent me" (v. 29). These people were proud of their covenant relationship and claimed to know God (Rom 2:17, 23), but Jesus shows that people cannot know the true God until they have come to know his Son. As John said earlier in 1:18, Jesus alone is "the one and only Son, who is himself God and is in closest relationship with the Father." He alone has "made [the Father] known," so these Jews who think they can know God from the law of Moses are tragically mistaken and know nothing of the God of the new covenant in Jesus the Christ. In this new covenant age God has revealed himself anew and shown new vistas of his being that can only be known through Jesus.

ATTEMPT TO ARREST JESUS (7:30–32)

There are three stages to this attempt: some try to seize Jesus but cannot do so (v. 30), the leaders send out the temple police to arrest him (v. 32), and then they are surprised when they come back without having done so (vv. 45–47). This was an ongoing plot to get rid of this troublemaking, blasphemous upstart (5:18; 7:1) and had been a long time coming (see 7:13, 25–26), but the leaders have finally had all they can take and feel they have to act.

The decision to seize him may have been a hasty one; it was futile and no one laid a hand on him because "his hour had not yet come." The authorities were not in charge; God was. This is a primary theme in John's Gospel and refers to the hour of destiny, the "set time" that would "fully come" (Gal 4:4) when God's plan of salvation would be finalized at the cross (John 2:4; 4:23; 7:6; 8:20; 12:23, 27; 13:1; 16:4, 32; 17:1). Their foolish attempt to arrest Jesus and stymie God's plan was doomed until the Father said, "It is time."

In contrast to the leaders, "many in the crowd believed in him" (v. 31). Certainly their faith was incomplete and was anchored in the miraculous signs, like the people described in 2:23-25, but this was an important first step (10:38). While their belief was inadequate in itself, they still realized that Jesus' deeds were worthy of the Messiah and so made a preliminary step of faith and began to follow Jesus (as in v. 27). Certainly, they reasoned, the Messiah will not "perform more signs than this man." They in our day would be called "seekers," or even "pre-disciples."

The leaders learned of the burgeoning faith of many in the crowds and felt they had to put an end to it. The attempt to arrest Jesus in verse 30 now leads to the official decision of the "chief priests and the Pharisees" to carry out the arrest (v. 32), unusual because they were normally opposing parties in the power structure of Judea. Yet they had united in their opposition to Jesus. This was probably an arrest warrant from the ruling council itself, the Sanhedrin, and carried out by the temple police or guards, primarily consisting of Levites whose duty was to keep public order in the temple and at times civic order in the city. So the Sanhedrin sent them to arrest Jesus while he was attracting crowds in the temple area. We will not see the results of this until 7:45-47.

JESUS TEACHES ABOUT HIS DEPARTURE (7:33-36)

As the guards are on the way to arrest Jesus, he explains to the crowds why they are unable to understand him and why his time among them will be short: "I am with you for only a short time, and then I am going to the one who sent me" (v. 33). The time of his passion is mere months away, and it will be time to ascend back to the Father (see 3:13-14; 6:62). Then he will return to the One who has sent him—the God in heaven who has given him his mission in the first place and sent him to earth (6:33, 38, 41, 42, 50, 51, 58). His coming death was not an end to his ministry but the beginning of the next phase of it as well as a return to his preexistent glory (1:1-2; 17:5).

The main point of this paragraph is Jesus' statement that "you will look for me, but you will not find me," which frames the whole passage (v. 34, repeated in v. 36). Jesus' words here contain a double meaning. On the earthly plane, they will seek often to arrest him yet will not be able to find him until the hour appointed by the Father. We will see this in 7:45–47. On the spiritual plane, they will search for God and for eternal life but be unable to find it because they are not willing to turn to Jesus in faith and find God's salvation, for it is contained only in him (14:6, "No one comes to the Father except through me"). Even his own disciples would look for him and be unable to find him (13:33). The difference is that his followers will eventually go to heaven and find him, while these unbelievers will face only judgment from God.

As expected, the Jews who are listening don't get it. With their earthly perspective, they fail to grasp his meaning and start murmuring to each other, "Where does this man intend to go that we cannot find him?" (7:35). Perhaps, they surmise, he is planning to sneak away from Judea and steal away to the diaspora communities, "where our people live scattered among the Greeks." Since his teaching in Judea is going nowhere, they reason, maybe he wants to "teach the Greeks." Most likely that meant he would teach Greek-speaking Jews and Gentile proselytes in other lands rather than live among the non-Jewish Gentiles. There is very little evidence of actual Jewish mission to the Gentiles in the first century. Later, the post-resurrection church would indeed involve a mission to the Greeks, but they through unbelief would have no part in it.

John's repetition of Jesus' words in verse 36 emphasizes the seriousness of their error. In reality Jesus' words served as both a rebuke and an invitation. The knowledge that they at present could not follow Jesus to heaven was a rebuke of their unbelief but at the same time an opportunity to repent and come to Jesus. Their inability and unwillingness to respond meant that they had no hope.

JESUS GIVES THE SPIRIT (7:37–39)

The second cycle of Jesus' ministry at the Feast of Tabernacles (see my comments at 7:14) begins on what John describes as "the last and greatest day of the festival" (v. 37). Tabernacles, like Passover, was a seven-day festival with a solemn assembly on the eighth day that concluded with a celebratory ending (Lev 23:36). Jesus inserts himself into this eighth-day celebration as the fulfillment or culmination of its meaning.

There were two special ceremonies on each of the seven days, and Jesus fulfills both. Every morning there was a water ceremony (fulfilled here in vv. 37–39), and every evening there was a light ceremony (fulfilled in 8:12).[5] These two did not take place on the eighth day, for it was a special joyous day of rest for disassembling the booths, with dancing and the singing of the Hallel psalms (Pss 113–118). Jesus stood and made this proclamation on that special morning, thereby presenting himself as the culmination of the water ceremony.

The water ceremony took place with a procession at dawn every morning. Each previous night the revelers would celebrate the crops God had given them and then in the morning thank God for the rain that made the crops grow. These ceremonies drew on Isaiah 12:3, "With joy you will draw water from the wells of salvation." Each morning the high priest drew water from the pool of Siloam in a golden pitcher. Then he led a procession up to the temple with the blowing of the shofar or trumpet at the morning sacrifices, with the pilgrims shaking *lulabs* or leafy branches, symbolizing the wilderness journey, and holding up a piece of citrus fruit (traditionally a citron or etrog) to symbolize the harvest itself. The procession marched around the altar seven times,

---

5. Both these ceremonies are described in the Mishnah, a rabbinic Jewish source. For the water ceremony, see m. Sukkah 4:1, 9–10; for the light ceremony, see m. Sukkah 5:2–4.

pouring water from the pitcher into a funnel on the side of the altar. As the water flowed around the base of the altar, the temple choir sang the Hallel.

When the water ceremony normally happened on the previous seven days, on the eighth day Jesus "stood and said in a loud voice" that thirsty pilgrims could come and drink of him. As God's envoy he became the source of "the wells of salvation" from Isaiah 12:3, fulfilling the symbolism of the water ceremony and continuing the imagery of the water of life from John 4:10, 11–14; 6:53–56. The joy that characterized the festival was quite evident in what Jesus said, as the Old Testament promise of living water is now realized, and the life the Jewish people have always longed for has now come to them. The two themes of the Feast of Tabernacles—harvest and hope—are combined in Jesus.

The statement itself has occasioned great debate among scholars. The citation of verse 38 ("Scripture has said") does not point to a particular passage but sums up a theme, and commentators debate whether Jesus or the believer is the source of the living water. If the believer is the source, it alludes to Proverbs 18:4 ("the fountain of wisdom is a rushing stream") and Isaiah 58:11 ("You will be like a well-watered garden, like a spring whose waters never fail"). If Christ is the source, it alludes to Zechariah 14:8 ("On that day living water will flow out from Jerusalem," a passage connected with the Feast of Tabernacles) and Ezekiel 47:9 ("where the river flows everything will live"). Jesus then would be seen as fulfilling the rock struck by Moses with the water gushing out (Exod 17:1–6; see Ps 78:16, 20).

The difficulty lies in the Greek itself. A literal translation will help: "Let anyone who is thirsty come to me and drink, the one who believes in me, as Scripture has said, rivers of living water will flow from within that person." The key is how we punctuate the statement. If a period is placed after "drink," the "one who believes" fulfills Scripture and becomes the source of the living water (as in the NIV translation). If we put the period after "the one who believes," then Jesus becomes the source of the living water—"Let anyone who is thirsty come to me and drink, *namely, the one who believes in me*. As Scripture has said, rivers of living water will flow *from him* [namely, Jesus]." We could also put the two aspects in the first part together and translate, "Let the thirsty person who believes in me come to me and drink."

Both translations are viable. The Eastern church fathers (like Origen) and many current scholars favor the interpretation with believers as the source. The Western church fathers (like Tertullian) and a nearly equal number of current scholars favor Christ as the source. If "the one who believes" begins verse 38 (as in the NIV), it would be the only place in the New Testament where the Scripture formula comes in the middle of a verse, but this is still quite possible and is found in virtually every translation. My problem with the "believer" interpretation is that the imagery would be of thirsty believers first drinking and then giving out the water to others, a possible but somewhat unlikely metaphor.

I think it is best in this context to see Christ inviting believers to drink and then himself distributing the water to them. Christ, rather than the believer, is the focus throughout chapters 7–10. The believers are the recipients of the Spirit, not the distributors of the Spirit—the giver of the Spirit in John is Jesus. This fits the Fourth Gospel better, with Christ sending out the Spirit in 14:26; 16:7. Moreover, Jesus speaking of himself in the third person ("flow from *him*") fits his use of "Son of Man" for himself, and so Christ pictures himself (rather than the believer) fulfilling the water ceremony.

We have already seen water as a symbol for the outpouring of the Holy Spirit in 3:5, a theme that continues here. Rabbis often linked the water ceremony with the promised Holy Spirit and called the temple courtyard "the house of the water-drawing" (y. Sukkah 5.1, 55a; Ruth Rabbah 4:8). So Jesus fulfills further prophecy by giving the Spirit to believers. The time for this is also clear in verse 39:

"Up to that time the Spirit had not been given, since Jesus had not yet been glorified."

The Spirit did not come during Jesus' life but awaited his entering into glory upon his death and resurrection, and then came at Pentecost (Acts 2). This in fact is the theme of Jesus' Farewell Discourse in chapters 14–17: he must depart so the Spirit may come. The Spirit would culminate Jesus' mission. Jesus provided the gift, and the Spirit was the operative force who carried out the directive. The age of the Spirit took place after Christ's departure and was launched in the resurrection appearances and Pentecost.

THE CROWD IS DIVIDED (7:40–44)

At the end of Jesus' message in the closing days of the Feast of Tabernacles, the crowd, similar to the Sanhedrin delegation's questions of John the Baptist in 1:19–22, asks Jesus whether he might be the prophet like Moses from Deuteronomy 18:15 (see 6:14) or the Messiah. The Moses prophet fits the manna imagery behind chapter 6, and the water imagery of 7:37–38 would fit the water from the rock in Exodus 17. Many Jews separated the two figures in messianic expectation, and that seems to be the case here.

However, as noted in 7:27, quite a few doubted that Jesus could be the Messiah due to his origins in Galilee. He grew up in Nazareth, and that excluded him, for Scripture prophesied that the Messiah would "come from David's descendants and from Bethlehem, the town where David lived" (7:42). Second Samuel 7:12–16 and Psalm 89:3–4 demand that the Messiah have Davidic origins, and Micah 5:2 identifies Bethlehem in Judea as his birthplace.

As a result the crowd is divided over Jesus and what they should do about him (v. 43). In verse 44 many "wanted to seize" and arrest him, "but no one laid a hand on him" because his hour of God-appointed destiny had not yet arrived (see 7:30; 8:20). Everywhere Jesus goes in John's Gospel he encounters the darkness in every person (1:5, 9), leading to negative reactions as the darkness rejects the light of God (3:19–20).

THE LEADERS ARE UNABLE TO
ARREST JESUS (7:45-52)

In verse 45 the group of temple police from verse 32 returns empty-handed to "the chief priests and the Pharisees" from their futile attempt to arrest Jesus (see 7:11, 30, 32). They had been gone about four days, since they left around the fourth day of the feast (7:14, 30, "halfway through the festival") and it was now the eighth day (7:37). In all that time they had been unable to arrest Jesus, even though he had been in the open, teaching in the temple courts (7:14). The dialogue recorded in these last verses must be a summary of this four-day ministry at the feast.

THE REASON: JESUS' INCREDIBLE MESSAGE (7:45-46)

It is not that there were no opportunities to arrest him. The crowds could not lay a hand on him (v. 44), and apparently neither could the temple guards. This seems very strange, but remember that they were not professional soldiers but Levites, and they may have got caught up in the religious fervor of the festival or been mesmerized by the power of Jesus' teaching. Perhaps they forgot their assignment and so could only respond to the leaders, "No one ever spoke the way this man does" (v. 46). They had ceased being police and instead became pilgrims spellbound by Jesus' deep truths. Amazingly, these police became witnesses to the Sanhedrin that his words were indeed "Spirit and life" (6:63). This does not mean they were converted but rather that they were stirred to the depth of their being. Some may have been converted, but we are not told.

THE COUNTERCHARGE OF THE LEADERS (7:47-49)

The officials react harshly and accuse these Levitical police of being deceived by Jesus and no better than the fickle crowds. Jesus then is a deceiver (7:12), a blasphemer who has led these Levites astray into dangerous heresy, and they have been so weak as to allow themselves to be caught up in this falsehood. There is a great deal of irony in the next two verses, for one of their own (Nicodemus) is about to speak up on Jesus' behalf.

In verse 48 these leaders ask the Levitical guards, "Have any of the rulers or of the Pharisees believed in him?" and then they answer their own question: "No!" They are about to be proved wrong one verse later. For the time being, they are correct as far as these Levites know, and now the officials shame them further by linking them with "this mob that knows nothing of the law—there is a curse on them" and apparently on these temple guards as well. The Pharisaical contempt toward "the people of the land" (in Hebrew, *am ha'arets*) is evident, and these leaders believe that their ignorance of the law places them under the covenant curse (Deut 27:26; Ps 119:21; Jer 11:3). They claim that these Levites should know the law and should never have allowed themselves to join this ignorant rabble in their deception.

NICODEMUS'S CORRECTION OF THE OFFICIALS (7:50-52)

In no time at all, Nicodemus proves them wrong. In verse 50 John reminds us that he "had gone to Jesus earlier" (3:1-15) and at the same time, as a Pharisee and member of the Sanhedrin, "was one of their own number" (see 3:1). He may not yet have become a believer, but at the same time he did not share their unbelief. There is no evidence that any of the members of the Sanhedrin had yet become followers of Jesus, but at Jesus' death and burial we are told of two members of the Sanhedrin who had become followers—Nicodemus and Joseph of Arimathea, described as a "secret disciple" due to fear of the other leaders (19:38). The pressure on commoners against speaking well of Jesus (7:13) was felt even more by the leaders, and it took a great deal of courage for Nicodemus to step up at this point.

Since these officials claimed they were experts on the law (7:49), Nicodemus raises a point of law. In verse 51 he says, "Does our law condemn a man without first hearing him to find out what he has been doing?" This is not a direct citation of Torah, but it comes close to several passages. Deuteronomy 1:16 says, "Hear the disputes between your people and judge fairly" (see also Deut 17:2–5; 19:15–19; Exodus Rabbah 21:3). "Find out" translates the Greek *gnō*, from *ginōskō*, to "understand" what Jesus is actually saying. Nicodemus realizes how the other officials are twisting Jesus' claims.

The leaders have no answer; he is right. So in verse 52 they resort to ad hominem slurs, deriding him as being "from Galilee," an insult equivalent to labeling him a provincial nincompoop. Then they turn to Jesus' origins, repeating 7:41 and declaring that "a prophet does not come out of Galilee." In reality they are wrong, for Jonah and Nahum were from Galilee, and the rabbis whose words were later recorded in the Talmud stated that prophets had arisen from every tribe (b. Sukkah 27b). They undoubtedly knew this but were so opposed to Jesus that they were not thinking logically. When they said, "Look into it," they were condemning themselves, for their error would take little time to discover. In one sense they are correct. Jesus' true origin is from heaven, as we have been reminded again and again in John (3:13, 31; 6:33, 50, 51, 58), but they remain ignorant of that essential truth.

———

At the beginning of this passage, Jesus' brothers parallel the temptation narrative from the Synoptic Gospels by trying to lure Jesus to produce a miracle that would make him famous (7:1–13). This Jesus would not do and refused to accompany them to Jerusalem under false pretenses. He served his Father and his calling and would not sully his God-appointed purpose in such a way. This is a very common temptation that many Christian leaders experience, and far too many yield and conduct their ministry to get ahead rather than to serve God. Jesus would not go publicly but would go in order to worship God privately. Still, when he went he had to teach as the Living Revealer and envoy of God (7:14–24).

In this he was characterized by a servant's heart, a lack of desire to "gain personal glory" (7:18) and a commitment to the centrality of God and his mission to the world. That is the model for servant leadership in our day as well.

In 7:25-36 we see a uniting of former opponents—the common people with the leaders and the chief priests with the Pharisees within the Sanhedrin. They came together in their opposition to Jesus (vv. 30-32), assuming that no Jewish peasant from Galilee could be the Messiah. John spells out their tragic error in verses 33-36. They have only an earthly perspective and fail to understand Jesus' true heavenly origins. As a result, they are completely unable to comprehend the divine truths he espouses and are doomed in their unbelief. This is the problem in our time as well, as sinful humanity wants nothing to do with Jesus and so invents reasons for turning away from him.

For those who do turn to Jesus, an incredible promise awaits, and this truly fulfills the meaning of the Feast of Tabernacles in Jesus. The water procession every morning signified the spiritual harvest and the Old Testament promises of the giving of the Spirit by the Messiah to the people of God. So in 7:37-39 Jesus pictures himself distributing the living water, the Holy Spirit, to his followers. This is one of the greatest of the events awaiting God's true people, who turn to Jesus and believe. For us, this takes place at conversion (Rom 8:14-17), when the Spirit enters us and begins to empower us to live the Christian life.

The rest of the passage (7:40-52) returns to the intense conflict between Jesus and his opponents. They are like many today who hate everything Christian and look for ways to make God's people look bad. They have "exchanged the truth about God for a lie" (Rom 1:25) and hate the light of God, preferring the darkness, which fits their chosen lifestyle (John 3:19-20).

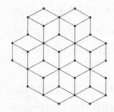

EXCURSUS: THE WOMAN CAUGHT IN ADULTERY

(7:53–8:11)

This is a famous story because it shows the grace of God in Christ through the forgiving of a woman who has committed adultery. However, at the same time it was undoubtedly not a part of John's Gospel and was likely added by Christian scribes early in the second century. The text-critical evidence is quite decisive. It is missing from nearly all the early manuscripts (𝔓66, 𝔓75, ℵ, A^vid, B, C^vid, L, N, T, W, 037, 038, 044). No Greek church father commented on this story before the twelfth century, and it is not found in the older translations of the New Testament (Old Latin, Syriac, Coptic). The only older manuscript containing it is D (Codex Bezae), but that codex is notorious for containing extra material. (Its version of Acts is 10 percent longer!) It is also placed in various places by later scribes—after Luke 21:38; John 7:36; 44; or 21:25. Almost certainly John did not have the story in his Gospel.

At the same time, nearly everyone believes the story actually happened. The church historian Eusebius in his *Ecclesiastical History* (39.16) mentions a similar story from Papias early in the second century, and it is also found in the third century *Didascalia Apostolorum* (ch. 7). Most current scholars place its addition to the Gospel of John in the second century, possibly because adultery was being treated then as a virtually unforgivable sin, and leaders wanted the church to realize God's forgiveness extended to sexual sins as well. So I would conclude that it is not canonical, but it is most likely a true story from Jesus' ministry.

The setting is in Jerusalem. Jesus is there possibly for one of the feasts or perhaps during passion week. The scene fits Luke 21:37–38, with Jesus staying on the Mount of Olives (probably in Bethany) and teaching in the temple courts every morning. His popularity with the crowds is evident, as is his opposition from the leaders.

The scribes and Pharisees interrupt Jesus while he is teaching and bring to him a woman who has been caught in an adulterous liaison, probably the night before. Scribes were legal experts, in a sense lawyers, who interpreted the laws for the rest of Judaism. In an act of wanton cruelty, they have held her incommunicado throughout the night without a trial, and they are using her shame to set a trap for Jesus. Their lack of concern for the woman is quite evident.

The law was clear. Stoning was demanded only if a virgin engaged to be married was caught, and then both the virgin and the man were to be stoned (Deut 22:23–24). But such legalities were not of interest to these scribes; they wished only to trap Jesus into saying something they could use against him (John 8:6). Jesus, not the woman, was actually on trial, and justice was not a part of the scene. If he said too little, they could accuse him of being ignorant of the law. If he said too much, they could accuse him before the Romans, who did not allow the Jews to execute people (see 18:31).

Jesus' reaction is noteworthy. Still sitting (his rabbinic teaching mode), he bends over and begins writing in the dust. Much has been said about his possible message: Augustine argued that it was Jeremiah 17:13 ("Those who turn away from you will be written in the dust"); Jerome, that it was the sins of the accusers. Or perhaps it was the sentence Jesus would deliver (the Romans would write down a sentence and then read it aloud). We cannot know for certain.

As he is writing, the Jewish leaders keep hounding him for a response, so he finally speaks: "Let any one of you who is without sin be the first to throw a stone" (8:7). This would fit the Jeremiah quotation above as Jesus shifted the focus from the woman to their own sins. In Deuteronomy 13:9 and 17:7 the official witnesses to a capital violation of the law would cast the first stones. Jesus would be following Matthew 7:1–5 ("Don't judge" when you have sin in your life) and saying in effect, "Who is ready to witness against her when God's witness stands against you?" Jesus then writes once more in the dust, probably the same message as before, to anchor their guilt before God.

None of the bystanders are "without sin," and so the former accusers drift away one by one, the oldest first (due to Jewish deference to the elderly, but probably also because they were more aware of their sins). Those who have shamed her now feel the shame of their own harsh actions, and they can only leave until she stands alone with Jesus. He then speaks for the first time and addresses her as she undoubtedly stands with head bowed, "Woman, where are they? Has no one condemned you?" They have all left, and the verdict is left to Jesus.

His sentence is clear: "Neither do I condemn you." Jesus had the God-given authority to judge (John 5:22, 30) and also to forgive (Mark 2:5–11; Luke 7:48–49). The point here is that forgiveness places a moral and spiritual obligation on the individual, so Jesus adds, "Go now and leave your life of sin." Jesus with his omniscient awareness knew the sins she had committed. She was clearly guilty, and her life of sin had to end with this experience of God's forgiveness.

———

This is a powerful model of forgiveness available to sinners. In this story the sin of the callous leaders is greater than that of the woman. Her guilt is evident, but their guilt supersedes hers, for they care nothing for truth and justice and want only to trap Jesus and turn the crowds and the Romans against him. So there are two messages here, the judgment heaped on those who are unforgiving and unrepentant and the forgiveness available to those who will stand before God with heads bowed and seek his mercy. A third message is also critical—when we are forgiven we are responsible before God to change our sinful ways and live righteous lives from that point on.

I believe the story of the woman caught in adultery is indeed true and quite meaningful today, but it was not part of John until the second century and is not inspired Scripture. Therefore, I could not make it the basis of a sermon or Bible study. But it could be used as an illustration of forgiveness in a sermon dealing with sexual sin in the church from a text like 1 Thessalonians 4:3-8, and that is exactly how I have used it in my own ministry.

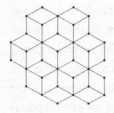

JESUS THE LIGHT OF THE WORLD
(8:12–30)

As mentioned in the previous chapter, two ceremonies were featured each day of the Festival of Tabernacles, the water ceremony each morning and the light ceremony each evening. Jesus is seen fulfilling the first in 7:37-39, and he fulfills the second in the "I am" saying here in verse 12, "I am the light of the world." As in chapters 5 and 7, conflict is featured in the rest of the chapter. The level of intensity is higher in this section, for in chapter 7 the crowds and leaders interrogated Jesus while here Jesus as the Judge (see 5:22, 30; 9:39) brings formal charges against this apostate Jewish people. The material breaks into two major sections, first the witnesses that authenticate the authority of the Son to judge (8:12-30), and second Jesus' charge that the devil, not Abraham, is their true father and that God is his Father, leading to his claim to be the "I AM" (vv. 31-59).

JESUS HAS AUTHORITY AS THE
LIGHT OF THE WORLD (8:12-20)

THESIS: THE LIGHT OF THE WORLD (8:12)

This is the second of the seven "I am" statements (see commentary on 6:35), and it forms the second exploration of themes from the feast of chapter 7. Remember that in the original Gospel this verse followed immediately after 7:52 and therefore constituted Jesus' second address on his fulfilling the two ceremonies, here the light ceremony in the evening. So it begins, "When Jesus spoke *again* to the people," designating the second of three messages (with 7:14–52 and 8:21–30).

At dusk, the priests would light four huge lamps in the court of women in the temple, high enough that they had to climb ladders to light them. At the top each lampstand had four golden bowls filled with oil, with the worn-out undergarments of the priests used for wicks. This took place on the Temple Mount, the highest point in Jerusalem, and it was said that all of Jerusalem was lit by these lamps. There was singing and dancing throughout the night, and the joyous celebrating became legendary in later Judaism. Jesus states in verse 12 that he as the light of God (1:4, 7, 9) illumines not just Jerusalem but the whole world. He spoke these words while standing in the treasury "where the offerings were put" (8:20) in the court of women, meaning he was standing beneath these golden bowls as he spoke.

As in 7:37–39, when he used the water imagery, Jesus' focus now shifts from himself to his followers and the blessings that will be poured over them. Here "whoever follows me will never walk in darkness, but will have the light of life." In 1:5 the darkness will never "overcome" the light, and in 3:20 those who walk in the light will triumph over darkness. In the Old Testament the presence of God was symbolized in the **Shekinah**, the pillar of fire by night and the cloud by day (Exod 13:21–22; Ps 78:14), and God's salvation is pictured as light in Psalm 27:1, "The LORD is my light and my salvation" (also Ps 44:3; Isa 60:19–20). Light symbolized God's word (Ps 119:105) and Israel as called to be "a light for the Gentiles" (Isa 49:6, also Isa 9:2).

While Zechariah 14:8 underlies the water ceremony (see the commentary on 7:37–38), Zechariah 14:6–7 undergirds the light ceremony, declaring that when the day of Yahweh arrived it would be "continuous day. ... There will be no normal day and night, for at evening time it will still be light" (NLT). Jesus is proclaiming here that he is bringing a new light from God not only for the Jews but for the entire world. His listeners can partake of that new gift of salvation by following him, with the result that the darkness of sin and death will recede and disappear (John 1:5; 3:19-20; 12:35-36, 46). Jesus' own people had rejected him and chosen the path of darkness (1:11), but if they turned back to him they would have "the light that leads to life" (NLT). Israel was delivered by the pillar of fire, and Jesus here promises the greater deliverance to eternal life by following him as the light of God.

FIRST CHALLENGE: THE VALIDITY OF HIS AUTHORITY (8:13-18)

The most vociferous of Jesus' opponents (John 4:1; 5:16-18; 7:32, 45-48), the Pharisees bring up a legal issue here. Jesus has been making claims about himself, so they charge, "Here you are, appearing as your own witness; your testimony is not valid." As Jesus himself admitted in 5:31, they are legally correct. Deuteronomy 19:15 demanded two or three external witnesses to validate any legal claim. Jesus in what follows clarifies his earlier statement.

It is true that his testimony about himself is not valid in a court of law (8:14), but this was not such a court, and he was not a normal witness. As the Son of God, he says, "I know where I came from" (descended from heaven) "and where I am going" (ascending to heaven). The Pharisees' judgment is fatally flawed because once again they were reasoning from an earthly rather than a heavenly perspective—they "have no idea" regarding Jesus' origins or his final destination. This was not ignorance but willful rejection: they "suppress the truth" because their "foolish hearts were darkened" (Rom 1:18, 21).

This new authority given to Jesus by God means that as the light he has the power to judge. He then contrasts their fleshly standards with his divinely bestowed authority. "Human standards" in

verse 15 is literally "according to the flesh" (*kata tēn sarka*), centering on the fleshly limitations behind their judging. Even though
Jesus earlier spoke of himself as a judge (5:22, 30), he here returns
to 3:17 and states, "I pass judgment on no one." This is not a contradiction, for Jesus did not mean in 3:17 that he never functioned
as a judge but rather that he mainly came to be Savior and became
Judge only for those who turned their backs on his offer of salvation. Here he is saying that he never makes superficial, human
judgments the way his opponents do.

He clarifies this in verse 16: "But if I do judge, my decisions
are true, because I am not alone. I stand with the Father, who sent
me." "If I do" means "when I judge" in light of his authority from
"the Father, who sent me." In other words, judging is actually part
of his mission. When that happens, it is always "true," or correct,
since it is grounded not in human standards but in his unity with
the Father. So Jesus' decisions are in reality God's decisions.

Putting all the material on Jesus as Judge together (3:17; 5:22,
30, 8:15–16), we understand that Jesus did not come to judge but to
save sinners, but his coming confronts people and forces them to
make a faith-decision, with the result that Jesus becomes Judge for
those who reject his offer of salvation. When he exercises his God-
given authority to judge, he is acting in concert with his Father
and as the agent of God, and his decisions are always absolutely
just and right.

THE TWO GREATEST WITNESSES (8:17–18)

Returning to 5:31 and 8:14a and the law's demand for two witnesses,
Jesus concludes that he is providing a new Torah of the Messiah:
his messianic authority means his witness is now valid. Therefore,
he and his Father are now providing the greatest witnesses possible, a trinitarian set of witnesses, so to speak. Jesus' witness to
himself transcends the legalistic Pharisaical brand of Torah interpretation because, as the divinely appointed envoy of God, he who
is the Son of God and on mission from his Father has an authority

that transcends that of earth-centered interpreters of Torah like
the Pharisees.

SECOND CHALLENGE: THE IDENTITY
OF JESUS' FATHER (8:19–20)

There was no way that the Pharisees could ever accept Jesus' claim
that God was his Father, so their question in verse 19 is a natural
one: "Where is your father?" Philip makes a similar error in 14:8,
when he tells Jesus, "Lord, show us the Father and that will be
enough for us." Both he and the Pharisees spoke from an earthly
understanding, and not even Philip could comprehend Jesus' claim
that his Father is in heaven and that is his place of origin.

Jesus makes the same response he has used frequently: they
neither know him (5:37–38) nor God (7:28). All along his message
has never wavered: you cannot know God without knowing Jesus,
for Jesus is the Revealer of his Father. This is at the heart of Jewish
self-identity, that they are the covenant people and the God of the
Old Testament is their God. Jesus' point is that the new covenant
has arrived, and God now is known in and through his "one and
only" Son (1:14, 18; 3:16). This key theme of God the Father will be
featured through the rest of the chapter as we move from God
the Father of Jesus to the question of who the father of the Jewish
people is in 8:31–59.

As in 6:59, John ends this portion of Jesus' teaching by relating that it took place (v. 20) in the treasury in the temple courts
near "where the offerings were put." There the priests had placed
thirteen trumpet-shaped receptacles for the offerings (Mark
12:41–44). It was also the place where the candle-lighting ceremony took place, so this was a natural site for this discourse. John
stresses the fact once more that "no one seized him, because his
hour had not yet come" (see 2:4; 7:6, 30). God is in control, not
the Jewish officials. They are powerless until God's appointed
hour arrives.

THE JEWS DISAGREE OVER
JESUS' ORIGINS (8:21-30)

This is the second addendum to Jesus' opening message at the festival, as indicated by "again/once more" (Greek: *palin*) in 8:12, 21. So the opening message consisted of 7:14–52 (with 7:53–8:11 deleted), centering on the identity and authority of Jesus. This then is followed by two clarifications in 8:12–20 (Jesus the Light of the World) and 8:21–30 (his heavenly origins). The sermon of 8:31–59 culminates the themes of the Feast of Tabernacles.

WARNING: YOU WILL DIE IN YOUR SINS (8:21)

This is a severe warning regarding the terrible destiny awaiting those who refuse to believe. Jesus establishes a series of oppositions between himself and these Jewish opponents. He is from above, they are from below. He is not from this world, they are of this world. His destiny is not theirs. His father is God, theirs is the devil.

In the opening contrast, which repeats 7:33–34, Christ focuses on his destiny. He predicts his coming departure from this world and the fact that they cannot follow him to heaven. When he says, "you will look for me," he refers to their continual search for the Messiah while remaining unwilling to accept that Jesus has fulfilled that role. When he says, "you cannot come," it could mean several things. In 7:35 they thought he was moving to another country, but he was referring to the cross and his departure from this life, when he would become the atoning sacrifice for sin. They knew nothing of that, for they had rejected him and refused to believe.

Therefore, he says to them that they will die in their sins because they will never receive the effects of Jesus' atoning sacrifice. They will never accompany Jesus to his final heavenly destination because the only path to heaven is faith (3:16; 5:24, 38; 6:35, 47; 7:38). The disciples will be told something similar but without the severe danger (13:33, 36). They are to remain on earth and

continue Jesus' mission, then follow him later (14:2–4). These enemies of Christ will never be able to go.

MISUNDERSTANDING AND CORRECTION (8:22–24)

With their usual misunderstanding from an earthly perspective,
they ask Jesus if he is planning suicide, thinking that by "you
cannot come" he means they will not want to join him in death.
This is quite ironic, for Jesus is indeed referring to his death but
clearly not in the way they think. He will surrender his life, but it
will take place in his God-given destiny (2:4; 7:6, 30; 8:20) as part
of the divine plan of salvation, not in a suicidal act.

Jesus responds in verse 23 by providing the next two contrasts
(after 8:21)—they are "from below," he is "from above"; they are "of
this world," he is "not of this world." This brings out clearly one
of the primary differences between Jesus and them: the heavenly
versus the earthly. The "below" is not the realm of Satan but the
realm of this world. of the gap between God and sinful humankind cannot be bridged through anyone other than Christ himself
(1:51; 14:6), for he has descended to this lower realm and opened up
heaven to fallen humanity. So Jesus and his opponents belong to
disparate realms and have nothing in common. Only by repenting and believing in Jesus can sinners bridge the gap.

So Jesus in verse 24 returns to his main point: "you will indeed
die in your sins." These people had chosen to turn their backs on
God's salvation and belong to the realm of sinful humanity, so they
would die not only physically but also spiritually, and that death
would be eternal. "Sin" (hamartia) only occurs once before (1:29,
"takes away the sin of the world"), but it occurs three times in 8:21,
24, stressing the absolute antithesis between the holiness of God
and sin, the ultimate barrier between humankind and God. To
die in your sins is to die without any hope of reconciliation with
God. The only hope lies in the faith-decision of coming to believe
in Jesus the Christ.

Jesus states the content of that belief as "that I am he," in the Greek *egō eimi*. This can be translated "that I am who I claim to be" or "that I am he" or "that I am Yahweh." All three catch aspects of the nuance here. I discuss the seven "I am" sayings in the commentary on 6:35, but this is the first of the "I am" sayings that have no implied predicate—known as absolute "I am" sayings—and should be translated, "I AM/Yahweh." These are found at 8:24, 28, 58; 13:19, and are direct allusions to God's revelation as Yahweh at the burning bush in Exodus 3:14–15 ("I AM THAT I AM") and the use of *'anoki hu'* ("I am he") in Isaiah 51:12 (also Isa 43:10; 47:8, 10) to signify "God and God alone." Jesus deliberately makes the phrase ambiguous to provide these levels of meaning.

They must believe the claims he has made here in John—that he is the Living Revealer, God's envoy, the Bread of Life, the One who descended from heaven, the Son of God, the Judge, the Savior, the Light of the World. And in this context in particular, they must believe that he is the One soon to leave and ascend to his Father above at the appointed hour of his sacrificial death. Then they must accept and understand the actual meaning of *egō eimi* as referring to the deity of Christ. Neither the crowd nor the leaders comprehend any of this, but as they want to stone Jesus for blasphemy, they must be beginning to catch on. The disciples will have no idea of this until Thomas's confession "my Lord and my God" in 20:28.

JESUS' TRUE IDENTITY (8:25–30)

These Jewish interrogators are quite confused, which is completely understandable in light of Jesus' "I am" statement. So they now ask, "[Then] who are you?" Pretty much everything Jesus has said in this Gospel thus far has gone right over their heads because they have read their earthly way of thinking into all the heaven-centered truth they have been told. This is no different.

Jesus' response in verse 26 is difficult, and interpreters have understood it in three ways: (1) as a question ("Why do I speak to you at all?" so NASB, NEB); (2) an affirmation in terms of his personal identity ("Just who I have told you from the beginning," so NLT); and (3) an affirmation in terms of his **christological** function ("Just what I have been telling you from the beginning," so NIV, RSV, NJB). The two affirmation views are more likely than its being a question, and since John's emphasis has been on Jesus' function even when discussing his identity, the third view is preferable. Jesus wants them to realize that everything he has said and done in his messianic ministry thus far has been to show them who he is and why he has come. Moreover, they need not ask, for he has been telling them these things all along.

Still, he has a great deal to add, but they won't enjoy hearing it, for it is all "in judgment of you" (v. 26). They have not truly listened before and have rejected what they heard. So his message will be one of condemnation due to their unbelief (5:45–47; 6:26–27, 41–42, 52; 7:7, 34). Most importantly, Jesus is not just speaking for himself, but his message stems from the one "who sent me," and so what he says will be completely trustworthy. In 5:19 Jesus does what he sees his Father doing, and in 5:30; 8:26, 40, he says what he hears from the Father. (In 3:32 seeing and hearing are combined.)

However, in spite of the fact that he "tell[s] the world" only what comes from his Father, they "did not understand" that he was speaking of his Father (v. 27). How often does he have to reiterate that he is on a mission dictated by "the one who sent me"? They have refused to consider both Jesus' messianic ministry and that his mission stems from God the Father.

Jesus has previously told them about his coming departure (8:21), and now in verse 28a he tells them that at that time they will finally understand who he is, but it will be too late. This is the second of John's passion predictions (3:14; 8:28; 12:32), and there is great irony in the fact that when the Jews crucify Christ, they will be actually lifting him up to glory. The cross will be his throne, his time of exaltation. In this sense, the cross, resurrection, and ascension will become a single event in salvation history, and so at that moment they will know "that I am he." (See comments on verse 24 for the absolute "I am" here.) This hardly means mass conversion. After Pentecost there were three thousand conversions (Acts 2:41), but the Jewish people as a whole remained opposed to Jesus. The national revival will not occur until the Lord returns (Rom 11:25–32). It is believing Jews who will know Jesus' true identity.

We can summarize the content of what they will know by identifying three items Christ has been saying at the feast in chapters 7–8: (1) that Jesus is the "I AM," Yahweh, the Son of God, and the "one and only God" (1:14, 18; 3:16, 18); (2) that he does nothing on his own but acts entirely according to the will of his Father (5:19 30; 6:38; 7:16, 28; 8:16); (3) that he "spoke just what the Father has taught me." As the Word or Living Revealer, his every word is absolute truth because his Father, who taught him what to say, is completely "trustworthy" (v. 26).

His opponents wanted to kill him (5:18; 7:1, 19), and many of his disciples had deserted him (6:60–66). He was soon to die the most horrible and shameful death imaginable, yet he was supremely at peace with it all. Why? Because "the one who sent me is with me." Jesus will go to the cross alone. His twelve disciples will run away in fear (Mark 14:50 and parallels), but Jesus' reply will be, "A time is coming and in fact has come when you will be scattered. ... You will leave me all alone. Yet I am not alone, for my Father is with me" (John 16:32).

There is a lesson in this for us. When we face opposition and trials of all kinds, we need to be aware of God's presence, as in Romans 8:31: "If God is for us, who can be against us?" So Jesus adds here, "He has not left me alone, for I always do what pleases him." The Christian life is a two-way street—we seek at all times to please God (Rom 12:1-2, "offer your bodies as a living sacrifice, holy and pleasing to God"), and God is always at our side watching over us and strengthening us.

Here "many" of his listeners put their faith in him (v. 30). The previous time this took place (2:23), the faith of those who believed was inadequate and false. John holds out more hope here that this time it will be stronger (see 4:41). This provides a good, positive conclusion to the challenges and warnings of this speech and an interesting segue into the negative material to come in 8:31–59. The purpose even of judgment passages is to bring people to faith in Christ.

In chapter 7 Jesus fulfilled the water ceremony and distributed living water, the Holy Spirit, to those who believed. Here in 8:12 he fulfills the light ceremony and illumines the world with the light of God, bringing salvation. Jesus as Light, however, invokes also the image of Jesus as Judge (8:15–16), for he has brought God's judgment to bear on those who reject his light. The conflict becomes increasingly severe, as the Jewish people and their leaders think up one excuse after another to reject the light of God in Jesus. In 8:19–21 they show they have rejected the Father and have no hope of joining Jesus when he returns to heaven. Their earth-centered religion is now opposed to the God of the new covenant and has closed the doors of heaven to them.

The above-and-below contrast in 8:23–24 is important for our day. If anything, our culture is even more centered on the earthly and has little room for the heavenly. People who think they can live for their earthly pleasures and get to heaven by a few good works (like attending church or giving to charities) are mistaken and playing dangerous games with their eternal destinies. True believers are heaven-centered and need to live for heavenly more than earthly treasure.

The emphasis on Jesus' true identity in 8:25–30 is also critical for our day. Even dedicated followers often have too low a view of Jesus. We can paraphrase J. B. Phillips's classic work as "Your Jesus is too small." His personhood transcends nearly all categories, for he is Yahweh, Creator of this world, and Savior who alone can bring salvation. Our worship of Jesus must be more central in our lives. Moreover, this One is both God and Savior, who will go to the cross all alone and will have no one to hold him up. But he will not be alone because his Father will be alongside him at every step. This is an immense comfort to us, for it tells us that we too will never be alone.

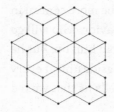

THE CHILDREN OF ABRAHAM
(8:31–59)

This dramatic dialogue culminates the conflict between Jesus and the Jews in chapters 5–8. The Jewish people here claim that they are the children of Abraham (8:37, 39), but Jesus counter-charges that they are actually the children of the devil (8:44). There are three parts to this interplay: the Jewish claim to be descendants of Abraham (8:31–41a), Jesus' counter that their true father is the devil (8:41b–47), and Jesus' claim to be deity (8:48–59).

THE JEWS CLAIM ABRAHAM AS
THEIR FATHER (8:31–41A)

THE NECESSITY OF ABIDING (8:31–32)

"The Jews who had believed him" are those who came to faith in verse 30, but they are soon to be described as slaves to sin (v. 34), those trying to kill Jesus (vv. 37a, 40), hardened (v. 37b), children of the devil (v. 44), unbelievers (vv. 45–47), and liars (v. 55). Some think this means the belief here is a false faith, but in John a word-based faith as in these two verses is a strong faith. Others think this was a problem in John's day rather than in Jesus' time, but Jesus is addressing a situation he is facing, not one that will arise later. It is more likely that the crowd contained both believers and unbelievers, and from verse 34 on Jesus will switch to address his opponents in the crowd. Some who had believed could have had the same quasi-faith as in 2:23, but they are presented as total opponents from the start, and it is best to see both groups, the saved and the unsaved, in the crowd here.

In these first two verses Jesus is speaking to the believers in the crowd and defines true disciples as those who "hold to my teaching," with "hold" translating the verb *menō*, "remain, abide in." This key term appears forty times in John and connotes a permanent relationship with God and his Word, an absolute commitment and abiding faithfulness to Jesus' teaching.

Those who are committed deeply to Jesus' teaching "will know the truth, and the truth will set you free" (v. 32). This means that such followers can discern truth from falsehood, discover the true way to live by God's will, and are committed to living that way (see Heb 5:14). "Truth" is Jesus' revelation of the Father. It is both dynamic, changing lives (see 8:36), and propositional, establishing true beliefs and doctrines.

This kind of truth will "set you free" from error and from sin (8:34; Ps 119:45). In Romans 6 Paul describes how Christ frees us from the slavery of sin so that we can become slaves of God and serve one another. The latter is a new kind of emancipation in which we surrender ourselves completely to our loving Father. This is a very important message for our time, in which so many churchgoers are half-hearted, yielding only a small part of their lives to Christ. Jesus said in Luke 9:62, "No one who puts a hand to the plow and looks back is fit for service in the kingdom of God." Those who live as if Christ freed them to do whatever they wish are sadly mistaken. We are free to live lives pleasing to God, not to seek whatever pleasure we want.

FREEDOM AND ABRAHAM'S DESCENDANTS (8:33–38)

Once more the earthly perspective of Jesus' listeners causes misunderstanding. They interpret "set free" as freedom from enslavement by other nations. Since they had kept their national identity in spite of subjugation under Assyria, Babylon, Persia, Greece, and Rome (conveniently ignoring their enslavement under Egypt), they center on the Abrahamic covenant and say, "We ... have never been slaves of anyone." In spite of political domination, they claim freedom of religion. This makes sense, for they were the only people given freedom to worship their own God by the Romans.

They assume that Abraham and the Abrahamic covenant have already set them free, so why would Jesus place their liberation in the future? Inwardly, they already have freedom even if outwardly they are under Caesar. They are children of God's kingdom, and that has precedence over the Roman realm.

Jesus responds in verse 34 with another double *amēn* saying (see comments on 1:51), which points to a solemn, important truth. He corrects their misunderstanding and makes it clear he has in mind spiritual and moral enslavement, and not political or religious. The true slave is "everyone who sins," literally "practices sin," referring to ongoing sin. Sinners sell themselves to a vicious taskmaster. In Romans 6:6–7, 14, 16–23, Paul tells us that everyone is a slave of something. People either belong to righteousness or sin, and apart from Christ there is no hope of being set free. Sin is an overwhelming power that cannot be conquered until we yield ourselves to the empowering presence of the Triune Godhead.

Jesus then develops this metaphor into an illustration contrasting the status of slaves and sons in the Roman household (vv. 35–36). His intention is to make these Jewish listeners aware of their misperception. They regarded themselves as the children of Abraham (vv. 33, 39), but in reality they were the slaves of sin (v. 34). Many think Jesus is telling a parable here, for the Romans considered slaves as well as parents and children to be part of the nuclear family. This is true, but not in the long run—slaves had no permanent place in the family since they could be sold to another family or earn their own freedom. (This happened often in the Roman world.) In Judaism a slave was to be given freedom after six years (often called a "sabbatical year," Deut 15:12–14), though this was not often practiced. In contrast, "a son belongs to it forever," even after death.

The contrast is clear: the Jewish hearers are slaves to sin while Jesus is the eternal Son of God. He descended from heaven and came directly from his Father, and they rejected God's Son and chose the path of sin. Jesus, however, is offering hope and liberation from their bondage. In verse 36 he promises, "So if the Son sets you free, you will be free indeed." In the first-century household a son (when he became an adult) could free a slave. Jesus has that authority from his Father (v. 36), and when he exercises it, those former slaves are "truly free." Paul called this "the old self," with "the body ruled by sin" completely nullified and the individual set free (Rom 6:6).

In verses 37–38, Jesus applies this understanding of freedom and slavery to his listeners. This Jewish crowd considered itself part of God's family as "Abraham's descendants," but this was not the whole truth. Physically, they were part of Abraham's lineage, but spiritually they were not (v. 39). They were Jews outwardly but not inwardly (Rom 2:28–29; see Jer 9:25–26).

Their alienation from God's family is shown by two realities: their repeated attempts to kill Jesus, and the fact that they had "no room" in their hearts for his "word" or teaching. They were completely unteachable and judged truth by the extent to which it fit into their narrow, preconceived categories. However, Jesus is the source of all truth (14:6), and his message constitutes the Torah of the Messiah: the final set of truths that will culminate God's revealed Word. As Jesus said in verse 31, the true disciple will remain faithful to his message. The Jews would agree with this if they agreed that Jesus was the actual Messiah, but they rejected Jesus, and everything flowed out of that tragic error.

The central point of this section is found in verse 38. Jesus and these Jewish interrogators have two different fathers. As in any family, the children "do" or act in accordance with what they have "seen" and "heard" from their fathers. Jesus followed the advice and patterns taught by his Father, God, and these Jews claim to do the same. The problem, as we will learn in 8:44, is that their actual "father" is the devil. They are enslaved to sin just like their true father, and that explains why they have no access to the God of the Bible.

THE WORKS OF ABRAHAM (8:39–41A)

The mistaken theology of the Jews continues to flow out of their earthly perspective. They fail to catch Jesus' actual point and continue to stress their physical lineage from Abraham. The spiritual problem continues, so Jesus can only repeat the point he already made in 8:37. Children always reflect the actions of their father; their father thus could not be Abraham, for he would never have turned against God's Messiah. The fact that they "are looking for a way to kill" Jesus (v. 40) disproves their claim. Abraham "did not do such things" as try to execute the "man who has told you the truth," which he has "heard from God."

Children always follow the example of their parent. My wife taught first grade for several years, and at parent-teacher conferences she could tell which parent belonged to which child within the first minute of meeting them. The children were the spitting image of the parents. That is Jesus' point here. These people's actions demonstrate conclusively who their father is, and it is not Abraham. Their desire to kill the Messiah and Son of God could only mean they have rejected the truth and followed the lie. To reject the Son is to reject the Father, for they are "doing the works of [their] own father," and that father is neither God nor Abraham.

JESUS COUNTERCHARGES THAT THEY ARE THE CHILDREN OF THE DEVIL (8:41B–47)

THEIR INABILITY TO HEAR (8:41B–43)

There is amazing consistency to Jewish reasoning throughout the Gospel of John. It is always devoid of spiritual awareness and centered on a this-worldly perspective. So once more they misunderstand and call out in verse 41, "We are not illegitimate children. ... The only Father we have is God himself." They have not been listening, as usual. Jesus has called both their lineage from Abraham and their relationship with God the Father into question. It is possible that this misunderstanding stems from the Jewish conflict with the Samaritans over who were the actual children of Abraham. The Samaritans were the result of the Assyrian occupation and their forced interbreeding of the Jews with pagans brought in by the Assyrians. The Jews thought of them as half-breeds, and the Samaritans likewise thought the Jews had descended from Cain rather than Seth.

Jesus and his listeners continue to debate the legitimacy of the Jewish people's descent from Abraham (Exod 4:22; Deut 32:6; Isa 64:8). Jesus retorts in 42 by returning to verse 37 a second time (see vv. 40, 42). If God were indeed their Father, they would love his Son rather than try to kill him. God "sent him," and so he has not come on his own. Their loving reception of God's agent would be tantamount to a sign of love for God. Throughout chapters 5–8 Jesus has repeated again and again how he came to earth from heaven (6:33, 38, 51, 58; 7:28; 8:14, 23) and was sent by God as his envoy (5:36, 38; 6:29, 57; 7:29, 33; 8:16–17). The Father and Son are one (10:30), so to love one is to love the other, and to hate one is to hate the other. Their attitude toward Jesus makes their actual relationship with God perfectly clear.

Jesus' deep frustration in verse 43 is apparent: "Why is my language not clear to you?" Anyone should easily catch what he has been saying, but he proceeds to answer his own question: they remain ignorant because they "are unable to hear what I say." In both Hebrew and Greek "to hear" (Greek: *akouō*) means both to understand and obey. It is their heart of unbelief that is at fault. In addition, their father Satan has plugged their ears to spiritual realities. They are spiritually deaf in both ways.

THEIR TRUE FATHER (8:44–45)

All along Jesus has been hinting at a mysterious father, and in
verse 44 we learn his identity: "You belong to your father, the devil."
No wonder they were the enemies of Jesus—they were slaves of
sin (8:34) and the children of Satan. They take a paternity test,
and their true father is the polar opposite of Jesus: the leader of
those fallen angels who were cast out of heaven by Michael and
his angelic army (Rev 12:7–9).

Jesus presents three reasons for their true kinship:

1. "You want to carry out your father's desires": they love the
    same kind of evil deeds the devil does. There is a twofold
    emphasis on the desires (*epithymia*, which could be trans-
    lated "lust for evil") and the deeds that result. The devil's
    basic desire is to establish himself as a god (as shown in Rev
    12–13), and this leads him and his followers to oppose God at
    every level. So these Jewish opponents of Christ turn their
    backs on the God of their fathers and reject his Son.

2. They join Satan, who "was a murderer from the begin-
    ning": Jesus here refers to his seduction of Adam and Eve
    and their expulsion from the garden, which introduced
    death into this world (Rom 5:12–14) and brought about the
    death of Jesus. All of this is ultimately attributable to Satan
    (John 13:2, 7).

3. The devil is "not holding to the truth, for there is no truth
    in him": Satan's primary strategy is deception (Rev 12:9;
    20:3, 8, 10); he does not so much overpower people as lead
    them astray. Falsehood is at the heart of his character, "for
    he is a liar and the father of lies." The only time he will
    ever tell the truth is when it enables him to deceive more
    easily. The false statements about Jesus from these Jewish
    leaders have their origin in the devil. Whenever Satan or
    these Jewish officials speak falsehood they are revealing
    their true nature and essence of being.

In complete contrast, Jesus says, "I tell the truth" (v. 45), for truth characterizes him (14:6). As the Living Revealer of God, he is the very voice of God. Since these people have followed the father of lies, they by virtue of their very character cannot believe in Jesus. Note that their unbelief arises *because* Jesus speaks truth. Their very internal makeup is incapable of truth, and they are thus repelled by it. This is a very strong definition of the "natural man" and the unbeliever.

THE PROBLEM: THEY DO NOT BELONG TO GOD (8:46–47)

Jesus uses two rhetorical questions to shift the focus from himself to his listeners. First, he asks them, "Can any of you prove me guilty of sin?" (v. 46). He uses a legal term, "convict" (Greek: *elenchei*). In 5:18 they formally accused him of Sabbath-breaking and blasphemy; in 6:41–42; 7:27, 41–42, 52, of being a messianic pretender; in 7:47, of false teaching; and in 7:20; 8:48, of demon possession. But Jesus demands legal evidence that would make all these charges stand up in God's court. They can accuse him, but they cannot convict him.

The second question builds on the last verse. Since Jesus has been "telling the truth," he asks, "Why don't you believe me?" The first question leads naturally to the second. They cannot prove him guilty of any sin, so they should recognize his sinless nature. Combined with his absolute truthfulness, there is no reason they should not believe.

Only one conclusion is possible: All the evidence shows conclusively that Jesus is without sin, and that they in spite of his perfectly truthful character still choose not to believe in him. The truth is that only "whoever belongs to God hears what God says" (v. 47). So Jesus has proved that in God's law court these Jews "do not belong to God." Jesus is returning to the Bread of Life discourse in 6:35–44. God has given some to Jesus, and they therefore rejoice in the truth. But these Jews refuse to listen, and that can only mean they do not belong to God. They have rejected God's Son and so are no longer the children of God. As in 1:11, they now belong to the world and to "the god of this age" (2 Cor 4:4). One could virtually say that they had switched fathers!

JESUS CLAIMS TO BE DEITY (8:48–59)

FIRST INTERCHANGE: JESUS' TRUE NATURE (8:48–51)

The Jewish reaction to Jesus' charge that they are the children of the devil and their legal accusations against him prove the truthfulness of what he has said. They had earlier accused him of being demon-possessed (7:20), and now we see they have learned nothing in the dialogue with Jesus since that occasion. Now they charge him with being a "Samaritan and demon-possessed." This may have arisen from his ministry and positive reception in Samaria in chapter 4. The Jews considered the Samaritans heretics, and Samaria was the source of many famous sorcerers like Simon Magus (Acts 8:9–24).

This constitutes further charges of blasphemy and sorcery as well as satanic delusion and control. They are trying to turn the tables on Jesus and accuse him of the very things he has just proved about them: "You say we don't descend from Abraham but instead belong to the devil; we say this actually describes you—*you* stem from the Samaritans and from demonic powers."

As he does in Mark 3:20–30, Jesus denies the charges here in verse 49 and returns to the theme of his honoring and glorifying God from 7:18. He is one with the Father and at the same time submissive to him, obeying his will (5:19–30). A heretic or demon-possessed person would never seek to honor God. Jesus at all times seeks to "honor my Father" ("honor" translates present-tense *timō*), while they constantly dishonor him, God's envoy and Revealer. John emphasizes the word *mou*, "*my* Father," stressing that while these people belong to Satan (v. 47), Jesus belongs to his Father.

Jesus seeks honor for his Father, and in return God seeks glory for his Son (v. 50). There is an A-B-A pattern here, with Jesus and his Father honoring each other and both surrounding and obviating the dishonor with which the Jews greeted Jesus. The fact that Jesus never sought glory for himself (again, see 7:18) was further proof he was not what the Jews claimed. The result of Jesus' perfect orientation toward his Father was the glory he received from his Father. This in fact is the theme of Paul's hymn in Philippians (Phil 2:6–11): Jesus sought humility and left the glory up to God. Since God is the true Judge, that glory (see John 1:14; 2:11) is both certain and right. The Jewish opposition was inconsequential in light of the fact of Jesus' Father's pleasure in him.

Using one of his double *amēn* sayings to communicate a critical truth, Jesus provides the central message (v. 51): "Whoever obeys my word will never see death." The emphasis in this section has moved from believing (vv. 24, 30–31; 45–46) to its result, obeying. In 8:31 he said "hold to [remain in] my teaching," and now he says "obeys [or keeps; Greek: *tēreō*] my word." One's belief must produce a reorientation of one's life away from the world and into the word of Jesus. Obedience is inherent in "hearing" the word (5:24; 8:43, 47). Jesus goes a step further here, challenging his hearers to "keep" his word, making it the priority in the synagogue and in their lives. Only then will they have eternal life and "never see death." The point here is just as important for our day: it is not enough to give lip service to our belief in Christ. Our faith must be shown in our works of obedience and righteous living. True piety should not be merely claimed; it must be performed.

SECOND INTERCHANGE: JESUS AS GOD (8:52–59)

These Jews were still interpreting what Jesus said at a superficial, earthly level (as in 8:19, 22, 33, 39, 41, 48), and so when Jesus said, "never see death," they thought he meant living on this earth forever. Their natural response in light of this is to think demonic forces have driven Jesus insane.[1] So they reply in verse 52, "Abraham died and so did the prophets." In spite of their spiritual power and the blessings God poured into their lives, the great men and women of God still died. This level of blasphemy could only have come from demon-inspired delusions.

They conclude Jesus thought of himself as greater than "our father Abraham" (8:53) and so ask, "Who do you think you are?" This is a great irony: the one who, more than any other human being, refused to seek his own glory (7:18; 8:49–50) is accused of magnifying himself, of being a glory hound. The truth is that Jesus is the paradigm of humility and has left his vindication and glory completely in the hands of his Father. These Jewish leaders are reading their own self-seeking pride into Jesus' words and actions. The "father of lies" (8:44) is actually guiding *their* thoughts, not those of Jesus.

In verses 54–55 Jesus states points he has already made to counter their false thinking. In fact, these verses serve as a summary of the main points in chapters 5–8:

1. Jesus never seeks his own glory or acts on his own. Everything he says and does arises out of union with his Father and seeks to glorify his Father (5:19, 30; 6:38, 57; 7:16, 18, 28; 8:16, 26, 28, 42, 50).

2. All his own glory comes from the Father (5:23; 6:27; 8:50). He is completely centered on the glory of God, so all personal glory is a gift from God (12:28; 17:1–5). However, this is not a glory the Jews or even Jesus' disciples could comprehend, for it came about when he was "lifted up" on the cross (3:14; 8:28; 12:32).

3. The Jewish people didn't really know God even though they claimed him as their God (5:37–38, 42; 7:28; 8:19, 47). This is the heart of the conflict in these chapters and stems from the Old Testament (Isa 1:3; Jer 2:8, 4:22; Hos 4:1). They reject

---

1. Ancient people linked insanity and demonic possession.

Jesus because they fail to realize he is more than Messiah—he is the Son of God. So they know neither God nor his Son.

4. Jesus both knows God and obeys him (5:19; 6:46; 7:28-29; 8:29). So there is only one path to God, through the one and only Son (1:14, 18).

Therefore, Jesus in 8:56 tells the truth about this Abraham to whom these Jews have appealed so often. In reality, "your father Abraham rejoiced at the thought of seeing my day; he saw it and was glad." They believe they are related to him, but Jesus has a far greater connection. This probably looks back to a combination of Genesis 15:17-21 (the covenant ceremony in Abraham's vision) and 17:17, his laughter at the news that a son, Isaac, would be born. Some rabbis understood Genesis 15 as referring both to this life and the age to come (Akiba), while others took it as only referring to this world (Johanan ben Zakkai). Since Jesus says here "to see my day," he applies it to the Day of Yahweh inaugurated in his coming. Then the birth of Isaac was a **typological** promise of Jesus' incarnation. So together they point to the incarnation as the dawning of the final age.

Needless to say, the Jews are shocked at this response and in verse 57 continue to interpret everything Jesus says from a this-worldly viewpoint: "You are not yet fifty years old." Jesus was about thirty-three years old (see Luke 3:23), so this was a round number. Abraham had been dead for two millennia, so they are aghast at Jesus' statement.

Jesus' response in verse 58 is the third double *amēn* ("truly, truly") saying in this chapter (vv. 34, 51, 58).[2] It is one of the most important verses in John, at the very core of the affirmations of Jesus' deity: "Before Abraham was born, I am!" This is the clearest example yet of an absolute *egō eimi* saying (having no predicate; see 8:24, 28; 13:19; 18:5-6). Jesus is proclaiming, "I am Yahweh," especially as understood against its background in Isaiah (Isa 41:4;

2. See comments on 1:51.

43:10–13, 25; 45:18–19; 48:12; 52:6) as a divine self-disclosure. He is saying in effect, "Before Abraham was ever born, I, Yahweh, was there." So this is not only a claim of divinity but of preexistence as well. As part of the Triune Godhead, Jesus existed long before Abraham. Jesus transcends the offices of both prophet and Messiah, for he is God of very God and the basis of our salvation.

The Jews could hardly have caught all this meaning, but they understand enough to know that from their perspective serious blasphemy has taken place, so they "picked up stones to stone" Jesus (as demanded in Lev 24:16; see also John 5:18; 10:31). In response, the NIV has "Jesus hid himself," but the Greek uses the passive "was hidden," hinting that God hid Jesus from them. His hour of destiny had not arrived (7:30, 44; 8:20), so once again the authorities were helpless in their attempts to remove this upstart peasant rabbi and "bring him to justice." He leaves the temple grounds, and many see in this a symbolic depiction of the **Shekinah** glory of God leaving the temple. In this sense it is a precursor of judgment, which in the **Synoptics** is stressed in the Olivet Discourse of Mark 13 and parallels.

This passage (8:31–59) has been called "an early Christ-sermon" because of its depth and penetrating insight into the person of Jesus and his conflict with the Jews. As one of the truly important passages in this Gospel, John presents the core of the conflict as Jewish dependence on their descent from Abraham along with their failure to conquer sin. Freedom does not stem from ancestry but from abiding in Christ (vv. 32–33) and being liberated in him (vv. 33–38). A person's actions show who their father truly is (vv. 39–41a), and so their father clearly was not Abraham. This is critical for today, for too many Christians depend on what denomination or church they belong to or what tradition they follow rather than truly surrendering to Christ.

In the middle section (vv. 41b-47), Jesus makes a legal declaration of the paternity test he has given these Jews—their true father is the devil. Their complete unwillingness to listen to the Son of God, their desire to kill him, and their evil deeds all show conclusively that they do not belong to God. This test is relevant for our day, but it is virtually ignored, and many who declare themselves followers of Christ but clearly prove themselves not to be are allowed to pretend to be what they are not. We by our lack of bold ministry are letting these people go to eternal damnation because we don't have the courage to tell it like it is. These days of shallow discipleship demand the kind of bold preaching that we see from Jesus here.

The final section (vv. 48-59), on the truth of Jesus' personhood, is the key to everything. He is so much more than prophet or Messiah. He is Yahweh, and until we both acknowledge and conduct ourselves under that reality we can never live the life God wants for us. As Paul says so well throughout his writings, Jesus is Lord of all, and we must make him Lord of our lives and live under that glorious reality. Then we will be "more than conquerors" (Rom 8:37) and truly live lives of freedom in him.

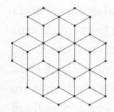

THE COST OF DISCIPLESHIP: THE MAN BORN BLIND
(9:1–41)

J esus is "the light of the world," a fact demonstrated in this story through his healing of a man who lived in the darkness of being blind all his life. Jesus fulfilled the major ceremonies of the Feast of Tabernacles (7:37–39; 8:12), and now he continues fulfilling the ceremonies as he gives sight to a blind man physically (9:1–7) and then spiritually (implicit in 9:28–34). In this way he stands in total contrast to the Pharisees. The healing of the blind had never been done before (9:32), so this is another quintessential messianic miracle.

It is a brilliantly narrated story, progressing via a series of interrogations (vv. 8–12, 13–17, 18–23, 24–34) sandwiched between an opening (vv. 1–7, narrating the healing) and a closing (vv. 35–41, narrating the blindness of the Pharisees). The conflict between the Jews and Jesus continues to occupy a central place, as the Pharisees go on the offensive against him. The message is seen in the plot development of the story: the man begins blind and proceeds to physical sight and then spiritual insight, while in contrast the Pharisees claim to have spiritual sight yet by the end are proved to be spiritually blind. At the same time, an important subtheme demands that the true disciple take a public stand for Jesus and be willing to suffer the consequences. Both the parents and the man are challenged publicly by the leaders and threatened with expulsion from the synagogue (and community). The man is never named (like the Samaritan woman); John's emphasis is on the message of the story, not the individuals involved.

At the same time, this episode has been central to the view of many critical scholars that this Gospel addresses more the church situation of John at the end of the first century more than actual events that took place in the life of the historical Jesus. According to this interpretation, John wrote this story to address Christian's expulsion of Christians from the synagogue in the 80s. I will discuss this in more detail at verse 22 below, but for now I will say that there is little evidence that John (and this chapter in particular) was written to describe the situation of the later church rather than of Jesus. All of this makes best sense in the life of Christ.

OPENING: JESUS HEALS A BLIND MAN (9:1-7)

This story takes place at sometime between the Feast of Tabernacles in the fall and the Feast of Dedication in the winter (ch. 10), so it likely occurred in October or November. As he is walking, Jesus passes by "a man blind from birth." We aren't told how the disciples come to know this, but they ask in verse 2, "Rabbi, who sinned, this man or his parents, that he was born blind?" Jesus was still considered primarily to be a miracle-working rabbi (see 1:38, 49; 3:2; 4:31; 6:25), so this was a natural query. It was a common Jewish view that physical deformity was the result of sin.[1] This passage, as well as the Old Testament book of Job, shows that this is not always the case and that God often has different purposes in mind.

Jesus makes it clear (v. 3) that this blindness did not result from sin but rather that "this happened so that the works of God might be displayed in him." This is similar to Exodus 9:16 (the plague of hail sent so God's name would be exalted) and Luke 13:1-5 (God

---

1. Based on Exod 20:5; Deut 5:9; Ps 89:32; see Genesis Rabbah 23:6; b. Shabbat 55a.

sending tragedies to bring about repentance). The goal of everything Jesus does is to glorify the Father, and this was the time for
good works to do God's work. Jesus is stressing the sovereignty of
God in this situation. He is in charge, and neither the sin of the
parents nor of the child can account for this blindness. Rather, God
allowed it to prepare for this very moment, when his works were
to be displayed. Everything done in this Gospel is a work of God,
either done by the Lord or by the disciples in his name.

In light of God's deeper purposes, Jesus and the disciples (Jesus
uses "we") are called on by God to "do the works of him who sent
me" (v. 4). The divine "must" (dei) makes this an absolute necessity. The task is part of his mission, and the disciples are privileged to assist in it. This is quite applicable to every one of us;
what we do is the Lord's work, and we will share in his glory as
we participate in it.

For Jesus, this is a further example of the war between light
and darkness in this world (see 1:4, 7, 9; 3:19-21; 8:12). The ministry among the Jewish people takes place during the "day" when
the light of God goes forth into this world. It is a time for going to
work for God with all our strength, and the urgency of the divine
"must" dominates this challenge. The truth is that "night is coming,
when no one can work." The day is the time Jesus is with them, and
the night is when he is taken from them. During this time "while
I am in the world, I am the light of the world" (v. 5).

The coming time of night/darkness has a twofold sense here.
First, it refers to the events at the cross and immediately afterward.
Judas leaves at night (13:30), and the women come to the tomb
after dark (20:1). During that time, the disciples did not work but
experienced the resurrection appearances and then waited in the
upper room. Before Jesus' departure, Jesus was the light of God in
the world and the disciples rejoiced in his "day." Second, the time
of night connotes the world we live in, where the powers of sin
and darkness resist the light.

The idea of Jesus spitting on the ground, making a mud pack of it, and then placing the mud pack on the man's eyes (vv. 6-7) is quite repugnant to the modern mind, which finds spitting offensive. Still, miracles involving spittle are found in two other places: Mark 7:33 (a deaf and dumb man) and 8:23 (a blind man). Some ancient Jews thought saliva had healing properties (b. Baba Batra 126b).[2] Jesus was likely accommodating himself to the level of the man's faith. This allowed the man to participate in the event and understand it. Many (several church fathers as well as modern scholars) see symbolic significance in the mud as an allusion to Genesis 2:7 and the creation of humankind from the dust of the earth. Jesus then is creating new sight, and this is part of the new creation (see 1:3-4), especially since this physical sight will make way for spiritual sight as the story develops.

Jesus then tells the man to wash the mud off his eyes in the pool of Siloam (v. 7). The washing is an allusion to 2 Kings 5:10-14 and the healing of Naaman the leper. John explains that the name "Siloam" means "sent," highlighting the work of Jesus as "the Sent One," the agent of God. There may also be a wordplay on Jesus' "sending" the man to the pool, stressing his sovereign authority to heal. Some have seen in this episode a symbol of baptism's saving role, but that goes beyond the text. There simply is no contextual basis for such an interpretation.

FIRST INTERACTION: HIS NEIGHBORS INTERROGATE THE MAN (9:8-12)

The man may have been a fixture in the community, probably begging in the same spot for years. His neighbors know him by sight and see him walking normally and are shocked; some of them are sure it is the same person, but others doubt it. To everyone who asks, he assured them, "I am the man" (v. 9). The follow-up

---

2. Though others thought spitting a wicked practice; see t. Sanhedrin 12:10.

question is also natural, "How then were your eyes opened?" They want to know who healed him.

This story is quite similar to the healing of the lame man in chapter 5, who was also asked who had healed him. That man was more thoughtless and said in effect, "Beats me!" He didn't really care—a symbol of the apathetic recipient of God's mercy. This man is far more aware: "The man they call Jesus made some mud and put it on my eyes" (v. 11). As he retells the story of his healing, he becomes another official witness to Jesus, initiating a process of understanding and thus of becoming a disciple.

The one question he cannot answer is, "Where is this man?" (v. 12). It seems likely at this stage that these neighbors are not filled with animus toward Jesus. They want to meet him rather than attack him, but the man simply doesn't know where he is.

SECOND INTERACTION: THE PHARISEES
INTERROGATE THE MAN (9:13-17)

The man's neighbors take him to the local religious experts, the Pharisees, so they can better understand the remarkable event that had occurred (v. 13). They have no idea what will be unleashed by this innocent act. There is no intent to cause a legal situation, and no need to take him to the priests, since no ritual uncleanness (like with leprosy) was involved. They have never seen a miracle like this and simply go to the Pharisees so they can make sense of it.

However, these Pharisees, like most of the leaders, are looking for ways to oppose Jesus and immediately turn it into a negative interrogation. As in 5:16 (the healing of the crippled man), the miracle has taken place on the Sabbath (v. 14). The Pharisees had created the oral tradition (an extension of the law of Moses) to define what constituted work and was prohibited on the Sabbath. Jesus broke their tradition in three ways: (1) healing was allowed on the Sabbath only for life-threatening situations; (2) some rabbis believed anointing the eyes on a Sabbath was wrong; (3) kneading (making a mud poultice) on the Sabbath was work, and so was not allowed.

As usual, there are mixed reactions when the man tells his story (compare 6:60–71; 7:12–13, 30–31, 40–44). Some Pharisees react as before: "This man is not from God, for he does not keep the Sabbath" (v. 16). On the other hand, others query, "How can a sinner perform such signs?" This was not your average everyday miracle; he had healed a blind man, indeed blind from birth, something that had never happened in history (see the introduction to this chapter). Those who emphasize the Sabbath-breaking are against him, and those who center on the supernatural miracle tend to be in favor of him.

So the Pharisees turn back to the man and ask for his opinion on Jesus: "What have you to say about him? It was your eyes he opened" (v. 17). In his response we see a critical difference between the lame man of chapter 5 and this man. The man in 5:15 reported Jesus to the authorities and cared nothing about him. Here the reaction is quite the opposite. This time, hesitation or equivocation, the man confesses, "He is a prophet." Like the Samaritan woman in 4:19, Jesus' supernatural powers convince him.

Note his developing understanding over the course of events. In verse 11 he identifies his healer only as "the man they call Jesus," but he has been mulling over the implications of the miracle since then. Now he is ready to deliver his preliminary conclusion. He does not yet realize Jesus is *the* expected "prophet like Moses," the Messiah (see comments on 1:21; 6:14); but he sees him in the Elijah/Elisha mold as a miracle-working prophet of God. His remarkable progression as a Jesus follower will develop from healer (v. 11) to prophet (v. 17) to one to be followed as a disciple (v. 27) to one from God (v. 33) and finally to Savior and Lord to be worshiped (v. 38).

THIRD INTERACTION: THE PHARISEES
INTERROGATE THE PARENTS (9:18–23)

The Pharisees are still divided, but the opposed majority are certain no miracle could have been performed by such a heretic. This man could not have been blind and then healed. They need more information and so turn to the parents in verse 18, asking them if he was indeed born blind and if so, how he can see now. They assume that he could not have been healed by this false prophet.

The informal interrogation has changed into a legal investigation, but not a fair one. They are not seeking truth but rather for evidence that will support the position they demand—that Jesus (and the man) must be guilty of fraud. They expected the parents to say he had not been born blind, for the second question would then come to the fore—"How is it that now he can see?" (v. 19).

The parents refuse to be used this way. This is a dangerous situation, for these officials can make life very difficult. So they opt to stay out of the debate, delivering bad news to the Pharisees on the first question ("he was born blind"), but avoiding the second question—"But how he can see now, or who opened his eyes, we don't know. Ask him. He is of age; he will speak for himself" (v. 21). A child became an adult at age thirteen and then could be legally interrogated. The leaders' ploy had failed to work. They could not use the parents against the man or Jesus.

John explains the reason for the parents' reticence in verse 22. They were "afraid of the Jewish leaders," who had predetermined that "anyone who acknowledged that Jesus was the Messiah would be put out of the synagogue." John describes the Pharisees as "Jewish leaders" because they represent the apostate nation (see comments on 1:11). Being put out of the synagogue was quite serious, one of the worst punishments a person could endure, for it meant removal from society as well. Total social ostracism would result, and all neighbors and even relatives had to follow it. No wonder they were afraid. There is a real tragedy in this, as these parents have seen their child wondrously healed but dare not celebrate because of these leaders' false demands.

This verse has become a focal point of scholarly discussion (see the introduction to this section) because many scholars think it reflects the situation of the church at the end of the first century rather than of Jesus. These scholars argue that such a ban expelling a person from the synagogue was not introduced until the 80s.[3] However, evidence of the expulsion of heretics existed even before the time of Jesus (see m. Ta'anit 3:8 from the first century BC). Everything written here could easily have taken place in the time of Jesus, so we are justified in considering the story to be historical.

FOURTH INTERACTION: THE PHARISEES INTERROGATE THE MAN AGAIN (9:24–34)

THEIR DEMANDS FOR THE MAN (9:24–27)

The parents have dodged their questions and become a dead end, so the Pharisees have to return to the man himself. They no longer want his opinion. It is too dangerous to their cause. Instead they try to put words in his mouth, couching the demand for a lie in pious terms: "Give glory to God by telling the truth. ... We know this man is a sinner." If ever there was an example of an oxymoron, this is it. This language is normally a demand for repentance, but here it is connected to one of the greatest falsehoods uttered in the Gospel of John thus far (see the comments on 8:46 regarding Jesus' sinlessness). "Give glory to God" is often a formal oath (Josh 7:19; 1 Sam 6:5), and here it is linked to their judgment that Jesus has to be seen as a "sinner."

The man's response is curt, but it is truth. He states what he knows and what he doesn't know. He has no idea if they are right that Jesus is a sinner. What he does know is simple: "I was blind but now I see." The Pharisees have not escaped from their dilemma—how can a sinner perform so great a miracle?

---

3. It is around this time that part of the Eighteen Benedictions, a liturgical document recited three times a day by Jews, was revised in a way that excluded Christians from the synagogue.

Now that the Pharisees' demand that he repent and support
their position has failed, they must return to the beginning. As
a result they ask, "What did he do to you? How did he open your
eyes?" (v. 26). In his answer the man seems to have realized the
absence of any search for truth on their part and goes on the offensive: "I have told you already and you did not listen." He has had
it with their double-edged questions, so he responds with biting
irony, "Do you want to become his disciples too?" (v. 27). It is quite
possible the man has started to think of himself as a disciple and
so is mocking their attempt to put words in his mouth.

THEIR ACCUSATIONS AND THREATS AGAINST THE MAN (9:28–34)

The Pharisees cannot answer the man. It is obvious that he has
correctly judged their intentions, so they too go on the offensive.
They now show their true colors as they begin to insult and curse
him for exposing a truth they don't want to face. This is not pro-
fanity but calling down covenant curses on him for what they considered blasphemy (Lev 24:10–16; Num 15:30). They begin by calling
him (with some truth to it) a disciple of Jesus while they in contrast are "disciples of Moses" (v. 28). They assume that this man
could not follow Jesus and Moses at the same time. God revealed
his law to Moses, and Jesus was a contrary upstart and heretic.
Yet Jesus had already stated that belief in Moses mandated belief
in him, for Moses "wrote about" him (see 5:46). Their tragic error
was a failure to accept the truth about Jesus' origins.

The man's sarcasm is evident in verse 30: "Now that is remarkable," he responds. His longest speech occurs here (vv. 30–33), and
it destroys the false logic of the Pharisees. The unbelief of the leaders is very strange in light of the simple undeniable fact—Jesus
has healed his eyes. That is the one thing their radical skepticism
is unable to answer. So he asks how they could say, "We don't even

know where he comes from" (v. 29). If he can heal the blind, he must have a very special relationship with God.

God would not listen to "sinners" (v. 31, looking back to v. 24), so the Pharisees have to be wrong. God "listens to the godly person who does his will," and that must be Jesus. Again, Jesus' status is proved by the fact that he is a miracle-working prophet (v. 17). The man may be looking back to the definition of the godly person in Micah 6:8, "To act justly and to love mercy and to walk humbly with your God." That must be Jesus, for the healing of a blind man had never been done before (v. 32), and that proves God's favor on Jesus. The man's logic is impeccable—"If this man were not from God, he could do nothing" (v. 33). A false prophet may be able to perform some miracles (for example, the Egyptian magicians in Exodus), but not this one.

These Pharisees are so blinded by their prejudice (as we will see below) that they do not even realize how extensively this man's simple logic has destroyed their poorly conceived arguments. They have been upstaged by him, and so they blow up at him. Their assumption, as we have seen (7:15), is that no one without proper training should be allowed to speak, this former beggar least of all. They assume that his blindness at birth proved him a sinner (disproved by Jesus in 9:3) and so scream, "You were steeped in sin at birth; how dare you lecture us!" Then they "threw him out," undoubtedly meaning they expelled him from the synagogue, the ban discussed at verse 22. To follow Jesus into discipleship means to follow him into religious and social ostracism. As stated so well in 3:18–19, darkness will always reject light.

THE CONCLUSION: JESUS DISTINGUISHES SIGHT FROM SPIRITUAL BLINDNESS (9:35–41)

The movement of the story now arrives at its proper conclusion. It has been apparent that two things have been happening. The man

born blind has progressed amazingly upward, from begging by
the side of the road to skipping and dancing down the road while
seeing everything around to the opening of his spiritual eyes to
amazing spiritual insight. At the same time, the Pharisees have
progressed even further downward, from the claim to be the eyes
of the Torah in the nation to greater and greater spiritual blindness. I will comment on both these movements in this section.

LIFE FOR THE ONE WHO HAS RECEIVED SIGHT (9:35–38)

The light (8:12) has been conquering darkness (1:5). The Pharisees
have been doing everything they can to impede Jesus and prove
him a false prophet. They have expelled the man from the synagogue, and now Jesus has found him. Jesus has often taken the initiative in seeking potential disciples (1:43, 48; 4:7; 5:6), and once
more he takes control, as will the Spirit at the next stage of salvation history (16:8–11).

The man has never laid eyes on Jesus until this moment. He was
sent to wash the mud poultice off his face as part of the healing
process (9:7) and then went home. His knowledge of God's truths
is still incomplete, so Jesus comes to fill in his gaps. Jesus' direct
challenge here ("Do you believe in the Son of Man?") seems abrupt,
but it is the perfect beginning.

Why does Jesus call himself "Son of Man" rather than "Son of
God"? The latter is the major title in John and would seem to better
communicate who Jesus is. However, the "Son of Man" in John is
the one who reveals the heavenly reality (1:51), reveals God, and
brings life and judgment to fallen humanity (3:13–14; 5:26–27; 8:28).
Note especially 6:27, "work ... for food that endures to eternal life,
which the Son of Man will give you." It is Jesus the Son of Man who
rewards the man's belief with eternal life and then brings down
judgment on the blind Pharisees (vv. 39–41). Certainly this man
could not have caught all this, but the reader is expected to do so.

The man immediately responds (v. 36), admitting his ignorance, "Who is he, sir? ... Tell me so that I may believe in him." All he knows is the wondrous thing this Son of Man has done in his life, and he is ready for the next step (in contrast with the crowd in 12:34). As with the Samaritan woman (4:26), Jesus replies that this "Son of Man" is the very one he is looking at (a second miracle of this gift of sight) and hearing. When the Pharisees looked at Jesus, they saw only a false prophet to be despised and disposed of. There is a difference between physical sight and spiritual insight. This man has the latter. He sees the face of the one who brings life and immediately cries out (v. 38), "Lord, I believe!" The scene ends with marvelous worship as this man enters the kingdom of God.

JUDGMENT FOR THOSE WHO HAVE BLINDED THEMSELVES (9:39–41)

The Son of Man brought life to the formerly blind man who had come to both physical and spiritual sight, and now he brings judgment to the Pharisees who have proved themselves blind. The thesis of the whole story comes in verse 39, "For judgment I have come into this world, so that the blind will see and those who see will become blind." This narrative is an acted parable of double reversal on the theme of light and darkness. The eyes of the man are opened step by step not only to the sights of this world but also to the greater vistas of God's truths.

On the other hand, the theme of judgment appears often in this Gospel (3:17; 5:22, 30; 8:15–16). Christ has come not to judge but to bring salvation. But for those who reject his offer of life, he becomes the judge, as here. Christ is explaining the other side of his messianic ministry, the rendering of judgment. He has come to give sight to those who realize they are blind and come to him, and he has come to judge those who claim they can see but remain closed to the gospel and render them blind. The man more than once confesses his ignorance and asks for help (vv. 12, 25, 36), and the Pharisees often arrogantly proclaim their knowledge (9:16, 24, 29). Most interpreters see here an allusion to Isaiah 6:9–10: "Be ever seeing, but never perceiving. ... Close their eyes. Otherwise, they might see with their eyes ... and turn and be healed." These Pharisees with their hardened hearts have now been rejected by God.

Jesus has been speaking loudly enough that some Pharisees hear and ask (v. 40), "What? Are we blind too?" They have caught just enough of it to realize dimly he could be speaking of them. His reply is devastating. He says in effect, "If you realized you were blind, you would not be guilty of sin; but now since you claim you can see, your guilt remains." They have all the light of the law with them, and the Son of God, the Light of the World, is present in their midst. Yet they reject all that light and greet Jesus with unbelief and hatred. They see only what they want to, and they have shut their eyes to God's salvation. Their guilt will remain for all eternity.

———

One of the longest stories in the Fourth Gospel, this is virtually a parable on the theme of light and darkness that permeates John. The man born blind is the quintessential disciple, reacting in the way God intends to the healing presence of Jesus and continuing to grow throughout the narrative. The Pharisees are the typical antagonist, exemplifying the power of a lie to turn those with sight blind. They move in the opposite direction from the man who has been healed, as their rejection of truth and opposition to Jesus renders them blind to the things of God.

There are three groups in the story: the man, who typifies discipleship; the neighbors, who might be identified as seekers who want to meet Jesus; and the Pharisees, who move further into unbelief and rejection as the story progresses. The understanding of the man grows deeper because he is both completely open to whatever he learns about Jesus and because as a result he has a natural ability to assimilate spiritual truth and come to understand it. His logic allows him to unmask the Pharisees in all their falsehood.

We find in this story that those who follow Jesus should never expect to be treated fairly by the world. Darkness hates light and at the same time wants to pretend it is light. When possible, believers will be tricked into supporting the lies of the world. Moreover, when that fails they will be persecuted and completely mistreated by the denizens of the dark. The Pharisees tried to get the man and his parents to lie and then threatened them with expulsion from the synagogue and community unless they complied.

The two sides of divine judgment also flow out of this story. The man is judged and found worthy; the Pharisees are judged and found wanting. Their blindness stems from their ability to brainwash themselves into thinking they are the paradigms of truth when in reality they are following Satan's lie and turning in unbelief against the only means anyone has of finding salvation.

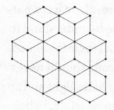

THE GOOD SHEPHERD
AND HIS SHEEP

(10:1–21)

In chapters 7–9 John develops Jesus' fulfillment of the Feast of Tabernacles, and in 10:22–42 Jesus fulfills the meaning of the Feast of Dedication (Hanukkah). The extended allegory here in 10:1–21 provides a transition, as sheep were part of both feasts. This passage also culminates the conflict narrative that has dominated since chapter 5. In chapter 9 the Jewish leaders blinded themselves to the truth and opposed Jesus utterly, threatening anyone who took his side. That narrative ended with the verdict that their sin remained (9:41).

Here Jesus expands that declaration of guilt and reveals that they are the false shepherds of Ezekiel 34:2, where God tells Ezekiel to "prophesy against the shepherds of Israel." They had forsaken their flock, so God had decided he and his servant David would stand against them. The Jews understood this as a messianic promise, and Jesus sees himself here as the Davidic shepherd fulfilling that prophecy as the Good Shepherd (v. 11). Moreover, the Jewish officials are thieves and robbers as well as hired hands who care nothing for the sheep (vv. 1, 8, 12). Jesus in contrast is the gate who provides a way for the sheep to come to God and find both care and safety (v. 7).

This is technically an illustration or extended metaphor rather than a parable, for there is no plot but rather the development of a particular metaphor surrounding the image of a shepherd. However, a story or plot implicitly lies behind it, so it can viably be called a parable as well. The illustration itself is found in verses 1–5, and it contains two images, the gate (vv. 1–3a) and the shepherd (vv. 3b–5). Jesus then develops it through two explanations, the gate in verses 6–10 and the shepherd in verses 11–18. This adds further to the picture of Jesus as water (7:38) and light (8:12). He is now the messianic shepherd as well.

JESUS TELLS THE ILLUSTRATION OF THE GATE AND THE SHEPHERD (10:1–5)

THE GATE FOR THE SHEEP (10:1–3A)

Jesus begins with another double *amēn*, which so often in John points to an important saying ("I tell you the absolute truth"; see comments on 1:51). The picture is based on a first-century sheepfold, an enclosure often built at the foot of a hill with walls on three sides and a small opening with a gate so the shepherd can come and go. Some interpreters think of this as a small single-family pen, but I prefer to see it as a large sheepfold, possibly housing several flocks with an under-shepherd or "gatekeeper" (v. 3) helping. He would man the gate to protect the sheep and make sure none were escaping. Villagers would have added a few sheep each, sending them into the countryside to graze under the care of a single shepherd.

The word-picture begins with the dangers often encountered in minding sheep in the first century. Thieves and robbers could easily climb over the walls, which were usually about waist high because you don't need much to keep sheep within an enclosure. The thieves would steal the sheep or even kill and butcher them right there. The job of the gatekeeper was also to protect the sheep and prevent either thieves or predators from entering.

The shepherd enters by the gate and is known by both the gate-keeper and the sheep (vv. 2–3a).

THE SHEPHERD OF THE SHEEP (10:3B–5)

You can tell the good shepherd from the false because he is the one who enters properly through the gate and knows each and every sheep. He maintains a deep relationship with his sheep. He calls them by name and they respond, following him out of the pen and coming to him in the field. They each both know his voice and the name he has given them. In Jesus' time (and today), a shepherd would assign each sheep a name or call (for instance, a certain set of notes on a flute), and this would enable him to recall one that had started to wander off. With these distinctive calls the shepherd could keep the herd together and following him (v. 4). Note the stress on "his *own* [*idia*] sheep" in verse 3, which brings in some of the predestinarian theology of 6:37–44. They belong to the Shepherd, and there remains a special relationship (to be developed further in 10:14). A stranger obviously could not do this, and the sheep would run away (v. 5).

There is a great deal of Old Testament background behind this picture. God is often depicted as Israel's shepherd (Gen 48:15; Pss 28:9; 80:1; Isa 40:11; Mic 5:4), leading his people to safety and watching over them (Ps 23; Ezek 34:11–16). The leaders who fail are called false shepherds who take the milk and wool for themselves and butcher the flock (Ezek 34:3; Isa 56:11; Jer 23:1–4). We should also note Numbers 27:16–17, where Moses asked God to appoint a new leader so Israel would not be "like sheep without a shepherd." That person was Joshua, the Hebrew form of the name Jesus.

In Jesus' day the "strangers" are the Jewish authorities who opposed the work of God, turned against his Son, and tried to steal his flock. In Paul's time and our day these are false teachers who falsify God's truths and force their own versions on the church (1 Tim 1:4). We today must be extra careful in centering on God's word as the basis for all truth and deeply scrutinizing these "new" teachings for falsehoods.

JESUS EXPLAINS THE GATE AND
THE SHEPHERD (10:6-18)

EXPLANATION REGARDING THE GATE (10:6-10)

In verse 6, we learn that the Pharisees could not understand, as before (see 8:19, 22, 27, 33, 41, 52, 57; 9:40–41). Jesus explains his illustration carefully, first the gate (vv. 7–10) and then the shepherd (vv. 11–18). This is not just built on the illustration in verses 1–5 but adds material and richly develops the picture further. With a second "very truly" (after v. 1), he begins with his third "I am" saying (after 6:35; 8:12), indicating that Jesus is the gate, the only way into God's community. In 10:2 he was the shepherd who entered the gate; now he is the gate itself. At night in the field where sheep grazed, shepherds would build makeshift pens, using rocks with thorns on top of them to keep the sheep in and wild animals out. The shepherd would then sleep across the opening, becoming in effect the "gate for the sheep."

Jesus is distinct from the "thieves and robbers" who came before him (v. 8). He isn't referring to the prophets of the Old Testament but to the Jewish officials of his own day who are linked with the false shepherds of Ezekiel 34. In passages like Mark 12:38–40 and Matthew 23:1–36, he derides them for their pride and for stealing the property of widows (i.e., their meager life savings) placed in their trust. The chief priests actually became quite wealthy through their control of the temple proceedings. Jesus was probably also thinking of the messianic pretenders of his own time, who led insurrections and brought great harm to the nation.

Jesus is the true "gate" or door to salvation, the only way people can enter the kingdom and "be saved" (v. 9). One thinks of the gate to heaven (Gen 28:17; Ps 78:23) that God's people enter at death or the gate into the kingdom of God (Matt 13:13–14) entered at conversion. Jesus pictures them going about freely and finding pasture, with Jesus as the shepherd leading his sheep into lush pasturelands (Ps 23; Rev 7:17).

Once more, he is totally distinct from the leaders who are thieves who come "only to steal and kill and destroy" (v. 10), an allusion to Ezekiel 34:2-3, picturing them as those who "clothe [themselves] with the wool and slaughter the choice animals." Jesus, on the other hand, has "come that they may have life, and have it to the full." With him the sheep have an abundance of divine blessings in every area. This embraces not only eternal life with God in heaven but also the daily earthly needs of God's flock. Christ has created a new flock, a new messianic community that is the recipient of the Spirit and of all human needs met by God. The picture comes from Psalm 23 and the idea of the rich pastureland given to God's people by their divine Shepherd.

EXPLANATION REGARDING THE GOOD SHEPHERD (10:11-18)

The Shepherd Willing to Die for the Sheep (10:11-13)

The fourth "I am" saying looks to Jesus as "the Good Shepherd," the noble, ideal shepherd. The beautifully conceived imagery reminds us of Psalm 23, the kind of God who "makes me lie down in green pastures ... leads me beside quiet waters ... refreshes my soul." The false shepherds take the lives of the sheep; Jesus the Good Shepherd "lays down his life for the sheep." In this passage, Jesus demonstrates his awareness that he would die as an atoning sacrifice for humankind (see John 1:29; 6:51; 10:15; 11:50-52; 18:14).

This is connected to the prophecy of Isaiah 53:10, that the Suffering Servant's life would be "an offering for sin." Jesus laid down his life "for" or "on behalf of" (Greek: *hyper*) the sheep, a proposition that in John always connotes vicarious sacrifice (6:51; 11:50-52; 18:14). Shepherds often faced dangerous predators (as David notes in 1 Sam 17:34-37), but few were willing to lose their lives in the process. Only Jesus deliberately gave up his life as part of the divine purpose for the sheep.

In verse 12 Jesus introduces the hired hand, and again he has the leaders of Israel in mind. They have no stake in the sheep, no pride or care of ownership. They care nothing for the sheep and so run away at the sight of a wolf (vv. 12–13). The **Mishnah** obligated a shepherd to fight if one wolf[1] came but not if two arrived. The hired hand is completely unconcerned and so abandons the flock at the first sign of danger, echoing Ezekiel 34:8: "You abandoned my flock and left them to be attacked by every wild animal" (NLT). In Acts 20:28–29 Paul warns the Ephesian elders of false teachers who like "savage wolves will come in among you and will not spare the flock." It is essential to choose church leaders not on the basis of their charisma or storytelling ability but on their walk with God and the centrality of scriptural truth in their ministry.

The Shepherd Who Knows His Sheep (10:14–18)

The vicarious sacrifice of the Shepherd for the sheep is grounded in Christ's omniscience and omnipresence, and in his deep relationship with his sheep. The core of this section is the atoning death of the Shepherd, stressed in verses 15, 17, and 18. Death produces life, and life works itself out in oneness. The mutual indwelling of 6:56 ("remains in me, and I in them") becomes mutual knowledge in 10:14, "I know my sheep and my sheep know me." This is built on verses 3–4, where the Shepherd "calls his own sheep by name and leads them out." This mutual knowledge is the anchor of our walk with Christ and defines the Christian life, preparing for the expansion of the mutual indwelling motif in 15:4, 5, 7, that will become the basis of the fruitful Christian life.

This new relationship between Shepherd and sheep is itself grounded in the mutual knowledge between Jesus and the father.

---

1. The wolf could symbolize Satan but more likely as in Acts 20:29 it depicts false teachers who will deceive and destroy many in the church.

The core of this is presented in 1:18, "the one and only Son, who is himself God and is in closest relationship with the Father, has made him known." The intimacy between Jesus and his Father translates itself into a similar intimacy with the flock. As God knew his people in both testaments (Pss 7:9; 119:23; Jer 1:5; 1 Cor 8:3; Gal 4:9), so his Son knows his followers. What makes all this possible is that he "lays down his life for the sheep." Intimacy flows out of sacrifice, for the love behind the sacrifice infuses the relationship as well.

Jesus has been talking about this relationship with the Jewish people, and in verse 16 he turns to "other sheep that are not of this sheep pen." The sheep pen would be Judaism, and the "other sheep" are the Gentiles. The Gentile mission would be launched during the resurrection appearances with the Great Commission (Matt 28:18–20), and it would begin with the coming of the Holy Spirit at Pentecost (Acts 2). So this constitutes a prophetic announcement like the messianic prophecies of the Old Testament. The Gentiles too are known by Jesus (10:14), and he will "bring them also" into his sheepfold when they "listen to my voice" calling them to the gospel. The Gentile mission is seen here as a divine necessity and part of Jesus' mission.

The coming of the Gentiles into the people of God was proclaimed in the Abrahamic covenant, where God told Abraham that a major purpose for his choice of Israel was so that "all peoples on earth will be blessed through you" (Gen 12:3; also 18:18; 22:18; 26:4; 28:14), and reiterated in Isaiah 49:6 ("a light for the Gentiles," also 42:6). It was always God's plan to bring the Gentiles into his larger fold, and he actually chose Israel to bring about the procession of the nations to Zion (Isa 2:2–4; 11:10, 12; 14:1; 56:6–7; 60:3). In John, Jesus is the "Savior of the world" (4:42) and the "light of the world" (8:12). While the world hates God and rejects Jesus, God loves the world (3:16), and the mission of Jesus and the disciples is to the world (17:18; 20:21).

The result of this redemptive activity is that "there shall be one flock and one shepherd," uniting his people the remnant of Israel with the "other sheep," the Gentiles, into a new Israel (10:16). Jesus is the "one shepherd," separate from the other shepherds who have been shown to be thieves and robbers. In 1 Peter 5:1–4 those who are chosen by God to lead the church are the under-shepherds assisting the Chief Shepherd, Christ. Oneness will take place within the flock but also between the one flock and Jesus the One Shepherd. Jesus will beautifully present this theme of unity in the church in John 17:20–23 ("that they may be one as we are one").

Such unity must be hard-fought, for human nature tends toward divisiveness, and that has been the case for the church in all the two thousand years of its existence. We must learn to "agree to disagree" over the many issues of minor doctrines (Calvinism versus Arminianism, the debate over charismatic gifts), worship styles (high versus low church), or cultural differences. The Spirit at work in our midst must forge oneness out of our differences, and this takes place when the love and unity of the Godhead works itself out in the midst of such divisions.

The basis for everything—from creation to redemption—is the Father's love (10:17). Salvation is possible because "God so loved the world" (3:16), but that salvation is anchored in the Father's love for the Son, and Jesus' mission was the outgrowth of that love within the Godhead. Here the Father's love is intertwined with his Son's submission to his will, Christ's perfect union with the divine plan, the salvation that flows out of his vicarious sacrifice for sinful humankind.

The wondrous truth, however, is that his death was not an end in itself. The purpose of his death is "so that" (*hina*) he might "take it up again." The two form a single act in salvation history—death produces life. His death constituted his being "lifted up" into glory (3:14; 8:28; 12:32) and is defined in this Gospel as his time of destiny (his "hour," 2:4; 7:30; 8:20) appointed by God. Moreover, in 1 Corinthians 15:20, 23, Paul tells us Jesus' death and resurrection were divinely intended to be the guarantee—the "firstfruits" (see also Rom 6:4–5)—of our own death to sin and resurrection to life. This is a trinitarian event, for it is the Spirit who dwells within us and empowers us to experience this glorious new life in him.

Certainly the Jews condemned Jesus to death on the cross, and the Romans carried out the sentence, but the reality is that "no one takes [Jesus' life] from" him, but rather he "lay[s] it down of [his] own accord" (10:18). He voluntarily gave himself up on the cross as the substitute for our sins, and all that transpired took place on the basis of his divine "authority." Neither Satan nor the Jewish leaders nor the Romans were in charge. Jesus was, and his authority combined with his obedience to produce this salvific act. Christ perfectly controlled these final scenes and at the same time perfectly obeyed his Father's "command," so it was Jesus' authority and God's command that actually led to the cross.

THE JEWS REACT (10:19–21)

Division as usual marks the day. The reaction to the illustration (vv. 1–5) is misunderstanding (v. 6), and the reaction to the explanation (vv. 7–18) is strong difference of opinion (as earlier in 6:52; 7:25–27, 40–43) and accusations that he is "demon-possessed and raving mad" (v. 20). As I said earlier (see comments on 7:20; 8:48, 52; see also Mark 3:20–30), these are a single charge, not two, for insanity was commonly considered to be demon possession. In C. S. Lewis's famous "trilemma," Jesus is either liar, lunatic, or Lord. Many then, as in our day, agreed that insanity must have been behind Jesus' claims about himself.

Yet on the other hand, as in 9:16, 32, one must also account for the undeniable fact that Jesus opened the eyes of the blind (v. 21). The question is valid: Could (or would) a demon do such a thing? The works Jesus performed had to be taken into account when judging his words. Thus many in the crowd are still inclined to see him positively. The result is typical—hopeless division.

Jesus develops the picture of a shepherd and his sheep (10:1-5) to demonstrate the differences between himself and the leaders of the Jews. This shepherd gathers and watches over all the sheep of the village, and he is different from the thieves who sneak in, steal, and kill members of the flock. He knows his sheep, calls them by name, and builds an enclosure in which he becomes the gate when he sleeps across the opening. Jesus is the gate of God's flock, providing entrance into the kingdom, as well as the shepherd of the flock who watches over and protects them from danger.

In the explanation (vv. 7-18), we see how Jesus and the leaders play opposite roles in this narrative. As the gate (vv. 6-10), Jesus is the only entrance to the kingdom of God and eternal life. The leaders provide entrance only to destruction, while Jesus leads his flock into God's rich blessings. The false shepherds are the leaders in Jesus' day and false teachers in Paul's day and ours. Church leaders are tasked with keeping these charlatans from preying on Christ's flock and leading them astray.

As the Good Shepherd (vv. 11-18), Jesus reverses the pattern. The leaders as thieves kill the sheep, but Jesus as the messianic shepherd dies for the sheep. The thieves take lives; the shepherd saves lives and gives life. Moreover, the shepherd knows his sheep intimately and calls them to himself. We live in a divided world, with racial tension everywhere we look. Jesus makes it possible for this divided world to find oneness, as love tempers divisions and enables us through the love of the Godhead to bridge the gaps and indeed become "one sheep" united under the one Shepherd. Jesus' mission to the world becomes our mission.

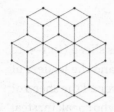

THE FEAST OF DEDICATION
(10:22–42)

The Feast of Dedication, known to us as Hanukkah, is the fourth and last festival Jesus encounters and fulfills (ch. 5: Sabbath; ch. 6: Passover; chs. 7-9: Tabernacles). The identity of Jesus is the central focus, especially the question of whether he really is the Messiah (v. 24) and Son of God (v. 36). This was the only festival in the Jewish calendar that had its origins outside the Old Testament. It originated in the events of 167-164 BC, when the Seleucid king Antiochus IV (Epiphanes), who was reigning over Palestine at the time, outlawed the Jewish religion and tried to force Greek religion on the people. He sent soldiers from village to village to make them sacrifice pigs to Zeus on pagan altars (1 Maccabees 1:41-50).

In the village of Modein an elderly priest, Mattathias, and his four sons rebelled. More and more gathered around him, forming a rebellion, then fighting a guerrilla war against the Seleucid armies (1 Maccabees 2:15-70). After a series of battles led by his oldest son, Judas (nicknamed Maccabeus, "the Hammer"), they liberated Jerusalem on 25 Kislev (= December), 164 BC, and rededicated the temple (1 Maccabees 4:36-61). The eight-day celebration that ensued was called "the festival of lights" due to the lighting of lamps in the homes and the procession to the temple. The more common name is Hanukkah, the Festival of Dedication.

JOHN SETS THE SCENE AT THE FEAST (10:22-23)

Two items in this passage are worthy of comment. John tells us Jesus is at the feast in "winter," a comment that would hardly need to be made, as everyone would know it took place in December. Several think "winter" has symbolic overtones similar to the "night" in 3:22; 9:4. However, this is the only place winter is mentioned, so it is unlikely. More likely John is telling why Jesus is in the colonnade of the temple rather than the open. Rabbis were known to seek shelter there from the cold winter winds, and it became known as a teaching area. Solomon's Colonnade was on the east side of the temple and was built on stone that preexisted Herod's temple-building project. The stone was believed to go back to Solomon's temple, though that was not the case. The colonnade was surrounded by magnificent columns and closed to the outside, making it an excellent shelter and a natural place for teaching.

FIRST INTERCHANGE: JESUS IS
THE MESSIAH (10:24-30)

The Jews there surround Jesus and challenge him, "How long will you keep us in suspense?[1] If you are the Messiah, tell us plainly." To this point Jesus has not identified explicitly in Jerusalem that he is the Messiah. The closest was the Samaritan woman; it was in Galilee where he was clear on the issue. At this point the crowds are not antagonistic and simply want him to settle the debates of chapters 5-9 once and for all. It is difficult for us to realize how politically volatile the issue of messianic expectation was at this time. It included strong nationalistic hope and had military overtones to it (see comments on 6:15).

Jesus' reply is unequivocal: "I did tell you, but you do not believe" (v. 25). This does not mean he has told them "plainly" but

---

1. This could also be translated, "How long are you going to annoy us?" implying hostility and opposition. However, it does not turn hostile until the next scene, and the more positive version is the better translation here.

that his implicit hints are sufficient. He has made clear that he
is the divine agent or envoy, the very voice of God making him
known to all. That should have been enough. The problem was not
their hearing; it was their unbelieving hearts. Every time he told
a crowd, they greeted it with unbelief (5:45-47; 6:36, 64; 7:48; 8:24,
45-46). In 5:36 the "works" he performed were an official "witness"
to his identity as Messiah, yet still they rejected him. Jesus' works
were in reality the works of his Father (5:17, 19-20) and were absolute proof of who he was.

Jesus now tells them why they have been so obdurate: "You do
not believe because you are not my sheep" (10:26). Jesus is drawing
on his words from 6:35-44—the sovereign God has not drawn them
to Jesus; they have not come, and so they are not his sheep. This
implies three stages by which people become Jesus' sheep (10:27):
they "listen" or hear his call; Jesus "knows" them; and they "follow"
him in response (see also vv. 3-4, 8, 14-16). The Jewish people did
not have eyes of faith and so missed the implications of both his
works and his words.

These next verses (vv. 28-29) form one of the most beautiful presentations of the security of the believer in Scripture.
Note the language, which teaches a two-handed security—the
believer is enfolded and protected in the hand of Jesus, which itself
is enfolded and protected in the hand of the Father—a double-
edged protection detail! No president has ever had better protection. This is the culmination of the rich, full life the Shepherd gives
the sheep (v. 10). In this Gospel eternal life is both a present possession (3:15-16, 36; 5:24; 6:40, 47, 51, 54, 58; 20:31) and a future promise
(5:28-29; 14:2-3). The sheep will "never perish." Certainly death is
still "the last enemy to be destroyed" (1 Cor 15:26), but at the same
time it is also a step upward to true life, our heavenly destiny.

This security is not grounded in any way in our own effort but
rather is centered on the power of Christ (6:37-40; 1 Pet 1:5) and
the empowering presence of the Spirit (John 16:13-15). The result
then is that "no one will snatch them out of my hand," neither

the thief nor the wolf (10:1, 8, 10, 12). The picture of sheep being snatched away is a violent one, depicting an enemy tearing us away from Christ (v. 12; compare Acts 20:29; 1 Peter 5:8). Similarly, in Romans 8:31–39 Paul teaches that nothing will ever separate us from the love of both Christ (v. 35) and God (v. 39). The love of the Godhead and its presence and power in us keep the believer completely secure.

Jesus made it clear in 5:19–30 that everything he did was anchored in his Father and flowed from him (see also 7:16, 28; 8:16, 29, 42). God's underlying strength guarantees the security of the Christ follower, for he is "greater than all" and more powerful than any other entity. Neither satanic powers nor human rulers have sufficient strength to derail God's people. Again, Paul develops this very well in Romans 8:31–39. No one, not the predatory leaders of Jesus' day or the false teachers of Paul's day, had the power to "snatch them out of my Father's hand." God's people are safe in him.

The conclusion to all this is one of the truly great statements in Scripture on the deity of Christ: "I and the Father are one." It is clearly a **christological** high point, restating the other clear statements of 1:1 ("the Word was God") and 18 ("the one and only Son, who is himself God"). Yet there is also debate, for the "one" is neuter (*hen*) rather than masculine, and most see it as teaching a functional unity of purpose rather than an ontological union of person. It could then be translated, "I and the Father have one purpose."

However, it clearly contains both aspects, as seen in the definition of the Trinity—one essence and three persons. This is a restatement of 5:17–30, the unity of Father and Son in doing the work of God. So the oneness points to a unity of purpose and work within the unity of the Godhead. The Jews would not have "picked up stones to stone him" for blasphemy (10:31) if he were merely saying he had the same purpose as God. They understood him as in 5:18, where they realized he was "making himself equal with God." So this passage proclaims both a unity of work and purpose and also a unity of personhood. Jesus and his Father work as one because they are one.

SECOND INTERCHANGE: JESUS IS THE SON OF GOD (10:31-38)

THE JEWISH CHARGE (10:31-33)

The detail about the attempt to stone Jesus both ends the previous section and begins this section. The law demanded that blasphemy was to be punished by stoning (Lev 24:16). Technically, it was outlawed, for the Romans reserved the right of capital punishment for themselves. Still, it did take place at times (Acts 7:54-8:1, the stoning of Stephen). The emphasis here is on Jesus' self-control. He is in mortal danger but refuses to flinch at all and in fact carries on his discussion as if nothing has happened. He simply points to the "many good works" he has shown them and asks, "For which of these do you stone me?" The point is that these "good works" "from the Father" are done at his Father's leading and thereby prove that what he said in verse 30 was correct.

The implicit question Jesus poses to them is the same one we have been seeing in recent chapters—could he have done these wondrous works if he were a false prophet, deluded, or under satanic control? The Jewish opponents don't catch the relationship between what Jesus does and who he is. They center just on his claim and so tell him the stoning is not "for any good work ... but for blasphemy, because you, a mere man, claim to be God" (v. 33). To them his works are irrelevant in light of his claim, which constitutes blasphemy and demands stoning. It is an affront to their monotheism and cuts at the very essence of their beliefs.

JESUS' RESPONSE (10:34-38)

Jesus begins with a legal question, "Is it not written in your law, 'I have said you are "gods"'?" "Your law" here does not constitute Jesus' separation from the Mosaic law but rather reminds them

that he is appealing to the same Scriptures they themselves avow.
By "law" Jesus is not just referring to the Torah or Pentateuch but
to the whole canon of the Old Testament (often called "the law"
by the Jews): the citation comes from Psalm 82:6, "I said, 'You are
"gods."'" The complete text is, "'You are "gods"; you are all sons of
the Most High.' But you will die like mere mortals; you will fall
like every other ruler." The context is the oppression of the poor
by Israel[2] and the judgment they would receive for their injustice.
They had received God's message at Sinai and been called God's
"firstborn son" (Exod 4:22), but both fell by worshiping the golden
calf and were guilty of injustice to the poor.

Jesus argues from the lesser to the greater in verse 36. If these
failed people could be called "gods," how could anyone object to
Jesus being called "Son of God"? They received "the word of God"—
the law—at Sinai, and Jesus adds, "Scripture cannot be set aside,"
meaning that those at Sinai were truly "gods" because they became
the children and family of God. It is stated in Scripture and cannot
be ignored.

If this is true, and it is because Scripture says so, then how
much more is Jesus worthy, who can be characterized as having
two advantages only he enjoys: (1) He is the one whom the Father
"set apart as his very own," his one and only Son; and (2) he is
the one consecrated to be "sent into the world" to accomplish the
divine mission only he could fulfill. Putting them together, Jesus
was set apart for his Father's holy mission. Of course, Israel was
also consecrated and sent, but not with the authority and power
of Jesus. Moreover, Israel failed in its mission. So Jesus fulfills
and carries out the very mission that Israel failed to perform, and
therefore he has a perfect right to call himself "Son of God." They
have no right to call that blasphemy.

---

2. Some take Ps 82:6 as referring to the corrupt judges of Israel, but it is difficult to see them as the recipients of "the word of God." It is best to see this
as referring to the people of Israel who received God's word at Sinai.

Having proved his right to label himself "Son of God," he in verses 37–38 lays out the reasons why they should believe in him. This is the same point Jesus made in 5:36; 10:25—if they will not believe because of his words, they should believe because of his works, which demonstrate that he is carrying out his Father's work. All he does—his words and his works—are anchored in the Father and show his inextricable connection to him. He is indeed his Father's Son, for he does his Father's works. The Jewish people greeted both earlier claims with unbelief and attempts to stone him (5:18; 10:31), but he is giving them another chance. In 2:23–25 sign-based belief is partial and inadequate, but 5:36 and 8:14 show that the works as signs provide legally valid witness because they come from God and should lead to faith-decision. They prove his oneness with the Father and show that the two act in concert.

Jesus' purpose here is so that the Jews might "know and understand." He wants them to realize the truth that unites his deeds with his claims, demonstrating that he is indeed the Son of God. Specifically, they must come to know the mutual union between Father and Son—"the Father is in me, and I in the Father." This formula will appear again in 14:10–11 and 17:21, where it will be the basis for the unity between believers and Jesus/the Spirit (see 6:56; 14:20; 15:5, 7; see also 1 John 2:24; 3:24; 4:15) as well as the internal unity of the church (John 17:20–23).

The Feast of Dedication celebrated the liberation and consecration of the temple and thus included a messianic component as the Jewish people looked forward to their final release under the Messiah. Jesus presents himself as the fulfillment that brings spiritual liberation to God's former people now in exile.

CONCLUDING EVENTS: REJECTION AND DEPARTURE (10:39–42)

Once again the officials try to arrest Jesus, undoubtedly to try him for a capital offense, blasphemy (see 5:18; 7:30, 32; 8:37, 40, 59; 10:31). But he slips away, for as has been said, his predestined hour of destiny has not arrived (7:30; 8:20). This time he goes "back across the Jordan" (to the eastern side) to Bethany, where the Baptist ministered (1:28, not the Bethany near Jerusalem, where Lazarus made his home). That took place in the latter days of the Baptist's ministry, and now this takes place in the latter days of Jesus' earthly ministry.

Finally, however, the Baptist's witness (1:19–34; 3:27–30; 5:33–35) bears fruit. In verses 41–42 the evangelist highlights Jesus' ministry as a fulfillment of the ministry of his forerunner. The "many people" who come show that even though the Baptist had been executed, his popularity continued and his witness to Jesus was still effective. John was the prophet like Elijah, but it was not his miracles he emulated but rather his prophetic witness. John said, "He must become greater; I must become less" (3:30). The Baptist was the faithful witness (5:36), and now people are saying, "all that John said about this man was true," and as a result "many believed in Jesus." John had truly fulfilled the purpose of his ministry; he had prepared for Jesus and brought many to him.

———

This final passage showing how Jesus fulfills the feasts and answers the charges of those who oppose him is the perfect conclusion, for Hanukkah celebrated the rededication of the temple and anticipated the liberation of the nation by the Messiah, and so it is fulfilled in the person of the Messiah and Son of God, Jesus. The first part of this section (vv. 22–30) centers on the unbelieving Jews' rejection of these truths and details the wondrous double security of believers in the hand of God superimposed on the hand of Christ, one of the most beautiful statements on security in all of the word of God.

The second half (vv. 31–38) proves that Jesus has the perfect right to call himself Son of God. The Jewish people were called "gods" (Ps 82:6) because they were part of God's family in spite of

their failure to fulfill their mission from God. However, Jesus, who
was set apart for a mission he did fulfill, is rightfully worshiped by
us as God's Son. If Judas the Maccabee ("Hammer") in 164 BC was
feted by the nation as their liberator, how much more is Jesus the
divine warrior to be celebrated as our eternal liberator. Christmas
as our "festival of lights" is a valid successor to Hanukkah, and
we experience an even greater joy at Christmas than the Jewish
people did in their Festival of Dedication in Jesus' day, for our liberation is certain and eternal.

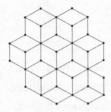

THE RAISING OF LAZARUS
(11:1–57)

M any doubt the historicity of this event, because not only is it the most spectacular of them all, but it is also only recorded in John. Some think it developed out of the parable of the rich man and Lazarus in Luke 16, but the two are quite different in theme and details, which makes it highly unlikely. The incredible detail and lifelike portrayal give us solid reasons for accepting this story. Jesus' raising the dead occurred more than once—Jairus's daughter in Mark 5:22-43 and the son of the widow of Nain in Luke 7:11-17 along with two general references in Matthew 11:5 and Luke 7:22. Moreover, the story fits its first-century context amazingly well and summarizes the emphasis in John on Jesus as the giver of life. So its function as the concluding event of Jesus' public ministry and as a transition into the events of passion week make it a natural instrument for this purpose. The death and resurrection of Lazarus provides the perfect introduction to the death and resurrection of Jesus.

LAZARUS DIES (11:1-16)

THE SETTING: NEWS OF THE ILLNESS (11:1-6)

Jesus' retreat in Bethany was short-lived because of the serious illness of his good friend Lazarus. He is not mentioned elsewhere, although his sisters Mary and Martha appear in Luke 10:38-42. Martha, the hostess in Luke 10, was probably the older sister. They so far as we know never became leaders in the church but were ordinary followers whose home Jesus stayed in when he was in Jerusalem. They were probably a wealthy family, since Lazarus was laid in a wealthy person's tomb and Mary poured expensive perfume on Jesus. Their home village, Bethany (not the same one as in 1:28), lay a couple miles east of Jerusalem on the road to Jericho. Jesus was actually resting in the other Bethany (10:40) when he received the bad news about Lazarus.

Mary is the better known of the two sisters as the one who anointed Jesus' feet (see 12:1-8), and John mentions this in verse 2 here to introduce the three. This had to be a well-known story, for John mentions it before he narrates it. It also demonstrates that Jesus had long known the family, so their request in verse 3 is from devoted friends. Their request is quite simple: "Lord, the one you love is sick." This relates several things at once. First, it is a serious illness, and they need Jesus quickly to heal Lazarus; it is a plea that he come to them ASAP. Calling Lazarus "the one you love"[1] shows the depth of the friendship. Second, they are not casual acquaintances, and they are more than anonymous followers. They are requesting that Jesus travel from the Bethany on the east side of the Jordan to the Bethany on the outskirts of Jerusalem. The three siblings had become very close to Jesus.

---

1. The verb here is *phileō*, and some read that as human affection, but it is *agapaō* in v. 5 ("Jesus loved" the three) with no difference of meaning. As I have mentioned, the two verbs in John's Gospel are virtual synonyms.

Jesus' reply (v. 4) is reminiscent of his statement about the man born blind in 9:3 ("this happened so that the works of God might be displayed in him"). Here he says, "This sickness will not end in death. No, it is for God's glory so that God's Son may be glorified through it." The divine purpose makes both of these miracles programmatic signs for the glory of the Godhead. This does not mean Lazarus won't die but that it will end in resurrection rather than death. The glory of God was the major goal of Jesus' life; all he accomplished was intended to reveal his Father's glory (12:28; 14:13; 17:1, 4). The glory of God is always found in the mutual union between Father and Son (10:38; 14:10–11, 20; 17:21), which implies a reciprocity of glory. The raising of Lazarus would bring about the glory of the Father in the Son and would prepare for the greater glory of the dying and rising of Christ himself.

In 11:5–6 an even stranger aspect of the story ensues, as Jesus remains in the other Bethany an extra two days. It seems at first that he is enjoying his R & R so much that he doesn't want to leave. Adding to the confusion, in verse 5 John says he "loved" them but in verse 6 tells us he "stayed where he was." Another way to translate it would be, "He loved them enough to wait two more days." Why?

The note on the deep love of Jesus for them is critical. He wasn't calloused or insensitive; rather, it was so his Father could be glorified and their needs met. The two Bethanys were three to four days apart, and in verse 17 John tells us Lazarus had been dead for four days when Jesus got there. Lazarus must have died shortly after the messengers had gone to see Jesus. It seems that Jesus, being omniscient, deliberately waited two days (see 1:48; 4:18). If Jesus had left immediately, Lazarus still would have died before he could get there. Especially in light of the impact this event has had on church history, it seems the way God engineered the events was best for Lazarus as well as for everyone involved.

In the end, there were two reasons for the delay: (1) It heightened the miracle, showing even more powerfully that Jesus was indeed "the resurrection and the life." The Jews believed that the soul remained with the body until the third day, so Jesus was ensuring it was not a resuscitation but a resurrection. (2) It was God's timing; Jesus knew that when he left, the "hour" (7:30; 8:20) would arrive for the passion events to begin. Jesus waited until the signal from the Father came, launching these final events.

RETURN TO JUDEA (11:7–10)

The fact that Jesus wants to return to Judea rather than just Bethany shows his coming passion is uppermost in his thoughts, and the raising of Lazarus is a preparatory event. The disciples are quite aware of the dangers and mention the attempt to stone Jesus, likely the one in 10:31, 39. The opposition was intensifying, and they were in grave danger. In a short time (11:16) Thomas will speak of going and dying with Jesus. So they are surprised Jesus is willing to go there again so soon.

In verse 9 Jesus replies in the form of a proverb, similar to 9:4. There are two twelve-hour periods in a day, separated into the light of day and dark of night. It is easier to walk during daytime, when "this world's light" enables you to avoid obstacles and not stumble over them. The spiritual thrust is that Jesus the "light of the world" (8:12) illuminates this world of darkness with the light of God (1:4, 7, 9). There is only a short time left before the darkness takes over and he faces the cross. There is little time left, and he has to use it carefully to do the work of his Father while he can.

The same is true for the disciples. As in 9:4, the daylight is the short time Jesus will still be with them, and the night will arrive when Jesus is taken from them. They have to follow the light so long as they can, and that means a return to Judea. Ironically, to walk in the light for them means to follow Jesus into danger.

THE DECISION TO GO AND HELP LAZARUS (11:11–16)

Jesus expects his disciples to understand: "Our friend Lazarus has fallen asleep; but I am going there to wake him up." They should have realized Jesus meant to raise him from the dead. They had seen him do so before.[2] However, they commit the same error seen throughout this Gospel, taking Jesus literally from an earthly perspective. So they respond, "Lord, if he sleeps, he will get better" (v. 12). It is also possible they didn't really know the euphemism. While sleep is a fairly common euphemism for death, the idea that "waking up" means resurrection from the dead was not commonly used. This makes sense, for the evangelist feels he must explain it for the readers (v. 13): "Jesus had been speaking of his death, but his disciples thought he meant natural sleep." It also serves to show that Jesus knows all that has happened and is in total control.

So Jesus makes it absolutely clear for the disciples in verse 14, "Lazarus is dead." Then he proceeds to tell them that it was good for everyone (including Lazarus) that Jesus wasn't there to heal him. It must have been confusing to hear Jesus say he was "glad" that he wasn't present when Lazarus was dying. Yet as with the blind man in 9:3 there were larger issues at stake. God had orchestrated the events "for your sake"; first, "for God's glory" (11:4), and second, "so that you may believe" (v. 15). If Jesus had been there, it would have been another healing miracle. But now it will be a powerful raising from the dead, proving his authority to give life (5:21, 25–26). Their faith was growing, and this would be a significant step forward.

Thomas still does not understand and focuses only on the danger they are walking into (v. 16). So he acquiesces and says, "Let us also go, that we may die with him." The tremendous courage he shows here is exemplary, and he should actually be known as "courageous Thomas" more than "doubting Thomas" (due to 20:24–29). We know almost nothing about him from the New Testament.[3] Apart from John 11, 20, he is no more than named as

---

2. See the introduction to this chapter.

3. Later extrabiblical tradition indicates that he became a missionary to Parthia (in modern-day Iran; see Eusebius, *Ecclesiastical History* 3.1) or India (see the third-century Acts of Thomas).

an apostle elsewhere (Mark 3:18 and parallels; Acts 1:13). Still, he is the perfect example of Jesus' command to his disciples to "take up their cross and follow me" (Mark 8:34).

JESUS IS THE RESURRECTION AND THE LIFE (11:17–32)

THE SETTING IN BETHANY (11:17–20)

After a few days' journey, they arrive to find Lazarus has been in the grave four days (the Jews buried people the very day they died). As mentioned above, this is likely the main reason why Jesus waited two days before leaving (11:6). The rabbis believed the soul lingered near the grave for three days, hoping to reenter the body, but as decomposition begins, it leaves (Leviticus Rabbah 18:1; Ecclesiastes Rabbah 12:6). The identification of a corpse also had to be done within three days. As a result, this would be an especially dramatic raising from the dead.

John might mention the proximity to Jerusalem (15 stadia, or 1.7 miles) in verse 18 to tell us most of the mourners were from there (v. 19). It was quite common for many to come to "comfort" and console the family, and with their wealth they were probably prominent fixtures in the community. Mourning was a serious duty within Judaism. There was a great deal of loud weeping and cries of grief. In fact, some families would hire professional mourners to ensure all knew of the sorrow for the deceased (see 11:33).

As Jesus neared Jerusalem, Martha rushed out to meet him, while Mary stayed with the other mourners. This was a slight breach of custom, as the family was expected to "sit *shiva*" (meaning "seven days" of mourning), waiting for arrivals, as Mary did. Yet this also fits their personality as seen in Luke 10:38–42, with Martha bustling about and Mary sitting at Jesus' feet.

GREETED BY THE TWO SISTERS (11:21–32)

Greeted by Martha (11:21–27)

Many take Martha's statement in verse 21 ("Lord, if you had been here, my brother would not have died") as an implicit rebuke ("you should have been here"). However, it more likely depicts her sorrow and sincere belief that Jesus could have made the difference if he had been there. At first glance, her next statement that "even now God will give you whatever you ask" (v. 22) sounds like a full-grown faith that he could still raise Lazarus if he wanted, but Jesus' rebuke in verse 40 shows that could not be the case. There is some faith in what she says, but it is incomplete. This is probably an indistinct hope that perhaps Jesus could still get God to do something, but she is not sure what.

Jesus responds to this partly developed faith by affirming, "Your brother will rise again" (v. 23), which for him meant very soon and to Martha meant someday in the future, which Martha shows when she replies, "I know he will rise again in the resurrection *at the last day*." Resurrection was the subject of a major debate between the Pharisees, who accepted the reality of a final resurrection, and the Sadducees (the priestly leaders), who denied any possibility of an afterlife (see Mark 12:18–27; Acts 23:6–10). The majority of the common people sided with the Pharisees. After the destruction of Jerusalem, belief in resurrection and afterlife became the official Jewish view. Martha centers on this and does not realize Jesus is promising something much more immediate.

The center and thesis of the entire narrative is sounded in 11:25, the fifth "I am" statement (after 6:35; 8:12; 10:7, 14): "I am the resurrection and the life." Resurrection is seen as a reality that inheres in Jesus himself. This is what Martha fails to assimilate. John has stressed Jesus' authority to give life several times—both eternal life as a present possession (5:21, 24–25; 6:27, 33) and bodily resurrection in the future (5:28–29; 6:39–40, 44). Martha does not understand a key aspect and needs to deepen her partial belief into a full-fledged affirmation that Jesus is life itself, the one who gives it. For the Jesus follower death is not an end but a transition, a path to life eternal in heaven. Life inheres in Jesus, and we attain it by belief in him. Life for the believer is actually eternal life as a present possession, giving way in the end to ongoing life with Christ in heaven. Here the two are combined, as Lazarus will be raised from the dead now and not just "at the last day."

The key is belief that the one who comes to faith-decision "will live, even though they die." This refers to the physical resurrection, the realization that death has no hold on the one who believes. It is "the last enemy," but its destiny is "to be destroyed" (1 Cor 15:26). The truth is that "whoever lives by believing in me will never die" (11:25). Martha believes in the general truth of resurrection but has not tied it to the personal authority and control of Jesus himself. Jesus is speaking of both physical and spiritual resurrection. Eternal life is the believer's destiny. Jesus is life and sovereign over it, and the only way to participate in it is via faith in him (in Rom 3:21–4:25 "faith" occurs eighteen times).

Jesus ends in verse 26 with a challenge, "Do you believe this?" This is an invitation that goes beyond raising Lazarus from the dead. Jesus is asking Martha to believe in his power not only to raise the dead but also to give eternal life. So in this sense the raising of Lazarus is a prophetic action like those performed by Jeremiah or Ezekiel, signifying the new life that God in Jesus offers to anyone who believes.

So when Martha responds, "Yes, Lord" (v. 27), she is taking a step of saving faith. Her language proves her true faith: "I believe that you are the Messiah, the Son of God." These correspond both to the titles in the first salvation drama, uttered by Andrew and Nathanael in 1:41, 49; and at the end of this Gospel as the definition of true faith in 20:30–31. In addition, she acknowledges him as the one "who is to come into the world," restating 6:14; 7:28–29; 8:29, 42. **Christology** and **soteriology** are united in the highest confession yet in this Gospel.

Greeted by Mary (11:28–32)

Both Martha and Mary go out to meet Jesus rather than have him come to them, possibly because of the danger to him in Judea, but more likely to have him to themselves. So Martha returns and tells her sister Jesus wants to see her. It is interesting she still calls him "the teacher" or "rabbi" after calling him "Lord" in 11:21, 27. This term appears elsewhere in the Gospel (1:38; 3:2) and is probably the term they normally used. The fact that she "got up quickly and went" (11:29) shows her great affection and regard for him.

The fact that Jesus is still keeping separate from the mourners (v. 30) is most likely to maintain the privacy of meeting with his friends, but the effort is very short-lived. The friends who have come to console them think Mary is going to the tomb and follow her to comfort her in her grief (v. 31). It is possible that they thought this an official development in the mourning process, the change of the scene of mourning to the tomb itself.

There is some debate as to whether Mary is rebuking Jesus for not being there for him. She says the same thing Martha did in verse 21 ("Lord, if you had been here, my brother would not have died") but without Martha's statement of faith. Still, she "fell at his feet" (v. 32), likely in worship and not just in grief. Thus it is best to see her, like Martha, characterized more by sorrow than rebuke—she is pouring out her heart to Jesus with much the same burgeoning faith Martha showed.

JESUS IS OUTRAGED AT THE POWER OF DEATH (11:33–37)

Jesus' reaction is surprising to say the least. Most translations water down the emotion in the description, reading, "he was deeply moved in spirit and troubled" (NIV; see also KJV, NRSV, ESV, NASB, LEB, NET). However, the first verb is *embrimaomai*, used of a horse snorting, and connotes deep-seated anger or rage. The NLT is much closer: "a deep anger welled up within him, and he was deeply troubled." Perhaps a literal translation may be best: "he was outraged in spirit and deeply troubled within himself." The evangelist will use the second term, "deeply troubled," later to depict Jesus' state of mind when he faces his passion (12:27; 13:21). The two together show a supremely agitated Christ as he faces Lazarus's tomb.

What was he so angry about? There are three possibilities: (1) anger that they were forcing him to perform a miracle, similar to 2:4 in Cana; (2) anger at their lack of faith as seen in their excessive mourning; (3) anger at the power of sin and death in this world. The first is very unlikely because Jesus intended to perform a miracle from the start. Certainly the context makes the second viable since they have been weeping and pouring out their grief. But the repetition of this verb in verse 38 when he arrives at the tomb makes the third far more likely. Jesus is overcome by the horror of the human dilemma under sin and death, and as a result he is filled with anger. The specter of death hanging over all humanity unsettles him. This is critical for us as well. Christ and Christ alone has overcome death, and we must direct our lives by that fact.

Christ can wait no longer; he must defeat death for his dear friend. He asks, "Where have you laid him?" Interestingly they use the same words Jesus used to invite the first disciples: "Come and see" (v. 34; see 1:39, 46). As he stood before the tomb, we are told, "Jesus wept" (v. 35). This does not denote the same wailing put forth by the mourners but a more gentle weeping in grief. (It is a different term in Greek.) Moreover, Jesus is not grieving just for Lazarus, whom he is about to raise from the dead, but for all who like him must suffer the same sorrow. Lazarus would have to go through that again, and Mary and Martha would pass through that dark valley as well. This is the other side of Jesus' reaction to the "last enemy," death. They stem from the two sides of Jesus' nature—his justice feels outrage, and his love feels grief. This is a perfect model for us as we "hate the sin and love the sinner." Anger and grief go hand in hand as we cope with the sad results of a sinful world.

The onlookers are also split in their reactions (vv. 36–37). Some are touched by the depth of his love for Lazarus and admire his reactions. Others are upset that the one who could heal the blind has not "kept this man from dying." Both are partly right. Jesus did love Lazarus and could have healed his disease, even from a distance. But on the larger issue they were very wrong, as they would soon find out. They understood neither Jesus' true purpose nor the extent of his power over sickness and death. God's timing is always perfect.

LAZARUS IS RAISED FROM THE DEAD (11:38–44)

Jesus arrives at the tomb still seething with anger (see comments on 11:33) over what sin and death have done to all those created beings that the Godhead loves so deeply. In what transpires he confronts the evil powers and overcomes their hold over humanity. He is the Divine Warrior, the conquering Messiah, defeating the powers of sin and death and liberating God's people. This is about much more than the raising of Lazarus. It is a foretaste of what would take place at the cross and empty tomb and also at his second coming, when he will raise the dead and reunite them with their eternal spirits (1 Cor 15:51–55; 1 Thess 4:13–18).

The cave in which Lazarus was buried—a sign of his wealth, for only they could afford such a tomb (see comments on 11:1–6)— resembled the later tomb of Jesus with a stone rolled into a groove to seal the tomb. Jesus commands them to roll back the stone to give him access. The purpose of such a seal was to allow family members such access so they could do things like bring spices and anoint the body (Mark 16:1–4). As it is being rolled away, there is still no realization of his authority over death, and Martha, ever the practical one, objects because Lazarus has been decomposing for four days, and the stench would be terrible (11:39). While Egyptians used extensive embalming techniques, the Jews simply buried the corpse intact. All the spices and perfumes used to anoint the corpse (see 19:39–40) were intended to counteract that smell.

Martha, in spite of all her discussion with Jesus in verses 21–27, still does not comprehend what he is about to do. Therefore he repeats his earlier point: "Did I not tell you that if you believe, you will see the glory of God?" (v. 40, repeating v. 4). Since he said that to the messengers rather than Mary, we can take the "glory of God" as a theological summary of what he has told her in 11:21–27. "Glory" in this Gospel is linked to the miracles as signs pointing to the power of God (see 9:3; 11:4). The death and resurrection of Jesus are seen as glory in 12:40–41; 17:5. To experience this glory, Martha and the others need the same faith shown by the disciples in 2:11. The glory will be there no matter what, but it will be perceived and appropriated only by those who see with the eye of faith.

They roll away the stone, and Jesus stands at the opening, lifts his eyes to heaven (the basic Jewish posture for prayer was with uplifted arms and eyes), and prays (11:41). The uplifted eyes are symbolic of Jesus' total dependence on his heavenly Father. We would do well to pray this way more often. Interestingly, this is the only mention of prayer before any of Jesus' miracles, and he says in verse 42 that he does so "for the benefit of the people standing here, that they may believe that you sent me." Everything he did stemmed from his reliance on his Father (5:19, 30; 7:16, 28; 8:16, 29, 42), yet at the same time he himself had the power to perform miracles.

All of Jesus' prayers apart from the cry of dereliction on the cross in Mark 15:34 begin with "Father" and show his submission to God. The decision to raise Lazarus had already been made within the Godhead, so he begins with thanks to his Father for hearing him. The Old Testament teaches that God hears the righteous (Pss 34:15; 145:19), and Jesus is perfectly righteous. The raising of Lazarus is proof positive of his special relationship with his Father, and he wants to draw his followers into that intimacy and allow them to share in his close ties to the Father. Here he states that a further purpose is to enhance their faith that God had indeed sent

Jesus as his agent or envoy to complete the God-intended mission to the world (11:42). He is indeed the one sent from heaven by God.

It is now, when his prayer is finished, that his command ushers forth, "Lazarus, come out!" (v. 43). Many have commented that Jesus' authority over death is so great and complete (5:28–29) that had he not specified Lazarus, the dead would have emerged from every grave in the world. The last days were indeed here, and we now see why Jesus did not heal Lazarus when he received the message in 11:3. God wished to use him to show that Jesus was indeed "the resurrection and the life" (v. 25).

At Jesus' command, the most dramatic scene yet ensues. Lazarus emerges from the tomb with "his hands and feet [still] wrapped with strips of linen, and a cloth around his face." The Jews buried their dead by laying the corpse on a long, wide cloth with the feet at the bottom. They would then draw the cloth over the head and drape it over the front of the body, then tie it at the ankles, securing the arms to the body with linen strips. The face would be covered with a head cloth to hide the discoloration. It would be very difficult for Lazarus to walk with the grave clothes still around him, so Jesus immediately orders, "Take off the grave clothes and let him go." To have been there and seen Lazarus step out of the dark cave still wrapped in the linens would be electrifying. Can you imagine the joy and the hysteria at that moment?

There is a further parallel with Jesus' resurrection, when Jesus left the strips of linen and the head cloth lying in the tomb (20:5–7). The difference is that Lazarus would have to die again, while Jesus conquered death with finality and forever.

JEWISH LEADERS PLOT TO KILL JESUS (11:45–57)

DIVISION AND THE DECISION TO KILL JESUS (11:45–50)

The public nature of the raising of Lazarus electrifies the Jewish people, and everyone takes sides. As before, the Jews are divided over Jesus (6:64; 7:12–13; 10:19–21). Those who believe in 11:45 are

primarily the mourners who were present with Mary and Martha
at the miracle. Theirs was undoubtedly the type of partial belief
centered on the sign-miracle as in 2:23–25, but it was still the
beginning stages of true faith. Others (11:46) report what Jesus
had done to the leaders and joined the opposition. Jesus' miraculous signs always galvanize the crowds and force them to take
sides. Faith-decision is at the heart of John's Gospel. Jesus encounters every person at gut level, and there are no neutral people in
John. In our time we must welcome the "seekers," but also warn
them that so long as they try to remain interested but neutral, they
are actually in the process of rejecting Christ.

Jesus' miracle and the ensuing disagreement over it cause the
authorities to call a meeting of the Sanhedrin, the governing council of the Jews (v. 47). There were three groups who made up the
Sanhedrin: the chief priests (the controlling group and adamantly
opposed to Christ), the Pharisees (lay leaders and expert in the
Torah, divided somewhat but mostly negative), and the aristocrats
or "elders" (no record of them on this). Many interpreters think
this an unofficial meeting, but they come to an official decision
on Jesus. They had intended to kill Jesus earlier (5:18), had mud-
dled repeated attempts to arrest him (7:32, 45), and had been thoroughly outclassed by a formerly blind beggar (9:30–33).

Now a true crisis has come that in their minds threatens the
very future of the Jewish people, and a final decision has to be
made. Jesus' sign-miracles have magnified his popularity, and
people are starting to believe in him (v. 48a). Lazarus takes that
to the next level. No longer can they afford indecision; they must
act firmly, lest the Romans "come and take away both our temple
and our nation" (v. 48b). Many of the first-century Jewish rebel-
lions were messianic in nature, and so the fear that the fervor
of the people toward Jesus could be interpreted as another anti-
Roman rebellion was valid. In fact, about thirty years later, in AD
66, a rebellion started that led to the destruction of Jerusalem and
the temple.

We should notice that they do not ever consider the possibility that Jesus might actually be the Messiah. The leaders and many in the crowds have hardened their hearts and minds and are no longer open to the truth (5:41–47; 7:27, 47–49; 8:48–59; 10:33). This is shown in the centrality of "our" in "*our* temple and *our* nation." While on the surface they seem deeply concerned for the temple, in reality they are primarily concerned for their own position in society. They want to keep power for themselves.

On their behalf, the head of the Sanhedrin, the high priest Caiaphas, takes over (11:49–50). He reigned for quite a length of time (AD 18–36), inheriting his office shortly after his father-in-law, Annas (AD 6–15). According to the Old Testament law a high priest reigned for life, but the Romans controlled all government positions, including the high priesthood, and would frequently replace a high priest who had fallen out of favor. To the Jewish people the deposed leader would always be high priest, so there would be two at this time (as with Annas in 18:12–24).

As head of the Sanhedrin it was expected for Caiaphas to speak up. He begins by accusing them of ignorance: "You know nothing at all!" (v. 49). The Jewish historian Josephus, writing toward the end of the first century, said the Sanhedrin was wild and barbarous toward each other (*Jewish War* 2.166), and that is certainly true here. Caiaphas means that the Sanhedrin has failed to see the logic of the evidence and their own earlier conclusions about this dangerous blasphemer, Jesus of Nazareth.

He then provides his own conclusion, the one that will carry the day: "It is better for you that one man die for the people than that the whole nation perish" (v. 50). He believes Jesus should be sacrificed both to keep the Jewish people from the wrath of Rome ("for the nation," with "for," *hyper*, constituting sacrificial language) and to keep them in political power ("better for you"). Jesus would become a scapegoat given over to death for their sake.

THE MEANING AND RESULTS OF THE DECISION (11:51-54)

Caiaphas failed to realize the true significance of what he said, so John intervenes with the true spiritual meaning of what he labels an unconscious prophecy (v. 51). Caiaphas was thinking politically but didn't realize what he was saying, for the Holy Spirit was actually speaking through him in his high priestly capacity. He was led to prophesy in spite of himself, much like Balaam's donkey in Numbers 22:21-38. According to the Old Testament, the high priest was God's spokesman and could determine God's will for the nation by using the Urim and Thummim, sacred lots that were cast to discern God's wishes (Exod 28:30; Deut 33:8; Ezra 2:63). High priests were not normally prophets, but a high priest could be led by God to speak prophetically, and that is the case here.

He prophesies two things (vv. 51-52): (1) "Jesus would die for the Jewish nation," with *hyper* ("for") as in verse 50 referring to his atoning sacrifice in which he would die in their place. John stresses vicarious sacrifice more than the writers of the **Synoptic** Gospels (1:29; 6:51; 10:11, 15; 11:50-52; 15:13; 17:19). The fact that John uses "nation" here rather than "people" may be significant, as the latter term often was used in the **Septuagint** (Greek Old Testament) and New Testament for the covenant people of God. This hints that in their apostate state they have ceased to be the covenant people.

(2) He prophesied also, John says, that Jesus died "for the scattered children of God, to bring them together and make them one." This goes beyond the Jewish communities in the diaspora (outside Palestine) to embrace the Gentile mission as well. This thought reiterates 10:16, where Jesus says that the Good Shepherd died also for "other sheep that are not of this sheep pen." Believing Jews and Gentiles make up the whole "children of God" because they have been given to Jesus by his Father (6:37, 44) and thus would be gathered into "one flock and one shepherd" (10:16; 17:11, 20-23). The object of God's love and mission is at all times "the world" (3:16). The Jews are part of the world (1:10-11); Christ has "come into the world" (11:27) to be "the light of the world" (8:12) and "the Savior of

the world" (4:42). All peoples of the world will thereby be brought together and made one in Christ. The answer to racial divides in our time and all times is simple—the love and salvation of the Triune Godhead (Eph 2:11–22).

The decision is now finalized, and "from that day on they plotted to take his life" (11:53). This consummates a string of preliminary decisions to rid themselves of the heretic and troublemaker, Jesus (5:18; 7:30, 32; 8:59; 10:31). The raising of Lazarus is the catalyst behind it, since it magnified Jesus' popularity and support from the common people, so the leaders feel they can delay no longer. What they fail to realize is that they are actually doing God's will, as Peter will note later in Acts 2:23: "This man was handed over to you by God's deliberate plan and foreknowledge."

As before (10:40), Jesus learns of the decision and "withdraws" from Jerusalem. His hour of destiny (see comments on 7:30; 8:20) was not quite here yet, so he goes to a small village called Ephraim that was twelve to fifteen miles northeast of Jerusalem. God, not the Sanhedrin, would dictate the exact hour, and Jesus alone had authority to surrender his life (10:17–18). For the short time remaining he wished to be away from the furor of Jerusalem yet still close enough to return for Passover (11:55).

THE ARRIVAL OF PASSOVER (11:55–57)

Events are now escalating as they lead to that most decisive moment of human history, when the Son of God is to become the Lamb of God who is to be "lifted up" to the cross and glory (3:14; 8:28; 12:32). This is the third and final Passover in this Gospel (2:13; 6:4), the most important Passover in all of history, the one to which all the others (even the first) pointed. The imagery associated with Passover (the blood liberating God's people from death) was finally to be fulfilled once for all (see Heb 9:28).

Lazarus was probably raised a couple weeks before Passover (see 12:1), and pilgrims had started to arrive from all around the Roman world for the festival. This was a pilgrimage festival, and

Jerusalem would swell from about 70,000 (see Rev 11:13) to nearly a quarter million, so people would be camping out everywhere. They would come as much as a week early for "their ceremonial cleansing before the Passover." To offer the paschal lambs they were supposed to go through seven days of purification (Num 9:6–12; 2 Chron 30:17–19).

Because of the Lazarus miracle Jesus is the hot topic at the festival. The pilgrims look everywhere for him, figuring that he would not dare to come with the death sentence hanging over him (11:56). The primary place of discussion was the temple, both as the focus of Passover activity and the place where Jesus taught whenever he was in Jerusalem (7:14, 28; 8:20; 10:23). The tone in these verses indicates that the pilgrims still think well of him. It is the leaders with their arrest warrant that produce the negative setting. They issue orders that anyone who sees Jesus must report him to the authorities.

———

The story of the death and resurrection of Lazarus is one of the great transition stories in the Gospels, for it sums up the meaning of Jesus' ministry thus far as the Giver of Life and anticipates the death and resurrection of Jesus. God is in charge of every detail of these events. It was critical that Jesus arrive in Bethany after Lazarus had been dead four days, for all were to know that Jesus indeed had raised the *dead*—that is, after the third day, when the Jews commonly believed the soul had gone to be with God.

This story proves the love of Jesus for his friends and the love of God for all of us. We especially see it in his compassion (his weeping, v. 35) and his justice (his outrage over the power of death in vv. 33, 38). Both are awakened in the plight of Lazarus, and of all of us. Jesus is caught up in our earthly as well as heavenly life and cares deeply. All the hopes of God's people throughout history have focused on sharing the life of God and thereby defeating the power of sin and death, and here we see all that is centered on Jesus, who is "the resurrection and the life" (v. 25). Lazarus foreshadows and becomes living proof of this promise.

We should see the miracle itself in verses 38–44 as preparation for both the death and resurrection of Jesus and our own final resurrection when Christ returns. God intended this as a springboard for faith, as proof that Jesus indeed does have authority over life and death and exercises it out of love for his followers.

Yet even this miracle awakens hatred among those who are in thrall to the world. The Jewish leaders' animosity toward Jesus culminates in verses 45–57 as the Sanhedrin meets and finalizes their plans to arrest and execute this small-town Galilean heretic. John shows us that in spite of their plans, God is still in control. The Sanhedrin's plan actually brings about God's plan. They didn't realize that in reality they were tools of God to bring final salvation to sinful humankind. When Caiaphas takes over and makes a political decision to kill Jesus for the sake of the nation, he is actually led by the Spirit as high priest to utter a prophecy of Jesus' substitutionary atoning sacrifice to save the world by dying in our place. The major enemy of Jesus becomes an inadvertent prophet! We can be confident that in spite of opposition, the cause of Christ cannot lose.

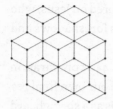

FINAL SCENES LEADING TO PASSION WEEK

(12:1–50)

John 12 consists of several scenes that take place leading up to Passover and Jesus' passion. With regard to the first of these, the scene of Jesus' anointing in Bethany, two issues need to be addressed: (1) The Gospel accounts need to be harmonized. Matthew (26:6–13) and Mark (14:3–9) are the same as John, but Luke (7:36–50) has different details and is a different episode. Luke has a dinner at the home of a Pharisee, an alabaster jar of perfume, and an immoral woman who has been forgiven by Jesus and anoints his feet with her tears and then perfume. There are differences between the other three—the home of Simon the leper in Matthew and Mark, an unnamed woman who breaks the jar and anoints Jesus' head—but there are greater similarities, and the story is the same. So Jesus was anointed twice—the one in Luke, and the one told in the other three Gospels.

(2) The chronology of the event is different—in Matthew and Mark, it occurs after Jesus' triumphal entry into Jerusalem, and in John it takes place before that event. However, this is only a problem if we demand a strict chronological order for the Gospels. Ancient historians did not demand such a thing, and that is true of the biblical authors as well. It has long been recognized that

the Gospel authors often followed a topical rather than chronological outline, especially the **Synoptic** writers. It is generally
agreed by recent evangelical scholars that John is more chronological, and that is the case here as well. Matthew and Mark have
placed it later to contrast the woman's worshipful act with Judas's
betrayal, and John places it where it originally took place, the day
before passion week began.

JESUS IS ANOINTED AT BETHANY (12:1–11)

THE SETTING (12:1–3)

Christ now returns to the Jerusalem area from Ephraim (11:54).
John tells us Jesus arrives "six days[1] before the Passover." There is
a vigorous debate as to whether John places the crucifixion a day
later than the Synoptic Gospels do (see discussion at 13:1). If that
is true, he would arrive on Sunday. I will be arguing John does not
do so, so this verse speaks of Jesus arriving on Friday evening (for
the Jews, days always began at dusk the evening before), six days
before Passover, with the banquet that following evening, Saturday.

The hour of destiny has arrived (see discussion at 2:4; 7:30;
8:20), so Jesus comes back to Bethany on the slopes of the Mount
of Olives a couple miles east of Jerusalem. When in Jerusalem he
likely always stayed with his friends Lazarus and his sisters. The
scene is now set for history's greatest Passover sacrifice, the "Lamb
of God, who takes away the sin of the world" (1:29). Lazarus was
a catalyst for the events, and his death and resurrection provided
a prophetic anticipation of the greater death and resurrection
soon to come.

---

1. Some see symbolic significance in the six days, but it is more likely just
a chronological marker telling us when Jesus arrived. If it is symbolic, one
possibility is that John in 1:19–2:1 presents Jesus' opening ministry over a six-
day period (see introduction to 1:19–34), and so this could frame Jesus' earthly
ministry with six-day scenes.

The Saturday meal that began the week of purification readying everyone for Passover becomes a banquet "in Jesus' honor"
(v. 2). Lazarus is the host, but Matthew 26:6 tells us the meal
took place in the home of Simon the Leper, undoubtedly another
believer. Some think he was the father of the three siblings, but
that cannot be known. Most likely it was a private celebration for
Jesus' followers. Martha, in keeping with her domestic tendencies (see Luke 10:40), is serving the guests, and in keeping with
custom at banquets, they are eating while reclining on couches
(see also 13:23, 25).

Mary, the younger sister, approaches Jesus as he is reclining
with a twelve-ounce container (NIV: "a pint") of "pure nard, an
expensive perfume" (v. 3). The plant is grown in the mountains of
northern India, and we are told it is "pure," the genuine article. It
is a sign of the family's great wealth and very well could have been
a family heirloom. This is an incredible amount, said in verse 5 to
be worth "a year's wages," in modern terms about $20,000. I have
never even seen a perfume worth that much!

John tells us she "poured it on Jesus' feet," while in Matthew
26:7 and Mark 14:3 she anoints his head. I believe she anointed both.
Since they were reclining, she probably anointed his head first and
then walked to the end of the couch and anointed his feet. Mark
14:3 tells us she broke the jar (likely the seal at the top) to pour out
the perfume, so she in effect emptied the whole amount on Jesus.
It would have run down his head onto his robes and dripped off
his feet onto the couch and floor. No wonder "the house was filled
with the fragrance of the perfume." In Mark 14:9 this signifies the
proclamation of her act throughout the world.

Mary then "wiped his feet with her hair," an unparalleled and
somewhat scandalous act, for only the husband was supposed to
see a woman's hair. In this banquet of close friends and followers
it would have been seen as unbelievably extravagant, a devotional
act that would have shocked all present. John centers on Jesus' feet
both to stress Mary's servanthood (looking forward to the washing

of the disciples' feet in 13:1–17) and especially to signify Jesus' destiny (the feet symbolized destiny). Matthew and Mark focus on the anointing of the head, a messianic act. Anointing in the ancient world commissioned a person to a special office (often high priest or king) and was a high honor (Exod 28:41; 1 Sam 10:1–13).

Mary's worshipful act was a prophetic acted parable, like those performed by the prophets Jeremiah and Ezekiel and like the triumphal entry that comes next in John's Gospel. The anointing points to Jesus' burial, and the wiping off with her hair may point to his resurrection. This latter may be too allegorical, but in any case her act as a whole was an unconscious prophecy (similar to Caiaphas in 11:49–52).

JUDAS'S FALSE COMPLAINT (12:4–6)

Judas in verses 4–5 speaks up on behalf of the others and utters what they all were certainly thinking, that it would have been far better to sell the expensive perfume and give the proceeds to the poor. Remember that none at the time realized Judas's true character (readers do because John in 6:70 called him "a devil"), and as treasurer of the apostolic band, he would have been a leader of the group. In the early church pastors usually controlled the finances. We don't know how he knew its worth, but it was a staggering amount, three hundred denarii, or "a year's wages" (a denarius was a single day's wage). This one jar of perfume could take care of an entire family for a year.

John then interjects so the reader can see the issue clearly (v. 6). Judas is not interested in the poor. He was a thief who as "keeper of the money bag" turned it into his own personal bank account, helping himself whenever he wanted some cash. In fact, money was one of the primary reasons he betrayed Jesus. In Matthew 26:15 he went to the priests and demanded money for delivering Jesus to them. The money bag held the monetary gifts from people like the wealthy women mentioned as Jesus' patrons in Luke 8:2. It paid for the needs of the group and also was used to give alms to the poor.

JESUS' EXPLANATION (12:7–8)

Jesus, still covered with the fragrant perfume, intervenes and defends Mary's act, since anointing was commonly done for the day of burial. To "save this perfume for the day of my burial" means that God had led her not to use it beforehand but to keep it for this occasion in order that it might prefigure his coming burial. Extravagant amounts were regularly used to anoint corpses (in 19:39 seventy-five pounds of spices will be used to anoint Jesus' body) in order to counter the stench of decomposition. Mary simply gives her gift early. Shouldn't it be perfectly acceptable for Mary to do so while he is still alive to enjoy her gift of love? It was unusual but accepted to wash the feet of important guests, to say in effect, "We are your humble servants and wish to serve you." Jesus will do exactly this in 13:1–17 at the Last Supper.

Jesus is stating that this is indeed an unconscious prophecy anticipating his death. He then adds (v. 8) that its extravagance is also acceptable, since you "always have the poor among you," while Jesus will not be around much longer. There was precedent for this in the Judaism of the time: the Talmud says that caring for the dead has precedence over almsgiving (b. Sukkah 49b). Devotion to Jesus and enjoying his actual presence has priority over everything else. Jesus is not minimizing the importance of giving to the poor so much as maximizing the value of enjoying the presence of the Son of God. This applies equally to us, as Peter says so well in 1 Peter 1:8: "Even though you do not see him now, you believe in him and are filled with an inexpressible and glorious joy."

TRANSITION AND PREPARATION FOR PASSION WEEK (12:9–11)

Word of Jesus' arrival spreads rapidly, and a huge crowd gathers from the surrounding area to see not only Jesus but Lazarus as well, who had probably been kept away from the public by his family and friends. Both have become celebrities, and Lazarus is receiving as much attention as Jesus. Crowds were looking for Jesus in 11:55–56, so the house may have been surrounded with onlookers.

The authorities are now doubly alarmed as Lazarus also draws many away from the leaders to the new movement. These formerly Jewish faithful "were going over to Jesus and believing in him" (v. 11), largely because of his raising of Lazarus. Not only have the people's loyalty shifted from the Jewish leaders to Jesus, but these people are accepting him as their Messiah. Lazarus has become as great a threat to them as Jesus, so they decide they have to eliminate him too. There is no evidence anything ever came of this, but John adds it to show how deeply their depravity had gone. Note the irony: Jesus raised Lazarus from the grave, and now the Jewish leaders want to return him to that very thing.

JESUS ENTERS JERUSALEM
TRIUMPHANTLY (12:12–19)

THE ROYAL PREPARATIONS (12:12–13)

The Synoptic Gospels stress the elaborate preparations and deliberate orchestration of Jesus' triumphal entry into Jerusalem at the beginning of passion week. John omits this, and instead emphasizes the event itself. Still, in all the Gospel accounts this is a prophetic acted parable, a prelude to the meaning of passion week and its messianic significance. Jesus openly declares who he is by riding into Jerusalem on a donkey in fulfillment of Zechariah 9:9 (see John 12:15). Jesus is in essence throwing down the gauntlet to the leaders and making clear his messianic intentions. Yet, by riding a donkey rather than a warhorse he is also declaring he is not the kind of Messiah they have expected. He has come to bring peace, not a sword.

The "next day" in verse 12 is Sunday, one week before the resurrection. As Jesus leaves for the short ride into Jerusalem, the news galvanizes the city and the pilgrims throng to him. A huge crowd of Passover visitors pours out to see the sight, waving palm branches to welcome Jesus (v. 13). These branches were a Passover tradition stemming from the Maccabean revolt, when the Jewish people welcomed Judas Maccabeus ("the Hammer") into Jerusalem for the rededication of the temple (the Feast of Dedication; see 10:22-39). They were also used at both Tabernacles and Passover to signify victory and new life for the community (1 Maccabees 13:51; 2 Maccabees 10:7). Here they demonstrate national hope for liberation and are a sign of messianic fervor.

The crowd also shouts out their high expectations. The titles are also messianic. They stem from Psalm 118:25-26, a royal psalm used in the processions of the king, stressing his rule under the authority of Yahweh. They are also part of the Hallel Psalms (113-118) sung by pilgrims in procession to festivals like Passover. At Tabernacles the temple choir would sing the Hallel every morning, and when they reached the Hosanna prayer of 118:25 the people would wave the *lulab* (branches of willow and myrtle tied with palm) and repeat the prayer three times.

The "Hosanna" that begins the cry in the psalm is a prayer, "Lord, save us," and that could be the thrust here. However, recent research shows that by Jesus' day it had become a cry of acclamation or praise to God. Most scholars believe that is the force here, though some want to retain the sense that it is a prayer for the kingdom to arrive. Both aspects may be part of its meaning here.

Then in verse 13 the pilgrims call down divine blessing on the one "who comes in the name of the Lord" from Psalm 118:26, which was understood in the first century as referring to the Messiah. They wished God's blessing on their messianic liberator, which many hoped Jesus was. This title, "the one who comes," is a primary theme in John, celebrating the descent of Jesus from heaven and his mission from the Father (John 3:13; 4:25; 6:14, 33, 38, 41-42; 11:27).

Finally they cry, "Blessed is the King of Israel," a title ascribed to Jesus by Nathanael in John 1:49 and found also in 18:33, 37, 39; 19:19, 21. This does not stem from Psalm 118 but is used here as a concluding hope for their royal Messiah, the conqueror descended from David. Their understanding of Jesus was primarily as a political leader. Still, they were centered on the messianic king and deliverer.

JESUS' PROPHETIC ACT (12:14–15)

As mentioned above, in the Synoptics there is a lengthy opening section on the preparations for the journey to Jerusalem, but here John simply tells us in verse 14, "Jesus found a young donkey and sat on it." There are differing understandings of the choice of a donkey over a horse. Most have thought it was to correct the political aspirations of the crowd. A horse was associated with military conquest (1 Kgs 4:26; Isa 31:1–3), and the donkey signified peace. Jesus would then be signifying that he was not coming as a messianic conqueror but as a Savior bringing peace. However, others have noted that it is a donkey in the messianic prophecy of Zechariah 9:9, and donkeys signified royalty, often used in royal processions (for instance, Solomon in 1 Kgs 1:33, 38, 44). On this view, Jesus would be accepting the crowd's hope-filled request.

I believe it is best to combine the two views. Jesus is accepting their messianic hopes but correcting them by demonstrating that he is not coming as the conquering king but as the lowly Messiah, the Suffering Servant of Isaiah 53. This was a fairly dangerous situation, with the crowd in its messianic fervor a tinderbox ready to explode into a full-scale riot. Jesus is trying to alleviate the pressure here.

John's citation in 12:15 draws on multiple passages. The phrase "do not be afraid" stems from Zephaniah 3:16 and Isaiah 40:9. "King of Israel" is from Zechariah 9:9 but also alludes to Zephaniah 3:15, and the two together state that Yahweh was in their midst as king and would deliver them. He would send a deliverer riding on a donkey. Zephaniah 3:9–10 adds a universal aspect, as people are gathered from all the earth.

Zechariah 9 then like Zephaniah 3 promises a lowly king, a messianic deliverer who will rescue God's people from their oppressors and "proclaim peace to the nations," establishing God's rule "from sea to sea" (9:10). Jesus' procession into Jerusalem on a donkey was a prophetic act to counter the desire of the Jews for a nationalistic Messiah. His universal kingship would not be brought about by his military victory but by his death. Jesus would be royal King at his first advent and conquering Messiah at his second coming.

THE REALIZATION OF THESE TRUTHS (12:16)

The disciples join the crowd in their failure to understand what the triumphal entry was all about. The full realization did not take place until "after Jesus was glorified." As Jesus will state in 14:26, it is the Spirit who is to remind them of everything Jesus has told them, even of those things they fail to understand at first. The mention of Jesus glorified is significant, emphasizing the passion as the time of glory. It was the glorified Lord along with the Spirit who enabled them to understand (as is also the case with us).

Many scholars struggle with this, for it seems contradictory that the crowds understand the messianic significance of the event (v. 13) while the disciples do not. But surely that is not really the case. The crowds understand only partially, and it is very doubtful that they caught the fulfillment of Zechariah 9:9 in the triumphal entry. All they express is their hope that Jesus will be the conquering Messiah, no more. There is no contradiction.

There are two things the disciples come to understand: (1) "these things had been written about him," referring to Jesus' fulfillment of the Old Testament, in this case Psalm 118 and Zechariah 9; (2) "these things had been done to him:" the events of the entry were part of God's predestined time at this point of world history. All the characters—the leaders of Israel, the crowds, and the disciples—are in the end under God's control.

THE INCREDIBLE RESPONSE (12:17-19)

The triumphal entry is framed by passages (12:9-11, 17-19) that contrast the belief of many with the rejection of the leaders. There are three groups in the scene here in verses 17-19. Two stem from the crowds. The first consists of those who were present at the raising of Lazarus. They "continued to spread the word" (literally, "were testifying"), thus becoming another group of witnesses to the reality of Jesus (see 1:27; 3:26; 5:31–40; 8:13–18). In fact, it is their witness that leads to the enthusiastic crowds that flock after Jesus (12:9, 12). This took great courage, for the threats of the Pharisees were quite real.

A second group of pilgrims respond to the witness (v. 18). They "heard that he had performed this sign" and "went out to meet him." Note that here the raising of Lazarus is called a "sign"-miracle, the seventh and last of these great events around which chapters 2–12 have been organized (see introduction to 2:1–12). This going out to meet Jesus has already taken place once, when he came into Jerusalem on the donkey in 12:12–13, and now it happens again. At this point his popularity is growing. It will be short-lived (see v. 39), and five days later will culminate in the cross.

The third group, the Pharisees, are greatly disturbed by all this positive excitement over Jesus (v. 19). Their carefully laid plans to arrest Jesus quietly have now seemingly become impossible. They are helpless in the face of the galvanized crowds, muttering among themselves, "See, this is getting us nowhere." At this point they don't know what to do.

This leads them to utter another unconscious prophecy similar to Caiaphas in 11:49–52: "Look how the whole world has gone after him." There is double meaning in "world." They mean pilgrims from all over the world have flocked to Jesus, but with further irony John emphasizes the universal impact the gospel of Jesus will have on all humanity, Gentiles as well as Jews. Unintentionally, the Pharisees are joining with the Samaritans of 4:42 in acknowledging Jesus as "Savior of the world." The universal implications of Zephaniah 3:16 and Zechariah 9:9 continue from 12:15. The whole world would indeed "go after" Jesus, and the explosion of the gospel throughout the world would be the major feature of the church age. In fact, the next scene (vv. 20–36), with "Greeks"

coming to meet Jesus, is an extension of this statement on the part
of the Pharisees.

GENTILES LEAD TO THE FINAL PREDICTION OF THE COMING "HOUR" (12:20-36)

John has decided to conclude his narration of Jesus' public ministry with this scene, and it becomes his final public statement. In
that sense this acts as a summary of his mission from the Father
and the purpose that his life and especially his coming death will
have for all the rest of the world.

INTRODUCTION (12:20-22)

The scene begins with "some Greeks" wanting to see Jesus. Some
have thought these to be Greek-speaking Jews from the diaspora
(those who lived in lands outside Palestine), but the term (*Ellēnes*)
refers to non-Jews. This means these were Gentiles, proselytes to
Judaism, or God-fearers—Gentiles who are attracted to Judaism
and have begun to worship Yahweh. The statement of 12:19 that
"the whole world" is coming to Jesus is already coming to pass!

It not unheard of that some Greeks would come for the
Passover Festival to worship the Jewish God and learn more about
the Jewish religion. The Jewish historian Josephus mentions this
(*Jewish War* 6.427), and in the book of Acts many God-fearers like
Cornelius would turn to Christ (Acts 10:2, 22, 35; 13:16, 26). They
were drawn to Judaism but were not willing to undergo circumcision and become full proselytes, or converts. They were allowed
in the court of the Gentiles in the temple complex and could participate in many of the ceremonies but could not enter the inner
courts (on penalty of death).

These Greeks wish to learn more about this Jesus and his followers. They somehow meet Philip, who has a Greek name and is
from the village of Bethsaida on the northeastern corner of the
Sea of Galilee, officially in the territory of Gaulanitis. It was near
the Decapolis, the "Ten Cities" of Syria, and some of these Greeks

may have been from there. They say, "We would like to see Jesus." So Philip and Andrew (also from Bethsaida; see 1:44) take them to see the Lord.

THE ARRIVAL OF THE HOUR OF GLORY (12:23-26)

It seems as if Jesus ignores these Greek seekers entirely, but his response provides the core of the salvation for which they are searching. He is telling the world how to find God's salvation, and the coming of these Greeks seems to stimulate this final response. Previously we have been told the authorities could not arrest Jesus because "his hour had not yet come" (7:30; 8:20). Now his hour of destiny has arrived. This is not just the culmination of the last couple of scenes. It is the reason for the incarnation, the destiny of all the ages for the coming of salvation to a fallen humanity. This monologue (vv. 23-26) is one of the key Son of Man passages (along with 1:51) associated with the glorification of Christ and the salvation that would result from it. For the Son of Man, suffering is not just the path to glory; Jesus' suffering is his glory. As in Isaiah 52:13, Jesus, the Servant of Yahweh, "will be raised and lifted up and highly exalted" in his vicarious suffering.

Jesus then clarifies the significance of his hour of destiny with another extended metaphor (see 10:1-5) introduced with a double *amēn*, which as always in John points to a critical saying (see comments on 1:51), essentially "I tell you the absolute truth" (12:24). Jesus often uses harvest imagery to illustrate the importance of his mission as gathering a harvest of souls (4:35-38). Here it explains the event that makes his mission possible—his sacrificial death. This agricultural metaphor is perfect, centering on the necessity that a grain of wheat "falls to the ground [= the grave] and dies" before it can produce a harvest, described as "much fruit" (v. 24; NIV: "many seeds").

The same image emerges from the parable of the sower, when the good seed produces a huge crop, "some thirty, some sixty, some a hundred times" (Mark 4:20), meaning that a single seed produces thirty, sixty, or a hundred plants. If Jesus had not died on the cross, his life would have affected no one but himself—but his sacrificial death has affected the whole world, a huge harvest of souls.

The harvest metaphor is used for evangelism in 12:24, and then this principle segues into discipleship in 12:25–26. To put it another way, Jesus moves from the seed to the crops that are produced. This is a guiding principle of Jesus' teaching. True disciples are Christlike, shaping their lives after the pattern of Jesus. As he proclaims in Mark 8:34, "Whoever wants to be my disciple must deny themselves and take up their cross and follow me." As Jesus' redemptive death produces life, so his disciples will not begin to live until they die.

For Jesus, life is produced from death, and that is the case for us as well. As he so often does, he states it two ways for emphasis: "Anyone who loves their life will lose it, while anyone who hates their life in this world will keep it for eternal life." The imagery of loving and hating life is found in five Synoptic passages (Matt 10:39; 16:25; Mark 8:35; Luke 9:24; 17:33), resulting in an antithesis between the destroyed life (= loving the world/self) and the preserved life (= hating the world/self). It is critical to realize that what Jesus actually says is "anyone who hates their life *in this world*," meaning to hate the world and its things. The disciple who focuses on worldly life rather than on Jesus will in the end have nothing. Moreover, by despising the worldly life and turning from it, we gain not just life but "eternal life." What a trade-off—giving up the temporary in order to gain the eternal. I cannot think of a more important lesson for all of us who live in a consumer-oriented society.

Jesus restates this in 12:26 with a different metaphor, that of the household servant (*diakonia*). Those who love Jesus and embrace the life of a Christ follower willingly accept the life of serving him rather than the world. Note the progression of thought: love and commitment to Jesus produce servanthood, which in itself centers on "following" him in every way, with the end result that our very existence is caught up in him ("where I am, my servant also will be"). Remember that Jesus is saying this on his way to the cross. The cross is the basis of Jesus' glorification, and dying to self and this world is the anchor of our new life in him. Think on this; dwell on this; orient your life to this!

Discipleship is servanthood, and servanthood must define our walk with Christ. Jesus received glory through the cross, and we receive "honor" from the Father when we yield ourselves to him. This is the imagery of baptism in Romans 6:4-5, "buried with him through baptism into death" and "united with him in a resurrection like his." We disciples define our life as a continual reliving of the life and ministry of Jesus.

THE TESTIMONY OF THE FATHER (12:27-30)

In this section Jesus has an experience that is reminiscent of his prayer in the Garden of Gethsemane, and some have even gone so far as to think John rewrote the Gethsemane event here. That is extremely unlikely, for the differences are too great, but Jesus is struggling with his impending death here in the same way that he does there. His opening "now my soul is troubled" reflects the deep-seated agony of heart he felt. The "now"-ness of his hour of destiny (12:23) is upon him, and he is experiencing great distress. Jesus is both God and man, and here his humanity comes to the fore.

He questions his own human response, asking himself, "What shall I say? 'Father, save me from this hour?'" This is quite similar to the Gethsemane prayer, "Abba Father, ... everything is possible for you. Take this cup from me" (Mark 14:36). In both places Jesus triumphs over his temptation, serving as an important model for us. In Mark he states, "Yet not what I will, but what you will," and here he says, "No, it was for this very reason I came to this hour." His entire life had pointed to this moment. The purpose of his incarnation was his death (Phil 2:6-8). The true meaning of Christmas is the cross. Jesus centered on his Father's will every moment of his life (John 5:19; 6:37; 8:29, 38; 14:31), and the glory of God in him could only be complete when his atoning sacrifice had brought God's salvation to fallen humanity.

His concluding cry, "Father, glorify your name!" (12:28), culminates this scene. The glory of God in the passion of his Son frames this monologue (vv. 23, 28), and it is this moment that will finalize the passion predictions (3:14; 8:28; 12:32). In the Synoptic Gospels Christ is primarily glorified in his resurrection from the dead, but John focuses on the cross itself as a time of glory. When Jesus is lifted up on the cross, he is lifted up into glory. So as Jesus brings glory to God throughout his life, God brings glory to Jesus in his death.

The Father's response in 12:28–29 is immediate and very powerful: "I have glorified it, and will glorify it again." The past element ("I have glorified it") refers to the incarnation and earthly ministry of Jesus. He "descended" from heaven (3:13, 31; 6:38, 42, 50, 51, 58), and he is that very divine power that unites heaven and earth (1:51). So he is the man of glory (1:14; 2:10–11; see Isa 35:1–2; Joel 3:18), with his glory manifested both in his revelation of divine truths and in his performance of divine deeds. The future element ("I will glorify it again") would soon be seen in his ascent to heaven (3:13; 6:62; 20:17), when he would reclaim his preexistent glory. In John, the passion events are regularly called the glory of Jesus (7:39; 13:31–32; 17:1, 5, 24).

The crowd (12:29) cannot tell what has taken place and fails to understand the message. In this they are similar to Paul's traveling companions on the Damascus road (Acts 22:9). Some focus on the power of the voice, saying "it had thundered." Others focus on its origin, mistakenly thinking "an angel had spoken to him." Thunder is often associated with messages from heaven (2 Sam 22:14; Ps 18:13; Rev 6:1; 10:3–4; 14:2). The fact is, they are confused.

Jesus corrects their mistaken thinking: "This voice was for your benefit, not mine" (12:30). But they fail to understand the message, so it is hard to see how what seemed to be gibberish to them could be for their sakes. In reality, all three times God speaks directly—the baptism, the transfiguration, and here—the message is intended for both Jesus and the onlookers. This is best seen in the baptism, as Matthew 3:17 has "This is my Son," announcing it to the crowd, while Mark 1:11 has "You are my Son," encouraging Jesus. That is likely the case here as well. Several point out that this is a "Semitic contrast" (a softer contrast than it comes across in English), meaning the voice is *more* for them than for Jesus, not that it was *only* for them. They may not have understood it then, but they would later, and even here they catch that the "voice" originated from heaven, and that is very significant. Once more, God is authenticating Jesus as his Son on his mission.

The Meaning of the Passion Events (12:31–33)

Jesus now spells out the implications of this final week in his earthly life. The "hour" has arrived (12:23), and his death is imminent (v. 24). This is now the hour of glory (v. 28), the turning point of the ages, the "fullness of time" (Gal 4:4), when all the Old Testament promises are about to be fulfilled. This is not just the time when salvation has come; it is "the time for judgment on this world" (v. 31). We saw earlier (John 3:17; 8:15) that Christ came to save the world, not judge it, but at the same time he became judge of all who reject his offer of salvation (5:22, 30; 8:16; 9:39). In fact, God made Jesus judge over the world (3:35–36; 5:22–23, 29–30).

Jesus as "the light of the world" (8:12) shines God's light on the world of darkness (1:4, 7, 9) and passes judgment over the evil that characterizes it (3:19–20). So judgment is not just a future event at the end of history; it is a present process that is coterminous with and involves the offer of salvation. Those who respond with faith are forgiven, but those who reject that offer go to the next level of judgment, convicted by the Spirit (16:8–11). Those who continually reject that offer will then face the final judgment at the great white throne (Rev 20:11–15).

At the cross judgment does not just fall on the sin-sick world; at that time also "the prince of this world [is] driven out." Jesus calls Satan "the prince [ruler] of this world" also at 14:31; 16:10; Paul calls him "the god of this age" (2 Cor 4:4), the "ruler of the kingdom of the air" (Eph 2:2); and John calls him "the great dragon" and "ancient serpent" (Rev 12:9; 20:2). Revelation 12:7-9 tells the story of how he led a great rebellion and swept a third of the angels with him out of heaven so that they became the fallen angels/demons who oppose us. He possessed Judas and used him to lead Christ to the cross (John 13:27; Luke 22:3).

The ultimate defeat of Satan is not awaiting the second coming but already took place at the cross (Rev 5:5-6). At the very moment Christ died on the cross, he told Satan and his forces that they had lost (1 Pet 3:19) and disarmed them, leading them in his victory procession (Col 2:15). We participate in this defeat of Satan when we surrender and depend entirely upon the Spirit in our Christian walk.

The final of the three passion predictions in John occurs here in 12:32 (along with 3:14; 8:28). All three picture Christ being "lifted up" on the cross as meaning he is "lifted up" into glory, building on Isaiah 52:13, where the Suffering Servant is "raised and lifted up and highly exalted." The cross is the high point of history, and together with the resurrection it is the high point of all eternity, the basis of Jesus' exaltation to glory.

The result of this exaltation of Jesus on the cross is that he will "draw all people" to himself. This is the same verb John used in 6:44 for God's drawing to himself those who come to him. The image is connected to the Spirit's work in convicting the world and proving them wrong in order to bring them to God. This is a trinitarian activity: all three members of the Godhead have a part. Yet in 6:44 God draws only those who come, while here Jesus draws everyone. I called this God's "universal salvific will" in 1:4, 7, 9, because it depicts God's desire that none perish and all come to repentance

(2 Pet 3:9). Those who respond will become "one flock" with "one shepherd" (10:16; 11:52; 17:20–23).

Finally, in 12:33 John tells his readers that "he said this to show the kind of death he was going to die." "Lifting up" was not some great Roman triumph but in reality depicted the horrible Roman crucifixion that Jesus would undergo. This is the great paradox: glory through suffering. In fact, there could be no glory without the suffering.

THE SHORT TIME WITH THE LIGHT (12:34–36)

The crowd finally catches on that Jesus is speaking of his death and that he is calling himself Messiah and Son of Man, but they are still confused. In this context Jesus does not say "the Son of Man must be lifted up" (as he does in 3:14), only that the Son of Man will be glorified (in 12:23). Also, they combine Son of Man and Messiah, understanding his glorification in light of their messianic expectations that the Davidic messianic line would be eternal (Ps 89:36; Isa 9:7; Ezek 37:25). If "lifted up" is a reference to his death, how is it possible for the Son of Man/Messiah to die if he will "remain forever"? Moreover, all their messianic hopes are on his being a conquering king, not a suffering servant. So they ask, "Who is this 'Son of Man'?" The kind of Messiah Jesus was describing was nothing they had ever contemplated.

Jesus refuses to answer their question, probably because all he has said in 12:23–33 has in effect already done so. Instead, he challenges them to respond to him as the light of God in their midst while there is yet time to do so. "You are going to have the light just a little while longer," he warns them. In fact, there are just five days left before Jesus will be taken from them.

Verse 35 ("Walk while you have the light, before darkness overtakes you") appears to be another short metaphor (see 12:24), this time picturing a person walking at sunset who must hurry to reach his destination before darkness overtakes him and he loses his way. Several interpreters call this a "parable of crisis" like those in Matthew 24–25, depicting a time of spiritual conflict when "the prince of this world" is at work. When we walk in the light, we conquer the darkness (1:5), but those who reject the light and choose the darkness (3:19–20) are overtaken by the night. They cannot see their way and think they are headed in the right direction but are on their way to destruction.

Jesus' final comment to the crowd builds on the path to salvation throughout this Gospel: "Believe in the light while you have the light, so that you may become children of light" (12:36). The darkness is in control of the leaders, but Jesus wants to rescue the crowds, and the only answer is faith-decision. Jesus, the light of the world (8:12), would soon be gone, and this was the last time they could respond to him directly.

If they respond with belief, they will become "children of light." "Child of" is an idiom used in Semitic languages (like the Aramaic Jesus likely spoke) describing a person's primary characteristic, so this means they would be characterized by the light of God within them. Jesus uses this image to contrast his followers with their opponents. This imagery is not unique in first-century Judaism; the Essenes of **Qumran** called themselves "the sons of light," and outsiders were "the sons of darkness."

This is a perfect way to end his public ministry with the crowds, with a challenge to leave the realm of darkness and enter the realm of light. There is an **inclusio** in this, as the light shining on all people began this Gospel (1:4, 7, 9, a central element of the prologue). Now his ministry closes with the call to become children of light.

Jesus signifies this closure by going and hiding from them (12:36), reenacting 8:59 after the crowd there had tried to stone him. His hiding has two thrusts here: Jesus has been awaiting the final "hour" God has established (7:30; 8:20), and it signifies God's judgment on those who reject him. He had been warning them and giving them chance after chance to repent and be forgiven, but their time was almost up.

UNBELIEF IS THE FULFILLMENT
OF PROPHECY (12:37–43)

This section begins with a summary statement from John, drawing together the many times Jesus' sign-miracles have been greeted with unbelief. These verses end the signs section of John (chapters 2–12), so unbelief frames these chapters (1:11; 12:37) and proves Jewish guilt before God. Even after all these wondrous demonstrations of divine power, these former people of God still refuse to embrace Jesus. This was a quandary so significant that Paul addresses it in Romans 9–11, responding to the question: If Jesus is indeed the Messiah and God is just, why have so few Jews been converted to him? Has God been faithful to his promises? Paul answers by pointing to the sovereign will of God and the guilt of the Jewish people (Rom 9–10); John answers that Old Testament prophecy pointed to this unbelief.

John's approach demonstrates that the same hardness of heart of the wilderness generation and Israel in the time of Isaiah still plagues the nation. It typifies the Jewish response to Jesus' earthly ministry and will continue after his death and resurrection. The majority remain closed to the gospel, exactly as Isaiah foresaw. There is a strong flavor of predestination here, with John stating that their unbelief came about "in order to fulfill" prophecy (my translation), but there is an equal emphasis on the guilt of the nation. This is the same question discussed in the comments on 6:35–44, and here as there we must find a balance between the two perspectives. God is sovereign, but people are responsible. There is a mystery here, and the final reconciliation between these two will have to await our arrival in heaven.

John cites two passages from Isaiah to prove that God saw their faithlessness ahead of time. The message here is that this salvation-historical tragedy of Jewish unbelief in itself fulfills prophecy. He first cites Isaiah 53:1 (12:38) from the fourth of the Servant Songs (52:13–53:12). While the Servant is exalted by God (52:13, in the background of Jesus' "lifted up" comment in 12:32), the nations are appalled to learn that he is disfigured and rejected. So 53:1 asks the natural question, "Lord, who has believed our message and to whom has the arm of the Lord been revealed?" God had often used mighty deeds like those of the judges or David, but the ministry of the one who was "despised and rejected ... a man of suffering" was greeted with unbelief. Jesus, the Suffering Servant, faced this same unbelief. The words ("our message") and deeds ("the arm of the Lord") of Jesus were ignored and rejected.

The second passage cited (12:40) is Isaiah 6:10, the primary passage quoted in the New Testament to explain Jewish unbelief (Mark 4:10–12; Acts 28:26–27; Rom 11:8). Leading into the citation, John further emphasizes God's sovereignty (12:39), telling us "they could not believe" because Isaiah had prophesied just that. Once more God's will is seen in his judicial hardening of Israel's hearts. It is the same issue as Pharaoh in Exodus, with God's hardening of his heart a judicial response to his hardening of his own heart. Divine sovereignty and human responsibility are intertwined in Israel's unbelief.

Isaiah had the most excited and at the same time most appalling commissioning service in history. In Isaiah 6, he was given a vision of God on his throne and told by the Lord that he would spend his life in a ministry of failure, sent to preach to a people who would not want or listen to anything he said. In fact, God would use him to *cause* that very rejection. John alters the sequence of Isaiah 6:10 to apply it to Jesus. Isaiah's order of lines is heart/ears/eyes, while John drops the ears and reverses the order to eyes then hearts in order to center on Jesus' miraculous signs and their effect on people's hearts. The purpose is to show how Jesus relives the ministry of Isaiah. Through his sign-miracles the eyes of the crowds have been blinded and their hearts hardened against Jesus and his Father. God wanted them neither to see nor to understand because of their unbelief.

We must note that God no longer wants them to repent (as in Mark 4:10–12): "nor turn—and I would heal them." For this reason, this is called a "judicial hardening." It is not a cold, calculated act but falls on a people who are already guilty. Once more we must recognize the interdependence and interaction of the divine and the human. They have been guilty of unbelief, and God is judging them by sending further hardening on them. Divine sovereignty is primary, but human responsibility is an essential component as well. This is the very principle Paul stresses in Romans 1:21–28; in reaction to the depravity of humanity, God "gave them over" to even deeper sin as judgment upon them.

John then explains that "Isaiah said this because he saw Jesus' glory and spoke about him" (v. 41). In Isaiah it was the glory of Yahweh, but John applies it to the glory of Jesus. How does this relate to judicial hardening? Divine glory is seen not only in the salvation of the faithful but also in the judgment of the faithless. The exalted Jesus is Judge of all, and in his judgment lies glory as it proves his exalted nature. This theme of glory through his function as judge is at the heart of the book of Revelation as well.

However, not all are guilty of unbelief, for even some of the "leaders believed in him" (v. 42). John wants us to realize that rejection was not universal, and there were even conversions among the leaders who led the attack against Jesus (like Nicodemus and Joseph of Arimathea; see 19:38–39). By implication, if some leaders had become followers, even more from the crowds had found Jesus. We have here the beginning stages of the church.

John has spent time discussing the many with weak and inadequate faith (2:23–25; 6:60; 8:30), and now we see a group who allowed peer pressure to make them cowards, afraid of undergoing the opposition of the Pharisees if their allegiance to Christ were to become known. In 9:22, 34, we saw the threat of being expelled from the synagogue, and the simple danger of neighbors turning against them would have been more than enough to dissuade many from making their faith in Jesus known very widely. The reason is clear in 12:43: "for they loved human praise more than praise from God." Nicodemus did not reveal his conversion until he helped bury Jesus (see 3:1–15; 7:50–51; 19:39). Joseph of Arimathea is described as "a disciple of Jesus, but secretly" (19:38). There were certainly many others.

There is no reason to think they were not true believers; they simply were afraid, without the courage of their convictions. There are all too many just like them in our churches as well. John shows us that there are several levels of faith, and it is difficult to determine where to separate seekers who are not believers from weak Christians who are. The task of church leaders is to continue to disciple all in the church to keep growing in Christ, and to leave many of these questions with the Lord. Those who "believed in" Jesus in 2:23–25 thought they were all right, but their true colors were revealed in 6:60–66. We must make weak Christians realize the seriousness of Jesus' statement in Matthew 7:23: "I never knew you. Away from me, you evildoers!" There is no greater danger than when we play games with our eternal destiny.

JESUS ISSUES A FINAL CHARGE
TO BELIEVE (12:44–50)

Like 12:23–28, this is a perfect summary of the message of the Fourth Gospel, drawing together Jesus' message to the Jewish people. Two of John's major theological themes are at center stage— belief in Jesus and his mission from God who sent him as the divine envoy.[2] The first emphasis (vv. 44–45) brings together the twin aspects of believing and seeing. Since Jesus is the divine agent, to believe or see him is to believe or see God. They are one (10:30), and to know one is to know the other. Jesus is the Sent One, the **shaliach** of God (see 3:17), and his mission is to make his Father known (1:18). He is the voice of God and the presence of God. He is the only way to God (14:6), and we can neither see nor believe in God without believing in his Son.

2. See "Major Theological Themes" in the introduction.

Jesus explains this further in 12:46 by using once more (see 9:4; 11:9–10; 12:35) the imagery of light and darkness. Through Jesus as the light of God (1:4, 7, 9; 8:12), we "see" the truth and come to belief. He shines in this dark world to expose its sin and rebellion, but the purpose is redemptive rather than punitive, bringing salvation rather than judgment (3:17). The light shines so sinners can find forgiveness and trust Jesus to light the way so they can overcome and leave the darkness behind (1:5).

In 12:47–48 Jesus moves from Redeemer to Judge, another major theme (5:22–23; 8:15–16; 9:39). Jesus identifies two groups here: the first group is characterized by the one who "hears my words but does not keep them"; these are the closet Christians of 12:42–43 and those with inadequate faith in 2:23–25. Jesus says, "I do not judge that person," reiterating the point he made in 3:17: "God did not send his Son into the world to condemn the world, but to save the world through him." Christ's work is redemptive. Even though they do not yet obey his teaching, his purpose is to bring them to repentance.

Christ does become Judge for the second group, characterized by "the one who rejects me and does not accept my words" (12:48). Their failure is more serious. The first group is willing to "hear," but this second group both rejects Jesus and refuses his words. The first group is on the path to true faith and partially accepts Jesus and his teaching. The second group is completely opposed, so as Jesus says, "the very words I have spoken will condemn them on the last day," meaning at the final judgment. This is similar to 5:45–47, where the words of Moses would judge the Jewish leaders since they had rejected God's truth.

The reason Jesus' words have such power lies in their source (12:49–50). They stem from the Father and come with the authority of the Triune Godhead. "I did not speak on my own, but the Father who sent me commanded me to say all that I have spoken," Jesus says, reiterating his submission to the Father in 5:19–30: "Whatever the Father does the Son also does." Jesus' every word and every action are in reality the Father speaking and acted in and through him.

The Father's "commands" give Jesus' teaching its authority, as in 14:31: "I love the Father and do exactly what my Father has commanded me." Jesus' mission receives its impetus from the divine commands and reflects the teaching of the prophet like Moses, prophesied in Deuteronomy 18:18-19: "I will put my words in his mouth. He will tell them everything I command him." Jesus is the **eschatological** prophet who fulfills this promise. Moreover, the result of these prophetic words from the Father is "eternal life," because these words are anchored in trinitarian truth, so that he becomes "the way and the truth and the life" (14:6).

————

John has placed the anointing of Jesus (12:1-11) in its proper place chronologically (before the triumphal entry) in order to show that his glory was present in him even before the passion events, and that Mary's loving gift of extravagant perfume had two purposes — to show Jesus' exalted status among his followers and to prepare for the glory of his death and burial ahead of time. As Mark 14:9 says so well, the story of her loving gift "will always be told, in memory of her."

This event, added to the raising of Lazarus, brings even more fame to Jesus and to Lazarus as well. It becomes such a threat to the leaders that they feel they have to kill both of them. This episode thus heightens the depravity behind their opposition. It also establishes a pattern that we see over and over for the next two millennia, as thousands of Christ followers will join Lazarus and others like James and Stephen as objects of hatred and martyrs for Christ. We all must be ready for the possibility of opposition and even persecution in this dark world (3:19-20).

Jesus' purpose in entering Jerusalem as he did (12:9-19) was to declare openly that he was indeed the Messiah, fulfilling

Zechariah 9:9. The Jewish people expected a conquering Messiah, but by riding a donkey into Jerusalem Jesus was showing he was the royal Messiah but would not conquer in a military sense like they wanted. He is the lowly Messiah coming as Suffering Servant to bring salvation and spiritual peace rather than a sword.

When the Greeks come to Jesus (12:20-36), we see the first stage of the universal mission to the Gentiles, but we also see the true meaning of Jesus' death as his glorification. Greatness and splendor are tied to surrender and sacrifice of all worldly things to Christ. The interchange between Jesus and the Father in 12:27-30 is the high point, in which Jesus submits his desires to his Father and accepts that his glory will be completely tied up with the cross. The message is for us as well: suffering is the path to glory, and humiliation provides the road to exaltation. The last part (12:31-36) centers on the battle between light and darkness. To find peace and victory in our lives we must become people characterized by light, turning away from the forces of darkness in control of this world.

The final section (12:37-50) centers on Jewish unbelief, as God judges them for their refusal to receive Christ and sends them a "judicial hardening" so that they would not repent. Jesus is reliving the ministry of Isaiah, who was sent by God to proclaim a message that would be rejected by the people as God poured out his judgment on them. This happens all too often in our churches today when people almost dare the pastor and other church leaders to make them care. The solution to this situation is found in the charge to believe in 12:44-50. Jesus is the light of God, illuminating the path and providing a beacon the lost can follow to salvation. We must develop in our churches a culture of listening and seeking, a willingness to follow the "light of the world" all the way.

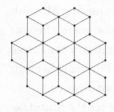

JESUS AND THE PASSOVER MEAL
(13:1–30)

The events of chapters 11–12 provide a transition between Jesus' public ministry (chapters 2–12) and the passion events (chapters 13–17). These next five chapters take place on Thursday of passion week at the Last Supper. John skips the events of Monday (cleansing the temple and cursing the fig tree), Tuesday (debates with the leaders in the temple, the Olivet Discourse), and Wednesday (Jesus and the disciples in Bethany as Judas plans his betrayal). The **Synoptics** provide the details of the events as they transpire, while John gives us the theological meaning of that week. He has decided to abbreviate passion week and cover only the one evening, for his focus is entirely on the cross and helping us to understand that Jesus dies as the Passover Lamb. Jesus' public ministry has ended, and it is time to begin the Passover celebration.

John also omits the elaborate preparations, the prediction of the desertion of the Eleven (minus Judas), the words of institution over the bread and wine, and the movement to Gethsemane (as well as Gethsemane itself), which all appears in the Synoptics. Undoubtedly aware of the Synoptic material, he decides to supplement it and focuses on two preliminary parts. For his Gospel these will serve to introduce the major element, the Farewell Discourse (13:31–17:26). The washing of the disciples' feet demonstrates to them that Jesus is indeed the Servant of Yahweh and that the life of discipleship is to be a life of servanthood. The one parallel with the Synoptic portrayal is the prediction of Jesus' betrayal (13:18–30 = Mark 14:18–21). The purpose of this narrative in John is to show that all attempts to thwart God's purpose in the cross will come to naught.

The focus has shifted from the crowds to Jesus' disciples, as Jesus turns inward to prepare his followers for the humanly terrible but spiritually wonderful events to come. The message is the same for us as it was for them. We too must look beyond the horror, for in reality the cross is the ultimate defeat of Satan and the demise of evil. At the cross "the lion of the tribe of Judah, the root of David, has triumphed" (Rev 5:5–6). The futility of Satan is not anchored in his final earthly defeat at Armageddon but in his eternal defeat at the cross.

EXCURSUS: THE CHRONOLOGY OF THE LAST SUPPER AND THE CROSS

Critics are divided over the chronology of the passion events in the Synoptics and John. At first glance it seems that John places the Last Supper a day earlier than the others. Mark places it on "the first day of the Festival of Unleavened Bread [= Passover], when it was customary to sacrifice the Passover lamb" (14:12), meaning that the Synoptic Gospels have the Last Supper on Thursday evening and the crucifixion on Friday morning. However, John places it "just before the Passover Festival" here in 13:1. The reason for the difference would then be that John wished to have Jesus' crucifixion (the next morning) coincide with the slaughter of the Passover lambs on Thursday, the day before Passover. The Last Supper then would be on Wednesday evening. To these scholars this is corroborated when John calls the crucifixion "the day of preparation" for Passover (19:14, 31, 42; see also 18:28), indicating it takes place on Thursday.

There are several possible solutions to explain the different chronologies: (1) The Last Supper was not a Passover meal but one of the preparatory meals, either the *Kiddush* ("prayer") or *Habburah* meal on Wednesday evening. The problem is that the details reflect Passover imagery. (2) John could be following a sectarian solar calendar, like the one used at **Qumran**, rather than the lunar calendar of the Pharisees, thus placing it a day earlier. But there is little evidence for this, and the sacrifices were offered in the temple on the official Thursday whatever calendar was used.

(3) The best answer is that the "day of preparation" on which Christ was crucified actually refers to the day before what was called the "special Sabbath" of Passover week (= Saturday) rather than Passover day (Friday). The Last Supper therefore takes place on Thursday and was the Passover meal, and the crucifixion was on Friday, the day of preparation for the "special Sabbath" of Passover week. Thus the Synoptic portrayal and John can be reconciled to one another.

JESUS WASHES THE DISCIPLES' FEET (13:1–17)

THE SCENE (13:1–2)

The two central themes of this unit are found in 13:1: Jesus preparing himself and his disciples for his departure from this world and his deep love for his followers. Jesus will never again speak to the crowds but now focuses entirely on those who will carry on his ministry. The footwashing begins "just before the Passover" meal. At this time Jesus realized anew "that the hour had come for him to leave this world and go to the Father" (see 12:23). This of course is the hour of destiny mentioned often in John (2:4; 3:14; 7:8; 8:28; 12:32) that would culminate his life and ministry and bring God's salvation to sinful humanity.

The world is the place of rebellion and rejection, yet it is also the focus of God's salvific love (3:16). He descended from heaven to this world in order to provide salvation, and now he is about to ascend back to his Father. In this final phase of his earthly life he is riveted on his disciples to prepare them not just for the terrible event soon to come but also for their life of ministry to the world that would follow.

His focus on his followers is dominated by love. Interestingly, in chapters 2–12 words for life (fifty times) and light (thirty-two) predominate over words for love (twelve), but in chapters 13–17 it is the reverse—love (thirty-seven) far outstrips life (six) and light (none). The phrase "loved them to the end" has a double meaning. "The end" refers both to time (to the end of his life) and degree (to the uttermost). Jesus' love for his own is the primary theme of the next five chapters. This also tells us that Jesus intended the footwashing as an anticipation of his death and that it passes on the responsibility of love to them, to be seen in the same servanthood exemplified in Jesus (see Mark 10:43–45).

The opening phrase of 13:2, "The evening meal was in progress," is debated. Some place these events at the beginning, as in the NLT "it was time for supper," while others take it as after the meal. I prefer to take it at the very beginning, which is certainly the time such an event would normally occur. John then says that "the devil had already prompted Judas … to betray Jesus." The Greek says Satan "entered the heart" of Judas, meaning that Satan took possession of him. Judas did it for the money (12:6; 13:27–30), but in reality Satan had planned this carefully and was behind Judas's evil desires. The passion is a cosmic battle against the powers of evil. This theme is prominent in this section (see 12:31; 14:31), but as we know from 1:5, darkness will not prevail.

THE WASHING OF THE FEET (13:3–5)

The footwashing is anchored in two things that Jesus "knew" in verse 3: he had power and authority from God over everything; and he was soon to return to God in heaven. For this reason there was no question how the battle against the powers of darkness would turn out, for he is Lord of all. The cross is not just an isolated skirmish but the central event in the greatest cosmic drama this world will ever know. The outcome was already settled, and God's plan of salvation would work itself out. God was in control, not Satan, and his Son had absolute authority over all the players in the drama. Jesus was soon to ascend back to his heavenly home, so his purpose now was to prepare the disciples for their part in the cosmic war.

In what ensues Jesus not only shows his disciples how much he loves them but even more passes on to them the responsibility of leadership in the new era he is inaugurating, as defined in Mark 10:43–45: "Whoever wants to become great among you must be your servant, and whoever wants to be first must be slave of all." He wants them to understand what his sovereign authority means and why he is surrendering his life. To follow his example and share his glory, their authority had to be exercised through servanthood. The Baptist defined it well when he said, "The straps of [his] sandals I am not worthy to untie" (1:27). Only a slave would wash the feet of a guest. It is also a family act, as wives would wash the feet of husbands and children the feet of parents. Jesus was making himself a model of love and humility, demanding that they imitate his model.

John describes Jesus' actions in some detail for emphasis. Just before the food was to be served, he "got up from the meal, took off his outer clothing, and wrapped a towel around his waist ... and poured water into a basin" (13:4–5). The shock of the disciples must have been incredible; Jesus was reversing the social order. Imagine the scene. It was a formal banquet setting, and they would have been reclining on U-shaped couches with Jesus at the head (in the center of the U), serving as father over the meal. When Jesus wrapped the towel around him, he took on the menial form of a slave.

When he began washing their feet and drying them with the towel (13:5), this One who was "in very nature God" deliberately took on "the very nature of a servant" (Phil 2:6–7). As Jesus states in Luke 22:27, "I am among you as one who serves." We must remember that one of those whose feet Jesus washed was Judas himself. What a model of unspeakable love, to wash the feet of the very one who would send him to his death! Successful Christian leaders are defined by the degree of humility and servanthood they demonstrate toward their charges.

THE DIALOGUE WITH PETER (13:6–11)

Peter's protest is quite understandable. Disciples served their rabbis, *never* vice versa. So he and the others were in shock. In the Greek "you" and "my" are side by side for emphasis: "You mean you ... my feet?" He wanted no one to see this scandalous breach of propriety. Jesus addresses them all in his words to Peter: "You do not realize now what I am doing, but later you will understand." "Later" should be read here as after the coming of the Spirit, who will "guide you into all the truth" (16:13).

Peter still could not understand (as Jesus had just said) and so continued to protest, this time with a stronger negative: "No ... you shall never wash my feet" (13:7). The Greek is stronger; literally translated it reads, "You shall never in all eternity wash my feet." The shame of it would simply be too great. He is not thinking spiritually or theologically, but from a worldly, sociocultural perspective. Jesus' response (v. 8) is equally forceful and settles the issue once and for all: "Unless I wash you, you have no part with me." "Having a part" means to share in Jesus' inheritance from God, which often refers to the eternal blessings awaiting the faithful (see Rom 8:17; Eph 3:6; 1 Pet 1:4). With this Peter finally understands the double meaning in "wash," that it refers to spiritual cleansing as well as physical. Washing means the cleansing of the cross, and unless one accepts this cleansing from Jesus, there is no sharing in the kingdom and no eternal life.

Peter wakes up and responds with his typical exuberance: "Then, Lord, ... not just my feet but my hands and my head as well" (13:9). There is no special meaning in the addition of "hands" and "head." He is referring to his whole body and is simply saying, "I want to be totally cleansed." It is often said that he continues to misunderstand and is only thinking on the earthly plane, but I don't believe that is the case. It is more likely he partially understands and is speaking of spiritual cleansing here. He does fail to realize that Jesus is speaking of the effects of the cross, but he could hardly be expected to do so. Peter is the type of disciple with lots of heart but not a lot of head knowledge.

In his next response (v. 10), Jesus builds on Peter's partial understanding, but the imagery is somewhat confusing, as he uses two words for washing up: "Those who have had a bath [*louō*] need only to wash [*niptō*] their feet; their whole body is clean." This is a short parable describing a person attending a feast who bathes at home so that when he arrives he needs only to wash the dust from the road off his feet. The message is clear. The disciples are already clean spiritually and need only to become servants of one another. Jesus' footwashing is really an anointing of the disciples' for Christian service. Spiritual cleansing occurs upon becoming a follower of Jesus, followed by an anointing to the service of God and one another.

The last point is one they could not possibly understand yet, but as Jesus said in verse 7, they would later. "And you are clean, though not every one of you." Jesus washed Judas's feet, but it was a purely outward cleansing and did not touch his evil heart. He remained covered by the far more serious dirt of sin. John explains this to the reader in verse 11. The filth of sin in Judas is the utter wickedness of betrayal. For the rest of human history he will become the paradigm of the traitor, and it is even worse than this, for he turned the Savior of the world over to be killed.

The Explanation of the Event (13:12–17)

Jesus finishes washing their feet, picks up the garments he removed in 13:4, and returns to reclining on the couch for the meal. Possibly while the food is being distributed, he begins to explain the significance of what he has done, moving from the "I-you" of his relationship with them to the internal relationships of the disciples to one another. There was no possible way they could have understood as yet, for everything Jesus had done was tied to the meaning of the cross.

They simply had no idea of a suffering Messiah, for all of Judaism interpreted Isaiah 52–53 as referring to the nation rather than the coming Messiah. The arrival of the Messiah was not oriented to salvation but to military liberation. Peter will react to Jesus' arrest by drawing his sword and cutting off the ear of the high priest's slave (18:10), thinking he is starting the war that will remove the Romans and begin the messianic kingdom. However, by washing the disciples' feet Jesus shows that he is indeed the Servant of Yahweh of Isaiah 52–53, and that the disciples are to emulate him as they serve others. That is the subject of John 13:13–17.

He begins with his authority, which they already know (v. 13), affirming that he is indeed their "Teacher" or rabbi as well as their "Lord." Both were common titles of respect and often addressed to Jesus, but obviously Jesus means much more. As rabbi he is the final interpreter of Torah, fulfilling the feasts (chapters 5–10) and summing up the Mosaic law in himself. As Lord he is Lord of the universe and Creator of all (1:3–4). "My Lord and my God," Thomas's cry of 20:28, speaks of deity. "Jesus Christ is Lord" became the core of all Christian confession (1 Cor 16:22; Phil 2:11). This confession forms the bedrock of all Jesus is going to say.

In 13:14 he applies the footwashing to the internal relationships within the group. He explains that he performed the scandalous act of washing their feet so they would follow his example and "wash one another's feet." This act of love establishes them as a family under God and becomes a lifelong pattern of service within the church of Jesus Christ. As they serve each other they will be knit together as one family (see 17:21–23). The disciples are bound to Christ and therefore bound to each other. Note the threefold movement of unity—love and oneness in the Godhead is lived out in the union of believers with Christ, resulting in the union of believers with one another.

Jesus now makes explicit what was implicit before, that he washed their feet as "an example that you should do as I have done for you" (v. 15). The "example" (*hypodeigma*) refers to a model or pattern to exemplify in one's life, not only for interrelationships but also for their future ministries. The self-sacrificial love Jesus shows is to guide them as leaders in the church. In fact, leadership without servanthood is an unbiblical affront to God.

This is important for debates about the place of footwashing in the church. Many churches have taken this literally as a command and have turned footwashing into a sacrament like baptism or the Lord's Supper, to be observed regularly, often as part of the eucharistic service. However, there is no evidence for this in the early church. The only other time it is mentioned in the New Testament (1 Tim 5:10) it is a qualification for ministry by widows. It was not practiced as a Christian rite in the earliest centuries of the church. It is best to see it as here, an example that can be a meaningful experience for the church but not a required rite.

This principle is anchored in another solemn and important double *amēn* saying (see comments on 1:51): "No servant is greater than his master, nor is a messenger greater than the one who sent him" (13:16; see also Matt 10:24–25; Luke 6:40). inhere the focus shifts from Jesus as the Sent One to Jesus as the Sender. His disciples are to continue Jesus' mission (17:18; 20:21). They are to imitate Jesus' self-surrender to his Father and his self-sacrificial love to his followers. True leaders define themselves by their call to serve their flock, not lord it over them (Mark 9:35; 10:42–45; 1 Pet 5:3). The true model of Jesus is one of servanthood, and if it characterizes him it must define the ministries of his followers as well.

So Jesus places the responsibility on them: "Now that you know these things, you will be blessed if you do them" (13:17). God will not bless the dictatorial Christian leader whose word is law. I know of far too many like that. A church secretary once told me of her boss, the pastor, "You have to understand something about him. He's never lost." This has always been a huge problem: all too few pastors have a pastor's heart for service. And all too often they don't know what they lack. I remember once speaking to a group about having a pastoral seminar on servanthood leadership. Their response was, "Why?" Knowledge is supposed to produce action, and once we know what Christ-centered leadership truly means, we must change.

JESUS PREDICTS HIS BETRAYAL (13:18–30)

THE CONTRAST WITH THE ELEVEN (13:18–20)

The prediction of Judas's betrayal in 13:18–30 is lengthier than in the Synoptics (Mark 14:18–21 and parallels). Jesus had already warned them (6:70; 12:24), even in this scene where he tells them not all of them are clean (13:10). So here, in telling them they will be blessed by God, he clarifies that "I am not referring to all of you." He had chosen each of them, including Judas (6:70), and he had been aware of his true nature from the beginning (6:64). At the outset, he first shows them the absolute difference between his betrayer (13:18) and the faithful eleven (vv. 19–20).

We now see why Jesus chose Judas in spite of his evil inclinations. He did so to fulfill Scripture. The early church generally understood Judas's betrayal in terms of scriptural fulfillment. In Matthew 27:9 the evangelist uses Zechariah 11:12–13 to explain Judas's betraying Jesus in exchange for thirty pieces of silver, and Peter in Acts 1:20 cites Psalms 69:25 and 109:8 to explain the betrayal.

Jesus cites Psalm 41:9 to show why Judas was chosen: "He who shared my bread has turned against me." David in this psalm is the righteous sufferer who has experienced the betrayal of a close friend while he was ill and persecuted by his enemies. David, here as elsewhere, is a type of the suffering Messiah. Judas in this sense is the antitype of the treacherous friend, and the psalm is fulfilled in his betrayal. The Greek behind "turned against" is literally "kicked up his heel," picturing a horse or mule kicking a person with their hooves.

Jesus wants them to know the extent to which he is in control even during this dark time. Yet he knows how hard it will be for them to handle what is about to transpire. So he is telling them ahead of time about Judas's treachery (v. 19) so that they will realize he is still in charge when it happens and so that through it "you will believe that I am who I am." Actually, this is like 8:24, 28, 58, an absolute "I am" (*egō eimi*) passage.[1] As the others, this should be translated, "I am Yahweh." He is giving this to them so at crunch time they can realize it and their faith be strengthened. Like Moses at the burning bush, they can come to know him as "I AM WHO I AM" (Exod 3:14), the God who is in charge.

We now come to the second double *amēn* saying of this section (13:16, 20): "I tell you the absolute truth" (see comments on 1:51). Jesus is ready and knows he is soon to be taken from them, so he is passing the baton to them. They are responsible to replicate his servant heart, and they are commissioned to continue his divine mission. This means that they go forth with his authority from God. There is a three-stage progression here, seen from the perspective of those to whom they will be sent by the Father and centered on the verb "accept" or "receive" (*lambanō*), drawn from 1:12, "to all who did receive him."

In 13:16 Jesus said that an agent or messenger is like the sender, so when people "receive" Christ's followers they are in reality receiving Christ, and when they receive Christ they receive God, the ultimate Sender (also in Matt 10:40–42). In this Jesus elevates the status and spiritual authority of the disciples, giving them the same power he has (as also in 15:5; 17:18; 20:21). He is one with the Father as the "I AM," just stated in verse 19, and now he is passing on that oneness to his followers. If we follow him, we are one

---

1. "Absolute" means there is no predicate; see comments on 8:24.

with the Son and thereby also with the Father. We go out with an authority we cannot even begin to imagine.

PROPHECY OF THE BETRAYER (13:21)

Jesus was earlier "troubled" at the death of Lazarus (11:33) and again as he contemplated the coming passion events (12:27), so here, when he is "troubled in spirit," is the third time he has his Gethsemane experience in John. His heart is breaking over the betrayal of Judas. He has known all along that this was to happen (see comments on 6:64, 70), but now that the time is here he grieves over Judas. We saw in 11:33, 38, the balance between the anger his sense of justice feels and the anguish his sense of loving compassion feels. Here the latter predominates. So he "testifies" in the form of a prophecy via a third double *amēn* saying (see 13:16, 20): "Very truly I tell you, one of you is going to betray me." He has commented on this earlier (6:64, 70; 13:10), and John told about Judas further in 12:4–6; 13:2, 10–11, 18, but now Jesus places it out in the open to prepare his disciples for what is to come.

DISCUSSION OVER WHAT IS TO COME (13:22–27)

Needless to say, this causes great consternation among them. We would think they would be somewhat ready given Jesus' earlier statements (see on v. 21 above), but they aren't. They look around at each other, perplexed. In Mark 14:19 and parallels they ask, "Am I the one?" If we remember the scene, they are all reclining on couches, and Matthew 26:25–26 records a private exchange there when Jesus told Judas that he knew. Still, the others missed that in the hubbub that likely ensued, and they had no idea which of them Jesus was accusing.

John adds to the Synoptic account and introduces the Beloved Disciple (BD) at this point. He is a fixture in the rest of the narrative (18:15–16; 19:25–27, 35; 20:1–10; 21:1–7, 20–24) and is presented as the archetypal or ideal disciple. It is striking that he never identifies this BD, though almost certainly John is speaking of himself.[2] Two important points are worth noting in 13:23. First, he is "the disciple whom Jesus loved," a somewhat unusual statement, for Jesus loved all the disciples deeply (13:1), loved Lazarus and his sisters (11:5, 36), and certainly with his Father "so loved the world" (3:16). John is *not* saying this out of pride ("he especially loved me") but out of a sense of awe and because he sees himself as emblematic of all true disciples. He wants us to share his wonder as he meditates on the love between himself and Jesus.

Second, he is reclining on Jesus' chest (literally "in the bosom of Jesus"), properly translated by the NIV as "reclining next to him," but the literal language helps us to picture the scene. They are all reclining on couches in a U-shaped configuration, with Jesus at the head and the BD obviously on a couch next to him and leaning over to converse with him. Reclining diners would rest on their left elbow and eat with their right hand. The picture is one of intimacy, and many have remarked that this re-creates the intimacy between Jesus and his Father in 1:18, "in closest relationship," literally "in the bosom of the Father." Jesus' followers share with him the very relationship he has with his Father.

Peter appears with the BD in virtually every scene where he appears in John. It almost seems like they are in competition with one another. Here it is the BD who asks Jesus about his prophecy and initiates the action. In 18:15–16 he gets Peter into the high priest's courtyard; in 20:1–10 he wins the race to the tomb; and in 21:1–7 it is the BD who recognizes Jesus. But this misreads the actual

---

2. Some have suggested the BD is Lazarus based on John 11:3, but that makes little sense since all four Gospels agree that the Last Supper includes Jesus and the Twelve, and 13:23 here has "the disciple whom Jesus loved." Others think he is purely literary and not an actual person, but there is little reason not to think he is both a real person and a model for the ideal disciple. As one of the Twelve and close to Peter in all the rest of the BD scenes, it makes most sense to identify him with John himself.

emphasis; there is no competition. Rather, they triumph together in the developing ministry of the apostolic band.

In 13:24-25 they work together to ask the identity of the betrayer, "Lord, who is it?" Likely Peter was reclining further away from Jesus, while the BD was next to him. The Greek has Simon Peter signaling by nodding his head to get the BD's attention, then the BD "leaning back" against the chest of Jesus to ask him. The scene portrays a deep intimacy and friendship. Some scholars have read a homosexual relationship into this, but that would be a serious mistake. It is common in many societies even today for two men to walk arm in arm or hand in hand as a sign of friendship with no sexual connotations whatsoever. This was the case in first-century Jewish society as well.

Jesus responds with another symbolic action (v. 26) like the washing of their feet, telling them that the betrayer is the one to whom he will give a piece of bread dipped in the bowl. In this bowl was the *haroseth*, a fruit paste consisting of dates, raisins, and sour wine. There is supreme irony in this, for passing this morsel to Judas would normally have been a great honor, marking him out as special. In this Jesus indeed loved Judas "to the very end" (13:1), but in reality it marked him out as the supreme betrayer and apostate. By passing it to Judas, he marks him as the object of God's attention for what he is about to do.

On the surface, it seems Jesus is favoring Judas, but in reality this is a sign of judgment, marking him as Satan's favorite, a tool for the evil deed that is to follow, and as the object of God's wrath. Now that his intentions and guilt are out in the open, Judas becomes resolute in his decision, and "Satan entered into him" (v. 27). The evil union is complete, a terrible copy of the supreme oneness between Jesus and his followers (6:56; 15:4; 1 John 2:24; 3:24). John strongly stresses Satan's part in the passion events (12:31; 14:31; 16:11), and Judas becomes a weapon in the cosmic war. Each act of Jesus' compassion toward him, like the washing of his

feet and now the morsel passed to him, simply hardened Judas further, and now he is possessed by Satan, totally consumed by evil.

Jesus, knowing that the hour has arrived, has only one desire
and so asks only one thing: "What you are about to do, do quickly."
The climax of the ages, the turning point of all history, had come.

THE FINAL STAGE IS SET (13:28–30)

John closes this part of the account with two things: the ignorance
of the disciples (vv. 28–29) and the departure of Judas (v. 30). Jesus
must have done all this quietly, for the others seemingly noticed
nothing, probably thinking Jesus was simply showing kindness
to Judas. The BD as well seemed to be in stunned silence, probably in shock. Since Judas was the treasurer of the group (12:6), the
others assumed that when Jesus said, "What you are about to do,
do quickly," he was sending Judas to purchase more supplies for
the meal or to give money to the poor. (Almsgiving was a part of
Passover festivities.)

Judas, his resolve complete, immediately gets up and heads out
into the night. Night and darkness in John are symbolic of evil (see
comments on 3:2), and that is certainly the case here. The deepest night was not outside the upper room; it was in Judas's heart.
The supreme evil act in all of history—putting the Son of God on
the cross—had now been set in motion.

The passion events in John are quite truncated compared to those
in the other Gospels, as John's entire attention is on the significance of the cross for eternity. The preparatory events in this
Gospel all take place on one night rather than throughout the
week as he focuses on the Last Supper and Farewell Discourse.
The Last Supper scene as well is abbreviated, as only two aspects
are related: the footwashing, which shows Jesus as the Servant
of Yahweh defining the meaning of leadership for his disciples,

and the betrayal of Jesus, which shows that God is completely in charge, even using the defection of Judas to accomplish his greater purposes.

The themes of love and servanthood dominate this scene, and both are as relevant today as they were then. I am certain that all who have personally experienced a footwashing ceremony would say it was meaningful. Leaders who are servants are desperately needed in our time and too few in number. In my first pastorate, I felt the biggest problem was pride in the leaders of churches around me, and that hasn't really changed. We all need to use our gifts to help and better the lives of those to whom we minister, and to refuse to manipulate them to our own ends.

Clearly humility and service to others is seen here as a weapon, part of the armor of God that would defeat the forces of evil in the cosmic war against Satan. Jesus in the cross defeated Satan once for all, and when we become servants like Jesus was, we too win the battle against the cosmic powers. Servanthood as seen in the dialogue with Peter (13:6–11) is an important element of our spiritual cleansing, something we must make part of our lifestyle so that we can be pure spiritually in our walk with Christ. Jesus here is our model or example (13:15), and to be Christlike we must be servants.

There are two further models for us in 13:18–30: Jesus as the quintessential righteous sufferer, betrayed by one of his own; and the Beloved Disciple, John, the ideal disciple who shares his life with Jesus and is faithful. Jesus chose Judas because of scriptural fulfillment, to show that even when he is pursued and betrayed by evil men, he and the Father are in complete control. They knew ahead of time all that was to transpire and are using this to increase the faith of their followers. The Beloved Disciple exemplifies selfless service, a humble type of leadership that is Christlike to the core.

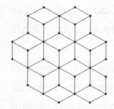

FAREWELL DISCOURSE: FIRST DISCOURSE

(13:31–14:31)

S uppose that after a series of tests, you discovered you had only twenty-four hours left to live. How would you tell your family and prepare them for life without you? This is exactly what Jesus has to do in this monologue, the longest speech in the New Testament. He has to make them ready for the horrors of the next twenty-four hours and commission them for their subsequent mission to the world. The basic theme of all Jesus is saying is, "I must depart so the Spirit can come." Jesus is about to finish his course, the "way" to the new era of salvation. The Spirit is to take over and complete God's plan, launching Jesus' followers to carry on his earthly ministry.

The form of the speech Jesus uses here—the Farewell Discourse—was frequently used in the Old Testament: Jacob in Genesis 47:29–49:33; Moses in Deuteronomy 32; Joshua in Joshua 23–24; Samuel in 1 Samuel 12; and David in 1 Chronicles 28–29. Each of these great men comforted their followers in the face of their impending deaths and both predicted and prepared them for what the future would bring. Jesus builds on and at the same time transcends these, for he is the Messiah and Son of God; and he alone would return from the grave.

There are three parts to the speech: The first discourse (13:31–14:31) consists of dialogues with four disciples—Peter (13:36), Thomas (14:5), Philip (14:8), and Judas (not Iscariot, 14:22). The second (15:1–16:33) consists of Jesus' elaborations on the first speech; and the third (17:1–26) consists of his high priestly prayer and concern to glorify the Father and his disciples. Some critics conclude this is not a whole discourse but is either two separate versions of the same material or a highly edited narrative consisting of several redactions by different authors. Neither satisfies, for it fits together remarkably well as a unified discourse (as I will be arguing as we go through verse by verse). It has a literary flow that shows careful construction with no evidence of clumsy compiling.

The one difficulty is 14:31, which breaks up the flow when Jesus says, "Come now; let us leave." This seemingly breaks the narrative into two parts, yet the themes of chapters 15–16 repeat those of chapter 14. But this is not an insuperable problem. It provides a neat organization in which Jesus first gives the basic theses in chapter 14 in the upper room and then builds on them as they walk to Gethsemane in chapters 15–16. This was a common Jewish literary technique (called "cycles") and fits well the original scene.

PROLOGUE: JESUS SPEAKS OF GLORY, LOVE, AND FAILURE (13:31–38)

There is some debate as to whether this section belongs more to the Last Supper scene (due to the prediction of Peter's denial in 13:36–38) or to the Farewell Discourse (due to the emphasis on glory and love, 13:31–35). Actually, it is another transition passage and thus belongs to both, but the themes in the opening verses prepare so well for chapter 14 that it primarily belongs there. The three themes here—glory, departure, love—are found in reverse order in the latter portion of the discourse: love (15:1–16:4a), departure (16:4b–33), and glory (17:1–26), forming a type of **chiasm**.

GLORY AND DEPARTURE (13:31–33)

Judas's abrupt departure (13:30) puts an end to the Last Supper scene and provides a powerful segue as Jesus now begins his explanation of these momentous events to come. In 12:23 Jesus predicted, "The hour has come for the Son of man to be glorified." Now that prediction begins to come true. The passion predictions from earlier in John all point to the fact that when Jesus is lifted up on the cross, he is lifted up to glory (3:14; 8:28; 12:32). Here is that supreme paradox—the most horrifying event in human history is at the same time the most glorious.

This is the last use of the title "Son of Man" in John, and it is fitting that it centers on **eschatological** glory. The full sense of Daniel 7:13–14 comes through, as it did in the first use, in 1:51: dominion, universal authority, and glory. Moreover, the glory of the Son, as in every aspect of the Father-Son relationship, means the glory of the Father. When God in supreme love gave his Son to die for us (Rom 5:8), the greatness and goodness of God was completely revealed. The sacrificial death of Christ is in itself absolute glory, and as such it manifests the **Shekinah** presence as an act of vicarious sacrifice. In John the cross is the throne on which he receives his crown as Davidic Messiah, and it is the mercy seat on which atonement comes to the world.

Since Jesus and the Father are one (10:30), the reverse is also true (13:32). Not only is the Father glorified in the Son, but also "God will glorify the Son in himself, and will glorify him at once." This combination of the future "will glorify" with "at once" emphasizes the imminent event of the cross. Amazingly, Jesus would be dead in about fifteen hours (near midnight Thursday to three in the afternoon Friday). Jesus was soon to glorify God by submitting to his will (Mark 14:36, "not what I will, but what you will") and fulfilling his hour of destiny (12:23). God would glorify Jesus by making the cross the final victory over Satan and the moment salvation comes to sinful humankind.

In light of the mutual glory of the Father and Son, Jesus now addresses his disciples regarding his imminent departure (v. 33). For the only time in John (seven times in 1 John) he calls them "dear children" to demonstrate his love and continue his role in the Passover meal as family head of the apostolic band. The Father-Son relationship with the heavenly Father is replicated in Jesus and the disciples (see 15:4, 9; 17:21–23).

His imminent departure is a major theme of passion week, and every detail looks ahead to the cross and empty tomb. Jesus has twice "told the Jews" the twofold message we see here, that they will seek him but never find him, for because of their unbelief they cannot come to his heavenly home (7:34; 8:21). The same is true for the disciples, but the reason for this massively differs for the disciples. His opponents can *never* come because they have rejected Christ's offer of salvation. The disciples cannot come for the time being because God has willed that they continue Jesus' earthly ministry. The separation of these Jewish opponents is eternal, but with the disciples it is temporary. As we will see, Jesus would "prepare a place" for them in heaven (14:2) and "come back" to receive them (14:28).

THE NEW LOVE COMMANDMENT (13:34–35)

The third major theme is love, and again the love relationship within the Godhead is to be relived in the love that binds together the members of the church. The command to love was hardly "new," as Israel itself was built on the command to love God (Deut 6:5) and neighbor (Lev 19:28). In John love is one of the three great eschatological gifts along with "peace" (14:27) and "joy" (15:11). Jesus made love an essential creed for the early church in Mark 12:29–31.

This was a "new commandment" because it was grounded in two things: God's love for Jesus and Jesus' love for them. This new level of love flows out of the Triune Godhead and forms the heart of the new covenant Christ has established for this new era. It is new in both quality and quantity, for it finalizes God's new salvation contract for his people. With Christ's sacrificial love as the paradigm, this new love has the potential to transform society and bring a whole new meaning to human relationships.

Jesus adds, "By this everyone will know that you are my disciples, if you love one another" (v. 35). The new age has begun, and a new depth of love now characterizes this new messianic community, anchored in the love demonstrated in the incarnation and sacrifice of Christ on the cross. As we experience divine love, we participate in it through love for one another. Christ's intention is that the world watch and see this love played out among the people of God. The result is that this proves to the world that the new way of Christ is superior. Throughout history this love—both external love for the unsaved and internal love for the brotherhood (Gal 6:10)—has played a major part in Christian outreach.

PETER'S BETRAYAL PROPHESIED (13:36–38)

Peter, probably speaking for the rest as well, is confused by all Jesus has said and centers on the key point: "Lord, where are you going?" He is still thinking on the earthly plane and wonders if Jesus is fleeing his persecutors. Like the Jews in 7:35 and 8:21–22, he fails to comprehend the prophecy about Jesus' departure, though he realizes that death is somehow involved (13:37).

Jesus' answer is quite different from what he told the Jews in 7:34, as noted above in the comments on 13:33. Peter cannot come now but will follow later. "Follow" is an essential component of discipleship in John (1:43; 8:12; 10:4, 27; 12:26; 21:19–22) and hints at the central aspect of the *imitatio Christi*, the "imitation of Christ," that the true disciple will follow and emulate Christ all the way, even to the point of death (Mark 8:34).

Peter protests that he is willing to follow Jesus, even if it means forfeiting his life (13:37). He is undoubtedly thinking of the final war in which Jesus as conquering King will destroy the Romans. He will show this at Jesus' arrest when he draws his sword and cuts off the ear of the high priest's slave (John 18:10), likely expecting the heavenly host to appear and begin the final war.

Jesus, who knows everyone's heart (2:25), exercised his omniscience (see 1:42, 48; 4:17–18) and tells Peter the truth. Far from dying for Jesus, he will "disown [him] three times" even "before the rooster crows" that night. Peter's bravado is misdirected, for he doesn't really know himself. The three times are in 18:15–18, 25–27. The mention of the rooster crowing is a common idiom. It doesn't point to any specific time but simply means early in the morning before dawn. The fact that his three denials are stressed in all four Gospels shows how important this was; the stress, however, is not on Peter's failure alone but on the failures we all undergo. Peter found forgiveness and reinstatement—and so can we.

JESUS IS THE WAY TO THE FATHER (14:1–14)

PREPARING A PLACE FOR THEM (14:1–4)

Clearly the disciples are very upset by all that Jesus has told them, and he is also "troubled" by the impending passion events (see 12:27; 13:21). They should be comforting and consoling Jesus in this tragic and desperate time, but they do not understand enough to do so. They are focused on themselves. So Jesus turns to them and says, "Do not let your hearts be troubled." I've heard several speakers say it's a sin to have a troubled heart, but if that's true, then Jesus himself was a sinner, since his heart was troubled (11:33; 12:27; 13:31). What he is saying is that we don't have to allow our worries to consume us. They are quite anxious about Jesus' imminent departure and his prophecy of their coming failures (13:35; Mark 14:27–31). Jesus wants them to know that they don't have to continue in this state.

His solution is simple: "You believe in God; believe also in me." There are three possible translations of the two "believes" in this verse:

(1) Indicatives—"You believe in God and also believe in me."
But the whole point here is that they are failing in this
very area.

(2) Indicative/imperative—"You believe in God; believe also in
me" (NIV). This is very possible, but does the context support that they are trusting God?

(3) Imperatives—"Believe in God and believe in me." I believe
this is best in a context where they are commanded to trust
in the Godhead as the antidote to fear.

As throughout John's Gospel, the Father and Son function
together, including as objects of faith. Trust in one demands trust
in the other, and that is especially encouraging at this point where
the disciples' whole world is being turned upside down. The antidote to worry is faith and prayer in the Triune Godhead (Phil 4:6–7).
With God and Christ in charge, all trials turn out for the best (Rom
8:28; Jas 1:2–4; 1 Pet 1:6–7). This prepares for the emphasis on believing prayer in 14:12–14; 15:7, 16; 16:23–24, 26.

At this moment it does not seem that God is on their side, for
he is taking Christ from them, and they are going to be alone.
However, that is rectified in 14:2–3 and turned completely around.
He is going away for their sakes, "to prepare a place for you" in
heaven, providing the perfect reason for them to put their trust
in him. Jesus imagines heaven as a huge home, telling them of
the "many rooms" waiting for them, all furnished by Christ himself. The emphasis is not on the lavish nature of the rooms (this is
why the "mansions" of the KJV is not a good translation),[1] but on
the ample provision Christ has made. There is more than enough
room to hold all the saints.

---

1. The use of "mansions" in the KJV came about through the influence of John
Wyclif, who in the fourteenth century followed the Latin Vulgate's *mansiones*.
However, we should avoid it due to modern connotations of extravagance and
luxury in the term.

So this pictures Jesus going home to heaven and readying dwelling places in his Father's heavenly home for the disciples, then at a later time returning to earth to gather his followers and bring them back to their final home in heaven. This is made clear in 14:3: "I will come back and take you to be with me that you also may be where I am." In light of 14:15–29, with its stress on Jesus after his resurrection coming back through the Holy Spirit (see below), there could be a double meaning in Jesus' "I will come back"—the coming of the Spirit anticipating his own second coming. Still, the primary thrust is not on the Spirit but on the second coming, the **parousia** (Greek "coming" and a technical term in English for his return).

Jesus is saying that his departure will take place via the cross, resurrection, and ascension. The disciples will join him at his second coming and their own resurrection to glory, as in 2 Corinthians 5:1: "If the earthly tent we live in is destroyed, we have a building from God, an eternal house in heaven, not built by human hands" but by Christ (as it says here in 14:2–3). In both texts the believers will dwell with the Godhead in heaven for all eternity.

Jesus concludes this opening part of his speech by reminding them, "You know the way to the place where I am going" (v. 4). This doesn't mean the disciples know all the details but that Jesus' previous teaching has given them the means of understanding this exciting truth.

Two Reactions (14:5–11)

Thomas: a person, not a place (14:5–7)

We see here that they truly do "know the way" but fail to realize it, for Jesus himself is the way to heaven (v. 6). Still, Thomas in his ignorance demurs, saying, "Lord, we don't know where you are going, so how can we know the way?" (v. 5). He is filled with doubts and questions throughout John (11:16; 20:24–25), but in his doubts he always speaks for the others. He does the right thing in bringing his doubts to Jesus (a lesson for us all). They are as before

thinking on the earthly plane and unaware of the heavenly realities. This is the third of four passages centering on the end of the
age and not just on the present situation (with 5:28–29; 6:39–40;
21:22), and the disciples are confused. They, like the authorities,
wonder where Jesus might be moving to. Jesus says, "You know
the way" (14:4), and Thomas replies, "No, we don't."

When Jesus denounced the ignorance of the Pharisees (8:14–21),
he did so in unstinting terms: "Where I go, you cannot come" (8:21).
The disciples, however, are faithful followers and honestly seek
the truth, so Jesus here responds with the sixth "I am" saying (see
comments on 6:35), which culminates Jesus' teaching on the salvation he provides for those who come to him: "I am the way and
the truth and the life. No one comes to the Father except through
me" (v. 6). Two important matters stand out. First, Jesus himself
is the way to the Father, a truth he clarifies in the second half of
this verse. Second, Jesus as the way is the central point, and the
other two support it. We could translate, "I am the way, namely,
the truth and the life."

"The way" describes the very heart of early Christian consciousness, as in the core Isaiah 40:3 passage that opens Mark 1:2–3 and
parallels: "Prepare the way for the Lord, make straight paths for
him." The first title the Christian movement used for itself was
"the Way," as seen in Acts 9:2; 19:9, 23. They viewed themselves early
on as a messianic sect of the Jews, joining the Pharisees, Sadducees,
and Essenes as another philosophy in first-century Judaism. This
self-understanding lends support to Jesus' identification of himself as the way to the Father and to salvation.

As the way, he is also "the truth" and "the life." He is truth
because he is the Living Revealer, the very voice and revelation
of God. He is the incarnate Shekinah glory of God, the "grace and
truth" (1:14). His words and deeds are the words and deeds of the
Father (5:19–30; 8:29), and all truth is summed up in him. He is
the "resurrection and the life" (11:25), because God has granted
him life-giving power (5:26), and he bestows life on whomever he

wishes (5:21). Eternal life only comes to those who believe in him (3:16, 36; 5:24). So Jesus is the way to God because he is the truth-teller and the life-giver.

For this reason, "no one comes to the Father except through" him. As Savior (4:42) and light of the world (8:12), all flows through him and his atoning sacrifice on the cross. In our world, people are highly offended and Christianity is viewed as oppressive because it dares to claim that it alone can bring people to heaven. The inclusive society we live in wants to hear that anyone can live up to their light and get in. The thought that Jesus is the only way turns Christianity into a hate religion for these people.

Yet why would God go to so much trouble and pain as to send his Son to earth to die on the cross if it didn't matter and people could get into heaven any way they wanted? That makes no sense at all. The truth is that modern people have spent their whole lives rationalizing their sins, failing to realize that you cannot enter heaven laden with sin and evil. How do sinners find forgiveness when they continue to sin with impunity? The truth is that sin is an internal force (we call it "total depravity") that makes it impossible to come to God on your own merits. With the atoning sacrifice of Christ, God paid for our sins himself and obtained forgiveness for us. There is no other way because there *can be* no other way.

There is an interesting text-critical problem in 14:7, for it yields two polar opposite readings. The first is a condition contrary to fact, which would be translated, "If you had really known me (which you didn't), you would then know my Father (which you don't)."[2] The second is a condition of fact, translated, "If you really know (which you do), you will know my Father as well."[3] The manuscript evidence is equal, but the context, I believe, fits better the more positive condition of fact with the NIV.

---

2. Supported by manuscripts A B C D¹ L and followed by NASB, NLT, LEB, ESV.

3. Supported by 𝔓66 ℵ D* W and followed by NIV, NJB, HCSB, NCV, NET.

In spite of frequent misunderstandings, the disciples have come to know Jesus, and so Jesus assures them that they are getting to know the Father as well. They have grown in their knowledge and know Jesus as Messiah, King of Israel, Son of God, and Son of Man (1:41, 49, 51). Since Jesus is the **shaliach**, the Agent of God, as well as the Word of God and has made God known to them (1:18), they can rest assured that to know him is to know the Father. So "from now on," from this point forward, they will both "know" and "see" the Father and grow in that knowledge every day.

Philip: mutual indwelling of Father and Son (14:8–11)

Out of the discussion with Thomas, Philip has a logical next request: "Lord, show us the Father and that will be enough for us." This is not a desire to look on the face of God, for in 1:18 John pointed out that "no one has ever seen God," which pointed back to Moses, who could not have looked on the face of God and lived (Exod 33:20). Most likely he is asking for a vision of God like Isaiah or Ezekiel were privileged to experience, God on his throne, high and lifted up. Moses asked, "Show me your glory" (Exod 33:18), and Philip wants that for himself too.

Philip's error is his failure to understand all that Jesus has taught them about his union with the Father. Jesus has "shown them the Father" all along, for when they look and listen to Jesus they are indeed looking upon the glory of the Father. How could Philip and the others have spent so much time with Jesus and not known this? Jesus answers, "Anyone who has seen me has seen the Father" (v. 9). All along, in Jesus' every word and deed, they have seen God's work in him and have listened to the truths of God in his teaching.

Jesus anchors this in their own faith and trust (v. 10). When they believed in Jesus, they embraced his union with the Father: "that I am in the Father, and that the father is in me." They have believed he is Messiah and Son of God but failed to perceive his actual relationship with the Father. The mutual indwelling of the Son with the Father is an essential part of the makeup of the Trinity. Jesus presented it in 10:38 and now explores it further in 14:10–11, 20, and 17:21–23. If the disciples can come to grips with this truth, they will have no problem understanding that to see Jesus is to see God.

This is especially true of Jesus' teaching. As he said in 8:28 and 12:49, his words are part of his Father "living in me, who is doing his work." Jesus' words are the Father's living deeds acted out in him. As in 5:19–30 Jesus does nothing on his own. All he says and does is the Father working through him. The challenge of Philip to believe here is not saving faith but illuminating faith, the Spirit-driven ability to see and understand divine truths. In 14:11 Jesus tells them how to develop such faith. If they struggle believing Jesus' own testimony to himself, they should turn to the "works themselves." His miracles are more than mere acts of power. They are signposts revealing the presence of God in him and telling us that the kingdom of God has arrived. In 5:36 Jesus said, "The Father gave me these works to accomplish, and they prove that he sent me" (NLT; see also 10:37–38).

JESUS PROMISES POWER VIA FAITH (14:12–14)

After challenging them to find faith, Jesus in this next short section shows them the potential of faith to change their lives and the world around them. Thus far he has centered on the works of God through him, and now he applies these truths to the works of the disciples themselves. We move from illuminating faith to appropriating faith. Those who finally comprehend the true nature of Jesus will now through the Spirit discover the incredible spiritual power available to them.

Jesus defines the results in two directions: First, they "will do the works I have been doing." This includes miracles but goes beyond to embrace all the "works" of Jesus: his deeds of servant-hood and love, his proclamation of divine truths, his life of piety and prayer, and his power to change the lives of those around him.

For us this means the age of miracles has not passed, and the power of God is available to the church today.

Second, Jesus goes beyond this to state that "they will do even greater things than these," using the language of 1:50; 5:20. Yet what can be greater than the raising of Lazarus or changing the water into wine? Many answers have been given, such as doing even more miracles than Jesus did (a shallow theory) or even more powerful miracles (what would they be?). Nearly all agree that Jesus is referring to the new age of the Spirit that will follow his death and resurrection. The post-resurrection power will involve eternal realities. This fits well, for Jesus explains that this is so "because I am going to the Father" after his earthly work is finished and he has been exalted to the right hand of the Father (Mark 12:36; Acts 2:34–35).

This is true, but there is more. The text says "greater *works*," and so we must ask what a greater miracle than the raising of Lazarus might be. The answer is that the greatest miracle is not new physical life such as Lazarus received but new spiritual life, the bestowal of eternal life on the unsaved. While Jesus made forgiveness for sins and salvation possible by his sacrificial death on the cross and by sending the Spirit to enter the new believer upon conversion, we are allowed to participate in God's mission to save the lost (20:21–23). So the "greater works" are both life in the new age of the Spirit and the resultant mission to the unsaved empowered by the Spirit. Once more we are dealing with trinitarian truths, as all three members of the Godhead are deeply involved in the lives of the saints on earth.

Part of these "greater works" of the new age is a new prayer power (14:13–14). These verses exhibit an A-B-A pattern, with the two prayer promises framing the purpose, "so that the Father may be glorified in the Son." Christ's death produced "a new and living way opened for us through the curtain" (Heb 10:19), meaning a new access to God for salvation and prayer. In each step his goal was to bring glory to the Father throughout his earthly life (7:18; 13:31;

17:4). By answering prayer, he would continue to do so in heaven. So through prayer we participate in the glory of the Godhead! The new prayer power we enjoy is proof positive that the kingdom of God has arrived (see 15:7, 16; 16:23, 24, 26; 1 John 3:22; 3:14–15).

So he promises, "I will do whatever you ask in my name" and then repeats it: "You may ask me for anything in my name, and I will do it" (14:13a, 14). On the surface these prayer promises are extraordinary: "Ask for anything ... I will do it." Mercedes Benz, here I come—McMansion, why not? I feel like being an NBA super-star. However, to assume we can get anything we want through prayer is not just wrong, it is exceedingly dangerous. We become "spiritual" hedonists, greedy people living for the things of this world and pretending they're spiritual. This is the problem with prosperity theology. It is a worldly approach to life under the guise of prayer power. If what prosperity preachers say is true, we and not God would be in control, and he would become a mere puppet serving our whims. This movement is heretical.

In reality, the key is the phrase "in my name" (see also 14:26; 15:16; 16:23, 24, 26). This is not a magical formula that we tack on to the end of a prayer to guarantee God will give us whatever we ask. In fact, nowhere in the New Testament does it appear at the end of a prayer. Instead, it provides a true perspective on prayer. In the ancient world a person's name portrayed who they were, the essence of their being. Parents chose the name as a kind of proph-ecy for the kind of person their child would become. The angel tells Mary in Matthew 1:21 to "give him the name Jesus, because he will save his people from their sins" (*yeshua'* meant "Yahweh saves"). So to pray in Jesus' name means to pray in union with who and what he is, to pray in accordance with his will. Self-centered prayers are not answered (Jas 4:3).

JESUS PROMISES THE HOLY SPIRIT (14:15–31)

There are three paragraphs in this section (vv. 15–21, 22–24, 25–31), out of which four themes emerge. The first three are found in the first two parts—the Spirit (vv. 15–17), the Son (vv. 18–21), and the Father (vv. 22–24); and the fourth is the new peace given believers by the Triune Godhead (vv. 25–31). In all this the gift of the Paraclete (the Holy Spirit) dominates, and the whole section introduces this astounding truth of the coming of the Spirit produced by the departure of Christ. In one sense one could argue that the doctrine of the Trinity begins here in earnest, for now the Holy Spirit enters this world in a new way and begins his work in the life of every saint.

THE PROMISE OF THE HOLY SPIRIT AS PARACLETE (14:15–21)

The ministry of the Paraclete (14:15–17)

As I said earlier, the primary theme of the Farewell Discourse is Jesus' departure so the Spirit may come. The Spirit is the primary sign of the new age, the final kingdom Christ would inaugurate. Jesus begins here with the ethical responsibility of God's people in light of all this: "If you love me, keep my commands." These are the by-products of the greater works and new prayer power Christ bestowed in 14:12–14. Love and obedience become the necessary qualification for experiencing the Spirit and at the same time are completely dependent on the Spirit within the believer.

John to this point has centered on the love of God for the world and for his people. In this discourse there is a slight reversal, and Jesus emphasizes our love for Christ and for God. This becomes the leading idea of this paragraph. The coming of the Spirit is the response of the Godhead to our deep love for Christ. Here love is the springboard to obedience. We cannot truly love Christ if we fail to obey him. In fact, the connection between them is a feature of this discourse (14:15, 21, 23; 15:14; see also 1 John 5:3). Moreover, we obey not just the ethical but also the spiritual commands, in fact, all that Jesus has revealed of the Christian life. We work at understanding and following all he has said, and we live our lives on that basis.

The giving of the Spirit is not dependent on our obedience. Rather, the Spirit gives us the strength to obey. Jesus now promises to "ask the Father, and he will give you another advocate" (14:16). It is the Spirit who enables believers to obey and gives them the power in prayer. This is the first of four passages on the ministry of the Spirit as Paraclete (NIV: "advocate," see 14:15–17, 26; 15:26; 16:7–15).

The Greek term *paraklētos* is rendered differently in many translations: "comforter" in KJV, "counselor" in the NIV1984, "helper" in the NASB, "advocate" in the NIV, NRSV, NJB, NLT. No English translation can suffice, for the term is too rich in meaning. For this reason I, like many, prefer to transliterate and use Paraclete.

The Spirit as "Paraclete" teaches, reveals, and guides God's people. He witnesses to, convicts, and prosecutes unbelievers. "Comforter" does not fit at all, and "helper" fails to describe the Spirit's ministry to sinners. "Counselor" fits the Spirit as guide and teacher but does not fit well the Spirit's convicting presence in the world. "Advocate" is probably best, for the term in the first century connoted a legal advisor and advocate but still doesn't fit his work in the world well. The English word refers to a defense attorney more than a prosecuting attorney. Still, it is closer than the others.

The term in itself etymologically would mean "called [*kaleō*] alongside [*para*]" another in some way, usually in legal situations. The basic idea behind it is a representative of God and parallels Jesus as the Agent or envoy of God. So John calls the Spirit "another Paraclete," the one who carries on the ministry of the earthly Jesus in this world. Everything that Jesus did, the Spirit continues. There is also some wisdom background to the term, building on Jesus as personified Wisdom. The Spirit is the presence of God and Jesus in the world. The trinitarian force continues here.

The Spirit is "given" by the Father. Twice the Spirit is sent or given by the Father (14:16, 26), twice by the Son (15:26; 16:7). This is part of the mission theme: the Father sends the Son into the world;

both Father and Son send the Spirit; and the Triune Godhead sends
the saints in mission to the world (17:18; 20:21).

Jesus then defines the Paraclete as "the Spirit of truth" (14:17;
also 15:26; 16:13), best understood as "the Spirit who is truth [=
14:6 of Jesus] and leads into all truth." Like Jesus, he reveals divine
truths and personifies all in this world that is truthful. He comes
first to the world that "cannot accept him," as does Jesus in 1:10–11,
because it "neither sees him nor knows him." The primary characteristic of the world in John is sin and rebellion. It is not that
God keeps them from knowing God but the deliberate rejection
of truth caused by depravity.

In contrast, the disciples do "know him" because they have the
Spirit. In fact, the Spirit "lives with you and will be in you." Both
their present and future are secure, for as in Romans 8:14–17 the
Spirit makes his residence in them, as we will see in the verses
that follow. When people are converted, the Spirit enters them
and makes them part of God's family. The movement from present
to future is much discussed, for the Spirit had not yet been given
to the disciples (7:39; that will occur in 20:22). The question is in
what sense the Spirit is *with* them (present), and in what sense
would be Spirit be *in* them (future). Likely it means the Spirit was
with them through Jesus' ministry to them and then would indwell
them after the resurrection and Pentecost.

The ministry of the Son (14:18–21)

The coming of the Spirit is the result of the Son's decision that
"I will not leave you as orphans." Without the Spirit they would
be as children without a father, a slave without a master, or disciples without a teacher/rabbi—all alone in the world. The next
statement is less clear: "I will come to you." There are three possible "comings" to which it might refer—the resurrection, the
coming of the Spirit, or the second coming. Several believe it is
the second, since this passage is bracketed with material on the

Spirit/Paraclete (14:16–17, 25–26). Others take it as the parousia/second coming on the basis of 14:2–3.

The most likely and simplest view is a reference to coming back from the dead in the resurrection appearances. When that takes place, the world will "not see me anymore"[4] (14:19) in the sense that there are no appearances to unbelievers apart from his brothers (1 Cor 15:7), but his disciples will "see me." The language is too personal and specific to fit Jesus' return via the Spirit. Moreover, Jesus' next statement is "Because I live, you also will live," which looks to him as the firstfruits and guarantee of their own resurrection (compare 1 Cor 15:20, 23).

Jesus' words in verse 20 may indicate a double meaning, as a new spiritual reality is inaugurated in the post-resurrection period. There is new life first in the guarantee of our own future resurrection and at the same time new life spiritually in Christ. "On that day" is an **apocalyptic** phrase found in the Old Testament (especially the Prophets) and referring to the coming of the kingdom of God. Here the "day" signifies the resurrection, an apocalyptic, world-changing event. When it arrives, God's people "will know." This refers not just to intellectual perception but to the participation of the whole person in the new age Christ is initiating.

All this means that in the period after his death the people of God will be taken care of because the Spirit will take the place of Christ among them and watch over them. Moreover, every one of the disciples will also be protected because they will not be alone. Christ will come back through his resurrection and be with them. He will come to them, not the world, and their new life in him will begin.

It is indeed a new life, involving a depth of union with the Triune Godhead they never could have imagined. As in 14:8–11, 17, the language here is of indwelling and progresses in three stages:

---

4. This parallels 16:16 and refers to his death ("not see me") and resurrection ("you will see me").

Jesus indwells the Father, the believers indwell Jesus, and Jesus in turn indwells them. The union within the Godhead is reenacted and reflected in the mutual union we have with Jesus himself. This will be deepened in 15:4–8 and 17:20–23, and the final stage comes in the union between believers when "all of them may be one" (17:21). Here there is a double union—the Paraclete indwells us (14:17), and Jesus indwells us (14:20).

This small paragraph is framed by love and obedience (14:15, 21). The central feature of this union is that "whoever has my commands and keeps them," the result of experiencing the love and indwelling of Jesus (14:21, also vv. 15, 23). It is impossible to love him without truly living this out in daily conduct. In the new age inaugurated by the resurrection there is a new intimacy with the Godhead and a corresponding new depth of adherence to his precepts. As we love and obey we enjoy this new union, as in the very act of obedience the love of the Father, Son, and Spirit will be enjoyed in ever new ways. Further, Jesus in this will "show" or "reveal" (*emphanizō*) himself to them, referring not only to the resurrection appearances but also to the progressive revelation to them that will mark the rest of their lives. As the Father "shows [Jesus] all he does" (5:20), so Jesus shows himself to his followers.

THE COMING OF THE FATHER AND THE SON (14:22–24)

The third disciple to interject with a question (after Thomas and Philip, 14:5, 8) is the other Judas (son of James, see Luke 6:16; Acts 1:13). He is probably the same one as Thaddeus in Mark 3:18; Matthew 10:3. He is confused, thinking "reveal/show" in 14:21 meant some kind of theophany—a visible manifestation of God. So he asks if it will be a private manifestation to themselves only and not a public theophany that will show the whole world his glory (as promised in Isaiah 11 or Daniel 7).

Jesus responds by contrasting his disciples who love and obey him (v. 23) with those opponents who do neither (v. 24). As Judas asks, he will indeed reveal himself to the first group. A life directed by Jesus' teaching is proof positive of love, and Jesus came for those people. They receive a double blessing: "My Father will love them," making them the recipients of all the promises of Scripture, and "we will come to them and make our home with them," making each of them the new temple of God.

While there will be an apocalyptic end of the world and an eternal home in heaven, Jesus reiterates here that before that event there will be an earthly home in every believer, inhabited by the Triune Godhead, who indwells each follower. Jesus is preparing a future "home" (14:2–3), but he with the Father is also making a present home in the life of the believer (14:23). This takes place through the Spirit, called both "the Spirit of God" (Rom 8:9a, 14; 1 Cor 6:11) and "the Spirit of Christ" (Rom 8:9b; Phil 1:19; 1 Pet 1:11), for he is the presence of the Father and the Son as he inhabits us (14:17). In this sense, the Triune Godhead indwells every saint. As in Revelation 21:3, "Look, God's home is now among his people! He will live with them, and they will be his people" (NLT). The first two returns have now been identified—Jesus' coming back in his resurrection appearances (14:18) and through the Holy Spirit (14:23).

The world, by contrast, neither loves nor obeys Christ (14:24). This is why he reveals himself (both in his appearances and in the indwelling of the Spirit) only to his followers. To ground this observation in his revelatory work, he reminds them that his teaching does not stem merely from himself but comes directly from God. These are divine truths, not just human observations. They must realize all he is saying consists of eternal truths coming from God himself.

Jesus' Departure and the Promise of Divine Peace (14:25–31)

With his death mere hours away, Jesus' departure from this world consumes him. His disciples need to know that while they will enjoy his physical presence only a little longer (v. 25), so Jesus is

saying all he can "while still with" them. With so short a time left
before his arrest, he has to watch every word.

His most important point is that the Spirit will soon take his
place and continue his abiding presence in their lives (v. 26). In
the same way that Jesus is the "representative" or Paraclete of
the Father, the Spirit is the representative of Jesus. As the Father
"sent" Jesus, so Jesus will "send" the Spirit "in my name." Jesus carries the authority of the Father in all he says and does, and the
Spirit has the authority of Jesus behind him. In the new era the
disciples can rely on him the way they do Jesus. As Jesus is the
"Word" or Living Revealer of the Father, the Spirit will "teach you
all things[5] and will remind you of everything I have said to you."
John has said the disciples failed to understand Jesus' certain sayings until after the resurrection (2:22; 12:16), so this tells how they
would do so. One thinks of the writing of the four Gospels and the
way the Spirit inspired every word as the evangelists wrote. Yet
it also relates to us today as the Spirit helps us recall passages[6] of
Scripture and understand those we are studying.

Jesus concludes with a promise of peace from God in light of
his departure (v. 27). "Peace I leave with you; my peace I give you"
becomes virtually a benediction in this context. Peace was associated with God's gift of salvation (Ps 29:11; Isa 57:19) and became
a primary messianic promise for the last days (Isa 9:6; 52:7; Ezek
37:26; Zech 9:10). Here it is a blessing they will receive with Jesus'
death and especially his resurrection (20:19, 21, 26). Jesus' peace
is a divine commodity beyond human understanding (Phil 4:7), a
major characteristic of the new order instituted by Christ.

---

5. "All things" doesn't mean all the knowledge that the world contains but "all
that they need" to walk in obedience and love.

6. "Remind" tells us that the Spirit is not involved in imparting new knowledge but in helping Jesus' followers to understand the revealed truth God has
already imparted in Jesus' teaching.

It is "my peace," not the world's peace. The world is unable to give such a peace, for it is characterized by random evil and uncertainty. Peace is a facade in this secular world order, upheld by military power then and now. The *Pax Romana* ("Roman peace") was a lie, for there were soldiers on the streets forcing it on a populace whose resources were used by greedy Romans to line their own pockets. Only Christ can provide inner peace through the cross, and only he can produce a peaceful world, though it will not come until he returns. When he said they need not be "troubled or afraid" in 14:1, he meant it in light of the Triune Godhead, who would be watching over them.

After this comforting promise, Jesus turns to his departure. He begins by repeating what he has said before about "going away" and "coming back" (v. 28; see 13:33; 14:2–3, 12, 18–19, 21–23). The problem is that his disciples have failed to comprehend all this teaching and are filled with consternation as well as confusion. The Synoptic Gospels contain three of the same passion predictions, and Luke has several others. John contains three different ones, all of them "lifted up" sayings (3:14; 8:28; 12:32). In spite of this volume of reminders, they are not ready for anything. When the women go to the empty tomb, they expect to anoint a corpse (Mark 16:1–2), and the Eleven doubt Mary when she tells them Jesus has risen (Luke 24:11).

Jesus' words "if you loved me" imply that in this instance they do not. He doesn't mean they have joined his enemies but rather that their love has not led to understanding and to concern for what is best for him. They are still in denial and do not want to face the reality. When we lose a loved one, it is natural that we feel grief for the loss and yet also joy that our loved one is with the Lord. This is what Jesus wants, that they "be glad that I am going to the Father."

He then adds, "for the Father is greater than I," meaning he is in complete control of the situation. Jesus' submission to the Father was the subject of 5:19–30, and this does not mean inferiority but equality. Everything Jesus does is part of his Father's work and done under his authority and power. That is true also of his approaching death on the cross. Every detail is under God, and both the death and the resurrection are orchestrated by God.

As he said in 13:19 and will say again in 16:4, Jesus is telling these details about future events ahead of time "so that when it does happen you will believe" (14:29). He wants them to be strong for the numbing events soon to transpire. They will need everything they can get, and he wants to give it to them. By knowing that God is aware of and has the power over every detail, they can be ready.

For the rest of their time in the upper room before beginning their walk to Gethsemane (vv. 30–31), Jesus wants them to be aware of the battle with the powers of darkness that surrounds the passion events. He has little time left to talk with them ("I will not say much more to you"), for "the prince of this world is coming." This means that Judas, possessed by Satan (13:27), was drawing near. The death of Jesus is clearly portrayed in John as a cosmic war (also in 6:70; 12:31; 13:27; 16:11). I used to think of Jesus' betrayal as a military error, Satan's Waterloo. But there is no way he could have failed to know what would happen—he knows the Old Testament much better than we do. But what could he do? He wanted Jesus to die, to bring pain to God. It was a small, brief victory, but at least he could enjoy the pain he inflicted on the Godhead. So the cross is not only the central event in the salvation of the lost, it is also the central battle in the cosmic war against the powers of evil.

Jesus calls Satan "the prince of this world" three times in John (with 12:31; 16:11). This refers to the fact that Satan rules over his own counterfeit kingdom inhabited by the fallen angels, described as one-third of the heavenly host in Revelation 12:4, which was cast out of heaven to earth by the archangel Michael's heavenly army in 12:7–9. Yet the real emphasis is not what we think. We should paraphrase, "he is *nothing more than* the ruler of this world." The same goes for 2 Corinthians 4:4, which could be paraphrased, "*merely* the god of this doomed world." His sphere of power is severely restricted to this fallen world. At this moment, he knew what was soon to transpire. He had been cast out of heaven, his time was short (Rev 12:12), and his final defeat was certain.

This is what Christ means by, "He has no hold over me." There is a legal connotation here. He can make no charge against Jesus, no legal claim that will stick. God is in control, not him, and Jesus knows this. The same is true for us. Satan cannot overpower the saints; he can only deceive and tempt us. We will only be defeated when we yield to his blandishments, for "God is faithful; he will not let you be tempted beyond what you can bear. But when you are tempted, he will also provide a way out so that you can endure it" (1 Cor 10:13). When we depend on Christ and the Spirit, we can say with Jesus, "He has no hold over me."

So rather than giving in to Satan, Jesus turns to the Father and to his imminent death on the cross. Part of his reason in doing so is to give a message to the world centering on two things: "that I love the Father and do exactly what my Father has commanded me." Satan may appear to be winning as the mob draws near to arrest Jesus. In reality, he can do only what God allows (Rev 13:5–8; 17:17). Jesus' love and obedience to the Father is a supreme example not only for us but for the world. The cross was an act of radical obedience to God, not a victory for Satan.

With this, the time in the upper room is at an end, so Jesus says, "Come now; let us leave" (v. 31). While many think this indicates a pause in the narrative that allows Jesus an interlude to finish his discourse, I take it literally to mean that Jesus gives them the rest of his Farewell Discourse on the way to Gethsemane. This allows us to picture them looking back on the temple and the vineyards for the dynamic background Jesus will be alluding to (see comments below). The main point is that Jesus is aware that it is now time to meet his destiny. He moves out as the Divine Warrior on his way to the most significant battle history will ever know.

———

The Farewell Discourse has delight after delight as we proceed through it. It begins with Jesus' departure as the culmination of all the hopes in the Gospel since the cross will be his messianic throne and the source of his glory (13:31–33). As the sign of God's amazing love, the cross is our model for loving one another. This love is the signpost of the new Christian movement (13:34–35).

The introductory section (14:1–4) tells us how we can overcome our constant worries by meditating on our future, which is guaranteed by Jesus' departure to heaven so as to ready our eternal heavenly home for us. While we have little control over our earthly troubles, we can bask in the certainty of our wondrous future. The key is to depend utterly on Jesus, who has provided "the way" to God (vv. 5–7). Like Philip we need to realize the trinitarian reality that in Jesus we have met God and heard his voice. We will never be alone, and we will always have both Father and Son at work in us (vv. 8–11).

There is a new power available in the new covenant age initiated by Jesus and the cross (vv. 12–14). There are two examples. First, in him the age of miracles is available to us, but we can perform the even "greater" acts of bringing the lost into the kingdom so that they gain not just new earthly life but eternal spiritual life. Second, a new prayer power is ours as we pray "in his name," that is, in union with him. Immense wonders are available to the people of God.

All of this is possible through the Spirit given us by both God and Christ (vv. 15–17). As Jesus is the voice and presence of God, the Spirit is the presence of Father and Son in this world, the one who mediates the divine truths and empowers God's people. In the next two sections (vv. 18–21, 22–24) Jesus presents a remarkable truth. Our hope is tied up with the return of Christ and the home in heaven that awaits us. But in actuality there is a coming of Christ that precedes this and involves a home he makes in us through the Holy Spirit. The final promise involves our making a home in heaven; this intermediate promise involves the Triune

Godhead making a home in us. So we already enjoy a touch of heaven, an exciting anticipation of what awaits us.

The final section (vv. 25–31) centers on Jesus' departure and the peace that is available to balance the consternation they have to be feeling. This is just as critical a message for us, for we have similar pressures and often feel a similar despair to the disciples. It is important to realize the tranquility of soul Christ gives us when we need it. Anxiety is a fact of life in this troubled world, but ours is reversed by the eternal promise of Christ that in the end nothing can harm us. The cosmic war that erupted with the cross has been won by Christ once for all, and he has done so for us as well. Satan is an already defeated enemy, and while he tries to destroy, we only know defeat when we fail to depend entirely on Christ and the Spirit. In other words, we are already victorious, even if it doesn't feel like it.

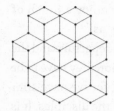

FAREWELL DISCOURSE:
SECOND DISCOURSE, PART 1
(15:1–16:4a)

The Farewell Discourse is organized as two cycles (13:31–14:31; 15:1–16:33) followed by a prayer of consecration (17:1-26). Cycles are a technique, common to literature written in Semitic languages, that goes over the same material twice, adding details the second time (compare Hebrews 8-10, 1 John, and Revelation, all of which employ this method). Jesus in 15:1–16:33 reworks the material from 13:31–14:31 and builds on the themes we have seen there, for instance, love in the community (13:34-35//15:17), the coming of the Spirit-Paraclete (14:15-17, 26//15:26, 16:7-15), spiritual warfare (14:30//16:11), and the prayer promises (14:13-14//15:7, 16; 16:23). At the same time, he adds nuances, centering more on the disciples who must remain in him and bear fruit. There is also the challenge to remain faithful in severe persecution.

This second discourse consists of four parts: the need for community love and unity (15:1-17), the need for strength to meet persecution (15:18-16:4), the work of the Paraclete (16:5-15), and the joy awaiting God's people (16:16-33).

LOVE AND UNITY IN THE COMMUNITY (15:1–17)

THE VINE AND THE BRANCHES (15:1–6)

This is another extended metaphor[1] like 10:1–18 on the shepherd and the gate, and the purpose of the vine metaphor here is the need to "remain in" Jesus in order to bear fruit for God. This has the same organization as 10:1–18 in the sense that the basic metaphor (15:1–6) is then explained in three sections—remaining and bearing fruit (vv. 7–8), love and joy in Jesus (vv. 9–11), and loving one another (vv. 12–17).

It begins with the last of the seven "I am sayings" (6:35; 8:12; 10:7, 17; 11:25; 14:6). The vine illustration draws its background from the use of vine imagery for Israel (Ps 80:8–18; Isa 5:1–7; 27:2; Jer 2:21; 5:10; Ezek 15:1–8; 17:1–6). In these the, vine metaphor is usually negative, centering on divine judgment for Israel's unfaithfulness. It is more positive here but still contains some negative overtones.

As Jesus and the disciples are leaving Jerusalem (14:31), they pass through the temple grounds and look up at the holy place where, at the entrance above the linen curtain, there is a large grapevine with clusters of grapes "the height of a man" (Josephus, *Antiquities* 15.395), made of pure gold and symbolizing Israel. When Jesus says, "I am the true vine," he fulfills this imagery and in effect replaces apostate Israel as God's true vineyard. Jeremiah 2:21 prepares for this: "I had planted you like a choice vine of sound and reliable stock. How then did you turn against me into a corrupt, wild vine?"

The nation had lost its place as the covenant people, and Jesus had become the only way to God (14:6). He has earlier fulfilled and taken the place of the temple (ch. 2), Passover (ch. 6), Tabernacles

---

1. There is no plot, just a series of metaphors on the topic of a vineyard, so many call it a *mashal* or extended metaphor, but technically, a parable does not have to explicitly tell a story. There is an implied plot behind it, so it can viably be designated a parable as well.

(chs. 7–9), and Hanukkah (ch. 10), and now he replaces Israel her-self. He now embodies the true people of God, and the disciples will become new Israel. In Sirach 24:17–21 Wisdom is seen planted among the people of God and bearing fruit. Jesus is the personifi-cation of divine Wisdom transforming God's people.

He adds, "my Father is the gardener," the one who controls the vineyard and decides what branches are to remain on the vine. In Isaiah 5:2 he is the one who "dug it up [= plowed the land] and cleared it of stones and planted it with the choicest vines." The Father tends the vine, seen now as Jesus himself. The picture is Jesus and his mission as planted and bearing the fruit of the dis-ciples, who now become God's vineyard in the world.

With this he moves into a new part of the metaphor, the branches (v. 2) consisting of two kinds—those bearing fruit and those failing to do so. Both types of branches are "in me" (= the dis-ciples), namely, part of the original vine. Jesus is using the ancient practice of viticulture as an illustration. Fruitless branches were removed, and the fruitful ones were carefully trimmed so they could produce even more. This points back to chapter 13, as Judas the dead branch is cut off and the disciples are pruned. For us the fruitless branches are quasi-Christians who are doing little to glo-rify God or follow him.

The removal of the fruitless branches will be developed fur-ther in 15:6; the point is they have become useless and ceased to be living branches. This removal took place in February-March, with the pruning of the good branches in spring and then again in August after they developed leaves. The gardener would press off many of the little shoots so the major branches could get all the moisture. Jesus uses this to describe the new life in him, and the idea of producing more fruit sums up the qualities of disci-pleship as found in this Gospel—increased faith, prayer, obedi-ence, love, mission—all of which bring glory to God (v. 8). The process of pruning symbolizes the difficulties in life, the trials that strengthen the believer (Jas 1:2–4; 1 Pet 1:6–7).

In 15:3-4 Jesus applies this to the disciples, encouraging them at the outset that they "are already clean because of the word I have spoken" to them. He has been developing them spiritually throughout his ministry, and they have been slowly learning to be fruitful. This might specifically refer to his teaching at the Last Supper (13:10, "you are clean"), finalizing the process of the previous months. The main point, however, is the necessity of Jesus' teaching (and for us, the word of God as a whole) in producing spiritual growth. We must help those in our churches and ministries to "crave pure spiritual milk" of the word (1 Pet 2:2).

Jesus then reintroduces the mutual-indwelling theme, a key concept in this discourse (15:4, 5, 6, 7, 9, 10) drawn from 14:16, 20, 23. The imperative in 15:4 probably has a slight conditional force, "If you remain in me, I will also remain in you." We are responsible to live entirely in union with Jesus and in dependence on his presence. Branches have life only to the extent to which they are attached to the vine, and fruitfulness stems only from the life-giving sap provided by the vine. All this illustrates the fact that the extent to which we rely on ourselves and our resources is the extent to which we will fail. So we must dwell entirely in Christ and the Spirit. As both Paul (Eph 2:8-10) and James (2:14-26) firmly state, works cannot produce faith, but faith must produce works. We are responsible to draw sustenance and life from our union with the vine, Jesus.

In 15:5 Jesus returns to the metaphor, repeating the theme, "I am the vine; you are the branches." His message is that only via mutual indwelling with him can there be fruit, for "apart from me you can do nothing." He is not only the model for spiritual strength and victory, he is the only path to incorporating that strength and finding victory. We rely on him for everything and rely on ourselves only for earthly needs.

The danger is incredibly great, as Jesus shows in 15:6. The branch that fails to remain, that dies and stops bearing fruit, is "thrown away and withers," then is "picked up, thrown into the fire and burned." It doesn't get much scarier than this. Jesus expands the image in verse 2 and is a very serious warning since it implies fiery judgment, alluding to the fiery judgment of Ezekiel 15:4–5 on apostate Israel. This has Judas especially in mind, but the warning is very important for other similar passages as well. The danger of falling away from the faith was constant and too often seen, as with the Judaizers in Galatians 1:8–9; the weak Christians in Hebrews 6:4–6; 10:26–31; the heresy in 2 Peter 2:20–21; and the cowardly in Revelation 21:8.

This passage contributes to a huge debate over apostasy and eternal security. Calvinists argue that those who are "thrown away" are unbelievers like Judas, who never was a follower. Those who apostatize were members of the church but not really true believers. Many also appeal to 1 John 2:19, "They went out from us, but they did not really belong to us." Others say the images of gathering and burning here are general images that encourage remaining in the vine rather than genuine warnings of apostasy.

Arminians, on the other hand, state that the text describes these branches first as "in me," meaning they are indeed believers, and then gathered and "burned," referring to the fiery judgment of the Great White Throne (Rev 20:11–15). This issue can never finally be solved, for God has provided passages that can be interpreted both ways. Still, it is an important issue, and we should work to find which view best fits all the evidence. It took me many years to decide, and I slightly yet firmly favor (the evidence is close to equal) the view that a Christian can fall away from their faith.

Explanation of the Parable (15:7–17)

Remaining and bearing fruit (15:7–8)

Many place verses 7–8 with the parable (so vv. 1–8), making it, with verse 4, the second application. I think it is better seen as the first of the three explanations. As the branches bear fruit only by remaining attached to the vine and receiving sap, so followers must "remain in me." This is new covenant language from the Old Testament (see Jer 31:31–34), with remaining leading to a new heart and a new reliance on God and the Spirit. In 15:4 Jesus links remaining to the promise that he will remain in them. Here he says, "my words remain in you," connected to the promise in 14:26 that his Spirit would teach and remind them of all he had said to them.

The indwelling presence of Jesus and his "words" results in the next all-sweeping prayer promise (see 14:13–14). When we center our lives on him and his teaching guides every decision (= the obedience of 14:15, 21, 23), then we truly exist "in his name" (14:13), that is, in union with him. In that situation, we may "ask whatever you wish, and it will be done for you," repeating the double promise of 14:13–14. Our prayer life is a reflection of that union with him, and the implication is that our prayers will not be self-centered but will seek God's glory (the thou-petitions of the Lord's prayer, Matt 6:9–10) and leave our needs with him (the we-petitions, Matt 6:11–13). Prayer in this sense is a major kind of fruit-bearing, a hallmark of true discipleship.

The goal of every disciple is to remain in Jesus and thereby to glorify God by bearing much fruit (15:8). This is first accomplished by total dependence on the Lord and placing all needs at his feet in prayer. The first we-petition is "Give us today our daily bread" (Matt 6:11), which we too often think means "Gimme, gimme!" but in fact means, "Lord, I surrender my needs to you."

This results in two things: first, God is glorified, as already stated in 14:13, asserting that Christ answers prayer "so that the Father may be glorified in the Son." Here this is extended to all fruit-bearing, not just prayer. In a real sense this is the basic goal of life. My daily prayer is that what I do that day will bring glory to God. I just prayed that this morning, and as I write I constantly ask that every word will glorify him. All fruit-bearing is the product of Christ and the Spirit indwelling us, and the goal is always, as the Westminster Confession says, to "glorify God and enjoy him forever." Second, fruitfulness shows "yourselves to be my disciples."

In 13:35 love in the community also shows "everyone … that you are my disciples." The world is watching, and the extraordinary life of the true believer will be a beacon light illuminating to all the joy and privilege of being a Christ follower.

Love and joy in Jesus (15:9–11)

The love (vv. 9–10) and joy (v. 11) the saints experience in Christ are further signs of the new covenant era Christ has brought with him. The primary image throughout this discourse is that the new relationship between Jesus and the disciples reflects that between Jesus and his Father. This is particularly true in experiencing Jesus' love, which is the outgrowth of the love he shares with his Father. The depth of this love is beyond our ability to understand and cannot be expressed in mere human language. It is our privilege to experience it and rejoice in it.

The verb translated "loved" is in the aorist tense, which in the Greek looks at an event as a single whole. Here it expresses the completeness of God's love for the Son and of the Son's love for us. It is perfect and all-embracing. We experience the eternal love that exists within the Godhead and now exists between the Triune Godhead and us. Paul shows this in Romans 5:8: "But God demonstrates his own love for us in this: While we were still sinners, Christ died for us." To experience its true depth, we must "remain in [his] love." It must be experienced continuously to be complete.

We must be careful to properly understand what it means to remain in Christ. It is much more than resting in Jesus or meditating on him. It is active and must always be reflected in obedience to his commands (15:10). It is obedience that enables us to actually experience that love. Moreover, like love, obedience is built on the relationship between Christ and his Father, as he adds, "just as I have kept my Father's commands and remain in his love." Christ's obedience as the basis and model for our own is a major emphasis in John's Gospel (4:34; 5:17, 19–20; 6:38; 8:29; 10:18; 12:49–50), especially in this discourse (14:15, 21, 23, 31). Jesus' love is the foundation

of our own, and our love for him is the source from which our obedience flows. This doesn't mean that when we fail to obey he stops
loving us (see Rom 8:31–39) but rather that disobedience keeps us
from experiencing the love of God and Christ.

The purpose of all this is joy (15:11). Jesus moves from peace
(14:27) to love and obedience (15:10) and now to joy. We will see this
again in the resurrection narratives, as messianic peace (20:19)
leads to messianic joy (20:20). All three of these **eschatological**
promises—peace, love, joy—are now available to his followers.
Even our trials can be greeted with "pure joy" (Jas 1:2); we may
not have happiness, since our trials are "painful" (Heb 12:11), but
we have joy because God and his Son are in control. When God's
joy is felt in us, our "joy [is] complete." The world's joy is finite
and temporary, but God's joy is perfect and eternal. Nothing else
in this world can help us to relate to the difficulties of life with joy,
and that is made possible by the presence of the Triune Godhead
with us as we pass through the dark times.

Loving one another (15:12–17)

The third implication of the vine metaphor is the deep love that
believers share with one another. This community love completes
the three stages of love: love between the Father and the Son leads
to love between Jesus and the disciples (vv. 9–10), and now his
love for us is reflected in our love for one another (as also in 13:34).
This triangular love itself reflects the Trinity. Our relationship
with each other grows out of the internal relationship of the three
members of the Godhead. All our relationships emerge and draw
their energy from our relationship with Christ. This is the case
at every level—husband-wife (1 Pet 3:7), parent-child (Eph 6:1–4),
slave-master (Eph 6:5–8), and Christian-government (Rom 13:1–2;
1 Pet 2:13–17). We cannot truly know the love of Christ without
loving one another. Love cannot be abstract but must be concrete,
lived out in daily life.

The greatest example of the depth of love God expects is the subject of 15:13. This "greater love" functions two ways: First, it is modeled in Jesus, who laid down his life, but his is the deeper love, for he died not just for "his friends" but for "sinners" (Rom 5:8). Second, it is the model for us, as in 1 John 3:16: "This is how we know what love is: Jesus Christ laid down his life for us. And we ought to lay down our lives for our brothers and sisters." Jesus would yield his life in just a few hours, and as we emulate this love, we must be prepared for a possible future in which we surrender our lives, as many martyrs have done throughout church history. God's word is clear on this: suffering is a special sharing or "participation in his sufferings" (Phil 3:10), and God will use it redemptively. As the church father Tertullian (ca. AD 155-230) wrote to the Roman authorities in Carthage, "We multiply whenever we are mown down by you; the blood of Christians is seed."[2]

The next two verses (15:14-15) are in a sense a graduation ceremony. The disciples are no longer "servants," a term often used of the disciples of a rabbi. Instead, they have become "friends," a term not normally used of the disciple-rabbi relationship. This clarifies Jesus' laying down his life for his friends in verse 13 as partly a reference to his dying for his present and future followers. These verses clarify that further. The disciples have transcended the old disciple-master relationship by becoming the objects of Jesus' love and friendship. The risen Lord will elevate their status further in 20:17, when he commissions Mary, "Go instead to my *brothers* and tell them." The progression of their "graduation" is in two stages— from disciple/servant to friend and then to brother.

Friends are those who obey Christ, who "do what I command." It is not actually a condition, as if every disobedient act destroys the friendship. Instead, it flows out of what he has been saying

---

2. Tertullian, *Apology*, 50.13, in *Tertullian's Apology and de Spectaculis*, ed. G. P. Goold and W. C. A. Kerr, trans. T. R. Glover and Gerald H. Rendall, The Loeb Classical Library (Cambridge, MA: Harvard University Press, 1931), 227.

regarding the link between love and obedience (14:15, 21, 23). When we obey we experience the depths of his love and friendship (15:10). Nothing can separate us from the love of Christ (Rom 8:35), not even disobedience. Still, following his precepts allows us to enjoy a special intimacy with him.

The term "servant" (literally "slave," *doulos*) is often used to describe the believer's relationship to God, meaning we belong to him and are part of his family. (Slaves were often included in family lists.) It isn't that this metaphor was no longer valid but rather is deepened due to Christ's love for his followers. The disciples now enjoy a new status as "friends of God," a concept the Jewish people reserved for the great leaders of the past like Abraham and Moses. The depth of this new friendship is cemented by the fact that "everything that I learned from my Father I have made known to you." This would never be true for a slave, for he would never be allowed to "know his master's business." The disciples have been brought within the circle of divine truth and knowledge. This is brought even deeper by the Spirit, who reveals the depths of Christ's knowledge to them (14:26; 16:13–15).

Christ took the initiative in choosing them as friends: "You did not choose me, but I chose you" (15:16). This was highly unusual, for normally disciples chose which rabbi they wished to study under (see comments on 1:37–39). But throughout John, Jesus often chooses his own followers—Philip (1:43), the Samaritan woman (4:4, 7), the blind beggar (9:1–2). The emphasis here is on the incredible privilege of being one of the chosen. Like Israel in the Old Testament, we are the special people of this world, and we are not only chosen but also "appointed" or "set apart" (*ethēka*) from the rest of humanity. We are those with authority to be the children of God (1:12), with the purpose to "go and bear fruit—fruit that will last," literally "fruit that remains [*menō*]," part of that which Christ indwells.

This fruitful Christian life is specifically to become part of Christ's mission to the world, and this enduring fruit is converts, specifically those who receive the gift of eternal life. Election, God's choosing of us, is not just to salvation but also to mission. In order to accomplish this glorious task, Christ once more grants us a new power in prayer, so that "whatever you ask in my name the Father will give you." This is the fourth all-embracing prayer promise of this discourse (after 14:13, 14; 15:7). Mission to the world is a difficult and dangerous enterprise given the world's hatred and opposition (as we will see in 15:18–16:4), so it is critical for us to bathe it in prayer and receive the Spirit's empowering presence as we go out. Prayer could be called the lubricating fluid for the engine of fruit-bearing; we need it to run smoothly.

Concluding this section, Jesus reiterates his command to "love each other," framing this section (vv. 12–17) with the necessity of brotherly love (15:12, 17). Jesus presents two things here as necessary to the success of the mission of Christ through the church— prayer (15:16b) and community love (15:17). Love also is part of the sap emanating from the vine and enabling the branches to grow and bear fruit. The love of the Godhead and of Christ for the believer strengthen each follower to love each other, and that provides impetus for bringing others into the community.

THE WORLD HATES THE DISCIPLES (15:18–16:4A)

A good title for this section would be that of Dietrich Bonhoeffer's classic *The Cost of Discipleship*. As disciples, we all share in Jesus and his ministry. Christlikeness includes "participation in his sufferings" (Phil 3:10). Opposition from the world is the natural conclusion from John's theology, in which the world is the place of sin, rebellion, and persecution (see on 1:10). We are part of the light of God sent into the world, and the world prefers darkness and hates the light (3:19–20), so we cannot expect the world to relate well to us. The message of this section can be presented as a syllogism:

Major premise: The world hates Jesus.
Minor premise: Jesus loves and indwells his disciples.
Conclusion: The world hates his disciples.

John has organized the section into an A-B-A pattern: opposition (15:18–25), mission (15:26–27), opposition (16:1–4). Jesus and the Spirit are with us in a special way on our mission, but the world hates us. As I said above, we shouldn't expect it any other way.

THE HATRED OF THE WORLD EXPLAINED (15:18–25)

Hatred as part of union with Christ (15:18–21)

Four conditional clauses govern this section (18, 19, 20a, 20b), all of them concrete conditions of fact (using Greek *ei*, "if") assuming the reality of the statement. The disciples are about to embark on a journey of mission that they cannot begin to comprehend. They have seen the opposition against Jesus intensify almost daily, but they have been shielded by him to a great extent. They are not ready for what is about to transpire. In fact, in about an hour or so when Jesus is arrested, they will all run for their lives and desert him completely (Mark 14:50).

Jesus in this section wants to educate his disciples about the reality of what is to come. They must understand that being a Christ follower will entail serious rejection from all around them. They have the words of life, but people don't want to hear them. So he begins, "If the world hates you"—and it does—"keep in mind that it hated me first." They should not be surprised (as 1 John 3:13 says) when people turn against them. They have seen that happen to Jesus for their entire ministry with him. In 1:11 John was explicit that the Jewish people were part of "the world," and here it is even more so.

In 15:18 Jesus tells the disciples that the world hates them, and in 15:19 he tells them why. The world loves its own, so "if"—the second of the four *ei* statements—"you belonged" to it, it would "love you as its own." But they belong to the light, not darkness, and Christ has chosen them to be his own (as in 15:16). The world hates the light (3:19–20) and wants nothing to do with God's special people, the chosen ones. Peter says it another way. We are

"foreigners and exiles" in this world (1 Pet 2:11; see also 1:1, 17) and
cannot be a part of it, and the people of this world despise those
they cannot understand.

In 15:20-21 Jesus asks them to "remember" their relationship
to him. They as disciples are "slaves" (*douloi*) of Jesus (a commonly
used metaphor for the rabbi-disciple relationship). Jesus has earlier said, "no servant is greater than his master" (13:16) while washing their feet, and now he wants to apply that to the issue of sharing their Master's suffering. They are ambassadors of the Word of
God, in direct opposition to the world. Since the apostate people
have rejected Jesus' message, of course they will reject the disciples as well.

The third and fourth "if" statements sit in contrast to one
another. The point is that Christ's followers should expect to
receive from the world exactly what happened to Jesus. Those
who "persecuted" Jesus will continue to do so with the disciples,
and those who "obeyed" his teaching (far fewer in number) will
follow them as well. This means that their treatment of them is
actually part of their treatment of the Lord. Their task is mission,
and they must leave the reactions of people to them with the Lord
and trust him for strength to endure.

The true reason for this rejection is not the disciples or their
message but "because of my name," namely, who he and his Father
are (15:21). The one they "do not know" and turn away from is "the
one who sent me." The truth is that God sent Jesus, and Jesus sent
the disciples (17:18; 20:21). There are three stages of rejection: their
rejection of the disciples is actually a rejection of Jesus the Christ,
who sent them, and that itself constitutes their rejection of God,
who sent him. These Jewish people claimed to know God, but when
they rejected his Son they turned away from his Father as well.
They are no longer God's people but part of the world.

The guilt and judgment of the world (15:22–25)

In words reminiscent of Romans 1:18–32 (on the depravity of the Gentiles), Jesus now explores the guilt that lies behind the hatred of the Jews. In both Romans 1 and here, a willful ignorance lies behind the rejection. The unsaved know the truth but deliberately suppress it. Jesus came to them with words (v. 22) and works (v. 24), but they have refused both. Their guilt would not be so clear if he "had not come and spoken to them." But he has come, and as a result, they have "no excuse for their sin." They stand before God with a guilty verdict in his courtroom.

When they reacted to Jesus with hatred, that constituted hatred of God as well (15:23). They had not just met a so-called prophet and pretend Messiah; they had met the Son of God, the one and only God (1:14, 18; 3:16, 18), and in rejecting him they had turned their backs on God and on final salvation. In responding to the Son and now the disciples with hatred, they have lost all hope.

So Jesus in 15:24 (centering on his works) repeats his point of verse 22 (centering on his words). They could claim innocence if he had never "done among them the works no one else did." The fact that "no one else" has done such works points to his sign-miracles, which proved who he was and revealed his true nature. So as a result of his wondrous words (v. 22) and works (v. 24), they now have no excuse and are proved "guilty of sin" before God.

Far from producing a crisis, God was more than ready for this hatred and opposition. God's revealed Word had prophesied it long ago, and it in fact has occurred in order "to fulfill what is written in their Law." In support of this Jesus cites Psalm 69:4 (and possibly 35:19), "They hated me without reason." In both psalms David grieves over the large number of enemies who oppose him. As the Davidic Messiah and righteous sufferer, Jesus suffers the same fate as David, and he fulfills it in himself. The treachery of the Jews who are part of the world is to be expected, and the disciples should not be surprised by it in the least. "Without reason" stresses for the third time (vv. 22, 24, 25) the fact that they have no excuse for what they are doing. Their own Scriptures prove them guilty (as in 5:45–47).

JESUS' MISSION CONTINUED (15:26–27)

Jesus is departing from this world, but his mission will continue, carried on by the "witness" of both the Paraclete (v. 26) and his disciples (v. 27). This saying is not out of place, as though it were artificially added by a later scribe, but in fact it fits quite well here. The hatred and persecution of the Jews will certainly disrupt the mission of Jesus quite severely (by killing him!). However, that opposition will come to naught when the Spirit and his followers take it to a new level. Jesus provided the basis for our salvation. The Spirit and his followers will proclaim this salvation to the ends of the earth.

This is the third Paraclete saying (after 14:15–17, 26) and gets to the heart of the message of the whole discourse: the coming of the Spirit to introduce the new age in God's plan of salvation. These two verses combine to stress the one mission of God as the Spirit empowers and indwells the new messianic community, inspiring their witness to Jesus (as in Matt 10:20; Acts 5:32; 6:10).

Note the trinitarian thrust—the Son and the Father send the "Advocate" (Greek: *paraklētos*). Once again, note the progress of authority for mission in this discourse: the Father sends the Son, the Father and Son send the Spirit, and the Triune Godhead sends the church to the world. All of heaven is involved in the mission to the world. The legal setting continues as the Paraclete "testifies" about Jesus to the world. As the "Spirit of truth" (see 14:17; 16:13) the Paraclete ensures that the world hears the divine truths concerning Jesus and his saving work. There will be no avoiding the light of God that illuminates these truths (1:5).

The disciples in 15:27 join the Spirit in witness and continuing Jesus' mission to the world. They follow the Spirit and become the Spirit's mighty tool in this holy enterprise. The reason their witness is so powerful is that "you have been with me from the beginning." Jesus himself has invested his time and energy in them from the start, and so they are filled to overflowing with these truths. Moreover, they are filled with the Spirit and empowered for this witness. It would be impossible to be better prepared for the ministry to the world God is giving them. The verb "must testify" is an imperative, and so it is a divine mandate. They are chosen envoys of the Trinity, and it is their calling to witness to the world.

THE PROBLEM OF PERSECUTION (16:1–4A)

We now return to the main topic of this section: as the disciples head out on their Spirit-empowered mission, they must expect fierce opposition to all they are doing. Jesus covered this generally in 15:18–25, but here he describes specific trials they will undergo. Moreover, the greatest danger is not just the persecution or the discouragement it will engender due to hard times but the possibility of apostasy, abandoning the faith to stop the suffering. This danger had already been presented in the vine and the branches parable and had already occurred in Judas. The entirety of the Letter to the Hebrews is devoted to this danger, showing how real it was to the early church (see 15:6 for the theological debate).

The first specific trial was already seen in the story of the man born blind in 9:22, 34 (also 12:42), being expelled from the synagogue (16:2). Jesus warned of this elsewhere (Matt 10:17; Mark 13:9; Luke 21:12). It was more than being removed from synagogue membership, for it was being put "under the ban" and meant being totally ostracized from the community.

However, that is only the beginning of problems. The phrase "the time is coming" seems to have an ironic double meaning. Throughout this Gospel it is used of the time of destiny for Jesus' passion events to begin (2:4; 7:20; 8:30; 12:23, 27), but here it refers to the beginning of the persecution of the disciples after the death and resurrection of Jesus. Most likely, the two "hours" become one eschatological hour here, stressing the persecution of the saints as a "participation in [Christ's] sufferings" (Phil 3:10).

Christians were seen as heretics (as was Jesus) by the Jews,
and so as Jesus says in 16:3, the Jews will think they are "offering
a service to God" when they take the lives of these blasphemous
Christians.[3] Jews more than Romans were the primary source
of persecution in the New Testament period. They believed that
so long as there was blasphemy in the land, the Messiah could
not come. Paul undoubtedly thought this was the case when he
arrested Christians, put them in prison, and had them killed (Acts
8:3; 9:1; 26:10). The saddest aspect in this is that we Christians too
often have done the same thing when we have been in power in a
society. We too have instigated (or failed to speak out against) similar slaughters of innocent people, as in the Jewish pogroms of the
nineteenth century or the Holocaust in the twentieth. I have some
friends who were taught racial bias at Bible schools.

The reason for this terrible hatred is "because they have not
known the Father or me" (16:3). John has emphasized this since
1:10-11, where he pointed out that the Jews are part of the world
for that very reason. Christ, who is one with the Father and is
his Agent, is the only path for knowing the Father, so when they
refused to recognize him they were also refusing the Father. This
refusal is much more than ignorance but connotes deliberate rejection of the truth. The message is that their opposition to Christ's
messengers is tantamount to rejection of God's Messenger and
therefore of God himself.

Christ is telling them of these things ahead of time to protect
them when these discouraging things take place (16:4). In 13:19
and 14:29 he prophesied these things to strengthen their faith for
enduring this opposition, and in 16:1 he did so to keep them from
falling away. Those two are combined here. Christ has "told them
this" to increase their faith so they won't fall away "when their
time comes" to endure the same persecution he has experienced.

---

3. The **Mishnah**, an ancient Jewish source, presents killing heretics as an act
of worship; see m. Sanhedrin 9:6.

This second half of the Farewell Discourse continues the themes of chapters 13-14 and centers on the disciples. The vine-and-branches illustration pictures the process of Christian discipleship, where we the branches remain closely connected to Jesus the Vine so we may partake of his life-giving sap and bear fruit for God. There are only two kinds of branches or people in the church: those who are fruitful and those who are fruitless, producing nothing for God. The latter are cut off and burned, picturing eternal judgment for the apostate, useless members of the church ("in me," 15:2, 6). The fruitful branches "remain in" the Vine and produce much fruit, so God "prunes" or uses the trials of life to help them grow.

The threefold explanation (vv. 7-17) is extremely relevant when applied. The first (vv. 7-8) centers on the fruitfulness that results from remaining in the vine and lists a new prayer power (= 14:13-14) as part of the fruit that we bear. The second result of remaining in Christ is the new depth of love and joy in him that we experience (vv. 9-11). As we bask in his love, we know a new all-embracing immersion in his joy that changes our perspective on life. Third, we learn to love one another in a new way (vv. 12-17). The love of the members of the Godhead for one another is reflected in the love we share with Christ, and that then provides a new depth of loving relationships in the community of Christ. We are now "friends" of Christ, with a new status and authority but also with a new depth of love from him that we then reflect in our internal relationships in the church.

The second major section of this discourse is the reminder that while we share Jesus' love, we also share his sufferings, and that includes hatred and persecution from the world (15:18-16:4). We are one with Jesus, and that means we share not only the good but also the bad. We are light in him, so the world of darkness will avoid us and actively oppose all we stand for. In rejecting us, they are rejecting Christ, and in rejecting Christ, they are actually rejecting God. When we pass through the dark valley of hatred, we must remember that in this persecution we are reflecting our oneness with Jesus and God.

Yet connected to this outpouring of hatred is the mission of the church. As Christ died for sinners who were his enemies (Rom 5:8), he sends us out to those who turn against us as well, and in this mission the Spirit-Paraclete joins us and enhances our witness of Christ to the world (vv. 26–27). Our witness is actually a major tool of the Spirit's witness, and he fills us as we go out to the world.

Jesus lists three specific dangers in 16:1–4: expulsion from the synagogue, heightened persecution, and the temptation to apostatize from the Christian faith. Jesus in this section prepares the disciples to face these dangers so they can find the strength to persevere when these hard times arrive.

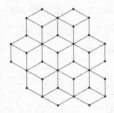

FAREWELL DISCOURSE:
SECOND DISCOURSE, PART 2
(16:4b–33)

J esus' departure from his earthly ministry to return to his
Father is now at hand, and this is why he is telling his follow-
ers of the difficult days that lie ahead. They need to know not just
of all the troubles that will soon fall on them but also of the help
God will send them to enable them to rise above these struggles.
This help consists of the Spirit of Christ as the presence of the
Lord among them. He has just told them of the trials soon to arrive
(15:18–16:4a), and now he wants to make them know of the coming
Paraclete, who will empower them so they can be victorious.

There are three sections in this chapter. The first (vv. 4b–15)
shows how the Spirit convicts every unbeliever and proves them
guilty before God. The result is that they are without excuse
(vv. 8–11). At the same time, he guides and empowers every believer
(vv. 12–15), enabling them to speak for and glorify God in everything they do.

In the second section (vv. 16–28) Jesus tells them that the Spirit
is coming because he will depart from them and go to the Father.
Yet because of that their grief in the midst of all their afflictions
will be turned completely to joy as they experience the Triune
Godhead—Father, Son, and Spirit—in their lives.

In the final section (vv. 29–33) Jesus predicts their failure during his passion, but he adds that in him (and the Spirit) their afflictions will also be turned to peace as well as joy.

JESUS DESCRIBES THE WORK OF THE PARACLETE (16:4B–15)

JESUS' DEPARTURE (16:4B–7)

Jesus tells them that he has been silent about their future problems because "I was with you;" he has been there to watch over and protect them by seeing to it that all the animosity was directed at him rather than at them. But this was to cease within the hour with Jesus' arrest, for he would never again have extended time with them. So now he has to get them ready for the difficult time that is coming, starting an hour or so from now, when they will desert Jesus and run for their lives to avoid arrest.

He begins by announcing that his departure is now at hand. He is "going to him who sent me" and is soon to finish his mission from the Father. The next thing he says ("None of you asks me, 'Where are you going?'") is quite difficult because it contradicts rather directly 13:36 (Peter asks, "Lord, where are you going?") and 14:5 (Thomas says, "Lord, we don't know where you are going"). This has led some to say this verse is a later addition and that the editor failed to change the original out of reverence for the tradition. But this seems rather far-fetched.

There is a simpler explanation centered on the present tense "none of you asks me." Jesus is concerned that the disciples have stopped asking about his departure, and he wants them to remain involved in the discussion. They are so filled with confusion and grief that they fail to realize the deeper implications of his departure for his divine mission to the world. He wants them immersed in the question of the end of his personal mission, for they are to carry it on in their mission to the world. Neither of the previous questions had the implications of his departure for his mission in mind. He wants them focused, for it involves them and their future mission.

Therefore, in the next two verses (vv. 6–7), Jesus clarifies the eternal implications behind what is soon to transpire. They are consumed with grief, and he had already told them that they should be filled with peace rather than be taken over by fear and a troubled heart (14:27). They should be rejoicing that he is going to the Father (14:28–29) rather than grieving.

In 16:7 he returns to the primary theme, introducing it with an equivalent to his typical solemn double *amēn* saying, "Very truly I tell you," and states it both ways to highlight its importance: "Unless I go away, the Advocate will not come to you; but if I go, I will send him to you." The next six verses are dedicated to this theme. God's plan can only be completed when the Son returns to heaven and the Spirit is sent to take his place on earth. The cross is absolutely necessary to inaugurate the new age of salvation, and only after that central event of salvation history can the Spirit come (see 7:39).

It is also for the good of the disciples, for they cannot find their destinies until that moment either. As Peter will say later in his life, times of trouble and trials must be ameliorated by the realization that we are living in the new age of salvation (1 Pet 3:3–9), the time the prophets had longed to see (1 Pet 1:10–12). That time the prophets longed for was indeed the age of the Spirit (Isa 11:1–2; 32:15; 42:1; 44:3; Ezek 37:14; 39:29; Joel 2:28).

THE WORK OF THE PARACLETE IN THE WORLD (16:8–11)

The Spirit will have a twofold ministry, convicting the world (vv. 8–11) and strengthening the church (vv. 12–15). He is coming to carry on Jesus' mission to the lost and "convict" (*elenxei*) or "prove the world to be in the wrong" in three areas: "sin and righteousness and judgment." The verb in a general sense means to "expose, show, or convince" others of a truth. It also can have a strong legal connotation, meaning to "prove a person wrong or guilty" in a

court of law, as it is used in 8:46 ("Can any of you prove me guilty
of sin?"). That is its thrust here.

So the Spirit as Paraclete is a prosecuting attorney here, presenting irrefutable evidence of the guilt of the world before God.
Moreover, this is not the final judgment, for the Spirit is not standing before God on his judgment seat but is convicting the people
of the world in their own hearts so as to bring them to repentance.
This is the primary area in which the Spirit works as an "advocate" bringing his convicting presence to bear on the unsaved. It
is the courtroom of the mind where the Spirit as Paraclete per-
forms his convicting work.

In the rest of this section Jesus identifies three areas in which
the Spirit operates (16:9–11).

(1) He convicts the world of "sin, because people do not believe
    in me." Sin itself centers on the centrality of self, so the
    basic sin is unbelief, the refusal to trust in anything other
    than one's self. If the unsaved were to come to faith, they
    would find the light of God (3:18–21) and eternal life (3:16;
    5:24). As a result of sin and unbelief, the world lives in dark-
    ness. Jewish opponents had accused Jesus of being a sinner
    (9:16, 24) when in reality they themselves were steeped in
    sin and unbelief (5:47; 6:64; 7:48; 8:24; 9:41; 15:22).

(2) The world is convicted of "righteousness" (16:10), primarily
    in the contrast between the true righteousness of Jesus and
    the spurious righteousness of sinful mankind. The basis
    of this seems strange at first: "because I am going to the
    Father, where you can see me no longer." The world con-
    demned Jesus and crucified him on the cross, but God dem-
    onstrated that the opposite was the truth by raising him
    from the dead and taking him to heaven. Jesus' true righ-
    teousness was demonstrated for eternity, and the unrigh-
    teous nature of humankind was proved once for all (12:23;
    13:31–32; 17:1, 5; 1 Tim 3:16). The disciples (Jesus refers to
    them rather than the world here) will no longer see him,

but they will depend on the Spirit-Paraclete, who mediates his presence in them and makes his supreme righteousness known as God's saving force in the world.

(3) The world is finally convicted of "judgment, because the prince of this world now stands condemned" (16:11). The world judged Jesus and in the end put him on the cross. Its judgment has been proved false (7:24; 8:16), and the true Judge is Jesus himself (5:22, 30; 9:39). The truth is that in the passion Jesus confronted and defeated "the prince of this world" (12:31; 14:30), and so both the ruler and his kingdom have been condemned by Christ. Satan may still be "the god of this world," but he is worshiped and followed only by the people of this world, and both he and they are doomed. When we put on the armor of God and stand against the powers of darkness (Eph 6:10–17), they must retreat. In other words, Satan still has a hold on this world (Eph 6:12; 1 John 5:19), but his power has been broken and his end is certain.

THE WORK OF THE PARACLETE IN THE CHURCH (16:12–15)

Christ has "much more to say" about the cosmic conflict and the passion events, but he has to demur because it is "more than you can now bear." They are so beaten down with grief and despair that they simply can't take any more. Likely Jesus means that the Spirit-Paraclete will finish his work and teach them "all things" that they need (14:26). This is similar to 13:7, when Jesus said "later you will understand." Complete understanding would be provided by the Spirit, probably after the resurrection (2:22; 12:16; 13:7; 14:26).

This is an incredibly deep teaching on the Spirit's ministry to the church. Jesus mentions four items here.

(1) It is "the Spirit of truth" who will "guide you into all the truth." In 14:26 Jesus said the Spirit would "teach" and "remind you of everything I have said to you," and he builds on that here. There is Old Testament background to the

Spirit as guide (Ps 143:10; Isa 63:14), and the Spirit is continuing the work of Jesus in taking the Word of God and
making it practical in their daily lives. Truth is a major
emphasis of this Gospel. The importance of understanding the Word and living by the truths that flow from it is
all important. One of the major needs today is for people
who want the depth of the Word to engage in deep Bible
study. There are exciting truths just waiting to be unlocked.
That is why I am dedicating the rest of my life to these commentaries. I can think of nothing as critical as being used
of the Spirit to guide you, the reader "in[1] all the truth" of
the Word.

(2) The Spirit also continues Jesus' practice in his teaching.
Jesus always spoke in accordance with what his Father told
him to say (3:34–35; 5:19; 7:16–17; 8:26, 28; 12:49–50; 14:10;
15:15), and in the same way the Spirit passes on what he has
been given by Jesus. The disciples receive these truths on
a trinitarian path from Father to Son to Spirit to them and
likewise pass them on in their own teaching and preaching (2 Tim 2:2). When we proclaim the Word, what we say
has an incredibly rich heritage behind it.

(3) The Spirit "will tell you what is yet to come." There are
quite a few views as to what this means. It could be the
immediate future, referring to the death, resurrection, and
ascension of Jesus, or perhaps the distant future, referring
to the final events of human history. It could also connote
the gift of prophecy in the Spirit-inspired prophets of the
early church. However, none of these quite fit. It probably
is intended in a comprehensive way to the Spirit guiding
the church into the future, building on all Jesus said and

---

1. There is a text-critical issue as to whether we should read "into" or "in" all
the truth here. Actually, "in" has good manuscript evidence behind it (א¹ D L
W) and reads better in the Greek.

did as the new kingdom of God advanced into the age of the Spirit. Christ has prepared his followers, and now the Spirit takes that into the developing ministry of the church in the world.

(4) The Spirit will bring glory to Jesus (16:14) in the same way that Jesus sought to glorify his Father (7:18; 13:31; 14:13; 17:4). Christ received the content he proclaimed from his Father, and the Spirit likewise receives from Christ "what he will make known" to them. Once more note the trinitarian process: Jesus receives the truths from the Father, passes them on to the Spirit, and the Spirit reveals them to the teachers of the church so that they can be proclaimed in the churches. I am amazed at the unbelievable depth of this concept. I always told my classes of the richness of 2 Timothy 2:2, that there is a passing of the baton of truth from Paul to the early teachers down the line to me, and I then pass them on to those in my class who will "be qualified to teach others." Now, this moment, I realize for the first time that that is only the second half of the actual equation! In reality, these truths have passed from Father to Son to Spirit before they even reached Paul. In fact, we could add Revelation 1:1–2 into the mix and say the Triune Godhead gave these truths and visions to the holy angels, who gave them to John and Paul to deliver to us. Wow!

Jesus concludes (16:15) by making certain that his and the Spirit's ministry is put into proper perspective. The work of them both stems from the Father: It is the Father's work that comes to completion in the Son, and the Spirit extends the work of both as he guides the people of God into the final era of salvation history. God has "put all things under his power" (13:3), and Jesus has now passed this authority on to the Spirit. So the Spirit's work stems entirely from the Father through the Son. What we preach and teach does not stem from Jesus or the Spirit but from the Trinity as a whole, with the Spirit making known what the Father has revealed through the Son. There is a serious mistake made in many charismatic circles, where often the emphasis is on the new ideas that leaders come up with as from the leading of the Spirit more than on the revealed truths from Scripture. The emphasis is clear here—the Spirit makes known what he has received from the Father and Son. No mention is made of new material or so-called truths.

SADNESS WILL BE TURNED TO JOY (16:16–28)

JESUS' DEPARTURE AND ITS AFTERMATH (16:16–18)

Jesus sums up his basic message once more and tells the disciples, "In a little while you will see me no more, and then after a little while you will see me." There are two short intervals here ("a little while"). Some have taken the first to be the short time between his death and resurrection and the second to be the time between his resurrection and second coming, but that is unlikely because the second interval is not a short time. Others see a complex triple schema in which Jesus simultaneously predicts his resurrection appearances, the coming of the Spirit, and his second coming (the **parousia**). While Jesus has discussed all three in chapters 14–15, that is a lot to read into this verse. Moreover, it makes a lot more sense to take the first as the short time (about fifteen hours) before he is put on the cross and the second time as the thirty-six-plus hours[2] he will be in the grave before his resurrection (see also 14:19). The context stresses their joy at seeing Jesus again, undoubtedly in the resurrection appearances.

As always the disciples are completely befuddled (vv. 17–18) and understand neither "see me no more"/"see me" nor "a little while." Even after the numerous times Jesus has taught them, they still have no categories for the kind of messiah who would die and rise

---

2. He died and was put in the tomb between three and five Friday afternoon and was raised at dawn (about six o'clock) Sunday morning.

again. The thought that this incomprehensible event will soon take place is just too much for them. Their two questions are taken from the previous verse. They comprehend neither "the little while" nor his "going to the Father" from 16:5.

DISCOURSE ON JOY (16:19–24)

The disciples have been corrected so often that they are afraid to actually vocalize these questions, but Jesus on the basis of his omniscience (see 1:42, 48; 4:17–18) "knew" (NIV: "saw") or "realized" how perplexed they were. In 16:19 he tells them exactly what they wanted to ask, repeating what he has said in verse 16.

His answer to them becomes almost an ode to joy. It begins with another solemn and important double *amēn* saying ("I tell you the absolute truth," see comments on 1:51), predicting the great turning point in human history, this time considering it from the disciples' vantage point and wording it in line with 16:16, 19. After the initial "little while" (Jesus' death), they would "weep and mourn" while the world would "rejoice." But after the second "little while," this will be totally reversed, and their "grief will turn to joy" as Jesus is raised and appears to them.

Neither the disciples nor the world is aware of the true import of the passion events. All fail to realize that the single most important event in the history of the human race is about to take place. The very core of God's plan of salvation will soon transpire. Jesus' followers will grieve as at a funeral (the women in Mark 16:1 were planning to anoint a corpse, expecting nothing). The world, also thinking only they have rid themselves of a blasphemous trouble-maker, will be filled with joy at their victory. However, mere hours later, God will raise Jesus from the dead and the glorious Risen One will appear to them. And all the sorrow will turn to exuberant joy at the victory that God has accomplished in his Son.

To illustrate this reversal, Jesus uses the image of birth pangs (v. 21), a perfect example of intense pain turning to wonderful joy. This metaphor is found often in the Old Testament (Isa 26:17–21;

66:7-14; Jer 13:21; Mic 4:9-10) and the Gospels (Mark 13:8) for the sufferings of God's people and the coming of deliverance. Isaiah 26:17-21 is especially apt, combing the imagery of childbirth and the idea of resurrection ("your dead will live, Lord; their bodies will rise") in depicting the deliverance of Israel. Then Isaiah 66:14 adds "your heart will rejoice." In both the Isaianic promise of salvation through suffering and the joy of God's deliverance are uppermost. The emphasis is on the divine initiative in bringing God's salvation to pass. He makes the "new baby" (= eternal salvation) possible; the eschatological new age instituted at the cross becomes the beginning of the end. The last days are initiated at the cross and finalized at the second coming.

In 16:22 he applies this particularly to the disciples, who after his death will have a "time of grief" that will turn to joy that "no one will take away" when they see the resurrected Jesus. Nothing the world can do in the way of persecution can rob them of the joy of resurrection, beginning with that of Jesus himself and then resulting from his resurrection as a "firstfruits" (1 Cor 15:20, 23) guaranteeing their own future rising from the dead. So Jesus is ushering in a new age of peace (14:27) and joy. This enables every one of us to greet all our troubles with rejoicing (Jas 1:2; 1 Pet 1:6).

Now for the fourth time Jesus promises them a new prayer power (16:23-24; see 14:13-14; 15:7, 16), but here it is linked to the new age of salvation that will follow the death and resurrection of Jesus; "in that day" refers to the culmination of the scriptural promises in the new "day" inaugurated by the death and resurrection of Jesus. There are two promises in this, for Jesus begins by telling them they will have a new understanding when they finally realize the implications of these passion events. Heretofore their lack of knowledge was remarkable; there was virtually no area they got right. But when the events take place and clarify everything, and especially when the Spirit is there to teach them all things (14:26; 16:13), much will become clear.

Second, and once again he begins with "very truly I tell you" (16:20) to stress its critical nature, we have another promise of answered prayer (see 14:13–14). In verse 23a they need not ask Jesus because they have the Spirit. Now in verse 23b they no longer need to do so because they have direct access to the Father. This deeper intimacy with God grows out of their union with the Godhead— they are one with Jesus and one with God (17:21–23).

When Jesus says, "you have not asked for anything in my name" (v. 24), he means asking *the Father*. This is another salvation-historical switch. During Jesus' ministry the disciples brought all their questions to Jesus. But this new depth of intimacy and access to the Father they enjoyed in the new aeon means that they can go directly to God with all their queries. This was also the point in 14:13–14, and so Christ is making sure they have caught the new reality that is the church age. Now they will "ask, using my name," and the Father will "grant your request because you use my name" (16:23, 24 NLT). As I said at 14:14, "the name" is not a magic formula designed to get God to do things for us but means "in union with me." This name, signifying that we belong to him, is the basis of our power in prayer and is a sign of the new era Christ has instigated.

The disciples have never done this before, praying directly to God on the basis of their authority as the children of God. The Father is one with Jesus, so our union with Christ gives us an access never before thought possible. Our newfound prayer life is an eschatological gift defining the new kingdom we inhabit. So when we ask and receive with this new eschatological power, it is no wonder that our joy is complete. God is always present in the Spirit, and we are never alone. Our present is completely secure, and our future is guaranteed. How can we not have "pure joy" no matter what the trials (Jas 1:2)?

PLAIN TALK ON HIS DEPARTURE (16:25–28)

The central refrain in this section has been "in a little while" (16:17, 19), and throughout this Gospel Jesus and John have spoken of his "hour" (2:4; 7:30; 8:20) as the hour of destiny on the cross. Here the hour is coming "in a little while," referring not to the cross but the arrival of the new era when the Spirit comes and all the promises of the Farewell Discourse come into realization. Even in this final speech Jesus has been speaking "figuratively" (*en paroimiais*, meaning proverb, parable, figure of speech), using illustrations that seemed opaque and obscure to the disciples (e.g., 16:21). Jesus noted this inability to understand in 16:12.

The days of enigmatic speaking are now over. He will in this new era "tell you plainly about my Father." The problem was not in the imagery but in the deeper mysteries they were uncovering. He is promising that these mysteries will be revealed and "plainly" (*parrēsia*, openly, publicly) understood. The passion will unleash a time of fulfillment when these mysteries will be laid bare and open to all believers. Note the contrast with Mark 4:10–12, 33–34, when Jesus spoke to the unsaved "in parables" to hide the truths. These truths are for God's people, not for his (and their) enemies. Jesus and God want his people to understand, and what was obscure then would soon be made clear. They could not understand yet, because they simply could not comprehend Jesus' departure and future exaltation. But when these key events have taken place and the Spirit has arrived, they will become the key to unlocking the rest (see 2:22; 12:16; 14:26).

Most of us are probably saying, "It doesn't seem much easier today; I'm still pretty confused." It is true that we are living in the new age of understanding, but like the disciples, we need the Spirit and hard work studying these truths to come to that understanding. The point is that these things are available and can be uncovered. They do not come automatically, but God provides his word, and we have pastors and teachers to guide us into these complex yet understandable truths. Good preaching and teaching in our churches will remove most of this confusion and give us a new excitement about God's truths.

We have had five all-embracing prayer promises to this point (14:13–14; 15:7, 16; 16:23, 24). Now Jesus gives the final promise (16:26–27). This new direct relationship with the Father produces a new depth of asking and receiving. Jesus previously promised he would answer their prayers directly (14:13–14), and now he goes so far as to say he no longer needs to intercede with the Father on their behalf, for "the Father himself loves you" (16:27). This does not mean we no longer need Jesus' intercessory work (stressed in Rom 8:34; Heb 7:25; 1 John 2:1), but rather that by this intercession Jesus produces a whole new depth of intimacy between God and his beloved children. That love produces a direct line of communication with God, an access we would never think possible otherwise (see Heb 10:19–20).

We still pray "in Jesus' name," that is, in union with him (14:13, 14; 15:16; 16:23, 24), because he inhabits us and fills us with his presence (15:5–8), but at the same time that new depth of relationship with the Father (Eph 2:6, God "seated us with him in the heavenly realms in Christ Jesus") yields an effective prayer power beyond all expectation (Jas 5:16). The Father loves the Son (17:23–26) and so loves his followers "because you have loved me and have believed that I came from God." There is a threefold love relationship between Father, Son, and believers as members of the same family. God sending his Son speaks of Jesus' mission, and that mission embraces Jesus' followers as well. We participate in that mission and thus also participate in that love.

Jesus concludes this emphasis on his relationship with the Father (v. 28) by reminding them of the descent-ascent motif stressed in the first half of this Gospel (1:51; 3:13, 31; 6:33, 38, 41–42, 50–51, 58, 62). He descended from heaven in his incarnation and "entered the world," and now he is "leaving the world and going back to the Father." As I have pointed out several times, his departure is the primary theme of this discourse (13:35–36; 14:2, 19–20,

28; 16:5, 16–17, 19). He descended from the Father as the God-man
in order to complete his mission of bringing salvation to lost
humankind, and now he is soon to ascend back to the Father as
the risen Lord.

JESUS PREDICTS THE DISCIPLES'
DESERTION (16:29-33)

The disciples seem to have turned the corner and claim to have
reached that deeper understanding (vv. 29–30). They respond,
"Now you are speaking clearly and without figures of speech."
They now tell Jesus, "you know all things," and they no longer need
anyone to ask him questions, probably meaning that his knowledge of God is deep and complete. They think they now have a hold
on what he is saying, though of course theirs is a false bravado,
a delusion of grandeur. Their confession that Jesus "came from
God" is a move in the right direction, similar to Peter's confession
in 6:69 that Jesus is "the Holy One of God," so they are growing in
their faith and understanding. They seem to realize the crisis is
coming to a head, though they haven't a clue as to what that entails.
They have no idea how little they actually know. Their confidence
shows how little they comprehend.

Jesus' response (16:31–32) will shatter their false confidence.
Note the sarcasm in his, "Do you now believe?" He is fully aware
of the amount of faith they actually have and knows they believe
in him, but he wants to bring them back to reality. Their faith is
real, but it is incomplete. The test will come soon, and they will
utterly fail. Peter has already been warned of his coming failure
(13:38), and none of the others will fare any better. He too was certain of his faithfulness ("I will lay down my life for you," 13:37) but
had to face his own finite weakness. Now it is their turn.

In verse 32 Jesus tells them, "A time is coming," which in 16:25
positively described that time after the Spirit introduces the new
era when Christ will speak "plainly" and understanding will come
to the disciples. Now it has arrived and the phrase negatively

describes the passion events and the desertion of the disciples. When they run for their lives at Jesus' arrest, they will be "scattered, each to your own home. You will leave me all alone."

As in Mark 14:27 and parallels, Jesus is alluding to Zechariah 13:7, "Strike the shepherd, and the sheep will be scattered," a passage on the apostasy of Israel. The disciples will fall away and abandon Jesus, deserting him and fleeing to the upper room, where they will cower throughout Jesus' time in the grave. They will still be there when Jesus appears to them in John 20:19–23. In the same way that Paul could never forgive himself for persecuting the church, they had to live the rest of their lives knowing that when Jesus was on the cross needing them so greatly, they were safely hiding behind closed doors.

However, Jesus was not actually alone, for his Father was with him throughout his travail. In 8:28–29, Jesus said about that time when he would be lifted up on the cross, "The one who sent me is with me; he has not left me alone." This was now to come to pass. His closest followers would desert him, but his Father would not. Yet what about Jesus' cry of dereliction: "My God, my God, why have you forsaken me" (Mark 15:34 and parallels)? Those words refer to Jesus bearing our sins, and *only at that moment* when he became sin for us (2 Cor 5:21) did God have to turn his back. He still did not leave Jesus alone.

Jesus gives them this distressing news not to discourage them or beat them down but "so that in me you may have peace" (v. 33). This at first glance seems incongruous. How do you have peace when you know you are going to fail? We must notice that the promise is for peace "in me," not for an easy or an error-free life. The key is the contrast between peace "in me" and trouble "in this world." We believers will always have difficulties so long as we are in this world. "Trouble" (*thlipsis*) means both trials and persecution. Spiritual failure like the disciples are soon to experience is part of this. But they like all of us have the empowering presence of Jesus and the Spirit, which will enable them to turn trouble into peace. The combination of the resurrection appearances and the coming of the Spirit at Pentecost will turn the weak, self-centered disciples into spiritual giants who will change the world. That can be us as well.

Jesus' closing words are perfect: "But take heart! I have overcome the world." "Overcome" (*nikaō*) is the term John uses in Revelation for "conquering" evil and pictures Jesus as the Divine Warrior defeating the forces of evil. At the cross Christ was victorious over "the prince of this world" (12:31; 14:30; 16:11). Satan and his fallen angels are a defeated foe. The war is settled for eternity, but the battles continue. Satan and the world of darkness are filled with rage (3:19-20) because he knows his time is short (Rev 12:12). In the midst of our personal battles, we must "take heart" and be aware that in Christ we are "more than conquerors" (Rom 8:37), and that nothing can "separate us from the love of God that is in Christ Jesus" (Rom 8:35, 39). We will always be victorious when we depend completely on the Triune Godhead in our lives (Jas 4:7-8; 1 Pet 5:6-9).

———

This part of the discourse centers on Jesus' departure and how the disciples will be able to handle the grief and the pressure. The basic point is that Christ's departure is necessary because it will lead to the next stage of salvation history, the coming of the Holy Spirit to convict the world (vv. 8-11) and guide the church (vv. 12-15). I doubt if we will find a biblical passage more important than this one for a proper understanding of the work of the Holy Spirit in the world and among the people of God. "Convict" means that as God's prosecuting attorney, he will prove to the world that they stand before God guilty of three things—their sin of unbelief, their lack of righteousness before him, and their allegiance to Satan, the ruler of this world. This is the Spirit's mission, and he has been sent by the Father and the Son with their full authority.

When we witness to the lost, we are not alone, and the Spirit is strengthening our witness for us (15:26–27).

His work among the saints is equally critical. He guides us into the truths of God and Christ and takes Jesus' place as the teacher of truth. Here it is important to recognize that these are not new truths coming off the top of a "prophet's" head but rather those traditional truths that Jesus has given us in his Word. There is way too much emphasis in many circles on "some new thing" that bypasses Scripture as the work of the Spirit. He also prepares us for the future as well as the past on the basis of these creedal truths passed on from one generation to the next.

The next section (vv. 16–28) is a wonderful promise to us as well as the disciples. They will be filled with grief at Jesus' death, but just thirty-six hours later will be overwhelmed with joy when the Risen One appears and turns their sorrow completely around. In the same way, all of our troubles and trials often fill us with despair, but God turns all of that around when he takes over and "works for the good" in all things (Rom 8:28). Christ has given us direct access to God and an incredible new prayer power so we can have this joyous response to life (vv. 23–24). We live in a new era of plain talk (vv. 25–28) in which God's truths are made available by the Spirit in all their depth and call us into a new, exciting life of discovery in him and his Word. Our prayers are all the more powerful (vv. 26–27) because we now speak directly to God.

We, like the disciples, will fail (vv. 29–33), but Christ and the Spirit are with us, and when we yield to them can change us as well from defeated cowards to change agents who will turn lives around wherever we go. We, like the disciples, serve a forgiving, compassionate God who with his Spirit empowers us to be victorious and filled with joy.

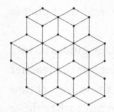

THE PRAYER OF CONSECRATION
(17:1–26)

This prayer functions as the conclusion of the Farewell Discourse and in some ways of the Gospel as a whole, as it sums up so many of the themes—glory, the mission from the Father, death and departure, discipleship, the future church. It is most famously known as the "high priestly prayer," and that is apt since it has priestly concerns like the glory of the Father, worship, and prayer for the people of God. However, perhaps a better term is becoming popular, "the prayer of consecration," as Jesus is dedicating these next hours to God and his righteous deeds accomplished in Jesus and is consecrating both his followers and the future church to God.

Many divide this into three sections—personal prayer (vv. 1–5), prayer for the disciples (vv. 6–19), and prayer for future followers (vv. 20–26). Others divide the last section into two parts—unity (vv. 20–23) and glory (vv. 24–26), but I see no real need for that and will use the three categories.

This powerful prayer is congruent with scriptural and Jewish parallels (Gen 49; Deut 32–33, Jubilees 22; 4 Ezra 8; 2 Baruch 48), but at the same time it is unique because it is prayed by the one and only Son, the incarnate Word of God (1:14). It is both the longest prayer of Jesus in the Gospels and the deepest theologically.

Jesus is praying as the God-man, pouring out his heart from the earthly perspective of himself as the incarnate Son of God and the heavenly perspective of the eternal Son of God. As such it summarizes key themes from the whole fourth Gospel, addressing Jesus' obedience, the glory of the Father, his death and resurrection as glory, Jesus the Revelation of God, the place of the disciples and of future believers, their mission to the world, and their unity as modeled on the unity of the Godhead.

At the same time, it is more than a prayer. It is the final teaching of Jesus in this world and so is a **christological** and ecclesiological masterpiece in its own right. It becomes the final preparation of the disciples so they can both be ready and understand the significance of the passion events as they unfold. The parallels between this and the Lord's Prayer in Matthew 6:9–13 are highly illuminating, with the concern for the things of God and then with the needs of God's people.

JESUS PRAYS FOR HIS GLORIFICATION (17:1–5)

As in 11:41 Jesus begins his prayer by looking up to heaven, very natural since heaven was his home and he was very soon returning there. As all prayers, it is addressed to the Father (six times— vv. 1, 5, 11, 21, 24, 25) and intends to place everything in his hands. The "hour" of destiny, with all the action directed this way (see on 2:4; 7:30; 8:20) has now "come," so the center point of history has arrived (as also stated in 12:23, 27, 31; 13:1).

Jesus states the theme of this first section right away: "Glorify your Son, that your Son may glorify you." All the "lifted up" passion predictions (3:14; 8:28; 12:32) proclaimed this, and John's unique message is the Great Reversal—the shame of the cross is transformed into the time of Jesus' exaltation. "Glory" means "praise, honor, veneration" as God elevates the horror of Jesus on the cross to the glory of the Risen One. Yet even here Jesus' concern is not for himself but for the glory of his Father. This culminates the glory theme of the Fourth Gospel. The glory shown in the sign-miracles

(2:11; 11:4, 40) was but a foretaste of what was to come at the cross. As Jesus is glorified by God (5:44; 8:54) he glorifies God in himself (7:18; 13:31–32).

The basis of Jesus' glory is the authority granted "over all people" (17:2). This is similar to "all authority in heaven and earth" in the Great Commission (Matt 28:18) and refers to universal, cosmic authority, especially the authority over life and judgment given by God in 5:21–23 (see Daniel 7:14). Both his glory and his authority in verses 1 and 2 are followed by purpose clauses. Jesus sought glory so that he could return that glory to his Father, and he sought authority so he could bestow eternal life on his followers. While his authority extends over everyone, saved and unsaved alike, unbelievers feel that power in judgment, and believers in the redemption that produces life. The cross as the moment of special glory comes about in the atoning sacrifice that brings life. The same stress on election from 6:37, 39; 10:29 is seen in "those you have given him" (see also 17:9, 24). Those who respond in faith-decision become the special people of God.

The result of the twofold glory experienced by the Son and the Father in 17:1–2 is found in 17:3: the eternal life for those who believe. The new creation made possible by the cross is eternal life, and the way (14:6) is "that they know you, the only true God, and Jesus Christ, whom you have sent." This is not just intellectual apprehension but salvific knowledge, experiencing Christ as Savior and coming to know the God who gives salvation. "The only true God" emphasizes him as the only God (1 Thess 1:9; 1 John 5:20), the only source of eternal life. As often stressed in this Gospel, to know God is to know Christ as the "only way" (14:6). We cannot know the Sender without knowing the One he sent (1:18; 14:7). Life is knowledge, not the trivial type gained off cruising the internet but the actual experience of God in a personal way, the kind of knowledge that leads to a changed life, to true salvation.

In the last two verses of this section (vv. 4–5), Jesus returns to the theme of glory, reversing verse 1 and centering on the glory of God, then the glory he will receive. Christ rejoices that he can bring glory to his Father by "finishing the work you gave me to do," mainly of course bringing salvation to sinful humankind through his atoning sacrifice on the cross. Still, every moment of his life from his incarnation to his death and resurrection was a moment of glory, as in 1:14, "we have seen his glory," and 2:11, "the signs through which he revealed his glory." Jesus' "work" refers not just to his miraculous works but to all of God's work he had been sent to accomplish, as in 5:17, "My Father is always at his work to this very day, and I too am working." This is primarily the work of salvation, centering on the cross and resurrection, when that work will be completed.

In verse 5 Jesus moves from his earthly glory to the preincarnate glory "I had with you before the world began." Jesus wants this preexistent glory to be reinstated to him in his exaltation to the "right hand" of the Father (Mark 12:36; Eph 1:20). This means the incarnation in some sense involved a surrender of that glory (Phil 2:6–7). He possessed glory during his earthly life, the glory of the incarnate Son (1:14; 2:11; 8:50, 54), given by the Father and recognized by his followers. But after his exaltation, he would return to the complete glory of the Godhead, a glory beyond human experience, entailing his transcendence over earthly realities.

JESUS PRAYS FOR HIS DISCIPLES (17:6–19)

Jesus' Work among the Disciples (17:6–8)

This is a transition section that many place with verses 1–5, referring to his glorious work among the disciples and centering on their relationship with his Father. Here he lists the reasons his prayer must now center on them. First, God has given them to Jesus from the world, the elect or chosen ones (see 17:2). They were at one time estranged from God, part of the world, but now they belong to God. This is John's encounter theology at its best—they have been chosen before the foundation of the world (Eph 1:4) to be God's special possession (Titus 2:14; 1 Pet 2:9) and made his own.

Second, as a result Jesus has "revealed your name" (NIV: "you")—by which he means the true nature and personhood of his Father—to them. Jesus is the Word, the Living Revealer of God (see on 1:1), and as he made God's name more real to his disciples, he revealed his person and character to them. They were progressively more aware of the place of God in their lives and of what that means. It was common within Judaism to think God's name would not be fully revealed until the final kingdom had arrived, so this is evidence that the final age has indeed begun.

Third, the result of this is that the disciples "have obeyed your word." There are two aspects of this: Jesus and the Spirit have revealed the meaning of his word, and they have kept those precepts in their lives. The purpose of this commentary is to make the depths of meaning of this Gospel accessible to you, the reader, so you can understand and obey what it commands you to do. Jesus has obeyed (8:55; 14:31; 15:10) and asks us to do the same (8:51–52; 14:15, 21, 23–24). This doesn't mean the disciples were paragons of obedience. We have seen their failures all too often, but they were committed to his word and sought to follow it. The implications of this for us are important. We too are imperfect followers, but when we dedicate ourselves to him and his Word, he fills us with his empowering presence to continue growing in these very areas.

The centrality of God's gift with respect to the disciples continues in 17:7–8. In verse 3 they came to know the true God, and here they "have come to know" (NIV: "now they know"; the perfect tense of this verb means this knowledge has become a state in which they are existing) "that everything you have given me comes from you." This means that they recognize every aspect of Christ's life and ministry as a gift from God to them and to all followers of Christ. Jesus has said clearly that every part of his life was tied to his Father, and his submission is the very heart of his power (5:19–30). Every single thing he has done or said has the authority of his Father behind it. Jesus is one with his Father (10:30), and God gave Jesus his message.

Jesus carries this truth further in 17:8. There are three stages of discipleship in this verse: (1) In the initial stage, God gives the message to Jesus, he passes it on to them, and they accept (obey) their calling as disciples. (2) The result is that they "knew with certainty that I came from you," meaning they came to know Jesus' mission as their own. (3) "They believed that you sent me": this mission is God's gift to them and is to guide their lives from this point on. Jesus passes his mission on to his disciples (17:18), and their obedience is seen in their acceptance of that message and the fact that God has indeed "sent" him on his mission (17:6). This is the path we must take as disciples—belief, acceptance, obedience. God too has chosen us in our own imperfection, and we are jars of clay holding God's treasures (2 Cor 4:7).

THE MINISTRY OF THE DISCIPLES TO THE WORLD (17:9–16)

Prayer for them, not the world (17:9)

They are chosen but imperfect vessels and desperately need Christ's intercession, so he prays especially for them (v. 9). Yet when he says, "I am not praying for the world, but for those you have given me," he hardly means he will never intercede for the world. The world, after all, is the object of God's love (3:16) and of Christ's salvific work (4:42). Indeed, it is the recipient of the mission of the Triune Godhead, with Father and Son sending the Spirit to convict the world (16:8–11), and the saints sent by the whole Trinity to convert the unsaved (17:18; 20:21–23).

The need for protection and unity (17:10–11)

However, the disciples are the true people of God, so he calls them "those you have given me, for they are yours." They have been chosen from the world to belong to God and to be given to Jesus (17:6, 9–10). They are the ones who most need divine protection and guidance. Christ's work on earth has come to completion, and the fruit of his labor is the disciples, who are the elect gift of the Father to the Son. They are unique in the world, the hope for the future, and so Jesus is asking his Father to especially watch over them.

They especially need divine protection and power, and Jesus anchors this by praying, "All I have is yours, and all you have is mine" (v. 10), which is quite similar to the father's words to the prodigal son in Luke 15:31. This means the disciples participate in Jesus' relationship with the Father since those the Father and Son "have" in tandem are the disciples. This reciprocity of possession means that believers belong to both, being Jesus' disciples and God's children at the same time. This leads to a remarkable confession by Jesus: "Glory has come to me through them." As we share in Jesus' glory, through our submission and obedience we share our glory with him. There is also a reciprocity of glory between ourselves and Jesus. The disciples perceived his glory in 2:11 and worshiped him as "the Holy One of God" in 6:69. They (and we) then proclaim his name to the nations as his sent ones in 17:18; 20:21, as we become a "show and tell" for his glory to the world.

These prayers for them are especially needed because, while Jesus departs to be with his Father, they are "still in the world" (17:11). He has earlier made them aware of the terrible opposition and persecution they will receive (15:18–16:4), and now they realize they will have to endure without the presence of their Lord to undergird them. This is why the emphasis on the coming of the Holy Spirit is so critical. When he says, "I *am* [present tense, not future like the NIV translates] in the world no longer," he is speaking as if he were already in heaven with his Father. Emotionally, he is. They know he is going to be back for them (14:2–3) and is sending the Spirit in his place (14:16–17), but as they go through the horrifying events of the next few days, they will be alone.

Jesus addresses his prayer to his "Holy Father," a title found only here in the Bible, but it was common in Jewish prayers to address God as "the Holy One" (Isa 49:7; 54:5; Hos 11:9; Hab 1:12;

1 John 2:20; Rev 16:5). This key characteristic of God prepares for the prayer in 17:17 to "make them holy" (NIV: "sanctify them"), and for 17:19, where he prays, "For them I sanctify myself, that they too may be truly sanctified." He is praying that God's holiness may fill them for the difficult days ahead.

As God's holiness gives them strength, Jesus asks him also to "protect them by the power of your name, the name you gave me," literally, "keep them in your name." The basis of the prayer is "the name" of God, the divine name he had also given Jesus. Most likely this name is referring to Yahweh, as in the "I am" passages of John (see comments on 8:58). Jesus partakes of God's holy name and is the final revelation of God. He now asks that the power of this holy name might protect and preserve his disciples in the troubles that lie ahead.[1] This is equally critical for us; we too as Christ's followers both share his name and will be protected through our troublesome times by the power of that name.

The purpose of this prayer is "so that they may be one as we are one." Jesus asks that the result of God's protection of his followers will be that they share the oneness of the Godhead. The disciples will never be alone. They have the Spirit and the powerful name of God watching over them, so their failing strength will be undergirded and magnified by the very might of the Godhead working on their behalf (see Eph 1:19–20). The goal of all this is unity—oneness with the Godhead reflected in the oneness of the church. This important concept builds on previous teaching in John (10:16; 11:52) and prepares for the major teaching of 17:20–23.

This unity cannot be achieved in our own strength; the unity of the Godhead is both the model and the means by which we can attain this difficult state in the church. In the last two millennia

---

1. There are two possible understandings of this. It could be stressing the location, "keep them *in* your name," and mean to keep them faithful to the name of God and all it means; or it could be instrumental, "keep them *by* your name," that is, by the power of your name (as in the NIV). The emphasis is on the act of protection, and the context, I believe, favors the second interpretation.

there have been all too few examples of this unity. Christians fight and divide over the most picayune issues, and Satan has a field day in creating fractured churches, as the New Testament and church history can attest. In fact, this prayer for protection may have in mind not just persecution from without but schism from within. The disciples needed protection from themselves as well as from enemies around them. As the cartoon Pogo said so well in the 1970s, "We have met the enemy, and he is us!"

Protection through sanctification (17:12-16)

After asking for protection (v. 11), Jesus reflects on his past protection of his followers. To this point he has always been there for them, but that is about to end. They will need his Father's power behind them more than ever. Heretofore he has been quite successful in keeping them "safe by that name you gave me." Not one "has been lost except the one doomed to destruction," Judas Iscariot. Literally this means "the son of perdition/destruction," with "son of" referring to his divinely appointed destiny—damnation or destruction.

The "Scripture" that this event fulfilled likely refers to Psalm 41:9, "Even my close friend, someone I trusted, one who shared my bread, has turned against me," cited earlier for Judas's betrayal in 13:18. Other passages used for Judas in the New Testament are Psalms 69:25 and 109:8 in Acts 1:20 and Zechariah 11:12-13 in Matthew 27:9-10. This is Jewish **typology** at its best, seeing Old Testament events as analogous and fulfilled in the life of Jesus and the early church. Even though Judas betrayed him, Jesus knew of it ahead of time, prepared for it, and his power was more than sufficient not only to nullify its force but also to use that betrayal to fulfill Scripture and increase the faith of the church.

Jesus' departure is now imminent ("I am coming to you now," 17:13), and he has a very short time left to teach and prepare his disciples. That is the goal of this Farewell Discourse, to instill "the full measure of my joy within them." Six of the seven occurrences of "joy" (*charis*) in John occur in this discourse (13:31–17:26), cul-minating in this verse (15:11; 16:20, 21, 22, 24; 17:13). All he has said is intended to impart his overflowing joy to them. In 16:20–24 he promised that their temporary grief at his departure would be turned to fullness of joy.

This must be understood in light of other parallels: all troubles are painful in the present (Heb 12:11) and become joy only when we allow our trials to turn us completely to God's loving control over our lives. It is this that transforms the pressure into "pure joy" (Jas 1:2) because it turns us into "gold" (1 Pet 1:6–7). Here the transforming factor is the resurrection of Christ from the dead as the firstfruits (1 Cor 15:20, 23) of our own future resurrection.

The basis of this joy is not only their communion with Jesus but also the fact that he has "given them your word" (v. 14). The "word" of God is the gospel message of Christ and the salvation he has brought. Yet "the world has hated them," as darkness will always hate the light (3:19–20), and this results in opposition and persecution (15:18–16:4). Jesus understands this, but the disciples do not and so are unprepared for what is about to happen. Those who follow Jesus now belong to God and so like Jesus are "not of the world" but instead are "foreigners and exiles" in this world (1 Pet 2:11; see also 1:1, 17). We have been chosen out of this world and no longer belong to it (15:19, 21), so we should never be surprised when the people of this world turn against us. One of the major problems of Christians today is the desire to be accepted and liked, so we compromise our walk with Christ in order to be popular.

One definition of holiness is to be set apart from the world and yet a part of the world. This is the point of 17:15. The disciples are to be holy and belong wholly to God and yet remain in the world. Jesus says, "My prayer is not that you take them out of the world"; they are to become the next stage of Christ's mission to the world, as we will see in 17:18. Instead, his prayer is that God "protect them from the evil one," possibly taken from the Lord's Prayer (Matt 6:13). Christ has conquered "the prince of this world" (John 12:31;

14:30; 16:11), but he is still "a roaring lion looking for someone to devour" (1 Pet 5:8) and wants to sift the disciples like wheat (see Jesus' words to Peter in Luke 22:31). Victory comes only from focusing on Christ (Rev 12:11), who with the Father shows us the way of escape from temptation (1 Cor 10:13).

While the disciples are to remain in the world and conduct mission, they "are not of the world" (17:16), for they belong to God and follow Jesus, who as their model is also "not of it." You cannot be a Christ follower and a person "of the world" at the same time. The world is under the control of Satan, so to be victorious in Christ demands that we live apart from the world and conquer Satan.

THE SANCTIFICATION OF THE DISCIPLES (17:17–19)

The best protection for the disciples is sanctification—growing in holiness. To make the disciples holy is to provide spiritual power that will enable them to rise above the burdens of this world. The "Holy Father" enables his children to partake of his holiness. In the Old Testament, "sanctification" was used of consecrating or setting people apart for God's service, either the nation as a whole (Exod 19:6) or a priest (Exod 28:41) or prophet (Jer 1:5). The sanctified become sacred vessels in God's sanctuary. In the Holiness Code (Lev 11:44; 19:2; 20:26), the command is "Be holy, because I am holy" (see 1 Pet 1:16).

Jesus begins, "Sanctify them by the truth" (17:17), and the preposition *en* here could have double meaning, referring to both sphere ("in the truth," that the disciples be immersed in God's truths) and means ("by the truth," that God's truth be a change agent in their lives). Jesus is truth (14:6), and the Spirit is "the Spirit of truth" (14:17; 15:26; 16:13). Holiness takes place in accordance with him and the Spirit in our lives. We surrender to the Triune Godhead and allow them to draw us to God in everything we say and do. Finally, "your word is truth," the third level (Christ to the Spirit to the word) and the means by which the disciple grows in holiness.

Holiness is thinking as God would have us think and living as God would have us live, and all that is defined in his word.

Holiness also involves mission (17:18). The sanctifying work of the Spirit in the disciples has as its goal to prepare them for their place in Jesus' mission to the world. Jesus prays for this mission here and then commissions them for it in 20:21. This is what it means for them to be a part of the world: they are chosen from out of the world, commissioned and filled with the Spirit, and then sent out in mission to bring the good news of God's salvation in Jesus to the world. So Christ prays, "As you sent me into the world, I have sent them into the world." There are two emphases—their status as "sent ones" and the object of their mission, "the world."

Here a further transfer from Christ to the disciples is taking place. It was glory in verses 1–5, name in verses 6–11, unity in verse 11, and holiness in verse 17. Jesus is transferring his mission to his followers in verse 18: "As you sent me into the world, I have sent them into the world." "Sent" is in the aorist tense, stressing the mission as a single whole from the beginning when Jesus chose them to the end when he takes them home. It is the defining factor of their life. One of the most frequent themes of this Gospel is their authority as "sent ones" (see on 3:17), describing them as *shaluachim*, agents or envoys of Jesus, as he was of his Father. They share his authority from God as they go out to the "world," the place of rebellion and rejection (1:10–11). They become the fourth stage of this critical enterprise: God ordains the mission (3:16), God sends Jesus (3:17, 34), the two send the Spirit (14:16–17, 26; 16:7–8), and then the Trinity sends their followers (17:18; 20:21–23). They (and we) carry on the ministry of Jesus in the world as his voice and presence in the same way that he as the Living Revealer was the voice and presence of his Father in the world.

In 10:36 Christ described himself as "the one whom the Father set apart as his very own," a good definition of the work of sanctification, "making holy" or "setting apart." So in verse 19 he states this once more, except now he is the agent: "I sanctify myself" or "set myself apart for" the Father's service. He does so "for them" (*hyper autōn*), and here he has his sacrificial death especially in mind, as in the NLT translation, "I give myself as a holy sacrifice for them." He is consecrating himself as a sacrifice (Exod 13:2; Deut 15:19, 21) for the salvation of the world, as in the words of institution, "This is my body given for you" (Luke 22:19).

Jesus passes on this act of consecration to Jesus' followers, "that they too may be truly sanctified." The process by which they were set apart for God and his work follows Jesus' supreme example, made possible by his atoning sacrifice. Jesus' death alone had the power to make the world mission possible, as seen in "lay down my life" (10:15, 18), the seed dying (12:24), and the concept of "lifted up" as "draw all people" (12:32). To be set apart is to dedicate one's self to the work of God, to make it one's life project. They join Christ's life's work and sacrifice all for the purpose of reaching the world with the saving message of Christ.

JESUS PRAYS FOR THE UNITY OF THE FUTURE CHURCH (17:20-26)

In this final section of his prayer, Jesus turns from his present followers to pray for future converts, "those who will believe in me through their message." These are the ones who will respond to the disciples' mission of 17:18. "Their message" is the result of John's chain of revelation—the gospel witness from Father to Son to Spirit to the disciples to the world.

PRAYER FOR UNITY (17:20-23)

The prayer itself (17:21-23) is for unity, expanding 17:11, "that they may be one as we are one." Several years ago Promise Keepers gathered about twenty scholars comprising a rainbow coalition of Caucasian, African American, Asian, Hispanic, and Native Americans. Over several days we hammered out theological policy positions (unpublished) on racial and denominational reconciliation. On denominational unity, the core statement was a summary of 17:21–23:

> The unity of the church on earth is a reflection of and witness to the unity of the Godhead in heaven, and the very mission of the church is at stake. The unity of the church is not an option but a mandate, and a fractured church (so often the case) is an abomination in the eyes of the Lord.

This summation is found three times in these verses, with the unity of the church stressed each time, the unity of the Godhead three times, and the mission of the church twice. This is a profound passage on the future Christ has planned for his messianic community. It will be grounded in a unity of love (13:34–35; 15:12, 17; 1 John 3:11) but cannot be reduced to love. The core is the power of God and the Spirit, a horizontal unity among ourselves made possible by the vertical, indwelling unity of the Father and the Son (6:56; 15:4–7; 1 John 2:24; 3:24; 4:15). Christ emphasizes, "May they also be in us" (17:21). There will be no unity until we are one with Christ and God and reflect their oneness. This will be a dynamic union with a strong sense of community (10:16; 15:5–6; see also 1 Cor 12:12–26; Eph 4:3–6; 1 Tim 3:15).

We must note the basis of the unity in the community: "just as you are in me and I am in you." The key concept of Jesus and the Father's indwelling one another is *en*, "in me/in you." The Father and Jesus interpenetrate one another, uniting in every area of their being. The church then must emulate their oneness and learn to work together in complete love and harmony. They can overcome their tendency to fight over minor issues by following Jesus' recipe for success—"May they also be in us." The idea is that we each indwell the Triune Godhead and find that oneness with each other through our oneness and meeting in them.

Another means by which we find unity is our shared "glory" (17:22). Again it is a threefold process, just like the love and the unity. God glorified Jesus, he glorified us, and we share his glory by honoring one another. When we honor each other we find unity, for as in Philippians 2:3–4, "in humility [you] value others above ourselves, not looking to your own interests but each of you to the interests of the others." When we imitate Christ and seek the glory of others rather than ourselves, we find unity as the natural by-product. Jesus' concern in 17:1–5 was that in his glory his Father would be glorified, and that is the model we must follow. As we share in his glory we share in his unity.

These ideas culminate in 17:23, where Jesus states the premise twice for emphasis—"I in them and you in me—so that they may be brought to complete unity." This perfect unity can only come from our emulation of the oneness of the Godhead. This mutual indwelling with the Godhead can overcome the many differences—temperament, theological outlook, worship style, personality conflicts, and so on—that keep us divided. Only in Christ and the Spirit can we triumph over our pettiness.

The goal once more is mission, found in both verse 21 and verse 23—"Then the world will know that you sent me and have loved them even as you have loved me." Christ's words in Revelation 3:9, to the beleaguered saints in Philadelphia, convey this well: he will make their persecutors "come and fall down at your feet and acknowledge that I have loved you." It is all-important that the world see how differently we live, and that by coming to Christ they can have the love of God they see in us and love each other in turn. When we bicker, we send a message that we are no different than they are and have nothing to offer.

PRAYER FOR GLORY AND KNOWLEDGE (17:24–26)

This short passage summarizes the two main themes of the prayer—glory (v. 24) and knowledge (vv. 25–26). Jesus' final request is for "those you have given me." There are two different possible understandings for "I want [them] to be with me where I am." One could read this as a prayer that they remain beside him throughout the present passion events as he goes through his terrible ordeal.

However, they will not be with him in the least, and the context makes this unlikely. It is far better to see that, in light of 12:26 ("where I am, my servant also will be") and especially 14:2–3 ("I will come back and take you to be with me that you also may be where I am"), Christ is speaking about their being in heaven with him. Jesus wants these promises to be fulfilled. This world will mean constant trouble and persecution, but the future will be glorious.

His second request flows out of the first. In heaven they will "see my glory, the glory you have given me." Of course, they have gained a glimpse of that glory through his sign-miracles (2:11) and in his person as the "one and only Son" (1:14). But they have not seen his preexistent glory as divine (17:5, "the glory I had with you before the world began"). His true glory will begin to be revealed in the cross (lifted up to glory, 3:14; 8:28; 12:32) and will be seen in power at the resurrection. We will not see the full glory, however, until we are in heaven with him. No one has ever seen God (1:18), and likewise no one has seen Jesus' true celestial glory (1 John 3:2, "we shall see him as he is"). So Jesus is praying for the realization of that glorious promise that we may see and share in his wondrous final glory.

This future revelation of glory is based on the fact that "you loved me before the creation of the world." The Father and the Son share a love that is eternal, that existed even before creation (Matt 25:34; Eph 1:4; Heb 4:3). This love is the source for that preexistent glory (17:5) and is the ground for the future as well. Love and glory are intertwined in the very makeup of the eternal Trinity.

In the conclusion of this prayer of consecration (vv. 25–26) Christ provides a further promise, beginning with "righteous Father," because every detail of this deep prayer results from God's righteous deeds. He begins by summing up the situation of the world—it "does not know" God (1:10–11; 7:28; 8:19, 55). This fatal and deliberate ignorance is overcome by the fact that Jesus does know God and indeed has made him known (1:18), as in verse 26, "I have made you known to them, and will continue to make you known."

The perspective shifts here: (1) The world does not know God, but (2) Jesus does and makes him known (3) to the disciples, not the world in this context. The world exists in deliberate opposition and ignorance, so Jesus works through the disciples, enlisting them in his mission to the world. The disciples are the focus here of both Jesus' present revelation to them in his earthly life and especially in this Farewell Discourse and his future revelation to them through the Holy Spirit ("will continue to make you known," see 14:26; 16:12–15). The process of revelation remains the focus: from the Father to the Son to the Spirit to the church, which is then commissioned and enabled to reveal God to the world (20:20–23).

There is a twofold goal in this continuing revelation: First, "that the love you have for me may be in them," an incredible promise. The love of the Father for the Son is an eternal, all-consuming force, deeper than any finite human being can ever know. We will both experience and live out this unbelievable love, and it can be known only through the Son, who demonstrated it on the cross (Rom 5:8), and brings it to us through his mutual indwelling with us (15:4–7). In this we have the basis also for the community love that infuses this final discourse (13:34–35; 15:12, 17). As we experience God's love in ourselves, we find the strength to extend that love to our brothers and sisters in the community of Christ. Our living relation with him moves outward to embrace those around us in the community (and then in the world).

The second goal/promise is that "I myself may be in them." This summarizes not only the mutual-indwelling theme of this discourse but also one of the central themes of all of Scripture, the promise of Exodus 25:8 ("I will dwell with them," also 2 Chron 6:18; Ezek 48:35) that will be fulfilled in the new heaven and new earth of Revelation 21:1, 3: "God's dwelling place is now among the people, and he will dwell with them. They will be his people, and God himself will be with them and be their God." The initial stage in fulfilling this promise is Jesus dwelling within the believer (6:56; 15:4; 17:23; 1 John 2:24; 3:24; 4:15) as a foretaste of the glory still to come. It will be finalized in heaven. So Jesus' final comment with his disciples before the arrest and the launching of the final events is his deepest desire, to love and indwell his followers.

———

This is the longest prayer of Jesus in the Gospels and functions as his final message to his followers before his arrest and crucifixion removes him from them. His entire concern is finishing his mission and work that the Father gave him and thereby to bring glory to God and a new strength and maturity to his disciples. The first item in his prayer (vv. 1–5) is this concern for glory, and it is clear that we have yet to see the true glory of Christ, the preexistent honor and veneration in heaven of Jesus as God. The earthly glory we do see is but a foretaste of an infinitely greater glory in which we will share, and it is the cross that will unlock this infinite glory as God's salvation is made possible for sinful humanity. We need to dwell more firmly on the glory that we currently share with Christ and the infinitely greater glory that will be ours in heaven. That will go far to alleviate the pressures we face in this world.

Jesus' second prayer concern is for his disciples (vv. 9–19). God gave them to Jesus, and he prepared them to carry on his own God-given mission to the world. To this end he prays for their protection and strength so they might carry out this mission. To that end a particular essential is for a united church to present their love and oneness to the world and show the world the difference that Christ can make. This is so important for us today. I know of several churches that do not have much of a mission consciousness. They focus on their narrow selves and are satisfied just to be together as a community. That is an act of deliberate disobedience, for the very fact of being God's community *must* (it is not an option) lead to our mission to the wider group around us to bring them into our community.

Jesus prays for divine protection, but the need is not just to be kept safe from outside pressures but to be protected from internal schism. The great need is for unity (vv. 11, 20-23), that we remain one in a fractured world and together reflect the unity of the Godhead in order to find personal victory and to show the world what it is missing. This is a major problem, for the church has all too rarely found unity. Calvinists look down on Arminians, low church rejects high church, and we all too seldom are able to "agree to disagree" even on minor issues (like church music). This prayer is so important for the church today, and we all need to join in Jesus' prayer here for the Spirit's unifying work to be successful.

Another marvelous prayer emphasis is for the joy and sanctification of the people of God (vv. 13-19). Like the disciples, we are all bombarded with the pressures of life and the animosity all too often of those around us. It is the Spirit alone who can give us the spiritual strength attained by growing in holiness so that we can set ourselves apart from the world and allow the joy of the Lord to fill us. We must realize we are aliens in this world, set apart from it for God (the meaning of holiness).

Finally, Jesus prays for the future church (vv. 20-26), for those who will come to faith as the church fulfills its mission. Again, the great need is unity, and this is the deepest reflection yet on this critically important theme. We have been united with Christ and so bask in the oneness of the Godhead, but if that is actually true, oneness in the church is an absolutely necessary by-product. Everything is at stake, and so fighting for the so-called purity of our preferred theological "community" can actually be a barrier to finding this unity that is so important to God. We cannot experience God in his fullness until we learn to put aside our differences and embrace one another.[2]

---

2. Of course, there is such a thing as heresy, and there can be no unity with false teaching. The problem is that a lot of what we fight over is not false teaching but simply minor theological differences. We must be careful to separate cardinal issues from peripheral ones.

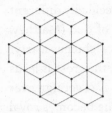

THE ARREST AND TRIALS OF JESUS
(18:1–19:16a)

The order of passion week can be harmonized among the four Gospels. The details differ somewhat, but the broad contours remain the same. John shares many of these details, like the movements of Jesus with his disciples to the Mount of Olives, his betrayal by Judas and subsequent arrest, and his trials before the high priest and Pilate. Yet at the same time John's portrayal has unique features. He omits many aspects, like the events on Monday to Wednesday—he centers on the Thursday events of the Last Supper, Farewell Discourse, his arrest and trials, and omits the words of institution at the Last Supper and Gethsemane.

In his account of the crucifixion itself, John omits Simon of Cyrene's carrying the cross, the mocking crowds, Jesus' cry of dereliction, and then adds several others—the soldiers falling to the ground at the arrest, the conversations with Annas and Pilate, the emphasis on the inscription above the cross, the details on the dividing of the garments, Jesus giving his mother into the care of the Beloved Disciple, the breaking of the legs and thrust of the spear, and Nicodemus at the burial. The result is a rather unique portrayal of events with a decided theological thrust centering on Jesus' sovereign control over his own passion.

John's portrayal of the crucifixion itself is decidedly different. Gone is the horror of putting to death the Son of God (Matthew and Luke) and the death of Jesus as the innocent, righteous martyr with a worshipful atmosphere (Luke). Instead, the cross is Jesus' exaltation, the culmination of his glory. Jesus is sovereign over his own death, and the cross is his throne as he becomes royal Messiah and Lord of Glory. John gives more space to the role of both the Romans and the Jews. Only John tells us of the presence of a Roman cohort at the arrest, and Pilate has a much more extensive role. Still, at the core is still the Jewish demand for Jesus' death ("the Jews" occurs twenty-two times in chapters 18–19). There is no anti-Semitism, as some have charged, but rather equal guilt for the death of Jesus. It is "the world," all of us, who put Christ on the cross.

JESUS IS ARRESTED (18:1–12)

BETRAYED BY JUDAS (18:1–3)

After the discourse is finished,[1] Jesus leads his disciples out of the city and across the Kidron Valley, a wadi or ravine that is a dry stream most of the year but becomes a river in the rainy season. On the other side of the ravine is the Mount of Olives, and on its slopes is Gethsemane (meaning "oil press") of Mark 14:32, simply called "a garden" here. They stay in the garden until the mob arrives (18:4). John probably omitted the **Synoptic** story to center on the arrest itself.

In 18:2 the scene shifts to Judas. This garden was a common meeting place for Jesus and the disciples when they came to Jerusalem, so Judas knew it well (18:2) and also knew Jesus would go there first. In Luke 21:37; 22:39 the evangelist tells us Jesus and his followers spent every night of passion week on the Mount of

---

1. The NIV has "finished praying," but the Greek is literally translated "after saying these things," meaning the discourse as a whole.

Olives, likely at this very spot. Jesus had stayed in Bethany at the start of the week (12:1), but starting Passover night they were to be in the near vicinity of Jerusalem. They could stay in Gethsemane but not Bethany. It is likely that one of Jesus' supporters owned the garden and allowed them to use it. Finally, the olive grove probably had walls around it.

Judas has agreed to betray Jesus so he can be arrested without much fuss, and the Sanhedrin (the governing council) sends a detachment of temple police along with "some officials from the chief priests and the Pharisees" (18:3). John adds that a company of Roman soldiers also accompanied them, calling it a "cohort," technically a battalion of six hundred soldiers but certainly here simply meaning a large company. They would want to make certain no riot broke out with so many volatile pilgrims around. They are said to be "carrying torches, lanterns and weapons," at least swords and probably spears as well. Perhaps it was a "maniple" of 200 (470 guarded Paul in Acts 23:23).

Jesus Goes Forth as a Sovereign (18:4-9)

Because of its strong supernatural elements, many doubt the historical reliability of this scene, which is found only in John's Gospel. We begin with omniscience—"Jesus, knowing all that was going to happen to him." This is a frequent emphasis in John (1:42, 47-48; 4:17-18; 13:1). The stress throughout the next chapters is his complete authority over all that is to transpire, including his death and resurrection (10:18). So he takes the initiative and goes out of the grove to meet his fate head-on.

John omits Judas's kiss of greeting, probably to continue Jesus' control of the situation. So Jesus reveals himself to the group and asks, "Who is it you want?" They respond, "Jesus of Nazareth"; "of Nazareth" functions almost as a surname much like Johnson (= John's son). Jesus' "I am he" seems innocuous at first, equaling "I am that person." However, this is not the case in John, where this becomes an "I am" saying (see 6:35), especially equivalent to an absolute "I am" saying (6:20; 8:24, 28, 58; 13:19), almost equivalent to "I, Yahweh, am here."

The results in the scene make this likely. As soon as Jesus says *egō eimi*, "I am," the entire arresting party of temple police and Roman soldiers "drew back and fell to the ground" (v. 6). The words of Jesus throughout John hold extraordinary power, since he is the voice of God, and this is strongly emphasized when John repeats the *egō eimi* in both verses 5 and 6. Some think this is little more than several soldiers clumsily tripping over one another due to their surprise at Jesus' boldness. I find that very doubtful. It is far more likely that John was creating an ironic scene of theophany—people fall to the ground when confronted with God's manifest presence (Judg 13:20–21; Ezek 1:28; Acts 9:4; Rev 1:17).

That is clearly the case here. Jesus is revealing himself as the "I AM," and people cannot remain standing before God's actual revelation of himself. Certainly the pagan soldiers do not understand what has happened. They are trained never to fall to the ground; to fall is to die in the midst of battle. As they picked themselves off the ground, they undoubtedly asked something like, "Was that an earthquake? What could have knocked us off our feet?" We the reader know exactly what happened. They were suddenly in the presence of deity.

They are so shocked that Jesus has to repeat his question (vv. 7–8), and when they give the same answer, he responds, "I told you that I AM," the third time he uses this title of deity. Think of the implications: God is standing before them waiting to allow them to arrest him! He is sovereignly allowing them to bind him and lead him away. For the only time in human history, God is bound, arrested, and led to jail. Note also that he is the one who gives the command, not them: "If you are looking for me, then let these men go."

Their acquiescence to his sovereign order is not stated but is implied, and in its place John restates the fulfillment of Jesus' prophetic words from 17:12: "I have not lost one of those you gave me" (18:9). The implications are enormous, for Jesus' words are treated as Scripture—this is the only place in John that a non-scriptural statement is seen as "fulfilled." In the prologue of 1:1–18 Jesus is the Word of God, his living voice, so this makes sense. Jesus as the Good Shepherd is watching over and protecting his sheep from the wolves (10:3, 12). Soon he will also lay down his life for them (10:11, 15).

THE ARREST (18:10–12)

The Synoptics tell of a disciple drawing his sword (Mark 14:46–47 and parallels), but it is John who tells us that the disciple was Simon Peter and the slave of the high priest was named Malchus. Several have recently argued that the addition of names in the Gospel accounts is a likely indication of their eyewitness value. An interested reader of the Gospel could check with them to discover the authenticity of the story. The sword (*machaira*) was likely a short sword or long knife hidden in Peter's robe.

It seems a reckless act with a company of Roman soldiers present, but we must remember that the disciples had no idea of Jesus as Isaiah's Suffering Servant. (They thought Isa 52–53 spoke of the nation.) Peter was thinking of the Messiah initiating the final war to destroy the nations. He undoubtedly expected the armies of heaven to appear as he drew his sword and wipe out the Roman soldiers, so Peter took to the offensive. This may have been a clumsy thrust, or he may have cut off the ear deliberately, since there is some evidence that a priest who had his ear sliced off would be disqualified from his office (Josephus, *Antiquities* 14.366). We cannot know for certain.

Jesus will have nothing to do with Peter's misbegotten attempt to start the final war. He came as Suffering Servant, not conquering King. Jesus' arrival as Divine Warrior would await the second coming. So he tells Peter, "Put your sword away!" (18:11). Luke tells us Jesus also healed Malchus's ear (Luke 22:51), and Matthew records Jesus adding, "All who draw the sword will die by the sword." That statement probably saved Peter's life. I can picture Roman soldiers about to impale Peter over his foolish act. Jesus does not allow them to do so and defuses the tense scene.

Jesus then anchors this by restating his sense of destiny: "Shall I not drink the cup the Father has given me?" Compare Mark 14:36, with "the cup" a symbol of suffering and wrath (Ps 75:8; Isa 51:17, 22; Jer 25:15; Mark 10:38). Throughout John the "hour of destiny" (7:30; 8:20) is uppermost, and Jesus is eager to complete his Father's calling. Peter has unwittingly placed himself in opposition to God's will, and Jesus will have none of that.

Jesus' order to put away the sword and his healing of Malchus save his disciples from retaliation by the soldiers, but they still take over to make certain there are no other abortive acts of defiance. The "commander" (*chiliarchos*) technically was the tribune or general in charge of a Roman cohort but here is simply the officer leading the large company of soldiers. They along with the officials from the Sanhedrin arrest Jesus (v. 12). Jesus is "bound" and led away, probably invoking the image of the paschal lamb bound for the sacrifice. (Compare the binding of Isaac in Gen 22.)

ANNAS INTERROGATES JESUS AND PETER DENIES HIM (18:13–27)

Many critical scholars deny the historicity of the trials before the high priest and Sanhedrin on the grounds that the **Mishnah** (the legal side of the Talmud, compiled about AD 200) forbids a nighttime trial and says they had to take place over a two-day period. However, there is evidence that these were not absolutely binding and could be neglected in emergency situations. Also, we can't be sure that later rules were in effect during the time of Jesus. One thing is clear: the authorities wanted to execute Jesus before the volatile time of the Passover began, and in that context a nighttime trial makes perfect sense.

In 18:13–27 and 18:28–19:16 John is at his dramatic best, interspersing scenes for dramatic effect. In this passage he places Jesus' interrogation by the former high priest Annas beside Peter's three denials and contrasts them with each other. Jesus is still in sovereign control and turns himself over to the officials while Peter, in far less danger, loses all control in light of his desire to save himself. The nighttime trial was necessary to deliver Jesus to Pilate at dawn, when the governor normally heard cases, so Jesus could be crucified and buried before dusk, when the Passover began. They had to find legal evidence by then to get Pilate to acquiesce to their desires. Annas and Caiaphas betray their high priestly office and look for lies to convict Jesus, while he is the paragon of truth and faithfulness to God.

The first order of business is tracing the legal deliberations, moving from the Jewish trial (18:13–27) to the Roman trial (18:28–19:15) and then to the final verdict (19:16). Annas's interrogation (18:13–14, 19–24) is interwoven with Peter's three denials (18:15–18, 25–27) to establish the contrast and to show Jesus as both the faithful witness (in contrast to Peter) and the true high priest of God (in contrast to Annas).

JESUS BEFORE ANNAS (18:13–14)

The Synoptic Gospels have the trial before Caiaphas, but John has decided to center on a preliminary interrogation by his father-in-law Annas, who had been high priest earlier (AD 6–15), with five of his sons eventually also becoming high priests. That was one powerful family. Caiaphas was the current high priest (he held the office until AD 36/37). Since according to the Mosaic law a person was high priest for life (Num 35:25), Annas would still have been respected, and so Jesus was brought to him first and then turned over to Caiaphas to finish the Jewish phase of the trial. It was Roman politics that kept switching high priests, and the Jews had to allow that but still looked upon Annas as a high priest.

In 18:14 John reminds us of Caiaphas's inadvertent prophecy that "it would be good if one man died for the people" (from 11:49–50). He is both identifying Caiaphas for the reader and reminding us of the significance of the events to come as well as God's complete control over those events. Even the evil high priest is a tool of God and is led by him to witness to the substitutionary nature ("for [hyper] the people") of Jesus' coming death.

PETER'S FIRST DENIAL (18:15–18)

John omits the desertion of the disciples (Mark 14:50–52) and centers on Peter's failure, set in contrast to Jesus' sovereign control over the events. We see the extent to which Jesus faces these terrible hours completely alone. Even those closest to him fail utterly. Peter begins well, following after Jesus as he tries to remain faithful. The "other disciple," possibly the Beloved Disciple, John (see comments on 13:23), is able to get Peter into the courtyard because he is "known to the high priest."

The language points to a close friend, and so there is some question as to his identity. How could a lowly Galilean fisherman be a friend of the high priest? Because of this, many think this "other" one was an official like Nicodemus. However, John regularly names such people (even Malchus, 18:10), and the only other unnamed individual is the Beloved Disciple. The connection with Peter would point this direction (13:23–26; 20:1–10; 21:7–8, 18–24). Moreover, fishermen were not at the bottom of the social scale, and John's father Zebedee had workers under him (Mark 1:20), indicating some wealth. A connection with the high priest is not out of the question, and the language here makes it likely this is indeed the Beloved Disciple.

Peter is forced to stand "outside the gate" until this "other disciple" speaks to the servant girl who is guarding the gate, and she allows Peter to enter. This is unusual, for normally a male was expected to guard the gate of the high priest. Still, it happened at times. Annas and Caiaphas both lived in the Hasmonean palace on the west hill of the city, which had an extensive courtyard.

The woman challenges Peter (v. 17), "You aren't one of this man's disciples too, are you?" This is significant, for this means

John was known to her as a disciple, and there is a double contrast. Peter's cowardice is not only the opposite of Jesus but of the Beloved Disciple too, as he denies any connection with Jesus. We should note that while Peter does fail Jesus here, he and John are the only two brave enough to come this far. The rest are hiding behind closed doors back in the upper room (20:19), unwilling even to go out into the light of day.

It is a cold night, so everyone is standing by the fire trying to keep warm (18:18). The mention of the "charcoal fire" (*anthrakia*) is a historical touch emanating from John's penchant for such authentic details. It almost looks like an intimate scene of friends waiting together, until we realize the sinister cast in which most are enemies of Jesus. Peter is standing among enemies, afraid for his freedom. There is a turnaround coming at another "charcoal fire" in 21:9, where Peter will receive forgiveness and be reinstated by Jesus.

INTERROGATION BY ANNAS (18:19-24)

John has decided not to narrate the main trial before Caiaphas and the Sanhedrin but rather to focus on the preliminary questioning by Annas, who gathers information for Caiaphas to use in the main trial. He interrogates Jesus regarding two things—"his disciples and his teaching." An actual Jewish trial would not proceed this way. The judge instead would interrogate witnesses to see if two or more would substantiate the charges. This is an unofficial query to gather information. Annas is looking for evidence of seditious teaching. He and the others assume Jesus' guilt and only want material to use against him to prove blasphemy and to implicate him in a plot with his disciples. The hope is that Annas can become a key witness at the forthcoming trial.

Jesus' response is fairly curt (vv. 20-21). He says nothing about his disciples but centers on his teaching, saying he has always "spoken openly," not in secret like an insurrectionist would. He has taught publicly "in synagogues or at the temple, where all the

Jews come together." In fact, he had been teaching in the temple courts all that very week (Luke 21:37). There was not one set of teachings in public and another for his followers, like the cults had. His views were a matter of public record and well known. In short, Annas should know his teachings.

Then Jesus takes the offensive and demands that Annas question witnesses, as he should have been doing: "Why question me? Ask those who heard me. Surely they know what I said" (vv. 21). This was proper protocol. (Roman courts centered on the accused, Jewish courts on witnesses.) Anyone in Jerusalem could answer these questions.

When the officials who are there hear this, they assume Jesus is showing disrespect, and one of the temple guards strikes Jesus in the face (v. 22). Jesus' reaction is quite different from Paul's humble deference when rebuked before the Sanhedrin in Acts 23:4–5. Some scholars charge Jesus with lower standards than Paul, but Paul is in a legal trial setting, and Jesus is responding to an unfair act. He challenges them for striking him and says, "If I said something wrong, ... testify as to what is wrong. But if I spoke the truth, why did you strike me?" (v. 23). He has told the truth, and they have no right to strike him. Telling the truth is never a sign of insolence, and he does not call the official a "whitewashed wall" like Paul did. Jesus wants a fair trial, but their animosity is so great they won't give it to him. We must also remember that Jesus is fighting a cosmic war against the powers of darkness (12:31; 14:30; 16:11), and these officials are tools of Satan. He goes on the offensive in this light.

There is nothing more to be said, and Annas realizes his gambit has failed. So he terminates the interrogation and sends him bound to his son-in-law Caiaphas for the formal trial before the Sanhedrin (v. 24). Here John shows his knowledge of the Synoptic story of this trial (Mark 14:53–65); those who argue that the Synoptics and John contradict each other are wrong. John centers on the Annas story to highlight Jesus' control of the proceedings. However, the

Annas interrogation had to be an unofficial questioning, for only Caiaphas and the Sanhedrin could deliver Jesus to Pilate.

THE FINAL TWO DENIALS (18:25-27)

The scene shifts to the outside of the palace, Simon Peter by the charcoal fire. "They" are questioning him now, meaning not just the servants but also the temple police and officials. They seem to be accusing Peter of being "one of his disciples too" just as in 18:17. For a second time he denies any connection to Jesus. The final challenge is another of "the high priest's servants, a relative of" Malchus (v. 10). He was there for Peter's abortive attempt to start the messianic war and so says, "Didn't I see you with him in the garden?" Peter for the third and final time denies any such thing. When the rooster begins to crow, Jesus' prophecy from 13:38 has indeed come true.

John's account is quite brief compared to the others (see Mark 14:70-72). He has omitted the series of oaths that accompany Peter's denial as well as the bitter tears when he realizes what he has done. John focuses on the contrast between Peter and Jesus and keeps the story simple. This was definitely the worst moment of Peter's life and his greatest failure, but in all the Gospels there is hope for the future. He will be reinstated (21:15-17) and fulfill Jesus' prophetic promise that he will indeed become Peter, "the rock" (1:42). We are so much like him, and we too must realize that in spite of our failures God is faithful and gives us a similar hope in the future, so long as we keep turning to him.

JESUS GOES ON TRIAL BEFORE
PILATE (18:28-19:16A)

It is interesting to note how John shortens the Jewish trial quite a bit from the narrative in the Synoptics and at the same time expands the Roman trial before Pilate into a very complex theological narrative. As with the Jewish trial, a few critics doubt the historicity of the details, but in reality they add not just drama but also authenticity, for the whole story holds together well and is both plausible and trustworthy.

It is now accepted by the majority of scholars that this narrative is organized as a dramatic seven-scene masterpiece with a **chiastic** order, making 19:1–3 the center of the story:

A Outside: The Jews demand Jesus' death (18:28–32)
  B Inside: Pilate questions Jesus about his kingship (18:33–38a)
    C Outside: Pilate finds Jesus not guilty (18:38b–40)
      D Inside: The soldiers scourge Jesus (19:1–3)
    C' Outside: Pilate finds Jesus not guilty (19:4–8)
  B' Inside: Pilate talks with Jesus about power (19:9–11)
A' Outside: The Jews obtain a death sentence (19:12–16a)

The contrasts between the inside and outside scenes are stark. Inside, there is more and more a sense of peace and a realization of Jesus' innocence, and Jesus remains incredibly calm and in control of himself. Pilate increasingly finds him innocent of the charges. Outside, where the Jewish officials and people are, there is continuously greater clamor and chaos, as they demand Jesus' death. As in the Jewish trial, the stress is on Jesus' sovereign control. Before he was the true high priest, and now he is the true king. Pilate is weak and vacillating, while Jesus stands in splendid isolation, accepting his destiny as royal Messiah and Suffering Servant. Clearly, this is a legal farce—the Jews bring him before a Roman governor when even legally his guilt is entirely Jewish, and his so-called political aspirations have nothing to do with Rome. There is nothing political about it, for the actual grievance is theological: his unity with the Father.

OUTSIDE: THE JEWS DEMAND JESUS' DEATH (18:28–32)

Pilate heard cases before dawn, so the Sanhedrin has to get Jesus there in "early morning." After they have condemned Jesus, they have to take him to Pilate's residence and headquarters, the

praetorium (*praitōrion*). The Romans alone had the right to execute prisoners, called the *ius gladii*, the "law of the sword" (see
18:31). So the Jewish authorities must go through Pilate for Jesus
to be crucified, and the actual execution must be carried out by
Roman soldiers.

Pilate ruled the province from a palace Herod the Great had
built in Caesarea on the coast, but would frequently come down
to Jerusalem with a detachment of soldiers for Jewish feasts, for
that was when riots often would break out. In Jerusalem he would
stay either in Herod's palace on the west hill or at the Tower of
Antonia, a Hasmonean castle adjacent to the Temple Mount that
had been rebuilt by Herod (Josephus, *Antiquities* 18.92). He was
"prefect" of Judea from AD 26 to 37 and was notorious for his contempt of Jewish ways and his brutal repression of any dissent (see
Luke 13:1).

Still, this was a complex and difficult situation even for him. No
governor of Judea had ever succeeded there, for they had to walk
a tightrope of Roman expectations and Jewish cultural and religious sensitivities that they simply could not understand.

The Jewish contingent cannot enter the palace because to enter
a Gentile home would mean "ceremonial uncleanness" that would
render them unable to "eat the Passover" that evening (18:28b).
Gentiles by nature were not unclean, but many household items
could cause defilement like yeast or road dust or even the presence
of Pilate's wife (Matt 27:19), since she would not follow the Levitical
rules for menstruation. So they stay outside throughout the trial.
The actual Passover meal was the night before, so the meal noted
here is the *hagigah* meal, a morning meal that would have been celebrated on the morning shortly after this trial. Every meal during
this seven-day celebration was a "Passover meal." Any uncleanness
at all, whether a one-day or seven-day defilement, would render
full participation in the festival impossible.

As a result, Pilate has to repeatedly go outside into the courtyard to meet with the Jewish officials, thus the continual movement

inside and outside the trial setting. The entire scene is quite plausible in light of Jewish sensitivities. In fact, it is hard to see how it could have been otherwise. Since Roman soldiers were there for the arrest, Pilate would have known the Jews would be coming and was prepared.

He begins with a formal question to determine the actual charges against Jesus (18:29–30). The Jewish authorities are defensive and sound somewhat insolent: "If he were not a criminal, ... we would not have handed him over to you." It is possible that they had a preliminary agreement with Pilate (he had sent soldiers to arrest Jesus) and expected him to rubber-stamp their judgment and order the execution. So when he asks for charges, they are nonplussed.

Since they have no formal charge, Pilate sarcastically tells them, "Take him yourselves and judge him by your own law" (18:31a). He certainly knew what had just transpired, but he felt little but contempt for them and wished to demonstrate their impotence. They both knew that the conclusions of a Jewish trial would have no power without Roman agreement.

This flushes them out and forces them to admit their tricky legal situation: "But we have no right to execute anyone." They have to admit their demand for Jesus' death, stressing from the outset their guilt. This is quite debated, for some think the Jews did have the right of capital punishment, as in the stoning of Stephen (Acts 7:57–58), and when a Gentile entered the inner sanctuary of the temple. However, Stephen's stoning is clearly mob action, and the right to execute in the latter case was a concession to the Jews, not the result of a general right to do so. The situation described here is legally correct.

John often stresses the Jewish leaders' desire to see Jesus dead (5:18; 7:19; 8:40, 59; 10:31; 11:50), and the authorities do not care about a fair trial. They could have asked for permission to put him to death themselves, probably by stoning or strangulation, but they want him to be crucified (19:6, 15), not just because it was the most brutal death but mainly because it would signify he was accursed by God (Deut 21:23; Gal 3:13). Yet in reality this death penalty would be in fulfillment of the prophecy that he would be "lifted up from the earth" (12:32; see also 3:14; 8:28). God is in control even over the decisions by Jesus' enemies.

INSIDE: PILATE QUESTIONS JESUS ABOUT HIS KINGSHIP (18:33–38A)

Now Pilate turns to Jesus and begins with the key question, "Are you the King of the Jews?" This is central to everything, as will be evidenced by the fact that it also becomes the inscription on the cross (19:19). This is the actual charge the Sanhedrin will use in presenting their case to the Romans, that Jesus believes he not Caesar is the true king of the Jewish people and thus remains a threat to Rome (Luke 23:2). There had been no king in Judea since Herod the Great. False messiahs had appeared several times, claiming to be royal messiah in the Davidic line, and several insurrectionists had recently appeared, like Barabbas and the two malefactors (18:39–40; also Mark 15:6–15, 27). But the differences between Jesus and them are readily apparent, so Pilate decides to probe Jesus and find out his claims for himself.

Jesus was greeted as royal Messiah at the triumphal entry (12:13), so the common people thought that of him; and Jesus spoke of himself as Son of God and coming king. So there is basis in fact for this question.

In the Synoptics Jesus responds to this query with "You have said so" (Mark 15:2 and parallels). John has this at 18:37, but here in verse 34 Jesus shows his political acumen, challenging the source of Pilate's question, "Is that your own idea, ... or did others talk to you about me?" If it is indeed his own idea, Jesus can probe as to whether Pilate perceives him as a threat and instruct him more deeply. If it comes from the Jews (as Jesus suspects), then it is antagonistic and stems from the leaders' misconception of the true nature of Jesus' kingship.

Pilate's response (verse 35) shows irritation. In Greek, his question ("Am I a Jew?") begins with *mēti*, which expects a negative answer: "I'm not a Jew, am I?" It is clear he has no personal interest whatsoever in this matter, as he adds, "Your own people and chief priests handed you over to me. What is it you have done?" He wants only to find out why he has been stuck with this troublesome situation. It is clear that the Jewish leaders are violently opposed to Jesus, and there has to be a reason for that. The one thing he knows is that he has no clue what it could be. Like all Romans, he is completely mystified with it all. Clearly Jesus is no military man or insurrectionist. What has he done to so inflame the leaders? That's all he cares about.

One thing has become clear—the issue comes from the Jews, so Jesus knows how to answer. He clarifies the nature of his royal office (v. 36). It is not what the leaders intimated. "My kingdom is not of this world." It is a spiritual kingdom, no threat to Rome. Pilate may have thought he had lost his mind, but he knew Jesus posed no danger to Rome. This is a very astute response, both removing the charges as false and challenging Pilate (and the readers) with the otherworldly character of Jesus' kingdom. Jesus has earlier defined his origin as "from above" rather than of this world (8:23; see also 3:31). He now defines his kingship in the same way, and by "kingdom" he means his kingly reign. So he is no threat to Pilate or Rome and at the same time is revealing to him an entire realm of reality he never knew existed. There is somewhat of an evangelistic attempt in this.

Jesus throughout his arrest and its aftermath has wanted to protect his followers (see 18:8) and so adds, "If it were, my servants would fight to prevent my arrest by the Jewish leaders." Pilate knows Jesus has simply surrendered himself without a fight. In one sense, Peter did try to start a fight (18:10–11), but Pilate would have been aware from his soldiers that Jesus had told him to put away his sword and healed Malchus. Here he wants Pilate to realize that he led no band of insurrectionists against Rome. Jesus is a ruler at an entirely different level, and his disciples function at that otherworldly level and not as political or military rebels. They are at work in this world, yet their ministry is not of this world. They are spiritual rather than political operatives.

Still, Pilate recognizes Jesus is making some kind of royal claim and so probes further (v. 37), "You are a king, then!" Jesus' answer is deliberately vague, literally, "So you say." Several commentators translate, "King is your word, not mine," but that isn't quite right either. The NIV is close: "You say that I am a king."

Jesus knows that he came into this world to be royal Messiah, and that when he is lifted up on the cross he will be enthroned in glory, but once more that is a spiritual rather than earthly reality. So he adds, "In fact, the reason I was born and came into the world is to testify [bear witness] to the truth." His kingdom is a kingdom of truth, and from the start a primary motif of the Fourth Gospel is that Jesus is the incarnate **Shekinah**, the Word made flesh, literally "full of grace and truth," meaning "full of God's unfailing love and faithfulness" (1:14). Jesus is characterized as "truth" (14:6), and his revelation is truth itself (8:31-32, 40; 17:17), made known to us by the Spirit of truth (14:17; 16:13-14). He was born to be king, but not the kind Pilate could understand; still, Pilate could comprehend truth, even of the spiritual kind (yet see the next verse). God is now revealing himself through Jesus to Pilate himself, so Jesus asks him to grapple with this new realm of reality.

In light of all this, Jesus has taken the offensive and is asking Pilate to respond. An educated Hellenist like Pilate could relate to the issue of "truth," because Greek philosophy spent so much time on the issue of truth, and the Romans considered it the apex of their judicial program. Jesus adds, "Everyone on the side of truth" (a side all Romans would claim to be on) "listens to me." He is saying in effect, "All who love the truth recognize that what I say is true." He has just reversed the roles—Jesus has become the interlocutor, and Pilate is being challenged to choose truth over falsehood. He is challenging Pilate in this sense to become his follower and turn to the side of truth.

Pilate will have none of this and rejects the invitation with his famous and curt response, "What is truth?" He doesn't even give Jesus a chance to respond but turns abruptly and dismisses Jesus' offer, leaving the praetorium and going outside to address the Jews gathered there. He knows Jesus poses no threat to Rome and that the charges of the Sanhedrin do not concern Rome and thus are invalid. At the same time, he wants no more of Jesus' message of truth and so sadly joins the legion of unbelievers, ironically in this way becoming an ally of the Jews against Jesus. This reply is justly famous and is the heart-cry of all seekers of truth. With this John asks his readers to search their hearts for any openness to truth, especially the truth of Jesus.

OUTSIDE: PILATE FINDS JESUS NOT GUILTY (18:38B–40)

Pilate apparently leaves Jesus inside and goes to the outer courtyard to give the Jews his preliminary verdict: "I find no basis for a charge against him." He doesn't care how guilty Jesus may be of crimes according to Jewish law. He has committed no crime against Rome. Jesus' aspirations in a religious sense are of no concern to him (as a Roman judge). While Pilate was weak, vacillating, and petty to the Jews, he cared deeply about Roman issues and tried to be scrupulously fair to Jesus, as is evident here.

Luke tells us (23:5–12) that the crowd at this point shouted that Jesus had caused problems everywhere, giving him an excuse to send Jesus on to Herod. John omits this and focuses on Pilate and the Jewish crowd. One wonders why he didn't just force this verdict on the Jews, but he had made mistakes recently and had to back down on more than one occasion when the Jews appealed to Rome. So he was unwilling to take the high road. To assuage the crowds, he tries a different tack and invokes the custom of releasing "to you one prisoner at the time of the Passover" (v. 39). This was calculated by the Romans as a gesture of goodwill. He is hoping the people will allow him to release Jesus. The people have to choose the one released, so Pilate cannot just do what he wants.

Many doubt this so-called paschal amnesty, for there is no definite external evidence for the practice. There is one passage from the Mishnah that mentions "one who has received a promise to be released from prison" in a list of those who could participate in the Passover celebration (m. Pesahim 8:6), and several believe it a reference to this amnesty. Moreover, the Jewish historian Josephus (*Antiquities* 20.209) and the Roman historian Livy (*History* 5.13) attest to analogous Roman practices. It is accepted by a growing number that it makes good sense and is likely a historical event.

When Pilate asks about Jesus, he cannot resist throwing out one more barb and ask, "Do you want me to release 'the king of the Jews'?" There is a distinct hint of sarcasm and contempt, presented as if he agrees with the title and thinks Jesus an apt king of this rabble. At the same time John sees a further unconscious prophecy (like Caiaphas in 11:50–52), for he was indeed the "King of the Jews," preparing for the inscription on the cross (19:19); and Jesus' own people were demanding the death of their royal Messiah.

Pilate's plan backfires, as he underestimates the resolve and hatred of Jesus' enemies. So the crowd "shouted back, 'No, not him! Give us Barabbas!'" John explains he had "taken part in an uprising" (v. 40), actually *lēstēs*, "robber," a first-century bandit and rebel. Mark 15:7 tells us he had committed murder in an uprising and was an insurrectionist. This was Pilate's mistake—to the Romans he was a murderous terrorist, but to many Jews he was a patriot and folk hero, an ancient Robin Hood. There is great irony here, especially in light of Matthew 27:16, which tells us that his name was "Jesus Barabbas." Barabbas means "son of Abba" (the Hebrew name for "father"), so the crowd is choosing between two who are "Jesus son of Abba." The name "Jesus" means "God saves/delivers," so one is offering spiritual deliverance via salvation, and the other offers earthly deliverance via the sword. Needless to say, the crowd chooses the wrong "Bar Abbas."

INSIDE: THE SOLDIERS SCOURGE JESUS (19:1–3)

It seems contradictory that Pilate would one moment be trying to release Jesus and the next moment having him scourged. The answer is in Luke 23:16, where his intention is to "punish him and then release him." It is a second ploy to appease the Jews, to satisfy their desire to see him punished. There were three kinds of beatings—the *fustigatio*, a less severe beating for light offenses; the *flagellatio*, a severe beating for hardened criminals; and the *verberatio*, the most severe type with the criminal beaten by a succession of soldiers, often with a scourge, a whip with several leather thongs tipped with pieces of metal or bone. A scourging could break a person's back and strip his skin off, leaving his entrails exposed and often killing him (Josephus, *Jewish War* 2.612). This was likely the first type, for he hoped to release Jesus. There is a second beating at the end of the trial (Mark 15:15) and just before the crucifixion. That is probably the third type, the scourging, meant to weaken Jesus so he will die on the cross more quickly.

As was typical for such situations, Jesus is made the butt of cruel jokes by the soldiers. Since he has been charged as "king of the Jews," they gave him mock homage, laughing at him the whole time. For the kingly crown, they weave together either the thorn bush mentioned in Isaiah 34:13 or the date palm, with very lengthy thorns up to twelve inches. The latter is the most likely and would add further irony because that same palm yielded the branches used in the triumphal entry (12:13) just five days earlier. They dress him in a mock emperor's robe of purple, likely the deep red of an officer's cloak (no one could afford actual purple). Several times (imperfect tense) they mimic "Ave Caesar," saying, "Hail, King of the Jews," then slap his face to show their contempt. This is further irony, as they are truly addressing the "King of Kings and Lord of lords" (Rev 19:16).

Outside: Pilate Again Finds Jesus Not Guilty (19:4-8)

Pilate is still convinced Jesus is innocent and hopes the beating and mockery have caused enough suffering to satisfy the Jews. So he tries one final time to free Jesus, telling them, "Look, I am bringing him out to you to let you know that I find no basis for a charge against him," much the same as he did in 18:38. Then he brings him out in the pathetic robe and crown of thorns, with the blood from the thorns and the flogging flowing down his face and body (19:5). Isaiah 53:2-3 is certainly fulfilled in this, with Jesus having "no beauty or majesty to attract us to him, nothing in his appearance that we should desire him." When Pilate says, "Here is the man,"[2] he does so not out of contempt for Jesus but to say he is no threat and should be released. With his beaten face and body and his oozing cuts, he would have been a sorry sight yet at the same time in reality "The Man," the incarnate Shekinah and glorious Son of Man.

The chief priests and other officials pay no heed to Pilate (19:6) and cry out (undoubtedly with the crowds echoing them), "Crucify! Crucify!" They will allow no mercy for Jesus. This also proves that their charge placed before Pilate was sedition against Rome, for crucifixion was used almost entirely for enemies of the state.

Pilate is angered at their refusal to acquiesce to his will, and he responds, "You take him and crucify him. As for me, I find no basis for a charge against him" (the third time he has stressed this, 18:38; 19:4). He knows they cannot do so (18:31b) but is filled with disgust at them. Still, he does not have the courage to release Jesus on his own authority and so resorts to legalities. However, they are not working.

This goads the Jewish authorities into revealing their true intentions. They now know the political charge won't work, for Pilate has three times rejected their arguments. So they turn to

---

2. Greek "Behold the man," with the "behold" reminding us of 1:29, "Behold the Lamb of God" and further irony hinting at the actual exultation of Jesus.

the religious reason behind it all: "We have a law, and according to that law he must die, because he claimed to be the Son of God" (19:7). This would be Leviticus 24:16: "Anyone who blasphemes the name of the LORD must be put to death." He may not be a threat to Rome, but he is to the Jewish authorities and their law, and he is guilty of blasphemy (see 5:18; 7:32; 8:59; 10:33, 39). They are now asking Pilate not to condemn Jesus by his laws but to respect their laws and allow him to be put to death. The Romans are duty-bound to do just that, so Pilate is now obligated.

The specific charge is "because he claimed to be the Son of God." This title could be used for angels (Gen 6:2; Ps 29:1) or kings (2 Sam 7:14; Ps 2:7). It is a major title for Christ in the Gospels, and Jesus' opponents rightly have seen that he used it to make himself equal with God (5:17–18; 10:33–37). A great deal has been said about what constituted blasphemy to the Jews: not Messiah, for there were many false messiahs, and they were seen more as political figures. This title "Son of God" is part of the solution, but there was more. Technically, a false use of the title "Yahweh" was the heart of blasphemy, because it was the primary title for God, and none, not even the archangel Michael could sit with Yahweh as an equal. So Jesus' use of the supreme divine name and his claim to be "the Son of Man sitting at the right hand of the Mighty One" (Mark 14:62) are at the heart of the guilty verdict.

Pilate's response, that he is now "even more afraid" (18:8), is quite strange, especially given the great disdain he has just expressed for the Jewish leaders. One thing we must keep in mind is that while Pilate's primary concern was for Roman interests, he was still required to keep the peace and look out for Jewish needs as well. While he never cared for that side of his duties, he was still held accountable for it by Rome. The context tells us the fear is connected to the "Son of God" title ("when he heard *this*"), and he would think Jesus was what Romans called a "divine man," perhaps a messenger from the gods or a person with "divine" powers. His wife has just warned him about Jesus (Matt 27:19) from a dream she had (a message from the gods?), and so Roman superstitions come into play. He is more right than he could know, for it is the one true God who is sending him the message.

INSIDE: PILATE TALKS WITH JESUS ABOUT POWER (19:9–11)

Pilate's superstition continues as he asks, "Where do you come from?" He wants to make certain Jesus is not a heavenly being, afraid that his fears are real. This is further irony, for throughout this Gospel John has emphasized Jesus' descent "from above" (see 3:31). He is quite upset when Jesus refuses to speak, but for the reader this evokes Isaiah 53:7: "As a sheep before its shearers is silent, so he did not open his mouth." Jesus has already told Pilate his kingdom is not of this world (18:36), so there is nothing more to be said. To Pilate, however, it seems insolent, and he reminds Jesus, "Don't you realize I have power either to free you or to crucify you?"

This unlocks the silence, and Jesus reminds him in turn that there are greater powers at play than he knows, telling him, "You would have no power over me if it were not given to you from above." God is the true and only source of Pilate's authority. The language is carefully chosen. Jesus is "from above" (3:31), and all authority stems from that realm. In fact, he is "one" with the source of that authority (10:30). The very authority Pilate possesses has been given over to Jesus by his Father (10:19–30), so in reality Jesus rather than Pilate is actually in charge here. Pilate, however, undoubtedly interpreted this to mean Jesus was recognizing the power of Rome.

Jesus now adds another comment that would have pleased the governor: "Therefore the one who handed me over to you is guilty of a greater sin." Pilate clearly lacks the moral courage to do the right thing and release Jesus—God has given him the authority to do it. Yet there is an individual who bears the greater guilt. It is difficult to identify "the one." It could be Judas ("handed over" = "betrayed") or Caiaphas the high priest (the leader of the Sanhedrin that condemned Jesus) or used collectively for the Jewish leaders as a whole. Probably a combination of the last two is best. Judas plays no part in the trial scenes. Caiaphas spearheaded every aspect of the events that led to this point, but he also worked through the Sanhedrin.

We need a careful understanding of the issue of Jewish guilt, since it has been terribly misused in the pogroms of Europe, the Holocaust, and anti-Semitism in general. The Jewish people are not "Christ killers." We all are! We in reality put Christ on the cross through our sin. The book of Acts clarifies how the early church thought of Jewish guilt for the death of Christ, for while the Jews demanded his death, the Romans participated and actually carried out the crucifying of Christ. In the sermons of Acts the message is "You put Christ on the cross, and he died for you [not "because of you"]. So put your trust in him, find saving faith, and attain salvation" (see Acts 2:36–39; 3:15–19; 13:27–31, 38–40).

OUTSIDE: THE JEWS OBTAIN THE DEATH PENALTY (19:12–16A)

For the fourth and final time, Pilate tries to free Jesus, but as before the leaders stop him. Throughout the trial he has realized Jesus has done nothing that threatened Roman rule. But he is up against an implacable foe. The turning point in the entire drama occurs when they shout again and again, "If you let this man go, you are no friend of Caesar. Anyone who claims to be a king opposes Caesar."

The phrase "friend of Caesar" is a semi-technical title with political repercussions. Pilate was under the protection of Sejanus, the chief administrator of the empire under the emperor Tiberius. He had got Pilate his position as prefect of Judea. The Roman historian Tacitus (*Annals* 6.8) said that any friend of Sejanus was a friend of Caesar. So it became almost a technical term for a close companion of the emperor. But in AD 31 Tiberius became convinced Sejanus was a threat and had him and several relatives and friends executed. Since it is now about AD 30 it is hard to know how serious a threat this was to Pilate at this time. For those who think the crucifixion was later, in AD 33, it is serious indeed.

I would argue for the earlier date, but even in AD 30 the political storms had likely started to blow, so Pilate with this threat would be afraid for his career and possibly for his life. We should note the further irony: he is being charged as "no friend of Caesar" by the one group in the empire who are in no way friends of Caesar, and at the same time the true King of kings is being executed for the charge of calling himself a king.

At any rate, this turns the tide against Jesus, and Pilate surrenders. In verse 13 he brings Jesus out to the public arena, signifying he is ready to render his decision. Before, he stood and dialogued with the leaders, but now he sits down as the judge to declare his verdict. The fact of Jesus' innocence no longer matters, and as usual politics wins out over truth. He brings out Jesus to face his accusers and sits in the *bēma* or judgment seat, called here the "Stone Pavement," or in Aramaic *Gabbatha*, meaning "high place" or "hill." It was likely a platform at the highest point of the courtyard of the governor's residence (Herod the Great's former palace) where public meetings were often held.

John now tells us (19:14) it is "the day of preparation," or Friday morning (see on 13:1), at "about the sixth hour," or noon by Jewish reckoning. There is a discrepancy with Mark 15:25, 33, which says Jesus was crucified at the "third hour" (nine in the morning), and darkness fell at the sixth hour or halfway through his time on the cross. Some think John is using the Roman reckoning, according to which the day begins at midnight and the sixth hour is six in the morning, but that doesn't work any better and is doubtful since John's Gospel is quite Jewish. The likely answer is the ambiguous way ancients spoke of time, centering on the four three-hour "watches" for daytime or nighttime. So "about the sixth hour" would be anytime between nine in the morning and noon. So one author (Mark) rounded it down to about nine in the morning, while the other (John) rounded it up to about noon.

Pilate has to give in to the Jewish demands and surrender Jesus to his fate, but he decides to taunt them one last time and so proclaims, "Here is your king," a beaten, bloodied wreck of a person, undoubtedly saying to himself, "This pitiful person is just what you deserve," not realizing he couldn't be more right. He was not just their king but the King of the Ages, the one who will reign over heaven for eternity.

The response of the crowd (19:15) is a tumultuous uproar: "Take him away! Take him away! Crucify him!" As the trial has gone on, their animosity and volume has kept getting worse. By this time they virtually tear the roofs of the houses with their noise. He asks a final time, his contempt quite obvious, "Shall I crucify your king?" This leads them to utter their own blasphemous claim: "We have no king but Caesar." At the very least, they should have recognized God as their king (Judg 8:23; 1 Sam 8:7; 10:19). Still, to choose Caesar over Jesus the Son of God is true blasphemy.

Now Pilate's capitulation is finally complete (19:16a), as he "handed him over to them to be crucified." None of the Gospels record the actual ceremony of sentencing Jesus, but all imply it. The "them" here would be the Jews on the basis of the emphasis on Jewish guilt. Of course, it was Roman soldiers who led him away and nailed him to the cross, but John could not be more clear that it was the Jewish leaders at every level who condemned him. Pilate allowed the Jewish officials to have their way and turned Jesus over to the soldiers to prepare him for crucifixion.

———

The arrest and trial of Jesus is one of the truly amazing scenes in history. Nothing like it has ever happened before or since. In the arrest of Jesus (18:1–12), history's greatest army is a side-point to the truly sovereign power at work. An entire company of Roman soldiers, possibly two hundred in all, along with a large group of Jewish officials, come to take away a rabble-rousing peasant preacher and instead are suddenly on the ground as the true deity of this person is suddenly revealed to them. He is in control of the arrest, not them. This is the major theme for the rest of this Gospel: the authority of Christ, who surrenders himself to his destiny and allows himself to be taken away. When Peter tries to start the final war, Jesus takes over and keeps it all from escalating out of control.

The denials of Peter (18:15-18, 25-27) show the human frailty all of us share and at the same time demonstrate how Jesus overcomes even our failures. An important message is the critical nature of humility. Peter is full of bravado, thinking of himself as above such things, and that makes his fall all the easier. We must learn how to surrender completely to Jesus and the Spirit, relying on them for the strength to overcome rather than on our own strength.

The interrogation by Annas (18:19-24) shows their determination to get rid of Jesus, as they even set up this unofficial questioning to gather information so as to indict him. It is a complete fiasco, as Jesus again dominates the scene. We need to realize he, not us, is in control at all times. Spiritual victory is totally dependent on realizing this and surrendering to him.

Most of the space here is taken up by the detailed trial before Pilate (18:28-19:16a), used by John to show Roman as well as Jewish guilt for the death of Jesus. The truth is that all of us with our many sins have placed Christ on the cross. Still, even here the Jewish guilt is stressed, for Pilate is convinced of Jesus' innocence and wants to free him, but every attempt (four in all) is met with louder and louder demands that Pilate give in to demands and crucify Jesus. John tells this story very artistically, with seven scenes in chiastic order showing Pilate's growing desire to free him (inside scenes) in contrast with Jewish shouts for his execution (outside scenes).

There is a strong **christological** emphasis in this trial as well. Jesus reveals himself as a king that is no threat to Rome (like the Jews are claiming) because his is a spiritual kingdom, not of this world (18:33, 36), and his purpose is to reveal a whole new realm to Pilate and to invite him to enter it. Pilate cannot understand that, so Jesus offers him "truth" and invites him into the realm of spiritual reality (18:37). Again, Pilate doesn't get it and asks, "What is truth?" John's point in this is to show who is on trial here—the spiritual ruler of this world who offers a whole new level of truth is on trial before a worldly court understanding only earthly things. Such a trial is doomed from the start; justice cannot be attained.

Pilate tries another tack (18:38–40), asking them to choose between the insurrectionist Barabbas or Jesus, the King of the Jews, to be freed on the basis of the paschal amnesty. Here Pilate joins Caiaphas as inadvertent prophets telling all and sundry of this new King and royal Messiah. So both governments unconsciously recognize Jesus as king.

In 19:1–16a the final verdict comes in, and Jewish threats finally force Pilate to acquiesce. As the governor of Judea, Pilate was forced by Rome to respect Jewish customs (which he never did very well), and so when the officials threaten to go to Caesar and especially when they threaten to denounce him as "no friend of Caesar," he becomes afraid for his job and career. He literally washes his hands of the matter and turns Jesus over to be crucified.

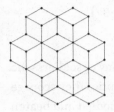

THE CRUCIFIXION AND
BURIAL OF JESUS
(19:16b–42)

The "hour" of Jesus' destiny (3:14; 7:30; 8:20) has now fully arrived, and Jesus is about to yield himself as the atoning sacrifice for sin. John's portrayal of this central scene of Scripture is very dramatic, tightly controlled, and unique. It parallels the **Synoptic** Gospels in including Jesus bearing his cross, the inscription, the dividing of the garments, the two criminals crucified with him, the women witnesses, the sour wine to drink, and his death. At the same time, John omits a great deal, including Simon of Cyrene carrying the cross for him, refusing the wine at the beginning, the taunts, the darkness, the cry of dereliction, the earthquake, the tearing of the temple veil, and the centurion's cry.

While John follows the basic contours of the others, he adds some important new material: the universal witness of the inscription, the details and significance of the dividing of the garments, the scriptural fulfillment citations, giving his mother to John, the final cry, and the piercing of his side. The result is a unique, well-crafted, and stylized portrait with theological motifs paramount: the sovereign control of Jesus, the cross as his throne, his anointing as royal Messiah, and the cross as a lifting up into glory.

JESUS IS CRUCIFIED (19:16B–37)

JESUS LED TO THE CROSS (19:16B–18)

The group to which Pilate hands Jesus is a company of soldiers who march him to the site of execution. In the Synoptics they scourge him further, mock him, and lead him away. Bloodied and beaten but unbowed, Jesus carries his own cross to Golgotha. John takes us immediately there. John omits the story of Simon of Cyrene carrying it partway in order to show Jesus facing his destiny in full control of everything to do with the cross. It was common practice to make a condemned criminal bear the crossbeam to the execution site, with the pole already there (see Plutarch, *Divine Vengeance* 9). This was not just for cruelty's sake but to tell the condemned they were already dead and break their will to live.

The destination was the site the Romans officially set aside for executions. It may have been named (in Aramaic) "Golgotha" or "Skull"[1] because it was a hill that resembled a skull or because it was the site for executions. We cannot know for sure. Most agree that the Church of the Holy Sepulchre (inside the walls of the Old City of Jerusalem today) is more likely than Gordon's Calvary (outside the walls today) as the true site. The walls of Jerusalem in Jesus' day were in completely different spots than they are today.

The pole was already placed in the ground. Upon arriving, Jesus would have been laid on the ground and his wrists and hands nailed to the crossbeam. The normal method was to tie his arms to the cross, but the Jewish leaders needed him to be dead in time to bury the body before sundown because it was Passover, so they used nails. Then he would have been hoisted up and the crossbeam fastened to the pole about seven feet off the ground, just high enough for his feet to be off the ground. Finally, they would

---

1. It is also called "Calvary" because the Latin term for "skull" is *calvaria* and appeared as such in the Vulgate, the popular Latin translation of the Bible.

nail his feet to the pole with one six-inch spike through the ankles. The blood loss from the nails would help him die more quickly.

It is hard to imagine the pain. Jesus' back would have been torn to pieces by the scourging, and with the nails through his wrists and ankles, his entire weight would be held by those nails through his flesh. The Romans would also place a *sedecula* or seat (a small block of wood placed slightly above the buttocks) on the pole that would enable to him to pull himself up occasionally to rest on it, prolong the agony (pulling himself up then falling off it), and get needed breaths.

Death would usually come by asphyxiation and could take several days if the arms were just tied to the beam. The hands and arms would also slowly turn gangrenous due to the cutting off of circulation. The agony for that entire time would be beyond imagination. Roman citizens could not be crucified except by direct edict of Caesar, and for the Jews it constituted being cut off from the covenant as "hanging on the pole" (Deut 21:23; see Gal 3:13). The Romans would normally leave the body on the cross to rot, but at Passover the Jewish law demanded that bodies be buried before sunset (Deut 21:23).

Two other criminals are crucified with Jesus, one on each side in fulfillment of Isaiah 53:12, which says that the Servant is "numbered with the transgressors." Mark 15:27 tells us they were rebels and conspirators with Barabbas. John has omitted their taunts and the conversion of one of them (Luke 23:39-43), again probably to center on Jesus and his control over the situation.

The Inscription on the Cross: A Universal Witness (19:19-22)

It was quite common to write the crime on a placard and place it around the guilty person's neck for the duration of the trip to the execution site and then to place it on the pole to be read by onlookers. This served as a warning to others. The "notice" Pilate has placed on the cross is "Jesus of Nazareth, the King of the Jews."

There were three types of crosses, an X-shape for crucifying a criminal spread eagle,[2] a T-shape without a sign, and a cross if there is a *titulus* or sign on the pole, as was the case with Christ. Pilate has this particular message affixed above Jesus' head to mock the leaders and show his contempt, but God turns this into a further unconscious prophecy (like 11:50-52), a universal proclamation designating the cross as Jesus' throne.

With serious crimes the inscription would be written in several languages so everyone could read it. Pilate does just this (19:20), having it written in the three main languages of Palestine: Aramaic for the general populace, Greek as the common language of the empire, and Latin as the official language of Rome and the military. The leading priests object (v. 21), wanting it to say, "This man claimed to be king of the Jews." They want it to be no more than Jesus' self-declaration, but Pilate, wishing to humiliate them, responds, "What I have written, I have written."

In doing so Pilate turns the notice of the crime into a virtually worldwide proclamation of Jesus' kingship. He joins Caiaphas as an inadvertent prophet, unknowingly telling all and sundry who this man is and why he is dying. God often uses strange things to accomplish his purposes, and here he uses Pilate's racial prejudice and religious contempt to turn him into a prophet. Pilate was laughing at the Jewish leaders, but the world was beginning to notice the reality of Jesus as royal Messiah.

DIVIDING JESUS' GARMENTS (19:23-24)

The Romans specified that the possessions of a condemned criminal belonged to the soldiers and were to be divided among them. All that Jesus has are the clothes on his back, so these are divided up. Normally criminals were executed nude, but Jewish sensitivities led to them here being allowed loincloths. So the pieces

---

2. According to tradition, Peter may have been crucified upside-down on this type of cross.

divided among the soldiers are his headpiece, belt, sandals, outer robe, and his undergarment or *chitōn*—a "seamless [cloth] woven in one piece from top to bottom."

The normal squad for a crucifixion like this would consist of four soldiers. They divide the first four pieces and decide to have a little fun and gamble over the undergarment rather than tear it into four pieces. John seems to emphasize this tunic or undergarment, so scholars have long speculated that the seamless tunic symbolizes either the unity of the church (10:16; 11:52; 17:20–23), or Jesus as high priest with a seamless robe (Exod 39:27; Josephus, *Antiquities* 3.161). However, the unity theme doesn't fit the context here well, and the high priest's seamless robe was the outer rather than inner garment. Neither works well here, and it is more likely that John is stressing the seamless nature of the tunic to explain why the soldiers gambled over it and didn't want to cut it into four pieces.

In verse 24, John points out that this scene shows the fulfillment of Psalm 22:18: "They divided my clothes among them and cast lots for my garment." Jesus is fulfilling another aspect of the Davidic Messiah, that of the righteous sufferer abandoned by all but held up by God. This begins a major emphasis in the crucifixion scene, with four fulfillment passages (19:24, 28, 36, 37). John wants to show that all that happened to Jesus was following the divine plan. In fact, John describes the unfolding details as in keeping with Psalm 22: the division of garments (v. 23a) followed by the gambling over the tunic (vv. 23b-24a). All earthly ties are released— clothes, family, and life itself.

GIVING HIS MOTHER TO THE BELOVED DISCIPLE (19:25–27)

We must remember that Jesus' brothers have steadfastly refused to believe in him (7:5), and Jesus needs to ensure his mother's care (she was a widow[3]) when he is gone. The Romans kept family and friends back but still allowed them to be in hearing range and let the crucified make in a sense a last will and testament to them. It is interesting that John mentions the four soldiers in verses 23–24 and then the four women bystanders in verse 25. The contrast between them is part of the story.

All the Gospels have lists of women who served as official witnesses of the death and resurrection. John lists four, two unnamed (Jesus' mother and her sister) and the second pair named (Mary the wife of Clopas, who is possibly the brother of his father Joseph and a leader in the church; and Mary Magdalene). The lists differ somewhat from Gospel to Gospel, but there were at least five women—(1) Mary the mother of Jesus; (2) Mary the wife of Clopas and mother of James the Younger and Joseph; (3) Salome (Mark 15:40–41) the sister of Jesus' mother as well as the wife of Zebedee and mother of James and John; (4) Mary Magdalene (Luke 8:2); and (5) Joanna (Luke 24:10).

So Jesus, near death, here surrenders his mother to his cousin John the Beloved Disciple (see number 3 above). He decides to forge a new family relationship to ensure the safety and security of his mother. The language he uses (vv. 26–27)—"Woman, here is your son. ... Here is your mother"—is found in Jewish family law for entrusting one person to another. A lovely scene is forged, demonstrating the incredible love of Jesus for his own, even as he is dying an excruciating death. Jesus tells Mary she has a new son to take care of her, and we have a new model for the church as a family. In a beautiful detail, John tells us, "From that time on, this disciple took her into his home."

Catholic exegetes have seen this more as the naming of Mary as the mother of John and thus of the church, but it is exactly

---

3. There are no scenes involving Joseph during Jesus' adulthood in any of the Gospels, so he had undoubtedly passed away at some time while Jesus was growing up.

the opposite. Mary is placed in the care of John and taken into his home, forming a new family. All attempts at symbolism (like the two forming a new Adam and Eve or portraying Jewish and Gentile Christianity) fail to convince. At best, this is simply demonstrating the new relationships that bind together the new messianic community.

THE DEATH OF JESUS (19:28–30)

Jesus' omniscience (see on 1:42) is still evident, as he knows "that everything had now been finished," specifically his hour of destiny (7:30; 8:20; 13:1; 17:1). So the time has now arrived for his final sacrifice, the surrender of his life for the salvation of sinful humankind (3:16; 5:24). According to Mark 15:25, 33, he was on the cross about six hours, from the third hour (nine in the morning) to the ninth hour (three in the afternoon). He was naturally thirsty, but his statement here was more so that he could fulfill Scripture than to fill a physical need.

When he says, "I am thirsty," he may be alluding to Psalm 22:15 ("my tongue sticks to the roof of my mouth") but more likely Psalm 69:21, "they offer me sour wine for my thirst," a psalm already cited in 2:17; 15:25; and again in 19:29–30 below. The soldiers take a sponge and dip it in a jar of sour wine to assuage his thirst. This is not the myrrhed wine of Mark 15:23, offered when he first arrived at the cross, but a cheap vinegar wine drunk by soldiers and the poor. Here it says the Scripture is "completed" or "finished" (*teleiōthē*) rather than "fulfilled," unusual and closely linked with the "completion" of his messianic task earlier in the verse and with "It is finished" in 19:30, the last words he will speak before his death. This threefold use of "finished" provides a fitting conclusion to his earthly life and destiny as the incarnate Messiah and Son of God. The work of God and the purpose of all of Scripture has now come to completion as Jesus departs to be with his Father.

Only John tells us they gave the wine to Jesus by soaking a sponge in it and placing it on "a stock of the hyssop plant ... lifted ...

to Jesus' lips" (19:29). In Mark 15:36 they simply place it on a stick. They did not grow very long and were not very strong stalks, so many have thought it too insubstantial for this task. However, Jesus was only a short distance off the ground, so a soldier could have got it to his lips easily. Hyssop was important at Passover because it was used to sprinkle the blood of the lamb on the door-posts and sides of the posts when the angel passed by at the original Passover (Exod 12:22). So the hyssop symbolizes Jesus' death as the Passover sacrifice (see also 1:29, "the Lamb of God, who takes away the sin of the world").

The last moments of Jesus' earthly existence now take place (19:30). He "receives" or tastes the sour wine from the stalk of hyssop, makes a final cry, and surrenders his spirit to his Father. The one-word cry (*Tetelestai*) is quite significant, meaning the entire work of God assigned to the Christ is "finished." There is double meaning here—he has "ended" his earthly life and at the same time has "accomplished" his divinely appointed destiny. With the Passover implications, it means Jesus has now carried out his atoning work on the cross (one of the primary emphases of John, found in 1:29; 10:11, 15; 11:50, 52; 18:14). The paschal sacrifice has been offered for the sins of humankind, and redemption has now been accomplished. The age of salvation has now been inaugurated.

Still in sovereign control, even at the last moment of his life, Jesus did not passively die but actively "bowed his head and gave up his spirit" ("breathed his last" in Mark 15:37; Luke 23:46). Jesus earlier stated, "No one takes [my life] from me, but I lay it down of my own accord" (10:18). This is precisely the case here. Obedient to his Father to the very end, Jesus relinquishes his life to him.

PIERCING JESUS' SIDE (19:31-37)

The Torah (Deut 21:22-23) demands that corpses "hanging on the pole" or "tree" must be buried before nightfall lest the land itself be desecrated. Moreover, this was the "special Sabbath" of

Passover week, so it is even more critical that this injunction be followed. For good reason the Jewish authorities did not trust that the Romans would respect this and so sent a delegation to Pilate to make certain the criminals (including Jesus) would be dead in time to be buried before sunset. Crucifixions could take several days (and the Romans commonly left the bodies on the cross to rot as a warning to others).

It was necessary to ensure the demise of the condemned, and the Jewish leaders ask Pilate "to have the legs broken and the bodies taken down" and buried. They would break their legs with a heavy mallet, speeding their death two ways: the physical shock to a system already severely weakened by scourging and six hours on the cross would often stop their heart; and the inability to push themselves up on the little seat for taking breaths would asphyxiate them. Death would usually come quickly.

The soldiers first break the legs of the two criminals on either side of Jesus (19:32), and according to Mark 15:33–34 this took place shortly after three in the afternoon, allowing for time to remove and bury the bodies before sundown. However, when they come to Jesus they realize this is not needed since he is already dead (19:33; these hardened soldiers were experts on death). Still, just to make absolutely certain, one of them reaches up and thrusts his spear into Jesus' side. This was not a gentle jab piercing the skin but a vicious thrust deep into his body, for it causes "a sudden flow of blood and water" (19:34).

Medical experts throughout history have speculated on what caused both blood and water to flow. Traditionally it has been thought Jesus' heart burst, but that is medically unlikely. Others have thought the spear pierced the heart (the blood) and the pericardial sac along with the abdomen, or pleural fluid gathered around the lung. We cannot know for certain. John is stressing here the reality of his death. There was enormous stress on Jesus' body, and the terrible nature of his death cannot be overstated.

There is also a great deal of discussion regarding the symbolic overtones of this scene, especially of the blood and water. Historically, the church fathers tended to see the water as baptism and the blood as the Eucharist (Augustine, Chrysostom), but this does not fit the themes of the Fourth Gospel as I see them. More likely is the blood as Jesus' sacrificial death and the water as the cleansing work of the Spirit. This would fit the themes developed in this Gospel. Further, John could be countering a docetic heresy (from the Greek *dokeō*, "to appear") of the type John combatted in 1 John. There, false teachers denied that the Messiah could be human and taught that he only appeared to be so (see 1 John 2:22–23; 4:2–4; 5:5–6). Such a Messiah could not die but would only appear to die. So John here wants his readers to realize that the royal Messiah had truly died.

In 19:35 John anchors the reality of Jesus' death with the blood and water in eyewitness testimony, namely his own. He wants his readers to recognize the absolute reliability of his account of Jesus' crucifixion. This is important for us as well, telling us the early church demanded as much historical accuracy as we do. This is paralleled in 21:24 ("we know that his testimony is true"), referring to the accuracy of his Gospel as a whole. Other important witnesses are Luke 1:1–4 (claiming eyewitness testimony behind that Gospel) and 2 Peter 1:16 (denying that Peter invented "cleverly devised stories" about the transfiguration). Clearly the early church claimed historical authenticity for its stories about Jesus. The purpose of this accurate testimony is "so that you also may believe," paralleling 20:31, "But these are written that you may believe." The goal of apologetics is not just theoretical accuracy but also spiritual conversion.

John concludes his narrative on Jesus' death with two further fulfillment citations (19:36–37). Since Jesus is already dead, the soldiers do not break his legs, and this fulfills the saying "Not one of his bones will be broken," found in three places—Exodus 12:46; Numbers 9:12 (both regarding the Passover lamb); and Psalm 34:20, stating God's protection of his righteous people. Since protection is not the thrust here, John more likely intended the first pair of passages, with Jesus the slain Passover lamb (1:29). He is the perfect Passover lamb (Num 9:12, no bone broken) sacrificed for forgiveness of sins.

The second fulfillment passage is the piercing of Jesus' side as fulfilling Zechariah 12:10, "They will look on the one they have pierced" (used also in Matt 24:30; Rev 1:7). The Zechariah passage speaks of apostate Israel looking on God's representative (the prophet or Messiah) and mourning for her unbelief. John hoped that Israel would once again repent of her apostasy, showing once more that Jesus died so the nations would repent and find forgiveness.

JESUS IS BURIED (19:38–42)

When Jesus was lifted up on the cross, he entered his glory (3:14; 8:28; 12:32), and this constituted the enthronement of the royal Messiah. So it is only fitting that he would be given a royal burial. The Davidic Messiah is buried as the true King of the Jews.

Joseph of Arimathea was a well-to-do Jew and a member of the Sanhedrin (Mark 15:43). As a Christ follower, he anxiously awaited the coming of the kingdom and had been opposed to the Sanhedrin's decision (Luke 23:51). We are told here that he was also "a disciple of Jesus, but secretly because he feared the Jewish leaders." In 12:42–43 John is critical of closet Christians, but here he is more positive, possibly hoping to use Joseph as an example to draw out other secret believers and help them take a public stance for Jesus. Joseph's was a step of real courage.

The Romans usually left the corpses to rot, especially those condemned for sedition, but the Jews had received permission to bury the crucified in a common grave outside the town. Pilate's granting permission to Joseph's request to "take [Jesus'] body away" (v. 39) would have been very unusual. Likely, he did so because he had been convinced of Jesus' innocence and was disgusted at the Jewish officials who had forced his hand, so he gave Joseph permission.

Only John tells us that Nicodemus, "the man who earlier had visited Jesus at night" (3:1–2), was there to assist Joseph in burying Jesus. It would have taken at least the two of them to transport Jesus from Golgotha to the tomb, and they may have also used the service of slaves, for handling the body themselves would have rendered them unclean for seven days and made it impossible for either of them to observe the Passover celebration.

Nicodemus had brought along a hundred *litrai*, or "about seventy-five pounds" (exactly 65.45 pounds), of a perfumed ointment made from "myrrh and aloes," to anoint the corpse. This was an extraordinary amount fit for a king. Myrrh was a fragrant resin used for embalming by the Egyptians. The Jews used a powder form mixed with the aloes, from aromatic sandalwood. The purpose of anointing was to counter the terrible odor emanating from the decaying body. (The Jews did not embalm and so had to bury corpses within twenty-four hours.)

The amount used here was quite unusual and very expensive, paralleling the extraordinary amount used to anoint Jesus at Bethany in 12:1–8. Mary at that time used one pound of perfume to anoint Jesus, and it was worth a year's wages. How much would this hundred pounds be worth? This results in a royal motif fitting the burial of a king. Consider the death of Herod the Great. There were 500 slaves carrying burial spices at his funeral (Josephus, *Antiquities* 17.199).

The spices are packed in and around the "strips of linen" (*othoniois*, long strips of cloth), which they wrap around Jesus' body (19:40). Some see a contradiction with Mark 15:46, with its reference to a *sindon*, a single long sheet of linen. However, several think the "sheets" here a generalizing plural for a single sheet. They would have packed the spices in with the cloth and covered the body in accordance with "Jewish burial customs."

Also in keeping with the royal atmosphere of the burial is the fact that "there was a garden, and in the garden was a new tomb" (19:41). John states it was "at the place where Jesus was crucified," meaning it was nearby. Undoubtedly it was owned by Joseph of Arimathea (stated clearly in the Gospel of Peter 24), who had just purchased it for his family (indicated they are recent arrivals in Jerusalem?), as it was "new." Its placement in a garden is a further indicator of his great wealth. He and Nicodemus give extraordinary gifts of opulence to bury Jesus with honor, Nicodemus with the spices and Joseph with the tomb. Both gifts became further "unconscious testimonies" (like Caiaphas in 11:50–52 and Pilate in 19:19), this time of Jesus as the royal Messiah.

This was a "new tomb, in which no one had ever been laid," undoubtedly dug into the hillside in keeping with common Jewish practice. The garden was likely a type of olive grove, using the same term as the garden where Jesus was arrested in 18:1. Later, Mary Magdalene will erroneously think Jesus is the gardener who tends it (20:15). There are Old Testament stories of kings buried in gardens (2 Kgs 21:18, 26; Neh 3:15–16 of David's tomb), further evidence that the imagery portrays a royal burial. In the same way the resurrection takes place in a garden, and there may well be Eden **typology** as the original garden where humankind was born now is re-created for the burial and resurrection of the quintessential Man, the heir of David and Son of God.

All this takes place on Friday, the "day of preparation" (19:42) for the traditional Passover, where now the final Passover celebration bringing salvation to sinful humankind has taken place. This will be the only tomb in all of history to hold a corpse for only three days, and the garden of death is soon to become the Garden of New Life.

————

More than any other Gospel, John demonstrates that this one who gave his life on the cross was the King not only of the Jews but over the human race, and he at the same time is also the atoning sacrifice who brings salvation to humanity. Truly the cross is the glory and exaltation of Jesus, but it also is the basis for the eternal glory we share with Jesus. Every part of the narration highlights Jesus' sovereign control. He doesn't just die as royal Davidic Messiah, he demonstrates a kingly resolve throughout by orchestrating every detail. The crucifixion was not an unfortunate accident.

There are five main scenes, and each adds part of the theological significance of the crucifixion. First, the inscription (vv. 19-22) tells all the world (written in every major language) that this one on the cross has now been enthroned as King of the Jews, the Davidic Messiah. As the passion predictions (3:14; 8:28; 12:32) have shown, the preexistent glory is seen in the exaltation of the cross—lifting up on the cross is lifting up into glory.

Second, the soldiers' dividing of Jesus' garments (vv. 23-24) could be stressing the unity of the church in the seamless robe but more likely emphasizes that the very details of Jesus' crucifixion were not only known by God but also guided by his hand to fulfill Old Testament prophecies. It may have seemed that the powers of evil were in charge that day, but they were not. God was in charge and guided even the smallest aspects of the event according to his predetermined plan.

Third, Jesus' giving his mother into the care of the Beloved Disciple (vv. 25-27) prepares the way for the forging of a new family, the messianic community of believers who are brought together and united in Jesus, the Son of God. The two stress the twofold fact that in Christ we all become members of the family of God and that we are brought into a new unity as brothers and sisters, mothers and fathers, in him.

Fourth, the death of Jesus (vv. 28-30) yields two emphases: (1) Jesus does not just die, he surrenders his spirit. This sovereign control is very important for us, for it is also exercised on our behalf. (2) He dies as the Passover Lamb to take away sin. The salvation of every single one of us is tied completely to his atoning death on the cross.

Fifth, the piercing of Jesus' side releasing the flow of blood and water (vv. 31–37) has several aspects to it. It stresses the reality and horror of his death, showing the deep love of both the Father and Son that they would be willing to go through all this for us. There are probably symbolic overtones as well, stressing the atoning sacrifice of Christ (the blood) and the cleansing of the Spirit (the water). Further, John wants to stress the authenticity of these details, highlighting his accurate eyewitness testimony. Finally, two final fulfillment quotations show once again that God prepared for everything that happened long before, and it happened entirely according to his plan.

Finally, the burial of Jesus (vv. 38–42) is a beautifully crafted narrative of the royal burial of the true King of the Jews. Three elements bring out the royal implications—the huge amount of perfumed ointment that anointed Jesus' corpse, the new tomb where no one had ever been laid, and the garden in which the tomb was placed. The result is the sumptuous burial of the king of the ages. The true Davidic Messiah is entombed, but only for three days, for the garden will become the new Eden, harbinger of the resurrection of Jesus as the firstfruits of all God's people.

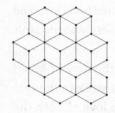

RESURRECTION, PART 1: JERUSALEM APPEARANCES

(20:1–31)

When Jesus cried "It is finished" as he surrendered his spirit to God, he was referring to his earthly life and mission. If he were speaking in salvation-historical terms, he would have cried, "It is beginning!" True life had been inaugurated on the cross, and its primary symbol, in fact its firstfruits (1 Cor 15:20, 23), was to take place about thirty-six hours later at dawn on the "special Sunday" of Passover week, when Jesus' eternal spirit entered his glorified body at his resurrection from the dead. Jesus had prophesied, "Destroy this temple, and I will raise it again in three days"¹ (2:19). That is now to come to pass and prove that he is indeed the glorified Lord.

Critical scholars have spent enormous effort and creativity doubting the historical trustworthiness of these accounts and reconstructing new scenarios to explain how the early church could have come up with such outlandish stories to believe. Several

---

1. In reality, Jesus died at three in the afternoon on Friday and was raised from the dead at about six Sunday morning, a total of thirty-nine hours. However, the "three days" was an idiom that was perfectly acceptable in Semitic culture, for it consisted of parts of Friday, Saturday, and Sunday.

theories have appeared through the centuries to explain what "really happened":

1. The conspiracy theory—The Jews spread the rumor that the disciples stole the body and made up a story of the resurrection (Matt 28:11-15). Yet the disciples would hardly be willing to die for a lie they created.

2. The political theory—H. S. Reimarus in the eighteenth century said the disciples were political opportunists (like Jesus) and made up the resurrection story to gain fame and fortune. But again, would they be willing to die for such a fabrication?

3. The swoon theory—The rationalists of the nineteenth century believed that Jesus fell into a dead faint (almost literally) on the cross, was mistakenly placed in a tomb, then revived and snuck away. But the Romans were experts at death and would never have made such a juvenile error. Nor would it have turned into a resurrection story.

4. The mythical view—Early Christians followed Greco-Roman precedent and created supernatural mythical stories of Jesus as a demigod who came back from the dead. However, no myths or legends have ever developed so quickly. One area of scholarly consensus is that on Paul's first visit with the Jerusalem leaders (Gal 1:18-20) he received this creedal set of truths about Jesus' death and resurrection, and as we can see, it was highly organized and full. This means that, for example, the creedal list of 1 Corinthians 15:3-8 was fully formed within three to five years of the event itself, and it radically differs from mythical patterns.

5. The subjective vision theory—Several have thought early leaders like Peter or John had dreams that they interpreted as reality. But Jesus appeared to unbelievers (like James and Paul) and to five hundred at once (1 Cor 15:6). This kind of mass hallucination is very unlikely.

6. The objective vision theory—Some believe these were actual visions sent from God, but it is very hard to see why God would do this and not have Jesus rise from the dead. Why just portray a vision as if it were real when God can just as easily accomplish the real thing?

In short, the most likely view is to understand the appearances as events that actually took place in history. The only true reason for doubting these stories is a prior belief that there is no supernatural realm and no God who has created this world. If we believe in the God of the Bible, there is no doubt that he has truly done these things. Jesus indeed did rise from the dead and appear to his disciples. And we will join him when we die and share his resurrection.

When we place the four Gospel accounts of the resurrection side by side, we almost wonder if these might be separate stories, the details differ so extensively. However, we need to understand certain facts: First, Jesus appeared to his followers over a forty-day period between Passover and Pentecost (Acts 1:3), and in all this time there are a total of ten appearances listed. It is doubtful that Jesus only came to them once every four days, and more likely that several appearances are not mentioned in the accounts. Each writer carefully chose which stories to tell. Second, each writer used these stories to sum up the themes of his particular Gospel and so was very selective in what he covered. They are so different because they had very different theological themes they were trying to culminate in their appearance narratives.

John has the most detailed narrative of any of the four. It is commonly believed his stories are theological and not historical, and that they are the furthest removed from the events themselves. However, I have tried to show throughout this commentary that John's account may well be the most history-driven of the four. He is the only one of the writers to include both Jerusalem appearances (ch. 20, with Luke) and Galilee appearances (ch. 21, with Matthew). His is the most comprehensive coverage. Chapter 20 contains the Jerusalem appearances as they take place that first week while the disciples remain in Jerusalem for the Passover and Feast of Unleavened Bread. Chapter 21 is a selection from the appearances in Galilee after they return home to that province.

John 20 is a beautifully dramatic portrayal of the problem of faith. There are four vignettes, and in each the problem of faith gets greater, moving from the Beloved Disciple's natural faith to Mary's sorrow, the disciples' fear, and Thomas's doubt. Each is a more severe problem, and in each case Jesus meets their need head-on, turns their life around, and the results become greater in each instance. The witness of the Christ followers becomes greater and greater as they attest to the reality of their risen Lord. This is an account of the overcoming of the barriers to faith via the presence of the risen Lord and of the resultant transformation of the disciples from defeated, crestfallen followers to victorious spiritual giants who are about to change the world.

THE DISCIPLES RACE TO THE EMPTY TOMB (20:1-10)

THE DILEMMA OF THE MISSING BODY (20:1-2)

In the **Synoptics**, a group of women start out just before dawn to anoint Jesus' corpse with no expectations stemming from his passion predictions. They see the stone rolled away and angel(s) at the tomb. John centers on one of the women (no contradiction), Mary Magdalene, a formerly demon-possessed woman who became a patron of the apostolic band (Luke 8:1-3) and a leader among the women (her name is usually first). He is aware of the larger story (evidenced in the "we" of 20:2) but centers only on Mary for dramatic purposes.

When Mary Magdalene arrives, she first sees "that the stone had been removed from the entrance" and immediately jumps to the conclusion that his body has been taken, either by grave robbers or by the Jews themselves. Grave robbery was a crime common enough to cause the emperor Claudius to make it a capital crime meriting the death penalty. So she leaves the group of women and runs back to the disciples in the upper room. Finding Simon Peter and the Beloved Disciple, she exclaims in horror, "They have taken the Lord out of the tomb, and we don't know where they have put him." She is hardly thinking straight and is filled with grief.

THE RACE TO THE TOMB (20:3–4)

This is a detail unique to John, but it is corroborated in Luke 24:12 (Peter's visit to the tomb and his doubt) and 24:24 (more than one "companion" at the tomb). Moreover, the vivid, realistic details fit the recollections of an "eyewitness" (19:35). The two disciples like Mary run full-blown to the tomb with both excitement and anxiety over what they may find. The mention of the Beloved Disciple outrunning Peter and reaching the tomb first has been seen as rivalry between the two (or between Jewish and Gentile Christianity, as some have hypothesized), but both of them are positive figures in the story. While John arrives first, Peter enters the tomb first. The traditional explanation fits well—the Beloved Disciple was simply younger and faster. The point in both cases is their overriding concern for Jesus and what happened to his body.

THE ENTRY INTO THE TOMB AND APOLOGETICS (20:5–7)

The first emphasis is apologetic, as the details in the tomb and the reactions of the two men center on the historical truth that Jesus has indeed risen from the dead. The Beloved Disciple is reluctant to enter but instead kneels down (the entrance would be about three and a half feet high) and looks into the tomb, seeing "the strips of linen lying there" (20:5). If grave robbers had come, they would never have left the expensive linen wrappings or spices lying there. Understanding begins to dawn on him.

Simon Peter arrives second but does not hesitate and goes right into the tomb, seeing not just the linen wrappings but also "the cloth that had been wrapped around Jesus' head" (20:7). This cloth is neatly "still lying in its place, separate from the linen." It is not visible until Peter has entered the tomb. The emphasis in this story is not on the rivalry or the race but on what is inside the tomb, the details of the grave clothes. Specifically, it is both the strips of linen and the face cloth that John stresses, and both are neatly placed by themselves, proving that grave robbers were not involved and strongly suggesting that the risen Lord himself had taken care of them quite neatly. This is evidence of an apologetic purpose in this story—John is proving that the resurrection truly took place.

Jesus' body would have been placed on a shelf to the right or left of the entrance with his head toward the entrance wall (so one could not see the grave clothes from the entrance). The graphic details point first to eyewitness reminiscence and second to theological emphases. The developing picture in 20:5-7 shows that the grave clothes are in the same position on the shelf that they were when Jesus' corpse was lying there, perhaps even retaining some of their shape due to the great amount of spices (compare Lazarus in 11:44). It is likely written to suggest that Jesus came to life, passed through the garments, and then laid all the grave clothes in their proper place. Grave robbers would never be so neat. For this reason it is becoming fairly common to label this the seventh sign-miracle of John's Gospel, with two official witnesses (Deut 19:15) along with the women whom God was also labeling witnesses of the resurrection.[2]

SEEING AND BELIEVING (20:8-9)

John now enters the tomb, and we are told simply that he "saw and believed." The linen wrappings and face cloth were enough to convince him that Jesus had truly risen. The second verb changes to the imperfect tense and is best translated "began to believe." This was an immense step, and he began the journey. Still, the conjunction of seeing with believing is the core of this section, and it points to a deep-seated faith that is beginning to develop. This is

---

2. See comments on 2:19.

much more than simply believing that Mary was right about the body taken from the tomb (as Augustine said) but encompasses the growing realization that Jesus was risen. The emphasis on seeing and believing is a lifelong journey and culminates the theme on faith-decision in this Gospel.

In verse 9 John explains that "they still did not understand from Scripture that Jesus had to rise from the dead." This does not mean that the Beloved Disciple had not yet come to this belief but rather that he did so in spite of the fact that for him his faith was not yet anchored in Scripture. It was the physical evidence from the empty tomb that led him to this belief (showing the value of apologetics). Belief is the primary theme of the chapter (20:25, 29, 31), and seeing the empty tomb was enough for John. For him, seeing is truly believing.

THE AFTERMATH (20:10)

Peter according to Luke 24:12 returned to Jerusalem confused and troubled. One would expect the Beloved Disciple to go to him and share his newfound understanding that Jesus was risen from the dead. One would think too that he would put his arms around the weeping Mary Magdalene (20:11) and tell her why she needn't grieve. But he does neither. This is a very anticlimactic ending to the first episode, for John reached the highest level of faith of the four and did nothing with it but simply "went back to where they were staying" (the upper room) with Peter. In short, he finds faith and then does nothing with it.

Several see in this an emphasis on the inadequacy of his faith, but that is not the case. It is not presented here as deficient. I think he was so filled with awe (remember, he did not enter the tomb at first either) that he was thunderstruck and couldn't speak for a while. In this there is a contrast with Mary, who did not attain his level of faith but with the risen Lord's help did so much more with it. His new faith virtually had no results.

MARY ENCOUNTERS THE RISEN LORD (20:11-18)

We now return to the "garden" that was introduced in 18:1, 26, and to the Eden imagery noted there. It is in the new re-created Eden that Jesus makes his first resurrection appearance and helps Mary Magdalene to overcome her grief and sorrow. The scene begins as the two disciples return to the upper room. Mary remains at the tomb, still weeping copiously, thinking grave robbers have stolen Jesus' body. Her deep love for Jesus has turned to sorrow, and as we will see, it has virtually blinded her to everything around her. It may also be the case that she had just arrived as the two were leaving and realizes she is now alone and needs someone to help her find and return the body to its rightful place.

MARY AND THE ANGELS (20:11-13)

With the tears pouring down her face, Mary "bent over to look into the tomb" (v. 11, echoing the action of the beloved disciple in verse 5). As she is looking, however, she is treated to a supernatural event quite unlike that experienced by the other two. She sees inside the tomb "two angels in white, seated where Jesus' body had been, one at the head and the other at the foot" (v. 12). They had not been there earlier, and it appears God has taken a special interest in her and sent two messengers to comfort her. Whenever angels appear in Scripture, it signifies heaven is deeply involved in the event.

The tombs for wealthy families dug into hillsides would usually have a small opening three to three and a half feet in size with a round four-plus-foot stone shaped like a wheel that slides into a groove to plug the hole. Inside would be a stone bench along the wall for preparing the body and burial grooves six by two feet dug into the wall to eventually hold the body. On the floor in front of the bench would be a "bone box" in which the skeleton would be placed after the body had thoroughly decomposed. The burial clothes are likely lying between the two angels who are sitting on either end of the bench.

There are two discrepancies regarding the angels in the four accounts: (1) John and Luke have two while Mark and Matthew have one; and (2) in Matthew and John they are angels while in Mark and Luke they are men. However, both are quite common changes, and neither is actually a contradiction. Angels are often described as men, for they always take human form when appearing on earth. Moreover, it is quite common in Gospel narratives to present a group by describing one member of the group for dramatic purposes.

So both variations are simply for dramatic effect. John has two angels as official witnesses (Deut 19:15) of the resurrection event. Moreover, this is a separate event than in Mark. The first appearance was to the group of women in Mark in order to commission them as witnesses. This here is a second appearance of the two angels a short time later to Mary alone, and their purpose is to witness to her of the reality of the resurrection. Some suggest an interesting possibility that their sitting at the head and the foot of the burial bench is intended to symbolize the golden cherubim at the two ends of the mercy seat of the ark of the covenant (Exod 25:18–19). This would then be a further emphasis on the atoning sacrifice of Christ. The glorified Christ has accomplished his purpose, and redemption is now available for humankind. God wants to prepare the women to be the official witnesses of the resurrection event.

Their question (20:13) sounds at first like an attempt to comfort her: "Woman, why are you crying?" Jesus addresses his mother as "woman" in 2:4; 19:26; and of two others in 4:21 and 8:10. In reality, it leads here into a rebuke similar to Mark 16:6, that the women have failed to understand the passion predictions and are still looking for a corpse. There should no longer be tears unless they are tears of joy. The tomb has become a vehicle for life, not death, but she cannot make the switch.

The problem is quite clear in her response. She pays no attention to the angels, fails to notice the significance of their position on the bench, and is completely consumed by grief. Her eyes are so blinded by her tears that she fails to recognize the heavenly visitors. In her numbed state she repeats what she said earlier to Peter and John in 20:2, "They [the grave robbers] have taken my Lord away, and I don't know where they have put him." Her lack of spiritual awareness and even of physical awareness is complete. Her weeping shows her doubt and ignorance in total contrast with the faith and developing realization of the Beloved Disciple in 20:8.

JESUS AND MARY (20:14–15)

Mary has entirely missed the first supernatural portent, the presence of the angels in the tomb. Her sorrow has overwhelmed her. So the risen Lord makes his first appearance and comes to her. But again her blindness caused by grief intervenes and keeps her from perceiving the truth. She believes he is nothing but the gardener and hopes he might have seen what happened.

Note the progression of scenes—she turns around from the tomb, sees Jesus standing beside her, completely fails to recognize her Lord, and thinks he is the gardener (19:41, this is a garden in the olive grove). The disciples frequently fail to recognize Jesus when he appears (21:4; Matt 28:17; Luke 24:16), probably due to the ravages of the crucifixion on his physical appearance. This points to their lack of expectation and spiritual perception, and Mary falls into this category.

For the third time (20:2, 13), she repeats her litany of misunderstanding (20:15). First, Jesus continues the rebuke of the angels ("Woman, why are you crying?"), except now there is all the more reason to rejoice, for the risen Lord himself is standing beside her. So he adds, "Who are you looking for?" probably to wake her up to her foolishness.

Instead, she looks right at him and thinks that as the gardener, he may have been in on the plot, asking, "Sir, if you have carried him away, tell me where you have put him, and I will get him." God has now sent two angels and the risen Lord himself, and still her sorrow is so deeply entrenched that nothing will remove the wall of blindness to reality. She may be hoping that Joseph of Arimathea had his gardener and other servants move the body for some reason, but all her thoughts are moving in the completely wrong direction. There is a certain irony in this, for Jesus is indeed the Gardener of the new Eden (see Rev 22:1–5) and is preparing a place for her (and us) in that final Garden. God is the Gardener in 15:1, and the risen Jesus is here. But she realizes none of this and remains totally defeated by her grief.

THE RESOLUTION AND TURNAROUND (20:16–18)

It is time for Jesus himself to take over. The solution could not be simpler. Jesus encounters Mary right in the midst of her grief-stricken blindness and reveals himself to her simply by calling out her name, "Mary." He is the Good Shepherd who "calls his own sheep by name," with the result that they "follow him because they know his voice" (10:3–4). This finally breaks through her barriers.

Mary indeed does recognize the voice and responds from the depth of her being in her mother tongue, Aramaic, with "Rabboni" ("my Rabbi"), which the evangelist explains for the readers as meaning, "Teacher!" This is a wonderful turnaround. But at the same time she is clinging to the old earthly relationship of rabbi-teacher, and the risen Lord is bringing a new age and set of relationships with him.

So the risen Lord now spells out what constitutes this new heavenly arrangement. He begins with the switch from teacher to family mode of relationships: "Go instead to my brothers." There are two steps to this profound change, first from disciple to friend (15:15) and now from friend to brother. As in Romans 8:14–17, at conversion God becomes our Abba, our heavenly Father, and we become his children and brothers or sisters of one another. Jesus becomes our brother and coheir (Rom 8:17).

The next part is where the difficulties lie. Jesus provides the reason for the salvation-historical switch: "Do not hold on to me, for I have not yet ascended to the Father. Go instead to my brothers and tell them, 'I am ascending to my Father and your Father, to my God and your God.'" There seems to be a surface contradiction between "I have not yet ascended" in 17a and "I am ascending" in 17b. Some have taken these literally and think Jesus doesn't want to be touched because he has risen but hasn't yet ascended to heaven. This is unlikely because later he does ask Thomas to touch him (20:27), and the ascension is actually not narrated in John. Others think that Jesus' ascension to his Father takes place between verse 17 and 27, so that by the Thomas episode Jesus has gone to heaven. Yet that doesn't make a lot of sense, for an event that important would not go unreported.

More likely, we should take this metaphorically. Mary in her excitement and worship falls down and grasps his feet (as the women do in Matt 28:9), but Jesus needs to correct her mistaken desire to return to the old set of relationships. This is a time for joy and the beginning of an entirely new era. Jesus rejoices in her love but wants them to move on and so says in effect, "Stop clinging to me" (NIV: "do not hold on to me"). The Greek for "hold on" or "cling" (*haptou*) also means "Don't touch me," indicating some physical contact. Jesus builds on this physical touch as a means to get across his message and tell her to stop clinging to the previous rabbi-disciple relationship, for those were earthly in force, and the heavenly or spiritual realm is now central. They are now entering a new era, the age of the Spirit, and a new set of family relationships. So Mary has to let Jesus go and accept his presence via the Spirit in this new realm of reality.

So Jesus is saying that he ascended to his Father at his resurrection, but this ascension is in transition during his appearances and will not culminate until his physical ascension at the end of the forty days (Acts 1:3, 9–11). So in the meantime he *is in the process* of ascending (after each appearance) but *has not yet* completed that process. Each appearance is a return to earth from heaven, and during this transition time of the appearances, Mary must yield to yield to all the joyous truths she is about to discover. She and the disciples are in an interim period, needing to forego the old earthly patterns and allow the new realities (primarily the presence of the Spirit) to take hold. So Jesus' appearances were temporary visitations from heaven, consummated in the final *ascension* of Luke 24 and Acts 1.

In the meantime, Mary has the glorious privilege of being the first ambassador of the resurrection tidings! God could have chosen Peter or John, who was the first to see and believe (20:8). But he deliberately chose Mary, and she ushered in the new age. It was to her that the exalted Jesus revealed the new family relationship that meant the disciples have now become friends (15:15) and then "brothers" (20:17), and she was the first to be told the wondrous truth of Jesus' resurrection and ascension to the Father. The deliberate "my ... your" language elevates the Christ followers to a place alongside the Son, stressing Jesus' unique status as "the Son of God" and then the new status of his disciples as "sons of God" in him. The crucifixion as "glory" culminates in the glorious ascension.

So Mary accepts her commission and takes the good news of the resurrection back to the disciples (20:18). The amazing truth is that God chose not Peter or John, the first to see and believe, but Mary to be the first herald of the resurrection tidings. She is the first to be privileged to see the risen Lord, so she goes back to the upper room and tells the disciples, "I have seen the Lord!" Note the progression of titles and how they demonstrate her growing understanding—from "Sir" (v. 15) to "Rabboni" (v. 16) and then "Lord" (v. 18). Her faith grows to full maturity as a resurrection faith.

JESUS APPEARS TO THE DISCIPLES (20:19–23)

If sorrow brought Mary's level of faith low, the ten disciples' fear (Judas was gone and Thomas was absent, 20:24) removes their faith entirely from the equation. It is as if they have no faith; they are too busy looking out for number one. On the evening of the third day after the crucifixion (Friday to Sunday) they are still cowering behind closed doors, afraid they might be arrested and suffer Jesus' fate.

Picture the scene. The doors are locked and the windows probably shuttered, with them quaking lest they be seen and recognized. They refused to accept the witness of Mary and the other women that they had seen the risen Lord, and John likely is still saying nothing. Out of the gloom (both physical and spiritual gloom), suddenly "Jesus came and stood among them." Another miracle has just transpired. As Jesus passed through his grave clothes, he now passed through locked doors. Their failure was every bit as great as Peter's. He denied Jesus three times (18:15-18, 25-27), but he was the only one with the courage to follow Jesus into the high priest's courtyard, while they had deserted him completely, running for their lives, and remained holed up throughout his death and burial. If anyone deserved rebuke, it would be them.

Instead, Jesus stands in their midst (20:19b) and says these wonderful words, "Peace be with you!" There is double meaning here. On one level it is a simple greeting, but on the deeper level (the main one here) Jesus is offering them his messianic peace, fulfilling his own promise of **eschatological** peace (14:27; 16:33) in keeping with Isaiah 9:6; 52:7.

Mary's low level of faith needed the Good Shepherd to call her by name, with his voice overcoming her sorrow. The disciples need more, and Jesus once again accommodates that need. He appeals to their sight, showing "them his hands and side" (20:20). Jesus in so doing proves both that he is the Lord who walked with them as their Messiah and that he is indeed risen from the dead. As Peter and the Beloved Disciple needed to see the grave clothes in the tomb (vv. 5-7), so the ten now need to see Jesus' wounds to realize he is everything he said he was.

At this moment, messianic joy (16:20-22) is added to their messianic peace. They now know the sacrificial Lamb has become the risen Lord, the greatest truth this world will ever know. The cross and the empty tomb are a single event in salvation history, and life is anchored in death.

The results are spectacular. Mary was given a mission as messianic herald; and the disciples become part of the very mission of Jesus to the world in verses 21–23. Note the progression of the mission theology in the Gospel of John. God loved the world so much that he devised a plan of salvation to bring these rebellious humans to him. He then "sent" Jesus as his *shaliach* or representative, making him part of that divine mission to the world (3:17; 5:23, 30; 8:16, 18). Next the Father and the Son sent the Spirit to the world (18:8–11). Finally, the three, the Triune Godhead, sent their followers to the world and brought them into the divine plan to redeem sinful humankind. So mission proceeds from Father to Son to Spirit to the church, all bringing salvation to the world.

The mission of each one in the drama is ongoing. Behind the sending is the authorizing, as the Father empowers the Son, Father and Son empower the Spirit, and the Trinity pours its power into us as we obey our commission to take God's salvation to the nations. So as we go out, we are filled with the empowering presence of the Godhead. Most of you readers feel inadequate. Not many of us are great speakers or natural-born leaders. We are not filled with charisma so that people just want to be in our presence. So what! What we are is filled with the Spirit. What we are is called to ministry, and God has made us exactly as he wants us to be. In each of us God has placed seeds of greatness, and all we have to do to unlock this power is surrender totally to Christ and the Spirit. The truth is that none of us should ever feel inferior again.

Let's look at the wonderful progression of thought in 20:21–23. Jesus begins by repeating "Peace be with you" from verse 19, probably because the disciples were in shock and were not there yet. To relinquish control to God and move out courageously in mission, we must bask in God's peace. Jesus then passes on his commission and authority from his Father to the disciples, "As the Father has sent me, I am sending you." Over thirty times John describes

RESURRECTION, PART 1: JERUSALEM APPEARANCES   467

Jesus as "sent" by God (e.g., 3:17; 5:23, 30; 8:16, 18). The program is complete with the sending of Christ's followers as the gospel proceeds from Jesus to the Spirit to the disciples and then from all to the world.

There is no way the finite believers could fulfill their mission in their own strength, so Jesus makes that power available by breathing on them and saying, "Receive the Holy Spirit" (20:22). A major theme in the Farewell Discourse is Jesus' promise to send the Spirit/Paraclete (14:16–17, 26; 15:26; 16:7), who would bring God's strength into the equation and enable them to become "sent ones." The idea of Jesus "breathing" on them alludes to God's breathing life into Adam at creation (Gen 2:7; see also Ezek 37:9; 1 Cor 15:45). In the new creation (John 1:3–4) life is manifest not only in eternal life but also in the gift of the Spirit. So the church as filled with the Spirit is a manifestation of this new creation. God gave the Spirit "without limit" to Jesus (3:34); Jesus gave the Samaritan woman "living water" (4:10, 14) and poured out the Spirit into his followers (7:37–39), who now are filled with the Spirit for mission.

There has been a great deal of debate over the connection of this giving of the Spirit to the Pentecost event of Acts 2. (1) Some simply see contradictory traditions and say they cannot be reconciled. But this is not necessary, for the other options provide satisfactory solutions. (2) A few think that *pneuma* (without the definite article) here refers to an impersonal power rather than the personal Spirit, but in the New Testament more than half the time the Holy Spirit does not have the article. (3) Many believe there is only one giving of the Spirit (Acts 2), and so this passage contains a promise of that future event rather than the actual sending of the Spirit, in effect translating verse 22, "You are going to receive the Spirit." This translation is not possible grammatically (it is an aorist imperative rather than a present-tense verb), though as a theological construct it may be possible that the future aspect is uppermost. It is definitely a command, and I am not satisfied with this future understanding.

I prefer to side with those who see (4) a two-stage sending of the Spirit, with this constituting a private infilling of the disciples on the first day of Jesus' resurrection appearances and then Acts 2 becoming a public empowering by the Spirit and the launching of the church's mission on the day of Pentecost.

Jesus spells out the authority for this mission in 20:23. With the reception of the Spirit, the disciples become God's agents or envoys alongside Jesus. With this Christ bestows on them his authority: "If you forgive anyone's sins, their sins are forgiven; if you do not forgive them, they are not forgiven." This authority to forgive and retain sins is closely connected to Matthew 16:19 and 18:18, when Jesus gives the disciples "the keys of the kingdom" and tells them, "Whatever you bind on earth will be bound in heaven, and whatever you loose on earth will be loosed in heaven." Both in Matthew and here the actual forgiveness of sins is God's purview (these are divine passives pointing to God), and the believers are God's emissaries.[3] We, the church, carry on the work of Jesus. He came to save, and in bringing salvation also became eschatological Judge. We participate in that mission and carry his authority as we go out.

JESUS SPEAKS WITH THOMAS (20:24–29)

This is the second Sunday after Jesus' resurrection, and his first two appearances were on this day. No wonder it became "the Lord's Day" (Rev 1:10) and the first day of the week in the Christian calendar. If Mary's sorrow crippled her faith and the disciples' fear lowered their faith even further, then Thomas's cynicism virtually destroyed his faith, for he flatly refuses to believe the witness of his fellow disciples. He was absent at Jesus' appearance in verses 19–23; and when the others tell him, "We have seen the Lord" (verse

---

3. A good example is the Catholic doctrine of the confession booth, based on this verse and Matt 16:19. Yet two of the greatest Jesuit scholars, Raymond Brown and Rudolf Schnackenburg in their John commentaries, admit that this is not speaking of the priest in the confession booth but the authority of the church in mission and proclaiming the gospel.

25), he is filled with skepticism and replies, "Unless I see the nail marks in his hands and put my finger where the nails were, and put my hand into his side, I will not believe." In a sense Thomas has become a philosophy major demanding final empirical proof before he will consider if it's true. He isn't satisfied with John's faith, who "saw and believed" (20:8), he demands to be able to *touch* the wounds. This is even worse than the official at Capernaum to whom Jesus said, "Unless you people see signs and wonders, you will never believe" (4:48).

He is not just "doubting Thomas"; he is cynical, unbelieving Thomas. However, Jesus responds with every bit as much mercy and understanding as he did with Mary and the other disciples. Thomas needs more help and has further to go, but Jesus meets his needs just as they are and lifts him up to understanding. Mary needed the *voice* of the Good Shepherd; the disciples needed to *see* Jesus' wounds and know it was truly him; Thomas needs to *touch* those self-same wounds. Jesus meets those needs right where they are and turns his life around.

Even eight days later, at the end of the Passover celebration, they are still hiding behind closed doors, afraid of being arrested. They have stayed for the weeklong Festival of Unleavened Bread, which was Jewish tradition and part of the Passover celebration. Can you imagine this scene! For the third time (after 20:19, 21) Jesus suddenly appears through locked doors and offers them his messianic peace. He accommodates Thomas's demands and says, "Put your finger here; see my hands. Reach out your hand and put it into my side" (v. 27). We can picture Jesus pulling back his robe to show his gaping wounds.

We don't know if Thomas actually did so, but he was undoubtedly on his knees, tears coursing down his face, awe consuming him. Jesus then adds, "Stop doubting and believe," literally, "Be not unbelieving [*apistos*] but believing [*pistos*]." His level of faith was the lowest of them all, but Jesus calls him back from the abyss. He has not committed apostasy and become an unbeliever, but he has refused to exercise faith in the witness of others.

Thomas rises to the challenge and responds by uttering one of the great confessions of history, "My Lord and my God" (v. 28). These words have become the fitting climax and theological core of the Fourth Gospel. While some have tried to turn Thomas's words into a mere part of the developing understanding of the disciples, they are so much more. With 1:1 ("The Word was God") this Gospel is framed by statements of Jesus' deity. It is an astounding leap of faith and understanding, as Thomas had spent the last seven days doubting Jesus' resurrection and now all of a sudden affirms that he is the one and only God. This shows a remarkable depth. Many critics refuse to believe it could have happened, thinking an affirmation of Jesus' deity was years away for the early church. Yet it actually makes sense logically, for all the while Thomas was saying, "I won't believe unless ..." he was also thinking, "What if?" By the time Jesus appeared to him, he had carefully thought through the implications and was ready.

The progression of Thomas's understanding makes a lot of sense. If Jesus had truly risen from the dead, then everything he had taught about himself and the Father was correct, for instance, "I and the Father are one" (10:30) and all of the "I am" sayings. The origin of this deep confession is most likely these teachings combined with the Old Testament confession of Yahweh as Lord God (2 Kgs 19:19; Isa 26:13; Rev 4:11).

Jesus in verse 29 comments on the confession and tries to encourage future believers. Some take this as a question ("Do you believe because you have seen me?"), which has the effect of emphasizing Thomas's failure. However, most rightly recognize it as a statement, which then puts the stress on the second half of the verse. Thomas does find faith but has to "see" in order to "believe." That was positive with the Beloved Disciple (20:8) but is a mild rebuke with Thomas because he rejected the witness of his fellow disciples. Future converts will not have that luxury, for the risen Lord will no longer be present. So Jesus gives them a special blessing from God for finding faith without the incredible experience of physically seeing the risen Lord.

"Blessed" (*makarioi*) introduces the second beatitude in John (with 13:17). As in the beatitudes of Matthew 5:3–12, this means that God pours out his blessings in a special way on those who find faith even when they have no opportunity to "see" and walk with Jesus. In this chapter all four who have been blessed by resurrection appearances have been privileged to "see" Jesus (verses 8, 18, 20, 27), but in the future that will no longer be possible. Their faith will be centered on the Good News, and this is along with the deity of Christ the other primary theme of the Fourth Gospel— the encounter with God in Jesus confronts the seeker and forces a faith-decision, and the result of that decision is life in all its richness. The truth of 1 Peter 1:8–9 is the experience of us all: "Though you have not seen him, you love him; and even though you do not see him now, you believe in him and are filled with an inexpressible and glorious joy, for you are receiving the end result of your faith, the salvation of your souls."

JOHN SHARES THE PURPOSE OF HIS GOSPEL (20:30–31)

The NIV does not translate the particles that introduce this verse (*men oun*) and mean "therefore, so," making these verses an inferential conclusion either to the Thomas episode or (more likely) to the chapter as a whole. John wants us to know that he has been very selective in choosing the sign-miracles he has included first in this chapter (the appearances as "signs," see intro to 2:1–12) and in his Gospel as a whole. He knew of "many other signs" that Jesus had done "in the presence of his disciples, which are not recorded in this book." There were too many to record (see also 21:25), but there were many others he could have used. In other words, there are countless reasons to see and believe (20:8, 29). In so doing, John is telling us that the death and resurrection of Jesus (as a single event in salvation history) is the greatest sign-miracle of them all.

The purpose of telling about these miraculous signs (indeed, of the Fourth Gospel as a whole) is clear: "that you may believe." There is a text-critical issue as to whether "believe" is aorist tense (with $\aleph^2$ A C D W) or present tense ($\mathfrak{P}^{66}$ $\aleph^*$ B 0250). The two options have become the basis of an extensive debate as to whether John was written to evangelize nonbelievers (aorist "believe" for a crisis conversion) or to strengthen believers (present "believe" for ongoing belief). Most likely the aorist tense has slightly stronger manuscript evidence, but in actuality either tense can fit either option. Furthermore, John was written both to evangelize the lost and to strengthen the saints, and it is a false debate. I doubt that either purpose was more important than the other for John, and John wrote with both purposes equally in mind.

This Gospel has always been about faith and the life of belief that results from it. This is the very essence of why God created the world and humanity. When God's creation fell into sin, his plan of salvation was initiated. He "gave his one and only Son" so that people could "believe in him" and "not perish but have eternal life" (3:16). John's two primary titles for Jesus here sum up the focus of faith: "that Jesus is the Messiah, the Son of God." The thrust here encompasses both the Davidic and Mosaic messiahs from the Davidic covenant of 2 Sam 7:5–16 and the prophet like Moses of Deut 18:15. The Son of God title refers both to the special Father-Son relationship so central to this Gospel and to Jesus' complete deity (1:1, 18; 10:30; 20:28).

Jesus was "sent" by his Father as the divine agent (3:17; 11:42; 16:27; 17:8), and the result of the Father-Son unity is that those who believe "may have life in his name." Life in this Gospel is the result of the faith-decision of the sinner who responds to Jesus and the Spirit with belief, and then for the believer "life" becomes a present possession as they place themselves under the power of Jesus and the empowering presence of the Spirit. Once more, John's Gospel is intended for both believer and unbeliever.

———

This is a remarkably well-written and carefully chosen drama encompassing both the reality of Jesus' resurrection and the transformation of the disciples' faith as they in four steps are transfigured from defeated cowards to victorious heralds of the new age. However low are faith is, the risen Lord meets it right where it is, turns our life around, and transforms us into something we never thought we could be!

The first step takes place with the race to the tomb (vv. 1–10). Peter and the Beloved Disciple, after Mary tells them Jesus' body has been removed from the tomb, race to it. Upon arriving, they observe the clothes folded neatly, and the Beloved Disciple begins to realize what has happened. This could not be grave robbers but must be the Lord risen from the dead. He sees and believes. His is a natural faith, but the results are disappointing. From the highest level of faith, he does little with it and tells no one (probably rendered speechless with awe) but goes back with puzzled Peter.

The second step centers on Mary (vv. 11–18), whose faith has been clouded by her sorrow at the missing body. She represents those of us whose difficult trials have left us so discouraged that we can do little. The level of her spiritual blindness is startling. God sends two angels to console her, and all of heaven is calling to her to realize the stupendous truth that has just happened. But she is completely consumed by grief and does not even respond to the supernatural manifestations. This continues even when confronted by Jesus, as she thinks he is the gardener. (He is, but it is the new Eden that has come.)

The Beloved Disciple needed no help in coming to faith, but Mary does. She needs the voice of the Good Shepherd calling her by name and revealing himself to her. This then transforms her, and she is able to accomplish what the Beloved Disciple could not, to accept the commission from the risen Lord and become the first ambassador of the resurrection tidings. Her privilege is immense, and it is a total turnaround, as she becomes the first God-chosen witness of this most wondrous event in human history.

The third step centers on the disciples (vv. 19–23), still cowering in a locked room and hiding, caring only about themselves. Their faith is lower than Mary's, destroyed by their fear (of the Jews). They represent those of us who are virtually afraid to move at all in our lives, we are so filled with trepidation at our uncertain future. They needed even more help from Jesus to overcome their virtually nonexistent faith, and once more Jesus met them right where they were and showed them his wounds, proving that he and his messianic peace were now theirs. Their joy turned them around, and as with Mary the results are even greater, as they are made a part of God's mission to the world, given the Spirit, and transformed into powerful agents/sent ones. As such they are given the power and authority to forgive sins and bring God's saving grace to sinful humankind.

The final step is with cynical Thomas (vv. 24–29), whose faith is lowest of all, virtually removed on the basis of his radical skepticism. While the disciples as a whole needed to see the wounds, he demands to touch them before considering the reality of the resurrection. Again, Jesus not only accommodates himself to those demands but gives them his messianic peace as well. It had to have been an incredible sight, with Thomas on his knees reaching out to put his hand in Jesus' wounds on his wrist and his side. The results are the greatest of all, as Thomas is ready to culminate the themes of this Gospel as a whole by exclaiming, "My Lord and my God." Thereby he recognizes that Jesus is not only the royal Messiah and Son of Man but is God of very God, Lord of all. In this way all the themes of this Gospel coalesce and are proved right in the risen Lord, the God-man Jesus.

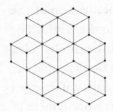

RESURRECTION, PART 2:
GALILEE APPEARANCES
(21:1–25)

There is considerable difference of opinion regarding the origin of this chapter and its place in John's Gospel. The majority of critical scholars believe it was a later addition, perhaps of what is called the "Johannine circle," a group of John's later disciples they think put together both his Gospel and his letters. Others think John wrote it but that he added it at a later time, and the original ended at 20:30–31. I strongly believe that John wrote this last chapter as the ending of his original Gospel. Analysis of language and style shows conclusively that John wrote it, and 20:30–31 as stating the purpose of the book does not have to be its concluding statement (compare 1 John 5:13; Rev 22:6). There is no evidence that the Fourth Gospel ever circulated without chapter 21. It is a natural conclusion to the interaction between Peter and the Beloved Disciple, and the threefold reinstatement of Peter (21:15–17) is also a fitting denouement to his three denials. It is a fitting epilogue, framing the Gospel with the prologue (1:1–18).

Chapter 20 centered on the issue of faith, and chapter 21 centers on the issue of mission. God's mission is carried out by the Triune Godhead and then passed on to the church (17:18; 20:21–23). This theme is at the heart of the message of this book, and each section of this chapter contributes to the mobilization of the church and the movement of the good news to the world. The miraculous catch of fish (21:1–14) reminds us of the similar miracle in Luke 5 and has the same message—when God's people surrender to the leading of the Lord, wondrous things will happen for those who "fish for people" (Luke 5:10). The reinstatement of Peter (21:15–17) centers on the responsibility of the leaders of the church to "feed" or care for God's flock; and the prophecy regarding Peter's death (21:18–23) reminds us that as we live out our mission we must follow the Lord's will for our lives rather than compare ourselves to others and their ministries. The prologue (1:1–18) focused on Jesus and his mission; the epilogue (21:1–25) centers on the Christ followers who live out the life of Christ and his mission in their own ministries.

JESUS APPEARS TO THE DISCIPLES
BY THE LAKE (21:1–14)

A DISAPPOINTING NIGHT OF FISHING (21:1–3)

"Afterward" of course means after the appearances during the eight days in Jerusalem. The first two were to the disciples through locked doors in the upper room. This takes place in the spacious vistas at the shore of the lake, called here the Sea of Tiberias because Herod had renamed it in honor of the emperor (see 6:1). After the festival ended, they returned to Galilee as the angel had commanded (Matt 28:7; Mark 16:7). Jesus' appearances are presented as "revelations" (*ephanerōsen*). Throughout this Gospel Jesus is the Living Revealer making God known to the world; now God is "revealing" the true nature of Jesus through his appearances. In this way the appearances are rightly labeled sign-miracles (20:30) that signify his true reality as the God-man. Like all the miracles of John, they are signs that "revealed his glory, and his disciples believed in him" (2:11).

Seven of the apostolic band are present at the lake (v. 2)—the inner circle (Peter, James, and John), Nathanael (called in 1:47–50), Thomas (who appeared in 11:16, 20:24–29), and two unnamed disciples. They were apparently waiting for Jesus to appear again and decided to bide their time with a little fishing. Seven seems to be important in this Gospel (seven sign-miracles, the seven-day opening ministry [see intro to 1:19–34]), and so this could designate the perfect number for launching the mission.

Peter decides to go fishing (v. 3), and the others decide to accompany him, perhaps for something to do. While John does not mention that Peter and Andrew, James and John, were professional fishermen, that would have been widely known. When Jesus called them to "fish for people," that didn't mean they quit their jobs. They were self-employed and kept their boats, as we see here. So they were free to leave their fishing whenever Jesus needed them, but they most likely fished in the in-between times when they were not with Jesus.

When they fished, there were two nets they would choose from—a hand net (a circular net about ten feet in diameter with weights on it so it could be wielded by a single person) or a large trawl or seine net with sinkers on the end, held between two moving boats, each one about 26.5 feet in length and 7.5 feet in width (the size of one recently discovered in Galilee). The net could entrap a large number of fish, and the fishermen would haul the fish into the boat with casting nets. Some see aimlessness or even deliberate disobedience in their actions, but that does not fit the atmosphere of the story. They are simply engaged in normal activities while they wait.

It was also normal to fish at night when the fish would come up to the surface to feed (Luke 5:5). When the sun rose, the fish would go deeper, and that lake was too deep to fish during the day; the nets would be useless. As in Luke 5, they fish all night and catch nothing. Unlike 3:2; 13:30, the night setting does not connote sin and darkness, but the scene does remind the reader that without Jesus they can do nothing. That will be the message here, as we will see.

THE MIRACULOUS CATCH OF FISH (21:4-6)

When dawn arrives, they are undoubtedly tired and somewhat dispirited. Suddenly, someone appears on the shore; it is Jesus. But in the twilight, they don't recognize him (v. 4). This is a common feature of the resurrection stories—the inability to recognize Jesus and doubt whether it is really him. As in the Emmaus Road incident (Luke 24:15-16), Jesus often appears as a stranger. The message is the need for openness and faith when we encounter him.

Jesus calls out from the shore with a term of endearment, *paidia*, which could be translated "lads" and in the NIV is "friends." He asks "haven't you any fish?" They answer, "No." Even here, Jesus' omniscience is evident, for he could certainly not see that their boats were empty. His reply to them is very strange (21:6), telling them to throw out their casting nets on the right side of the boat, and this without even moving their trawling net to gather the fish.

It is hard to know why they complied with this extremely unusual command. The authority of this stranger must have seemed evident to them, and they also may have thought, "What do we have to lose?" It was worth a try. The scene is quite similar to the miracle in Luke 5:4-7, where again Jesus told them to "let down the nets for a catch." The message is also the same in both stories—obey even when it seems hopeless or crazy, for miraculous things follow.

I have no doubt that when we get to heaven, Peter will tell us that the two greatest catches of fish he ever enjoyed in his life took place on these two occasions. There were so many large fish (153 in all, 21:11) that they could not even lift the net into the boat. The symbolic significance of the miracle in both episodes is evident: when we obey Jesus, even if the command does not seem logical, amazing things will happen. The missiological overtones are also evident. As in Acts, every crisis we go through is in actuality an opportunity to watch the Spirit work. This magnificent catch is a promise of the results of the worldwide mission Christ was about to commission them to undertake.

THE RECOGNITION OF JESUS (21:7–8)

Their obedience is not occasioned by their recognition, for they don't realize the stranger on the shore is him until now, after the miracle has occurred. In every appearance thus far, Jesus has had to reveal himself to be recognized, but the message is still the same—even when our faith is low, Christ will meet as where we are and reveal himself, turning our life around in the process. We must remain open to his miraculous presence in our lives. Here the Beloved Disciple responds to that revelation and tells Peter, "It is the Lord!"

Peter had been wearing a worker's smock for the night of fishing and had taken it off, working naked to gather the fish into the boat. Impetuous to the end, he either hastily throws it on and gathers it into his belt or puts on a loin cloth and jumps in the lake, swimming to get to Jesus. The other six disciples row the boat the hundred yards to shore with the catch of fish (21:8). John does not tell us what transpired when Peter first reached Jesus; John waits until 21:15–17 for the reunion. We also are not told what happened to the fish (apart from the few used for breakfast). Presumably, they did what is always done—stored them in some type of bin or tank. The emphasis is on Peter's single-minded obsession to reach Jesus. He abandons everything, even his fellow disciples and the fish, in his haste to Jesus.

THE BREAKFAST SCENE (21:9–14)

The focus now shifts to a meal already prepared, except for the fish the disciples would supply from their catch (v. 10). Jesus continually provides and cares for their needs: in 13:1–20 he washed their feet; now he prepares breakfast for them. Fish cooked on the fire and fresh bread were the basic Galilean meal (as in the multiplication of loaves in 6:1-15). Jesus possibly had some fish already prepared and now asks that they fetch some of their catch. There is a decided symbolic message in this—Jesus' followers participate in his mission with him. They share in the mission and in its wondrous results.

In verse 11 we discover there were two miracles. They had caught the astounding number of 153 fish, and in the process the net was not even torn with the incredible weight of the fish. There have been a ridiculous number of interpretations regarding the 153 fish, but let me highlight the main ones: (1) many see gematria (the sum of the numerical value of the letters in a word, as in the 666 of Rev 13:18), coming up with phrases (in Greek or Hebrew) like "Jesus Christ, God," or "church of love" or "children of God," but none of them work well here. (2) Since 17 is the triangular number of 153 (that is, adding the numbers 1-17 = 153), some see an allusion to Ezek 47:9-10, where a stream flows from Jerusalem to the Dead Sea, filled with fish from En-gedi (numerical value of 17) and En-eglaim (numerical value 153). This is interesting but impossible to prove. (3) Some simply find allegories in the numbers, like Augustine (taking the triangular number 17 as the ten commandments and the seven gifts of the Spirit) or Origen (the three parts of the Trinity are 50 × 3 + 3 = 153). Again, this does not make much sense here.

All of these imaginative solutions engage the creativity of the interpreter but have little value in the context of 21:1-14. So most rightly see the symbolism at a general level: this extremely large catch of fish signifies the abundance of the blessings Christ pours out upon his followers when they obey him and embark on their God-appointed mission, following the leading of the Spirit.

The net not being torn in all this is a second miracle. The unbroken net could signify the unity of the church or perhaps the limitless number of converts (there is always room for more). There is a contrast here with Luke 5:6, where the nets are torn. The significance seems to be with the limitless nature of the mission. It will continue to go on, winning converts, so long as this world lasts. Our mission will never stop.

Now we come to the meal scene itself (21:12-13). It too is a little strange. When Jesus calls them to breakfast, we would expect them to rush to him like they did when they saw the man on shore was him. Yet they appear reluctant, and John tells us, "None of them dared ask him, 'Who are you?' They knew it was the Lord." Why would they want to ask him such a question? This is certainly part of this doubt motif that is so evident. They are face to face with what has never happened before in human history, and their confusion is quite natural.

I think it is because Jesus is so much more than a man brought back to life. They are now coming to grips with the God-man in a new way. Before, his glory had shown through his humanity as the incarnate Son of God. Now his preexistent glory has taken over. He is still the Jesus they have walked with these last years, but he is now the exalted risen Lord, and they are experiencing his Godness in ways they had never imagined in their wildest dreams.

The meal itself (21:13) is closely connected to the multiplication of the loaves. As in 6:11, he "came, took the bread and gave it to them, and did the same with the fish." Some think this is a eucharistic celebration, but this doesn't really seem probable because fish did not become a eucharistic symbol until later. The theme is better seen as table fellowship. In sharing the meal they are sharing the new life they have forged for themselves as the church of God. The mission concerns a church in intimate fellowship with Jesus and with each other. Christ is watching over them, and as they follow him they are assured of his constant care.

John labels this "the third time Jesus appeared to his disciples." This is literary rather than chronological, for it does not include the appearance in the Emmaus journey of Luke 24:13-35 or the appearances of 1 Corinthians 15:3-8. It refers to the appearances to the Twelve (not Mary Magdalene) in 20:19-23, 26-29. "Jesus appeared" (*phaneroō*) occurs twice in this section (vv. 1, 14) and frames the episode with the fact that all this is made possible by God's revealing ("appeared" is a divine passive) the exalted and risen Lord to the Christ followers and thereby initiating his new creation, the church. The reason for choosing only appearances to the disciples is that John wants to establish the inauguration of the church age. His point is that Jesus has really and truly been raised from the dead and in so doing has established the church through his disciples and launched their mission to the world.

JESUS REINSTATES AND COMMISSIONS PETER (21:15-17)

The scene on Jesus' inauguration of the mission of God's people begins corporately with the disciples as a group, constituting the launching of the mission of the church as a whole. These next two sections center on the individual incorporation of the leaders of the mission, here Peter and the Beloved Disciple. This is not Jesus' first appearance to Peter. In fact, it is the third after his inaugural appearance in Luke 24:34 and 1 Corinthians 15:5 (probably the same appearance) and the group appearance to Peter and the others in John 20:19-23. So Peter has already repented and been forgiven.

The earlier appearance to him constituted his personal reinstatement by Jesus, and this passage details his public (six other disciples were present) reinstatement to ministry. In fact, this is even more his commissioning to ministry and to leadership in Christ's new creation, the church. This scene becomes Peter's marching orders. He denied Jesus three times (18:15-18, 25-27), and here he is commissioned three times to "feed" and "take care" of Christ's flock, the church.

After breakfast was finished, Jesus probably took Peter a short distance away (v. 20, Peter "turned and saw" the Beloved Disciple) for a semi-private discussion. Jesus' formal introduction, "Simon, son of John," repeats the initial call in 1:42 and almost seems to be a reformulation of their relationship. In this sense, they are starting over; in the larger sense, Peter has already established his ministry and is building on that.

The first question, "Do you love me more than these?" can be understood three ways: (1) "more than you love these other disciples"; (2) "more than you love these other things"; or (3) "more than these other disciples love me." It is common today to prefer the third on the grounds that Peter had boasted earlier that he was the most faithful of the group (13:37–38). While possible, that injects more negativity into the context than I believe is warranted. More likely, Jesus is asking him whether he is first in Peter's life and heart, and a combination of the first two is best. Peter's love for his brothers and sisters in the church ("love one another" in 13:35; 15:12; 17:11) must be secondary and flow out of his love for the Lord.

Peter's positive response, "Yes Lord, you know that I love you," leads to the commission to "feed my lambs." This is the major message of this scene, that true love for Jesus must result in caring for Christ's flock, the Christ followers. Christ then repeats this two further times, with stylistic variations to emphasize this point again and again.

This leads to the primary debate over this passage, the use of the two major verbs for love, agapaō and phileō. Many have interpreted this as two levels of love, but a paraphrase as if this is the case shows the difficulty with this view:

> Jesus said, "Simon, son of John, do you love me with a divine love [agapaō]?" "Yes, Lord," he said, "you know I like you a lot [phileō]." A little discouraged, Jesus tries again, "Simon, do you love me with a divine love [agapaō]?" Peter responds, "Lord, I'm really fond of you [phileō]." Jesus gives up, "So, Peter, you like me [phileō]?" And Peter concludes, "That's what I've been trying to say: I really like you [phileō]."

The inevitable implications of this would be that Simon Peter cannot raise himself up to Jesus' demands, and that Jesus capitulates and in the end accepts his inadequate level of love. This is quite unlikely and hardly fits the context, which is one of victory in the risen Lord. Moreover, in the Fourth Gospel this is another example of synonymous usage, as both verbs are used for the Father's love for the Son (3:35; 5:20), the Father's love for the saints (14:23; 16:27), and Jesus' love for Lazarus (11:3, 5, 36). So most agree that John uses two terms synonymously.

In these three short verses there are four word pairs, and the message of the passage flows out of these—two synonymous terms for "love," for "know," for "tend," and for "sheep." With this variety of terms John is stressing the comprehensiveness of the message; deep love for Jesus will produce an intense desire to take care of all the sheep of Christ's flock. By restating his point three times, Jesus gives it ultimate importance. The mission of God and Christ now has two foci: feeding and taking care of Christ's sheep in the church, and reaching out to and bringing the lost into the church.

Note how Peter is "hurt" (21:17) when Jesus asks the question a third time, replying, "Lord, you know all things; you know I love you." He did not understand why Jesus kept hammering him on this issue. The reason is not just that Peter had failed three times but even more the meaning of threefold repetition. To repeat something a second time makes it emphatic (example, "Truly, truly," the double *amēn* in John, see comments on 1:51), but to stress it a third time gives it ultimate significance, as in the *Trisagion*, "Holy, holy, holy" in Isaiah 6:3; Revelation 4:8, which makes holiness the defining characteristic of God and of our worship. As such love becomes a virtual covenant obligation for Simon Peter and for all followers of Christ.

Maintaining the flock of God is one of the keys to the mission of the church. The lost cannot truly be reached with success until the saints are deeply fed and mobilized. This was the heart of Paul's message to the Ephesian elders in Acts 20:28 ("Feed and shepherd God's flock") and Peter's challenge to the leaders in 1 Peter 5:2-4 ("be shepherds of God's flock"). In fact, I think 1 Peter 5:1-4 results from Peter's reflections on this very experience. The message is quite emphatic. The flock/church belongs to God and Christ, not to Peter or to any Christian leader. Christ is the chief Shepherd of the flock, and we are under-shepherds (1 Pet 5:2, 4) charged with feeding, guiding, and caring for his sheep. Our task is humility and obedience that leads to quality care. Shallow programs and teaching will not do; we are responsible to do our utmost to care for the flock well.

JESUS PROPHESIES REGARDING PETER'S DEATH: "FOLLOW ME" (21:18-23)

Jesus now goes back to 13:36 when he told Peter, "Where I am going [heaven], you cannot follow now, but you will follow later." Peter boldly promised he was ready to die for Jesus, and now Jesus tells him how that will take place. Jesus' prophecy takes the form of a double-*amēn* saying (see comments on 1:51) to stress a solemn truth that Peter has a twofold calling—to be a shepherd of God's flock but also to find glory by dying for the Lord (another major theme in John).

Jesus builds on an illustration (some say a Jewish proverb) about old age. This is a difficult verse for me to explain because at my current stage of life I am living out this story. I am seventy-five years old and have to walk with a cane, sometimes a walker. When I go down any incline, I have to hold on to someone's arm to balance myself. Unfortunately, this is my verse: "When you were younger you dressed yourself and went where you wanted" (I remember those halcyon days!) "but when you are old you will stretch out your hands, and someone else will dress you and lead you where you do not want to go." That is all too often my story lately.

The second half of the verse moves into the prophecy, for "stretch out your hands" refers to stretching out your arms to be bound or nailed to a cross. When he was "led to where you don't want to go," he would be taken to his death, as John will explain in 21:19. Church tradition says that Peter was crucified upside down during the reign of Nero (Acts of Peter 37-39; Eusebius,

Ecclesiastical History 3.1). We cannot know if that is true (it is a late tradition), but it is quite likely he was crucified.

John explains in 21:19 that Jesus was "indicating the kind of death by which Peter would glorify God." Jesus' death would constitute his being "lifted up to glory" (3:14; 8:28; 12:32), and Peter with his death would share that same glory. This is an important principle, called "the messianic woes." Suffering for the Lord is a "participation [or fellowship] in [Christ's] suffering" (Phil 3:10), and when Christians are martyred for Christ, they in reality "triumph over [Satan] by the blood of the Lamb and by the word of their testimony; they did not love their lives so much as to shrink from death." When the beast (Antichrist) "conquers" the saints (Rev 13:7), they actually conquer him in a far greater way (12:11). He triumphs only in that he takes their life; they conquer him for eternity. Every martyrdom is an ultimate victory over the powers of evil and brings glory to God.

The central theme of this section is expressed twice (21:19, 22): "Follow me." This essential discipleship motif is found in 1:43 (to Philip) and appears often (1:37–38, 40; 8:12; 10:4, 27; 12:26). Peter and John (see v. 22) were not to question God's will but "follow" his path wherever it led, even to the death. However, Peter always spoke his mind, even when it got him in trouble. He turns around and sees the Beloved Disciple "following them" (an ironic comment).

When Peter sees him he blurts out, "Lord, what about him?" He was virtually saying, "Why me and not him?" This is important for all of us. When we face difficult crises, we often look at someone who seems to have everything going well and ask a question just like Peter's. We all the time compare ourselves to others, but always when they appear to be having everything go smoothly.

Jesus' response to Peter (v. 22) is the same one he would give to us: "If I want him to remain alive until I return, what is that to you? You must follow me." Peter's responsibility was to follow Jesus and the path he had chosen, not to worry about the destiny of another. We dare not compare ourselves to others but must seek and accept

God's personal will for us. John did in fact live until a very old age. He wrote the book of Revelation in AD 95, close to thirty years after Peter's death. This did not mean God preferred John to Peter. Each was given that life and ministry that God deemed best for him. Nor could one say John had a better ministry than Peter's. Each fulfilled his calling and glorified God accordingly. In fact, when we get to heaven we may think God loved Peter more, for he brought him home sooner!

Whether we are called to a short but intense ministry like Peter's or a lengthy life and ministry like John's, we will be told the same thing as Peter, "So what? Follow me!" We are called to that life God in his sovereign wisdom and love knows is best for us and for the kingdom. This is true in so many ways, like pastoring a big church or a small one, writing but a single book versus many volumes, and so on. Neither one is more important to the Lord, and both are blessed by him for their service. It is Christ who is uppermost, and our place *and joy* is to follow his lead and serve him wherever he takes us.

Apparently Jesus' prophecy to Peter also touched many about John as well, and a rumor developed "that this disciple would not die" (v. 23) and it was apparently still around in the 80s as John was penning his Gospel. Since that rumor concerned him, John felt he had to dispel it. It may even have led to a cult following that centered on the Lord's soon return. On the basis of this rumor, as John got older the fervor regarding Christ's imminent coming would have made it necessary to correct the misunderstanding. So he gives an interpretive paraphrase regarding what Jesus actually meant, "If I want him to remain alive until I return, what is that to you?" This way nobody's faith would be seriously damaged if and when John died in the near future. (He would have been close to eighty when John was written.)

CONCLUSION: THE TRUE WITNESS (21:24-25)

In 19:35 John emphasized the historical reliability of the eyewitness evidence behind the resurrection narratives, and now he restates that premise, obviously feeling the readers need that affirmation. The truth and accuracy of the apostolic witness is necessary in light of the astounding nature of the claims. Along with Luke 1:1-4; 2 Peter 1:16, these tell us that the early church claimed to be writing factual history, and that reliable proof exists to establish their veracity. The old rationalistic premise that supernatural occurrences cannot be proved is wrong. So the burden of proof is actually on those who would deny the historical trustworthiness of the Gospels.

The affirmation in these two verses probably stems from the elders at Ephesus and the leaders of the church as a whole, telling the readers that the testimony of these chapters, indeed of this Gospel as a whole, can be trusted. It is more than just chapter 21. The entire Fourth Gospel is claimed to be reliable. So this concludes the witness theme in the Gospel of John, seen especially in 1:7-8, 29-34; 5:31-40; 8:13-18, where we are challenged to accept the official witnesses—the Baptist, Jesus' works, God, and the Old Testament prophecies—and realize these stories truly happened. These are summarized here in verse 24 in the testimony of John himself and of the leaders of his church, found in the narratives of his Gospel.

Two primary options exist for the "we" of this verse and thus for the author of these two verses: (1) It could be editorial "we" like those of 1 John 1:2, 4, 5, 6, 7; 3 John 1:12, referring to John himself; or (2) it could refer to the imprimatur of the church, perhaps the elders of Ephesus, to the veracity of this Gospel. This second fits the context slightly better, adding the church's official affirmation to that of John himself in 19:35. It demonstrates how important historical trustworthiness was to the early church.

Verse 25 in light of this affirmation of reliability turns to the deeds themselves, changing from the "we" of verse 24 to "I," as the evangelist himself adds his witness to that of the church in verse 24. He intends here to put everything in proper perspective. In his commentary he has only told us a small part of all that Jesus said and did. In reality, if he were able to achieve comprehensive coverage, "even the whole world would not have room for the books that would be written." When we consider 1:3-4, with Jesus the Creator of the universe and the divine figure behind the new creation, this is not as great an exaggeration as we may think. When we compile all four Gospels, even the miracles we know about are far more numerous than what John has been able to record. His lordship over the universe then increases this exponentially.

———

All John could do is relate a few representative stories to provide a sampling of all Jesus said and did. His purpose was to enable the readers to comprehend as well as possible the truth about the God-man, Jesus the Christ. In reality no single book could begin to capture the full reality and power, the majesty and glory of the Son of God (see 20:30-31). This is also why God inspired four Gospels rather than one, to allow his people a richer and fuller grasp of the wonderful reality.

While chapter 20 centered on the implications of the resurrection for faith, chapter 21 centers on the implications for the mission of the church. All humanity must be invited to participate in the new creation and the age of the Spirit inaugurated with the resurrection of Jesus. So each scene is included to culminate that central ministry of God's people. The miraculous catch of fish (vv. 1-8) re-creates Luke 5:1-11, a similar miracle that launched the mission that took place during Jesus' earthly ministry. Now the second fishing miracle launches that mission that will dominate the post-resurrection period, the age of the Spirit. The point is the same—when we submit and obey, even when it seems illogical, miraculous things will happen. Christ is in charge of each of our ministries, and we are to surrender to his power and leading in all that we do. What we attempt in our own strength (= the night of fishing) will often be discouraging, but when we allow Christ to be in charge (= casting their nets on the other side of the boat), there will be wondrous results.

The breakfast scene (vv. 9-14) turns the emphasis around to show that as the church engages in mission we are assured that the risen Lord himself is watching over us and caring for our every need. As we go out representing Christ, we mutually indwell (John 15) and depend on him, and he guides and empowers us in our mission. The meal itself signifies the depth of fellowship we enjoy with Christ as we share every detail of our lives with him. Again, the promise is the great abundance of the blessings (= the 153 fish) Christ pours into our lives.

The commissioning scene (vv. 15-17) is a beautiful and profound passage. The message is simple and yet life-changing. If we truly love Christ with all our heart, we must care deeply for his flock and take care of them well. The mission cannot be accomplished without a church that is well-fed and eager to take Christ to the masses. The mission of the church desperately needs a quality teaching ministry in the church to prepare the people to live for God in every area of their lives.

The final episode has a clear message—follow the Lord no matter what. Peter has been reinstated and commissioned, but he is also told he will not have a lengthy ministry but rather a short-lived one (literally). There are two points here: first, if God asks us to give our lives for him, it means we will not only share Christ's suffering but his glory as well; and second, our life must at all times center on one key thing, following Christ and his will for us. The one thing we must be ensured about is this—our lives will count for something, and that something will matter. There are no easy lives when we follow Christ, but there is no boring one either. None of us is irrelevant to the cause of Christ.

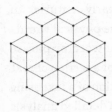

GLOSSARY

apocalyptic Refers to truths about God's plans for history that he has hidden in past generations but has revealed (the Greek *apokalypsis* means "unveiling") to his people. The name also describes a genre of ancient literature (including Revelation and parts of Daniel) that communicates these truths using vivid symbolism.

chiasm A stylistic device in which a passage is organized into two sections, with the contents of the statements in the first half repeated in reverse order in the second half (ABC:C′B′A′).

christological (adj.), Christology (n.) Refers to the New Testament's presentation of the person and work of Christ, especially his identity as Messiah.

eschatological (adj.), eschatology (n.) Refers to the last things or the end times. Within this broad category, biblical scholars and theologians have identified more specific concepts. For instance, "realized eschatology" emphasizes the present work of Christ in the world as he prepares for the end of history. In "inaugurated eschatology," the last days have already begun but have not yet been consummated at the return of Christ.

gnostic (adj.) Refers to special knowledge (Greek: *gnōsis*) as the basis of salvation. As a result of this heretical teaching, which developed in several forms in the early centuries AD, many gnostics held a negative view of the physical world.

inclusio A framing device in which the same word or phrase occurs at both the beginning and the end of a section of text.

midrash (n.), midrashic (adj.) A Jewish exposition of a text using the techniques of ancient rabbis to give a detailed analysis of the meaning and theology of a text.

Mishnah An ancient Jewish source, compiled around AD 200, that contains the sayings of the rabbis. While it was not written down until later, it tells us about oral traditions that were in existence in Jesus' time.

parousia The event of Christ's second coming. The Greek word *parousia* means "arrival" or "presence."

Qumran A site near the northwest corner of the Dead Sea where a collection of scrolls (called the Dead Sea Scrolls) was found beginning in the 1940s. The community that lived at this site and wrote these scrolls separated themselves from the rest of Jewish society. Many scholars believe they were a branch of the Essenes, one of the three major Jewish sects mentioned by Josephus (*Antiquities* 13.171–72). The Dead Sea Scrolls include manuscripts of Old Testament books as well as other writings that are not part of Scripture. They do not refer to Christianity, but do shed light on aspects of Judaism around the time of Jesus.

shaliach Hebrew for "sent one," a representative or ambassador who is the voice and presence of the sender. In John, Jesus is presented as the *Shaliach* of the Father.

Shekinah A word derived from the Hebrew *shakan* (to dwell), used to describe God's personal presence taking the form of a cloud, often in the context of the tabernacle or temple (e.g., Exod 40:38; Num 9:15; 1 Kgs 8:10–11).

soteriological (adj.), soteriology (n.) Relating to the doctrine of salvation (Greek: *sōtēria*), including such subjects as atonement, justification, and sanctification.

Synoptic A term applied to the Gospels of Matthew, Mark, and Luke because of their many similarities and parallels, from the Greek meaning "having the same look."

typological (adj.), typology (n.) A literary device in which Old Testament persons or events are the types that correspond to and are fulfilled in New Testament realities.

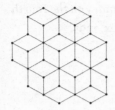

BIBLIOGRAPHY

Blomberg, Craig L. *The Historical Reliability of John's Gospel.* Downers Grove, IL: InterVarsity Press, 2001.

Brown, Raymond E. *The Gospel According to John.* 2 vols. Anchor Bible. Garden City, NY: Anchor, 1966–70.

Carson, D. A. *The Gospel According to John.* Pillar New Testament Commentary. Grand Rapids: Eerdmans, 1991.

Hughes, R. Kent. *John: That You May Believe.* Wheaton, IL: Crossway, 1999.

Keener, Craig S. *The Gospel of John.* 2 vols. Peabody, MA: Hendrickson, 2003.

Köstenberger, Andreas J. *John.* Baker Exegetical Commentary on the New Testament. Grand Rapids: Baker Academic, 2004.

Milne, Bruce. *The Message of John.* The Bible Speaks Today. Downers Grove, IL: InterVarsity Press, 1993.

Morris, Leon. *The Gospel According to St. John.* New International Commentary on the New Testament. Grand Rapids: Eerdmans, 1995.

Westcott, B. F. *The Gospel According to St. John.* London: Macmillan, 1881.

Whitacre, Rod A. *John.* IVP New Testament Commentary. Downers Grove, IL: InterVarsity Press, 1999.

Witherington, Ben, III. *John's Wisdom: A Commentary on the Fourth Gospel.* Louisville: Westminster John Knox, 1995.

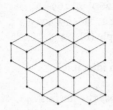

SUBJECT AND AUTHOR INDEX

of Jesus' Father, 212
idia, ta, 31
ignorance, of Nicodemus, 80–81
illness, of Lazarus, 268–70
imagery, apocalyptic, 44–45, 60,
    81–82, 106, 135
imitatio Christi, 332
immorality, of the Samaritan
    woman, 105
incarnation, the, 30–34, 37–38,
    160, 481
inclusio, John's use of, 304
independence, of John's Gospel,
    8–9
indwelling
    of Father and Son, 338–39,
        345–56, 403
    mutual, 51, 171, 345–46, 357,
        363–64, 403–7, 490
    of the Spirit, 21, 344, 347,
        359, 368
innocence, of Jesus, 426–31, 435
inscription, on the cross, 439–40
inspiration, of Scripture, 172,
    207
insurrectionist, Jesus as not,
    423–25
interrogation, of Jesus, 414–19,
    435
intimacy, of the Father and Son,
    36
Isaac, and Jesus, 231
Israelite, true, 56–57
ius gladii, 421

J
Jacob
    and Jesus, 103, 328
    and Nathanael, 56–57, 60–61
James (disciple), 5, 310, 477
jars, of water, 64–65, 110

jealousy, of John the Baptist's
    disciples, 91
Jehovah's Witnesses, 25
Jerusalem
    and Bethany, 272
    destruction of, 6
    Jesus' entry into, 291–96
    Jesus in, 123–24, 183, 205,
        209, 284
    Pilate in, 421
"Jesus creeds," 59
Jews, the
    and the Father, 212
    vs. Gentiles, 160, 195, 254–55
    and Jesus' death, 432
    and Lazarus, 279–80
    before Pilate, 420–23
    as rejecting Jesus, 31–32
    vs. Samaritans, 101–2, 105–6
Joanna, 442
Johannine circle, 5, 475
"Johannine thunderbolt," 9–10
John (disciple), 50–51, 477, 487
    as author, 2–6, 471–72
    as the Beloved Disciple, 324
    commentary of, 84, 89, 96–97
    at the Last Supper, 323–27
    and Mary (Jesus' mother),
        441–43, 450, 461
    as the "other" disciple, 416
    and the resurrection, 455–61,
        464–65, 470, 473–75
    at the Sea of Galilee, 479,
        482, 486
    witness of, 446, 488–89
John Mark, as the Beloved
    Disciple, 4
John the Baptist
    as a forerunner, 34, 37–40,
        45, 48–61
    as a planter, 113–14

and darkness, 86
and death, 276
and illness, 127
and Jesus, 227
of Jesus' enemies, 213–14
leaving, 206–7
and lies, 142
and slavery, 221–23
and spiritual blindness, 246
of the world, 367
sindon, 448–49
sinner, Jesus as, 241–42
sklēros, 176
slavery, and sin, 221–23
sleep, as death, 270–71
snake, bronze, 82–83, 88
soldiers, Roman, 414, 422, 428, 434
Solomon's Colonnade, 259
Son of God, Jesus as, 20–21, 128–37, 262–64, 472
confession of, 274
and God's voice, 301
and Jesus' charges, 430–31
and Jesus' resurrection, 481
and Nathanael, 57–58
as one with the Father, 145
prayer of, 390–91
as sent, 84–86
as setting free, 223
Son of Man, 82, 135–36, 244–45, 429
as being lifted up, 20, 297, 303, 330
sayings of, 59–60
soteriology, 7, 18–19, 177
and Christology, 133, 274
and faith, 162–64, 173
of Jesus, 411–12, 444, 450–51
and suffering, 235–36
and unbelief, 177–78, 306–7
sōzō, 127

sphragizō, 94
Spirit, 21, 328
baptism by, 43
and believers, 196–99, 472–73
and conviction, 85–86, 301–2
giving of, 196–99, 203
and Jesus' baptism, 46–47
and Jesus' second coming, 335
and John the Baptist, 45
knowing the, 344
and life, 177
and living water, 102
and power, 340, 387–88
and prayer, 382–83
promise of, 341–48
and rebirth, 78–82, 88
receiving, 467
and remaining, 359
and sanctification, 400–401
and truth, 384–85
and witness, 368–69, 372, 388
and the Word, 94–97
work of, 373–80, 388–89
and worship, 107–8
Stephen, 310, 422
stone, rolling away the, 277–78
storm, and the disciples, 152–53
structure, of the Farewell Discourse, 329
style, of John's Gospel, 1, 8–10, 23–24, 172, 234
subjective vision theory, 453
submission, of the Son, 20, 130–37, 145, 255, 278
and authority, 142, 309–11, 349–50, 394–95
and glory, 228, 330
Suffering Servant, 293, 420
as being lifted up, 297, 302
and the fulfillment theme, 305–6

of John the Baptist, 29, 41–49,
138–39, 265
of the Samaritan woman,
109–11, 120–21
of the Scriptures, 141–45
of the signs, 139–40, 260, 339
and the Spirit, 368–69, 372
woman, caught in adultery,
204–7
"woman," meaning of, 64, 460
women, and men, 109–10
Word, 20, 140, 378
Jesus as, 23–38, 94–95
word, of God, 399
words, of Jesus, 359, 412–13
work, on the Sabbath, 126, 129,
238–39
works
of Abraham, 224
of the disciples, 339–41
and faith, 157–58, 357
of the Father, 128–30,
235–36, 269
of Jesus, 262–64, 393
world, the, 81, 160, 166, 295
and darkness, 185–86, 236
and the disciples,
364–72, 395–401
and Jesus' enemies, 214
Jesus' mission to, 19,
114–15, 282–83
and peace, 349
and Satan, 19, 350–51
and the Spirit, 375–77
and the Word, 30–31
worship, true, 105–8

Y
Yahweh
as God's name, 397
and "I am," 109, 153, 161, 215–17,
231–33, 322, 470

and Jesus, 430
yeshua', 341

Z
zeal, messianic, 67–69
Zebedee, 416, 442

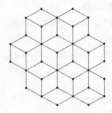

INDEX OF SCRIPTURE AND OTHER ANCIENT LITERATURE

Old Testament

New Testament

Matthew

Deuterocanonical Works

Old Testament Pseudepigrapha

Dead Sea Scrolls

Josephus

Classical and Ancient Christian Writings

Greek Manuscripts of John